Cuba Under Raúl Castro

Cuba
Under
Raúl Castro

Assessing the Reforms

Carmelo Mesa-Lago
Jorge Pérez-López

LYNNE
RIENNER
PUBLISHERS

BOULDER
LONDON

Published in the United States of America in 2013 by
Lynne Rienner Publishers, Inc.
1800 30th Street, Boulder, Colorado 80301
www.rienner.com

and in the United Kingdom by
Lynne Rienner Publishers, Inc.
3 Henrietta Street, Covent Garden, London WC2E 8LU

Library of Congress Cataloging-in-Publication Data
Mesa-Lago, Carmelo, 1934–
    Cuba under Raúl Castro : assessing the reforms / Carmelo Mesa-Lago and
Jorge Pérez-López.
        pages cm
    Includes bibliographical references and index.
    ISBN 978-1-58826-904-1 (hc : alk. paper)
    1. Cuba—Economic conditions. 2. Cuba—Economic policy. 3. Cuba—Social
conditions. 4. Cuba—Foreign economic relations. 5. Social change—Cuba.
6. Castro Ruz, Raúl, 1930–   I. Pérez-López, Jorge F. II. Title.
    HC152.5.M464 2013
    330.97291—dc23

                                                        2013006138

British Cataloguing in Publication Data
A Cataloguing in Publication record for this book
is available from the British Library.

Printed and bound in the United States of America

⊗   The paper used in this publication meets the requirements
     of the American National Standard for Permanence of
     Paper for Printed Library Materials Z39.48-1992.

5   4   3   2   1

To the Venerable Father Félix Varela,

activist in favor of Cuba's independence from Spain,
advocate of freedom and opponent of slavery,
social reformer and defender of civil and human rights,
teacher, exiled in the United States,
where he cared for the poor and the downtrodden

"The man who taught us how to think"

The only thing that could result in the failure of the Revolution and of socialism in Cuba . . . is our inability to overcome the errors that we have made over more than 50 years, and the new ones that we might incur in the future.

Our worst enemy is not imperialism . . . but rather our own errors.

We have the basic obligation of correcting the errors that we have made over the last five decades.

—Raúl Castro,
April 16, August 1, and December 18, 2011

Contents

Tables and Figures

Tables

Figures

Preface

In our book *Cuba's Aborted Reform: Socioeconomic Effects, International Comparisons, and Transition Policies* (2005), we examined the period from the collapse of the Soviet Union and the dissolution of the socialist bloc at the turn of the 1990s through 2003–2004. As we concluded that book, Fidel Castro had launched the "Battle of Ideas," which reversed the modest market-oriented measures implemented in Cuba during the first half of the 1990s to confront the most severe economic-social crisis during the revolution.

Significant changes have occurred on the island since then. In August 2006, overtaken by a grave illness, Fidel transferred power to his brother Raúl Castro. On July 26, 2007, in a major speech, Raúl discussed quite candidly the serious economic situation facing the nation and the imperative to undertake "structural and conceptual reforms." He called for a national debate, within socialist parameters, on the changes that were needed. While consensus on numerous policy prescriptions was achieved fairly quickly, inertia took over with respect to implementation—in part because of the global financial crisis, which dealt a heavy blow to the island's economy—and only a few isolated policy changes were made. In 2008, Raúl was chosen president of the Council of State and the Council of Ministers, thereby consolidating his leadership.

Beginning in 2010, the pace of reforms accelerated, resulting in the deepest actions in half a century to expand the private sector and to strengthen the role of the market. The key mechanism for approving the reforms was the Sixth Congress of the Cuban Communist Party (PCC), held in April 2011. As we concluded writing this book, at the end of November 2012, the reforms after the Sixth Congress were still unfolding, with many laws and regulations still to be issued and implemented. The Sixth Congress also elected Raúl as first secretary of the PCC, the last official title relinquished by Fidel. Even though Fidel is now officially out of power and often the subject of stories about his ill health and premature reports of his demise, he continues to be influential through his opinion pieces (called "Reflections"), which are carried extensively by the Cuban media.

Another important development has been the proliferation of magazines, blogs, and other media containing articles, debates, dossiers, and interviews of individuals inside and outside Cuba expressing different viewpoints. The Catholic Church, which publishes several electronic and print journals, has played a key role in this regard; in addition, it served as intermediary in obtaining the freedom of more than a hundred political prisoners in 2010.

This book begins with an overview of Cuban socioeconomic development since 1959. This is followed by a detailed analysis of developments in the domestic economy, international economic relations, and social welfare since Raúl's takeover in August 2006 and through the end of November 2012 (through mid-December for a few important issues), when we completed our manuscript.*

Finally, the book summarizes the national debate around reforms, as well as the agreements reached by the Sixth Congress of the PCC and ensuing measures; assesses the impact of the reforms; and presents our recommendations to improve the reforms in the future.

The research underlying the book is based on more than 400 published sources: statistical information from official sources and from international organizations compiled for the period 2005–2011, which we critically analyze and systematically compare with statistical information for 1989, the eve of the economic crisis of the 1990s; speeches by Raúl and speeches and statements by other key government officials, including pertinent "Reflections" by Fidel; and academic articles and books published inside and outside Cuba, including Cuban journals that deal with socioeconomic issues, proceedings of conferences held by the University of Havana's Center for the Study of the Cuban Economy (CEEC), and proceedings of the annual meetings of the Association for the Study of the Cuban Economy (ASCE), called *Cuba in Transition*. Finally, the book also relies on hundreds of other sources, among them items published by *Granma, Juventud Rebelde, Trabajadores, Bohemia,* and other official newspapers and magazines, by for-

---

*At the end of November 2012, Cuba's National Statistical Office (ONE) had released on its website most sections of the 2011 *Anuario Estadístico de Cuba,* but not the important sections on national accounts (macroeconomic statistics), finances, and the external sector. Similarly, the Economic Commission for Latin America and the Caribbean (ECLAC) had not yet published its *Cuba: Evolución económica durante 2011 y perspectivas para 2012.*

eign news agencies reporting from Cuba, and by newspapers and magazines published outside the island. All translations from Spanish to English are our own.

Throughout our academic careers, we have consistently documented our work on Cuba and tried to be balanced and objective, considering both positive and negative aspects of the Cuban revolution. Although this approach has brought us criticism from both extremes of the ideological spectrum and has thrust us into several unpleasant exchanges with some scholars, we are nevertheless gratified that our work has made a contribution to the academic study of Cuba's economy and society. In 2005, Mesa-Lago began to write for journals published in Cuba by the Catholic Church (*Vitral, Espacio Laical,* and *Convivencia*), which has allowed his work to become more widely known on the island.

While we are responsible for the content of the book, we are grateful to Lynne Rienner and Jessica Gribble for their enthusiasm about its publication and to the Christopher Reynolds Foundation for a research grant. We also want to thank several colleagues who generously reviewed our writing and made useful suggestions: Antonio Santamaría and an anonymous reviewer for the entire manuscript, Pavel Vidal Alejandro for Chapters 2 through 6, Alejandro de la Fuente for Chapter 4, María Dolores Espino on tourism, Jorge Piñón on energy issues, Carlos Romero on Cuba-Venezuela relations, and Kanako Yamaoka on the Vietnamese model. In addition, we are grateful to Oscar Espinosa Chepe, Marc Frank, Joaquín Pujol, and a Cuban American colleague who wishes to remain anonymous for providing us with important materials. Finally, we acknowledge Néstor Castaneda-Angarita's research assistance, the Center for Latin American Studies of the University of Pittsburgh for administrative support, and Jason Cook's careful eye and copyediting talent.

We acknowledge the permission to reproduce parts of the following articles or chapters by Mesa-Lago: "La economía cubana en la encrucijada: El legado de Fidel, el debate sobre el cambio y las opciones de Raúl," in *Cuba: Presente y futuro* (Madrid: Real Instituto Elcano, Documento de Trabajo, 2008); "La economía de Cuba hoy: Retos internos y externos," *Desarrollo Económico* 49:195 (2009); "Cuba: ¿Qué cambia tras el VI Congreso del Partido Comunista?" *Nueva Sociedad* 234 (2011); "Las reformas de Raúl Castro y el Congreso del Partido Comunista de Cuba," *Documentos CIDOB* 35 (2011); and *Social Protection Systems in Latin America and the Caribbean: Cuba* (Santiago de Chile: ECLAC, 2013).

It is our sincere hope that the analysis embodied in this book will contribute to the success of the structural reform process taking place in Cuba by fostering economic and social development on the island; increasing harmony and understanding between Cubans everywhere; and giving rise to an environment of prosperity, inclusion, civil and political liberties, and respect for human rights in the country where we were born.

1

Cuba's Economic and Social Development, 1959–2012

As necessary background to understand the reforms that are being implemented by Raúl Castro, this chapter summarizes the history of Cuban economic and social policies during the revolution (1959 to 2012), following a typology of "idealist" and "pragmatist" cycles.[1] In the chapter we identify eight such cycles and for each of them we analyze internal and external causes, describe policies that were implemented, and evaluate outcomes.

Idealist and Pragmatist Cycles in Cuba's Economic and Social Policies

The socialist central-planning or "command economy" model, introduced in Cuba in 1961, remains today as the basic form of economic organization, although substantially transformed and without some of its original elements. Economic and social policies have swung eight times since 1959, giving rise to cycles of different intensity and length that have alternated from movement toward or away from the market. For the sake of simplicity, herein "idealist" cycles are those dominated by policies that move away from the market, while "pragmatist" cycles are market-oriented.

During idealist cycles, the political leadership generally set ambitious goals—for instance reaching the highest level of industrial production per capita in Latin America within four years, producing 10 million tons of sugar annually and subsequently reaching annual production of 20 million tons, creating an unselfish "new man," and reaching food self-sufficiency within a five-year period. These goals were not achieved and their pursuit contributed to adverse economic and social performance and even crises.

Such failures raised the threat (real or perceived) of regime instability and prompted the political leadership to adopt market-oriented policies in order to boost economic performance and preserve or strengthen the regime and maintain control. Pragmatist cycles have resulted in moderate improvements in economic performance[2] and living standards, but have also brought about some adverse social effects, such as rises in unemployment or inequality. Typically, once the political leadership felt that the regime had been sufficiently strengthened under pragmatist policies, it launched a new idealist cycle, thus perpetuating a policy seesaw.

Economic logic dictates that Cuban authorities would maintain and strengthen pragmatist cycles that bring about positive economic results. But such rationality has not been followed by the Cuban political leadership because, in our opinion, it has perceived that market-oriented policies entail a certain loss of economic influence, decentralization of decisionmaking, and emergence of economic actors independent from the state and hence a loss of the latter's economic power and, potentially, political control. Thus, we argue that political logic (preservation of the regime and control) has surmounted economic logic, giving rise to recurring idealist cycles. Moreover, increases in unemployment and inequality and other negative effects associated with the market seemed unacceptable to the political leadership, at least through the decade of the 1990s.

Most of the cycles have lasted between five and six years, creating instability and uncertainty and hampering long-term economic growth. During the first pragmatist cycle, market-oriented policies were introduced slowly and timidly, while they were implemented more boldly in the second and third such cycles. In contrast, idealist cycles tended over time to become weaker.

The Eight Cycles: Characteristics and Effects

Since 1959, there have been eight policy cycles under Cuba's revolutionary government, with the first one divided into three subcycles. Four of the cycles have been idealist, three have been pragmatist, and one has been characterized by policy stagnation:

> 1959–1966: Although difficult to classify, this was mostly an idealist cycle, with some facets of pragmatism particularly in 1964–1966; this period is divided into three subcycles: market erosion, introduction of orthodox Soviet central planning, and debate over socialist models.
> 1966–1970: Fidel's adoption and radicalization of the Guevarist model, a strong idealist cycle.
> 1971–1985: The Soviet timid (pre-Gorbachev) economic reform model, the first well-identified pragmatist cycle.
> 1986–1990: The so-called Rectification Process, the third idealist cycle.

1991–1996: Crisis and market-oriented reforms, the second and strongest pragmatist cycle up to this point, under the "Special Period in Time of Peace."

1997–2003: Slowdown and halt of the reform, a cycle of policy stagnation.

2003–2006: Reversal of reforms, the fourth idealist cycle, although weaker than previous idealist cycles.

2007–present: Raúl Castro's structural reforms, the third and strongest pragmatist cycle of the revolution.

During each of the cycles there were changes—often contradictory—with respect to eleven policy areas: collectivization of the means of production; centralization of economic decisionmaking; role of the state budget; foreign investment; allocation of goods through rationing (rather than through markets and prices); agricultural free markets; self-employment; voluntary (unpaid) work and labor mobilization; egalitarianism; moral versus material incentives; and expansion of free social services.

Idealist cycles are characterized by an increase in the degree of collectivization and centralization in decisionmaking, decline in the role of the state budget as an instrument of macroeconomic management, de-emphasis or phasing-out of foreign investment, rise in the importance of administratively set ration prices rather than market-determined prices, increased restrictions or disappearance of free agricultural markets and self-employment, upsurge in labor mobilization and use of voluntary work, escalation in egalitarianism and predominance of moral incentives over material incentives, and expansion of free social services.

Policies during pragmatist cycles are diametrically opposite, albeit with divergent degrees of intensity according to the cycle: de-collectivization, decentralization of decisionmaking, greater role of the state budget in macroeconomic management, increased receptivity to foreign investment and steps to promote it, wider use of market prices versus rationing and controlled prices, introduction or expansion of free agricultural markets and self-employment, reduction or elimination of labor mobilization and voluntary work, decline in egalitarianism, predominance of material incentives, and cutback of free social services.

We assess the effects of idealist and pragmatist cycles through the performance of seven economic and social indicators: economic growth, monetary liquidity (excess money in circulation or monetary overhang), fiscal deficit, deficit in the goods trade balance, open unemployment, income distribution, and poverty incidence. Unfortunately, the latter two indicators cannot be evaluated quantitatively because of the lack of official statistics, but they will be assessed qualitatively and through estimates from foreign and Cuban analysts.

Internal and External Factors That Influence the Cycles

The ideology and decisions of Fidel Castro were the principal internal factors shaping the policy cycles on the island for nearly fifty years, until illness forced him to turn over his leadership role to his brother Raúl. As unchallenged leader of the revolution and founder of the regime, Fidel wielded immense power, holding concurrently the key political posts in the country: chief of state, president of the Council of State and of its Executive Committee, first secretary of the Cuban Communist Party (PCC) and head of its Political Bureau, and commander in chief of the armed forces. As president of the Council of State, he nominated the president of the Supreme Court, an institution subordinated to the Council of State. The only significant political institution that Fidel Castro did not head was the National Assembly of People's Power (ANPP), the top legislative body in the country. In practice, the ANPP has limited power; it meets twice a year for two to three legislative days at a time, with the Council of State governing during the rest of the year through decrees. Finally, as chief of state, Fidel was constitutionally granted the power to declare a state of emergency and under such conditions to modify the exercise of constitutionally enshrined rights and duties.

Fidel's proclivity for centralization, collectivization of the means of production, egalitarianism, and labor mobilization strongly predisposed him toward antimarket policies. And yet he was willing to adopt ostensibly pragmatist policies and economic reforms—although reluctantly—when a major crisis made it necessary to preserve the regime and his power. The "maximum leader" resisted changes to the political system, and hence it has been more stable than the economic system, notwithstanding the political institutionalization that occurred in the 1970s. In our opinion, Fidel's charismatic leadership and ideological bend prevented the logic of pragmatism from institutionalizing state socialism and implementing comprehensive and stable market reforms.

There are notable similarities between Cuba under Fidel and China under Mao Tse-tung; in both instances, a powerful and charismatic leader shaped the economic policy cycles. It was only after the death of Mao that China's economic reforms were consolidated, expanded, and deepened to create the "market socialism" model. Fidel has consistently rejected Chinese and Vietnamese economic reforms; the limited and timid market reforms implemented by Cuba in 1993–1996 did not come even close to the Chinese reforms and were virtually stopped by Fidel in 1996. Even Raúl, after replacing Fidel, was not able to put in place and accelerate pragmatic structural reforms until illness made it impossible for Fidel to interfere and stop them, although through the publication of his "Reflections" and statements during public appearances he tried to obstruct the reforms, at least through 2011, when he began to concentrate on foreign affairs and withdrew from the domestic policy arena (see Chapter 5).

Numerous exogenous factors, positive or negative, contributed to the launching, continuation, or end of a policy cycle. The two most important international actors, who played antagonistic roles, are the former Soviet Union and the United States. The former played a positive role from 1960 to 1990 through its economic aid, trade, and price subsidies, but its support declined beginning in about 1985 with the rise to power of Mikhail Gorbachev. The end of the vital Soviet assistance and the ensuing deep economic crisis at the start of the 1990s forced a change toward the implementation of market-oriented policies. The United States meanwhile has been a negative factor as a result of the economic embargo in place since 1961, subject to periods of hardening (presidencies of Richard Nixon, Ronald Reagan, and George W. Bush) and flexibility (presidencies of Jimmy Carter, Bill Clinton, and Barack Obama). The threat—whether real or imaginary—perceived by the Cuban leadership that political instability on the island would open the door to intervention by the United States was an important factor in the persistence of idealist cycles. Other historical actors have been the Organization of American States (OAS), the European Union, Cuba's international creditors, and foreign investors. Since 2002 the economic support of Venezuela has been essential for the survival of the Cuban regime.

Policies During the Cycles, Contributing Factors, and Effects, 1959–2012

This section describes eight policy cycles from 1959 to 2012. For each cycle, we describe policies implemented, identify internal and external factors that influenced the start and end of the cycle, and assess economic and social effects with respect to the seven indicators identified above.

Market Erosion, Soviet Orthodox Model, and Socialist Debate, 1959–1966

This mostly idealist cycle is divided into three subcycles. The first, which involved the elimination of capitalism and erosion of the market (1959–1960), resulted by the end of 1960 in the virtual elimination of the market through the rapid collectivization of the means of production. The vacuum created was filled with a Stalinist-type "command" economy during the second subcycle, which involved adoption of an orthodox Soviet central planning model (1961–1963), supported by foreign aid and trade with the Soviet Union. The establishment by the United States of a commercial embargo on Cuba in 1961, and its extension to most of the hemisphere in 1964 by the OAS, combined with the statements by Fidel in 1961 about the socialist character of the revolution, isolated Cuba from other countries in the Western Hemisphere and facilitated the adoption of the Soviet model.

There were important policy continuities during these two subcycles: expansion of collectivization of the means of production, elimination of foreign investment (through the nationalization of foreign assets on the island), centralization of economic decisionmaking, introduction and expansion of rationing, reduction in the role of the market and of market prices in resource allocation, growth of egalitarianism, and rapid expansion of free social services, particularly in rural areas. The economic development strategy centered on import substitution industrialization (Ernesto "Che" Guevara predicted that by 1965, Cuba would be the leader in Latin America on industrial production per capita), reduction of dependence on sugar, and increased agricultural diversification.

The Soviet central-planning model was ill-suited to Cuba, given that its economy was heavily dependent on a single agricultural commodity (sugar), and given its shortage of managers (who had left the country fleeing the revolution) and lack of experience with and weak statistical base in support of central planning. To compound the problem, collectivization proceeded at a fast pace and cut across all areas of the economy, while planning was introduced haphazardly. The industrialization plan set ambitious short-term targets that required imported capital goods and raw materials, which did not arrive as timely as needed. Agricultural diversification did not meet the anticipated targets and resulted in a significant decline in sugarcane cultivation, which led to declines in sugar production and exports and to a worsening of the merchandise trade deficit.

The failure of central planning and industrialization brought about the third subcycle, which involved debate and experimentation with alternative socialist models (1964–1966). During this cycle, two factions within the leadership, espousing differing ideologies regarding socialist development, engaged in an intellectual debate. Ernesto Guevara and his followers, partly influenced by the ideas of Mao embodied in the "Great Leap Forward," proposed an idealist, antimarket approach: an even higher degree of collectivization; reliance on the central plan and use of centralized budgeting; creation of a "new man" free from selfishness, moral incentives, voluntary work, and labor mobilization; egalitarianism; and universal and free social services. In opposition to Guevara and his followers, a pragmatist, pro-Soviet faction, led by economist Carlos Rafael Rodríguez (one of the founders of the pre-revolutionary Cuban Communist Party), who had been influenced in part by the Libermanism in vogue in the Soviet Union at the time, argued for a socialist reform model: some decentralization of decisionmaking, use of selected market-oriented mechanisms, preference for the use of material incentives, and halt to collectivization, egalitarianism, and expansion of free social services. In a Solomonic decision, Fidel divided management of the economy between the two groups, with the Guevarists controlling roughly two-thirds of economic ministries and the pro-Soviet group controlling the remaining one-third. Although this split in control makes it difficult to characterize this subcycle, economic policy tended to veer away from the market.

Overall, this cycle lasted seven and a half years, divided into subcycles that lasted two, three, and two and a half years, time spans that were too short for policies to take hold. Performance is difficult to assess because few statistics are available for 1959–1961 and because the introduction of the Soviet model in 1962 brought about a radical change in the methodology for calculating macroeconomic national statistics that was not compatible with the previous methodology. Economic results were mixed: economic growth initially rose, then declined, and later experienced a slight recovery; monetary liquidity and the commercial trade deficit increased throughout; the fiscal deficit apparently remained stable (although reliable statistics are not available); open unemployment initially rose but later declined; and poverty and inequality decreased (although there are no supporting statistics).

Fidel's Adoption and Radicalization of the Guevarist Model, 1966–1970

Although Fidel did not intervene directly in the policy debate, by the end of 1965 the leaders of the two contending factions were no longer at their posts: Guevara had left Cuba to promote guerrilla movements first in Africa and then in South America, and Rodríguez had resigned as director of the National Institute of Agrarian Reform. With the two faction leaders out of the picture, in mid-1966 Fidel publicly endorsed several elements of the Guevarist model and ordered their implementation, although he took the model to a higher level of idealism and distorted it with his own views. For example, he virtually eliminated the central plan and the state budget (essential in the Guevarist model), strengthened centralized decisionmaking (since the central plan had been eliminated, decisionmaking increasingly fell under Fidel's control), and gave even higher emphasis to moral incentives, labor mobilization, and the use of voluntary work.

Not only did Fidel diverge from the orthodox Soviet model, but he also affirmed that Cuba, with its idealist approach, had surpassed the Soviet Union in building socialism and communism. Moreover, through sponsorship of the guerrilla "foco" doctrine as a way to overthrow sitting Latin American governments, Cuba undermined traditional, pro-Soviet communist parties in the region. Despite this confrontation, the Soviet Union continued to support

Cuba economically until 1967, when Soviet leaders ran out of patience and reduced oil shipments to the island. Fidel responded by holding public trials of several prominent pro-Soviet government leaders and PCC officials (the so-called micro faction), who were found guilty of treason and "sectarianism," adding to the already tense relationship with the Soviet Union. In 1968, however, Fidel publicly defended the Soviet Union's invasion of Czechoslovakia (he argued that the Prague Spring was a counterrevolutionary and procapitalist movement, against worldwide criticism of the invasion), and such defense paid handsome dividends: resumption of oil shipments, better relations with the Soviet Union, and an overall increase in economic aid.

Cuba's development strategy shifted after 1964 from "inward" (import substitution industrialization) to "outward" orientation (export promotion). The previous policy of reducing sugar's role in the economy was reversed; a 1965–1970 sugar plan was adopted with the gigantic goal of producing 10 million tons of sugar in 1970. Perhaps the zenith of Cuba's distancing from the market occurred in 1968, when Fidel launched a "revolutionary offensive" consisting of the following policies: increased collectivization through the elimination of free agricultural markets and individual family plots within agricultural cooperatives; nationalization of some 58,000 small businesses (including barber shops, shoe repair shops, and street food stands); expanded centralization of economic decisionmaking through the creation of sectorial plans (e.g., for sugar, cattle) directly controlled by Fidel; setting aside financial controls (the state budget disappeared for nearly a decade); restricting and sanctioning self-employment; boosting voluntary work and labor mobilizations in agriculture; and emphasis on egalitarianism through reductions in salary differentials, promotion of moral incentives, and expansion of free social services (e.g., public telephones, burials, admission to sports and cultural events), all aimed at forging a socialist "new man."

This idealist cycle lasted four and a half years. Performance during this cycle is also challenging to assess, because of a government decision to cut back on collection and publication of statistics. Available information shows that most results were negative: the economic growth rate declined and was zero or negative in 1970, and sugar production fell short of the 10-million-ton target for that year by 15 percent and was accomplished at the cost of severe disruptions in other sectors of the economy. Monetary liquidity reached a record high and the excess currency in circulation brought about a significant decline in the purchasing power of the peso and a 25 percent rate of labor absenteeism (dealing a heavy blow to moral incentives and ending the myth of the creation of a "new man"). There are no statistics on the fiscal deficit because the national budget vanished, but the trade deficit increased considerably. Open unemployment fell to a record low (at the expense of increases in hidden unemployment and a sharp fall in labor productivity) and income distribution was the most egalitarian under the revolution, as indicated by estimates by foreign academics.

The Soviet Timid Economic Reform Model, 1971–1985

The failure in 1970 of both the sugar plan and the efforts to create a "new man," combined with overall economic deterioration, provoked a dangerous crisis and led to a timid oscillation of the pendulum toward the market beginning in 1971. The failure of Cuban-supported guerrillas in South America and the death of Che Guevara in 1967, combined with Fidel's public support of the Soviet invasion of Czechoslovakia in 1968, had facilitated reconciliation with the Soviet Union. Soviet soft loans, technical assistance, supplies of goods needed by Cuba, and price subsidies reached record-high levels during this period. For instance, the Soviet Union paid prices for Cuban sugar and nickel imports far above world market prices and sold oil to Cuba at below world market prices. Moreover, in 1972, Cuba was admitted into the Council for Mutual Economic Assistance (CMEA), an economic association composed of the Soviet Union and the socialist countries of Eastern Europe, which also opened up additional trade and financing opportunities. These positive factors were decisive at the start of the cycle and contributed to its continuation over a long period of time.

The United States, under the presidency of Gerald Ford (1974–1977), engaged in secret negotiations with Cuba and in 1975 the OAS lifted its multilateral sanctions, leaving it up to each member state to establish commercial and diplomatic relations with the island. But in giving military support to the socialist government of Angola, Cuba aborted its brief attempt at reconciliation with the United States. During the first years of the presidency of Jimmy Carter (1977–1981), tensions between the two countries were relaxed somewhat and an agreement was reached to establish political "interest sections" (at a level below that of embassies) in both countries. However, Cuba's military intervention in the war between Somalia and Ethiopia, as well as the arrival in the United States in 1980 of 125,000 Cubans in small boats from the port of Mariel, launched with Fidel's backing, gave rise to new tensions and paralyzed the process of improvement of diplomatic relations. During the presidency of Ronald Reagan (1981–1989), tensions between the two countries rose and Cuba organized "territorial militias" to defend itself from a presumed invasion by the United States. An offsetting positive external factor during this period was the availability of hard-currency credits to Cuba from international creditors.

During this period, the Cuban leadership essentially reversed its earlier idealist policies and initiated a timid journey toward the market. While there was an expansion of state-controlled cooperatives and a gradual absorption of private farms into cooperatives, a number of measures contrary to collectivization were implemented: the reintroduction of free agricultural markets and of family plots within state farms; reinstatement of self-employment and authorization of private farmers to contract workers, of citizens to build their own homes, and of individuals to swap homes (*permuta*); and enactment of a law to permit foreign direct investment (although the law imposed so many conditions that it was unsuccessful in attracting foreign investment). At the same time, central planning and the state budget were reinstated as macroeconomic management tools. Fidel criticized as "idealist errors" the previous calls for egalitarianism, moral incentives, voluntary work, and labor mobilization. The pendulum swung to the other side, with Cuba now adopting policies justifying salary differentials, reestablishment and expansion of the use of material incentives, reduction and near elimination of voluntary work (because of its inefficiency), creation of "parallel markets" where goods were sold to the population at prices set by the law of supply and demand, and charging users for certain public services that were formerly offered free of charge. During this period, an economic and political institutionalization process also took place: a new socialist constitution was promulgated, the National Assembly of People's Power was established, and the Cuban Communist Party was restructured. The new planning technocracy faced resistance; for instance, some of the measures were publicly criticized by Fidel (e.g., the free farmers' markets and self-employment), while others were not fully implemented (e.g., enterprise self-financing, profit-sharing with workers).

The development strategy was more rational and balanced than in previous cycles. An export-led orientation was maintained, with the sugar industry tapped to generate the bulk of export earnings; policies to spur sugar production—without adversely affecting the rest of the economy—included the construction of new mills and the mechanization of sugarcane cultivation and harvesting. With support from the Soviet Union and other socialist countries, Cuba also expanded nickel production and exports. Finally, the Soviet Union allowed Cuba to reexport (for hard currency) Soviet oil that had been committed to the island but not consumed. Tourism was reestablished as a generator of export revenues and production, and exports of citrus fruits and fish and shellfish were expanded.

This cycle is the longest (fifteen years) of the cycles identified here. Available statistics (during this period, Cuba also increased the quantity and quality of statistics) show stronger economic performance than in previous cycles. Economic growth recorded the highest average annual rate, particularly in 1971–1975, spurred by historically high world market prices for sugar, large sugar crops that averaged over 7 million tons per annum (in 1976–1985), and good performance in nonsugar sectors. Monetary liquidity declined through 1980 and the fiscal deficit was brought under control from 1978 (when the national budget was reinstituted) through 1985. The deficit in the trade balance remained essentially unchanged for a number of years and actually declined slightly in the 1970s (as a result of generous Soviet price subsidies for Cuban exports) but began to rise again in the first half of the 1980s (when some of such subsidies were cut back). For the first time since the start of the 1960s, pockets of unemployment appeared (because of the efforts to increase labor productivity, the decline in the demand for labor, and the entry into the labor force of the baby boomers conceived between 1959 and 1965) and inequality probably rose, although there are no statistics to support the latter inference.

Process of Rectification of Errors, 1986–1990

The economic recovery experienced in 1971–1985 resulted in economic growth and some improvements in population living conditions. However, internal and external forces conspired against the continuation and expansion of the timid market-oriented reforms that had been implemented. Fidel and the orthodox leaders resented the growing economic power of the technocrats who were leading the planning agencies, the elimination of some revolutionary institutions that were dear to them (such as voluntary work), the growth of inequality, and the emergence of a "new class" of individuals who were profiting from the reforms: private farmers, intermediaries who participated in the free agricultural markets, self-employed workers, and those engaged in the construction and swapping of homes. Although the magnitude of these activities was small, Fidel criticized them as early as 1982 and subsequently the government imposed heavy taxes on them. Fidel stepped up his attacks on private activities, accusing participants of being greedy and corrupt, a harbinger of policy changes to come. Externally, the rise to power of Mikhail Gorbachev in the Soviet Union in 1985 and the launch of his perestroika and glasnost policies, drove pressure within the Soviet Union to reduce trade and subsidies to Cuba and to demand more efficient use of the assistance given to the island. To make matters worse, in 1986 Cuba suspended servicing of its foreign debt with Paris Club members, resulting in a freeze of new credit to the island that continues to this day. In the United States, Presidents Ronald Reagan and George H. W. Bush maintained the economic embargo, providing Cuban authorities with justification to tighten internal controls as an alleged imperative to defend the country against an invading power.

The improving social and economic situation, coupled with important policy changes in the Soviet Union and pressures on the island to use Soviet assistance more judiciously, should have resulted in changes in Cuba along the line of those occurring in the Soviet Union and Eastern Europe. However, Fidel and the old guard feared that perestroika and glasnost in Cuba would weaken the revolutionary spirit, lead to social tensions, destabilize the regime, and erode their power and control. A new idealist cycle, involving rectification of errors and negative tendencies, was launched by Fidel in mid-1986 and lasted until 1990. In theory, the new policies sought middle ground between the "idealist errors" of 1966–1970 and the "economic (pragmatist) errors" of 1971–1985. In practice, most of the policies of the rectification process shared the same antimarket tenor of those of the previous idealist cycle, although not as extremely: acceleration of the process of elimination of private farms; halt of decentralization and return of economic policymaking to the political leadership (replacement of the Central Planning Board—JUCEPLAN—by a new agency led by a politician from the PCC's Political Bureau);[3] expansion of rationing and elimination of parallel markets; termination of free agricultural markets and of self-employment (the rationale for their elimination was that they were unnecessary and the state would assume their functions); severe restrictions on housing construction and swaps of private homes; reintroduction of voluntary work through the creation of military-style construction brigades; massive use of labor mobilization in agriculture; drastic reduction in the use of material incentives and reinstatement of moral incentives; and renewed emphasis on egalitarianism and free social services.

A new development strategy, centered on a food production program, set unrealistic targets, predicting that within five years the island would be self-sufficient in food production and would generate surpluses of food for export. A second, more pragmatic strand of the strategy was the development of the biotechnology industry, heavily promoted as a source of export revenue with the expectation that Cuba would become a world power in this industry. A third element of the strategy—and the most sensible—was the promotion of foreign tourism with foreign investment.

This idealist cycle lasted four and a half years, the same as for the 1966–1970 idealist cycle. Although publication of the Cuban official statistical yearbook, *Anuario Estadístico de Cuba*, was suspended after the 1989 issue, information from other sources shows that policies implemented during this cycle caused a recession, and Cuban society deteriorated according to virtually all socioeconomic indicators: the rate of economic growth was negative, monetary liquidity expanded significantly, fiscal deficits returned and expanded, the merchandise trade deficit reached historical highs, and open unemployment continued to rise. There is no information regarding inequality, but it probably declined in view of the measures taken. The urban population "at risk of poverty"—a euphemism for the internationally used term "poverty incidence"—was estimated in 1988, for the first time, at 6.3 percent.

Crisis and Market-Oriented Reforms, 1991–1996

At the start of the 1990s, Cuba suffered its most severe economic crisis under the revolution and probably since the Great Depression. External and internal factors were behind the crisis and the launch of a new pragmatist cycle. The first and most significant external factor was the disappearance of socialism in the Soviet Union and in Eastern Europe as well as of the CMEA, which resulted in the immediate loss of price subsidies and soft loans that had amounted to US$65 billion from the Soviet Union alone between 1960 and 1990; the halt of hundreds of Soviet investment projects and the return home of Soviet technicians; and the virtual end to all trade and economic aid from Eastern Europe. Cuba's foreign trade contracted by 75 percent, because about 70 percent of it was with the Soviet Union and that nation stopped importing Cuban nickel, citrus fruits, cigars, and other products; stopped exporting consumer, intermediate, and capital goods; and severely cut back on oil shipments. In a matter of a few years, trade between the two former allies was pared back so drastically that it basically turned into bartering sugar for oil at reduced volumes and at world market prices.

A second external factor that contributed to the crisis was the hardening of the US economic embargo, through the Torricelli (1992) and Helms-Burton (1996) legislation. The Torricelli Act banned subsidiaries of US corporations from trading or investing in Cuba and banned foreign ships used in Cuban trade from entering US ports. The Helms-Burton Act resulted in tougher provisions: for example, it banned imports of Cuban products from third countries and allowed US citizens to sue in US courts persons or corporations that "trafficked" in property confiscated by the Cuban government, and restricted the issuing of US visas to persons convicted of "trafficking."[4] The European Union, Canada, and Mexico protested the extraterritorial reach of the Helms-Burton Act, enacted countermeasures against the United States, and threatened to challenge the law before the World Trade Organization. Based on a provision of the law, Bill Clinton suspended every six months during 1996–2000 both the suing of "traffickers" and the imposition of sanctions, a practice that subsequently has been continued by all US presidents through the end of 2012.

The internal factor was the recession of 1986–1990, which had its roots in the Rectification Process. Contrary to trends in the rest of the world, the Rectification Process reversed the timid but positive economic reforms of 1975–1985, returned to moral incentives, and embarked in a failed food self-sufficiency plan. The recession left Cuba in a vulnerable economic position to confront the collapse of the Soviet Union and the socialist camp. In our opinion, had Cuba maintained the market-oriented reforms of the pragmatist cycle, it may have been better equipped to face the economic challenges of the 1990s and perhaps mitigate to some extent the effects of the crisis.

The economic crisis reached bottom in 1993; comparing 1993 and 1989 levels, real gross domestic product (GDP), adjusted for inflation, fell by 35 percent, per capita GDP by 41 percent, and physical production of sugar by 48 percent, of nickel by 36 percent, of citrus fruits by 32 percent, and of fish and shellfish by 63 percent. Monetary liquidity rose by 22 percent, to 73 percent of GDP; the value of exports declined by 80 percent and of imports by 75 percent, provoking a sharp shortage of foodstuffs, fuels, manufactured products, and raw materials and parts. The only positive developments were increases in the production of crude oil and of hard-currency revenue generated by the international tourism industry and a decline in the trade deficit resulting from a sharp fall in imports.

The crisis had other adverse effects as well. The rationing system was expanded to encompass nearly all consumer goods and rations were cut such that they covered barely half of monthly food needs of the average consumer. The black market grew rapidly and so did prices. The loss in the value of the Cuban peso resulted in a drop to one-tenth of the real average salary, which, combined with generalized shortages, spurred illegal activities and theft from state enterprises. This also had a negative impact on worker effort, bringing about an increase in absenteeism and a drop in productivity. The quality of all social services deteriorated severely. These developments offset many of the gains of earlier years and fed feelings of frustration and alienation among the population, eroding the regime's political base. In August 1994, hundreds of residents of Havana rioted in the streets to protest against the government, the first popular action of such nature and magnitude under the revolution.

At the beginning of the 1990s, a debate about economic policies and strategies resumed after a long hiatus since the 1964–1966 debate over the appropriate model of socialism to pursue. The debate this time was not over whether or not market instruments should be used, but rather the degree of their usage and how to do so within the context of a socialist system in order to avoid or mitigate potential negative effects. At the risk of oversimplifying a rather complex situation, there were essentially two positions. The most advanced reformers supported deep structural changes (but not neoliberal) that would reach to the roots of the economic problems and guarantee sustained economic growth in the long term, although they were concerned about the negative social effects of such policies. Meanwhile, orthodox thinkers (minimalists) supported only selected market-oriented measures to stop the economic freefall, reduce inflation and the fiscal deficit, strengthen the value of the peso, promote economic growth, and reduce social adverse effects, while keeping to a minimum the risk of destabilizing the regime.

The reformists were principally academics (economists and other social scientists) and technicians, who saw market reforms as the lesser of two evils. Some of them argued that repressing markets was futile, as they would emerge under any circumstances, as had been demonstrated by the black market. Besides, to the extent that the state was unable to meet the urgent basic needs of the population, the reformists argued that the state should permit regulated markets or private enterprise to fill the gaps. Others supported the privatization of personal services that they were convinced the state was incapable of delivering to the population, and reestablishment of free agricultural markets, self-employment, and other mechanisms that had been de-emphasized or abolished during the Rectification Process. The reformists believed that the private sector could make positive contributions; for example, it could check the state monopoly in certain areas, promote competition and increase efficiency, create productive employment opportunities, and spur economic growth. The minimalists feared a snow-balling effect, as a growing private sector would put additional demands on the state sector for inputs, create and accumulate wealth, and present a challenge to the government. A common apprehension was the adverse consequences that market reforms had caused in the Soviet Union and Eastern Europe, particularly the potential sharp reduction or disappearance of the social safety net: high open unemployment that would create serious political and social problems, income inequalities that would weaken population unity, increases in prices that would reduce significantly the purchasing power of low-income groups, and deterioration of social services.

Fidel initially opposed market-oriented reforms. In 1992–1993 he rejected commercial relations between state enterprises, including farms, and the private sector, as well as free agricultural markets and self-employed public vendors. In fact, he warned that the revolution would continue to expand state ownership of the means of production, nationalizing even the remaining small farms, and that any existing economic ills would be resolved through state action. He criticized supporters of reform within Cuba, calling them disaffected, defeatists, pseudo-revolutionaries, and traitors.

To confront the crisis, the government enacted an emergency plan (called the "Special Period in Time of Peace") that allocated scarce resources to the country's most vital needs. This was in fact a structural adjustment program, although it tried to protect social services as much as feasible. To halt the economic freefall and promote economic growth, several measures to stimulate the external sector were taken: promotion of international tourism, efforts to attract foreign investment, and redirection of foreign trade to Western nations. The new development strategy sought to keep the changes within enclaves in order to prevent "contamination" of the domestic economy and the socialist system. The results of these policy measures were modest at best and the economy continued to deteriorate. As the crisis deepened, in 1993 the government reluctantly introduced market-oriented reforms geared to the domestic economy; these measures were of limited scope, were taken in a piecemeal fashion, and were implemented cautiously to prevent the reforms from getting out of control.

This second pragmatist cycle embodied the most significant market-oriented reforms implemented up to that time under the revolution, through

the following measures: (a) reduction in collectivization through the transformation of state farms into a new type of cooperative—the Basic Unit of
Cooperative Production (UBPC)—with some degree of autonomy from the
state and the granting of small plots of lands within the UBPCs to farmers
for production for family consumption; (b) decentralization of economic
decisionmaking, initially regarding foreign trade and later also extending to
the national economy through the creation of quasi-private and mixed enterprises; (c) reinstatement of the central budget as a key fiscal policy tool
and implementation of measures to diminish public expenditures (e.g., cut
subsidies) and increase revenue (e.g., impose new taxes), and reduce the
monetary overhang; (d) enactment in 1995 of a more flexible foreign-
investment law, creation of free trade zones, authorization for foreigners to
buy real estate to be used for offices, homes, and tourism development, as
well as authorization for Cuban citizens to rent a portion of their homes to
tourists, legalization of the holding and use of foreign currencies (principally dollars), as well as of the receipt of hard-currency remittances sent
from relatives and friends abroad, and increased flexibility of family visits
to the island; (e) reduction in the scope of the rationing system, ability to
purchase some goods in free agricultural and artisan markets at prices set
by demand and supply, creation of the "convertible peso" (CUC), and opening of state-run hard-currency exchange houses (CADECAs) to buy and
sell foreign currencies as well as of foreign-currency stores (TRDs) to sell
goods to the population who are able to pay in hard currencies; (f) reopen-
ing of free agricultural markets and opening of artisan markets; (g) self-
employment authorization in 157 specific occupations, among them small
restaurants (paladares) and private taxis; (h) virtual elimination of voluntary
work and substantial rollback of labor mobilization; (i) reduction of egalitarianism, broader acceptance of income differentials, and preference for
economic incentives over moral incentives; and (j) increase in the price of
certain public services and charge for others that were formerly free, although public health and education continued to be free.

This cycle lasted approximately six years, although the most significant
and most market-oriented reform measures were implemented between
1993 and 1995. Beginning in 1994, the market-oriented policies began to
generate an economic recovery, although precrisis economic levels were
not recovered. Compared to 1993, the trough of the economic crisis, economic indicators in 1996 showed considerable improvement: GDP growth
swung from negative (–14.9 percent) to positive (7.8 percent), the strongest
growth rate since 1985; monetary liquidity fell from 73 percent to 42 percent
of GDP; the inflation rate fell from 26 percent to negative (deflation); the
fiscal deficit declined from 34 percent to 2.5 percent of the budget; exports
and imports rose by 72 percent and 80 percent respectively (the merchandise trade deficit grew by 89 percent, but was still about half of its absolute

value in 1989); the value of the peso (CUP) with respect to the US dollar in CADECA exchange houses appreciated from 95-to-1 to 19-to-1. Negative effects included increases in open unemployment, from 6.2 percent to 7.6 percent, and in inequality, although there were no statistics on the latter.

Slowdown and Halt of Reform, 1997–2003

The aforementioned pragmatist policies stopped the sharp drop in GDP and started a partial recovery. However, in our opinion, they generated distrust from Fidel and the minimalists due to their concern that the processes of de-collectivization, decentralization, delegation of governmental economic power, and growing economic independence of farmers, self-employed workers, and others would weaken the state and the power wielded by the leadership. Additional angst was caused by the growth of open unemployment and inequality; the latter particularly ran counter to the ideological preferences of the orthodox.

Pragmatist policies were subjected to strict government controls that prevented them from reaching their full potential and often led to their demise. For example, foreign investments exceeding US$10 million had to be approved by the Executive Committee of the Council of Ministers; foreign investors were normally limited to 49 percent participation in joint ventures; moreover, joint ventures were not permitted to contract or pay workers directly, as there was a state agency charged with the duties of collecting the salaries from the employers in convertible currency and paying the workers in pesos. The agricultural cooperatives (UBPCs), unlike their Chinese and Vietnamese counterparts, lacked independence to decide which crop to plant, to whom to sell their output, and at what price; the state essentially made those decisions and purchased nearly all of the output produced by the cooperatives at government-fixed prices that were well below market prices. Substantial licensing fees and taxes were levied on the self-employed, at the same time that their businesses were subjected to frequent inspections and heavy fines for alleged violations. Small private restaurants (*paladares*) were first authorized, then banned, and finally authorized again, but subject to heavy regulations: a limit of twelve seats, employment of family members only, restrictions on which meats and seafood could be sold, and high taxes. Private taxi drivers suffered initially the same uncertainty as did the *paladares,* and later were prohibited from serving tourists. The exchange rate of the so-called convertible peso (CUC) is fixed unilaterally by the government—that is, it is not determined by international currency markets and is exchanged on the black market at lower rates.

In March 1996, Raúl publicly discussed the negative effects of the market-oriented reforms, many of which he had supported, as well as the political challenges they posed. Several reformers were censured and removed from their posts, among them three internationally known economists who had published an important book about the need to move faster and deeper with the reform process within socialist parameters.[5] This purge put an end to the public debate on economic policy. While some additional reform measures were implemented after 1996 (for example, one reforming the banking sector and another creating free trade zones), from that point forward and through 2003 the process stagnated. Some measures that were discussed in 1995–1996 were never implemented: the elimination of redundant workers in the state sector, achieving the convertibility of the peso, authorizing individuals to operate their own businesses, a general reform of prices, and the requirement that all workers contribute to their social security pensions (only 11 percent of the labor force made contributions in 2012).

With production costs higher than prices in the international market, Fidel launched a major restructuring (dismantling) of the sugar industry: 45 percent of the sugar mills were shut down, 60 percent of sugarcane lands were shifted to other purposes, and 100,000 workers were laid off. The logic of the plan was that the downsizing of the industry would free up resources that could be used more productively in other economic endeavors.

The government judged—erroneously—that the problems associated with the economic downturn, the fiscal deficit, and inflation had been overcome, and so had the risks of political instability. The leadership probably judged that additional moves toward the market would enhance the risk of loss of economic and political power as well as adverse social effects. As in 1986, the political logic of Fidel and of the minimalists prevailed over the economic logic of the reformists, with the anticipated adverse impact on the economy and living standards. To address popular discontent and confront the looming peaceful dissident movement, in 1999 Cuba enacted Law no. 88, on the Protection of Cuban National Independence and Economy, which provided for jail sentences of between eight and twenty years and seizure of assets from citizens convicted of political crimes such as collaborating with foreign journalists, accepting payment for such collaboration, possessing or distributing "subversive materials" (independent publications not authorized by the government), disrupting the public order by participating in demonstrations, and so on. Based on a right enshrined in the Cuban Constitution, the Varela Project, spearheaded by Oswaldo Payá, a human rights activist and winner of the Sakharov Prize for Freedom of Thought (awarded by the European Parliament), collected over 11,000 signatures from Cuban citizens calling for a referendum to permit freedom of expression, hold free elections, grant amnesty to political prisoners, and permit the creation of small businesses. During a visit to Cuba in 2002, former US president Jimmy Carter made a speech (in Spanish) on national television, in which he described the elements of the Varela Project. A pastoral letter issued by Roman Catholic cardinal Jaime Ortega in 2003 called on the government to allow a political and economic opening and echoed some of the same proposals as in the Varela Project. In the aftermath of government-organized public demonstrations against the Varela Project, not only was the latter soundly rejected by the National Assembly of People's Power in July 2002, but the Constitution was amended as well with the addition of a new article proclaiming the "irrevocability" of Cuba's socialist system. In the spring of 2003, the government arrested seventy-five dissidents (economists, journalists, writers, librarians, supporters of the Varela Project, human rights activists), who were charged with violating Law no. 88 and condemned to long jail sentences. These actions provoked criticism from the international community, including from world personalities who up to that time had supported the revolution. At about the same time, several Cuban officials who had supported the reforms were dismissed from their posts.

The stagnation of the reforms had negative economic consequences. Comparing 1996 and 2003: the GDP growth rate slowed in 1997–1998 and in 2000–2002; monetary liquidity increased in absolute terms beginning in 1998 and reached a peak in 2002 (43 percent higher than in 1996); the rate of price change, which was a negative 4.9 percent (deflation) in 1996, turned to positive 7 percent (inflation) in 2002; the fiscal deficit rose to 3 percent of the budget in 2002–2003; the merchandise trade deficit almost doubled over the period, reaching a historical high of US$3 billion in 2003; and the aftermath of the September 11, 2001, terrorist attack on the United States led to a brief decline in Cuban tourism in 2002. The restructuring of the sugar industry provoked a 47 percent fall in production in 2004–2005, although the plan expected that the sugar plantations and mills that remained in operation—adduced to be the most productive—would partly compensate for those that were shut down. There are no statistical indicators that would permit a comparison of the social situation between 1996 and 2003, but those that are available suggest that there was a deterioration. Inequality increased markedly, with the Gini coefficient jumping from 0.250 to 0.407 between 1989 and 1999, while the ratio of revenue between the richest quintile and the poorest quintile grew from 3.8-to-1 to 13.5-to-1. The average monthly salary fell by 45 percent between 1989 and 2002. The urban population "at risk of poverty" rose from 6.3 percent in 1988 to 20 percent in 1999, while the share of the population who had a "perception of being poor" in a survey conducted in the city of Havana in 2002 was 31 percent. The only positive performance was with respect to open unemployment, which fell from 9 percent in 1996 to 3.3 percent in 2002, but at the cost of expanding labor surplus in the state sector.

Reversal of Reform, 2003–2006

Active reversal of the reforms began in 2003 under the aegis of the "Battle of Ideas," an ideological construct that returned conscience and voluntarism to the center of policymaking, consistent with previous idealist cycles. In

2004, José Ramón Machado Ventura, member of the PCC's Political Bureau (and in 2012 its first vice president), strongly criticized government officials who had been copying capitalist management techniques so well that they had become capitalists themselves, and warned that liberalism, tolerance, and lack of control were harming the nation. The reversal of the reforms was centered on three policy strands (some of them also were geared to control hard-currency expenditure due to the severe scarcity, as well as to fight corruption).

First was the re-centralization of economic policymaking, attained through ten measures: (a) central control of imports and exports, which had been delegated to state enterprises and were brought back under the Ministry of Foreign Trade; (b) ban on state enterprises conducting their activities in convertible currencies; (c) sale (transfer) of all hard-currency holdings and future hard-currency earnings generated by enterprises from exports to the Central Bank of Cuba (BCC); (d) requirement that all enterprises purchase hard currencies from the BCC (with a surcharge) to finance imports; (e) ban on state enterprises with respect to providing eighty-seven services formerly billed in hard currencies, and transfer of such activities to the state; (f) creation of a single account at the BCC, where state enterprises were required to deposit all earnings in hard currencies and convertible pesos, irrespective of their source; (g) requirement that all state enterprises obtain BCC permission to make payments exceeding 5,000 convertible pesos; (h) prohibition on state enterprises and banks from accepting payments or deposits unless approved by the BCC; (i) re-centralization of state tourism enterprises under the Ministry of Tourism and strong controls on tourism personnel; and (j) weekly review and approval of the budgets of state agencies by the BCC. The second policy strand consisted of curbs on the already small private sector: a ban on state employees, managers, and military officers engaging in self-employment; removal of some forty self-employment categories that had been previously authorized; cutback of licenses for about 28 percent of the self-employed who had received authorization to operate (including the virtual ban of private taxis); and closure of nearly all *paladares,* besieged by heavy fees and taxes and frequent inspections. The third policy strand consisted of implementing a de-dollarization policy: disallowing the use of the dollar as a means of exchange throughout the nation, imposing a 10 percent surcharge to exchanges of dollars for convertible pesos, and "appreciating" the CUC by 20 percent; moreover, to soak up more dollars being held by households, prices of consumer goods offered at TRDs were increased between 10 and 30 percent in 2004.

With sugar output falling by two-thirds of its average output between 2002 and 2007, the development strategy shifted from goods exports (except for nickel, which experienced record-high prices in international markets), toward export of professional services, such as those provided by physicians, nurses, teachers, sports trainers, and security personnel.

The three previous idealist cycles not only were incapable of addressing the country's socioeconomic problems, but also actually worsened them, provoking a succession of crises and requiring subsequent policy corrections. Why, then, a fourth attempt at centralization of policymaking and reduction of the role of the private sector? According to the official discourse, the new ideological thrust had the following objectives: combat corruption and lack of discipline, correct neoliberal and capitalist errors, reduce inequalities, curb hard-currency self-financing by enterprises and stop hard-currency "leakages," restore revolutionary morality, and confront US threats. But another probable cause for the shift was that the decentralization of economic decisionmaking to hundreds of enterprises, in the hands of thousands of managers, and involving hundreds of thousands of persons in the small but dynamic private sector, was distrusted by the leadership because of the potential risk of autonomy. Finally, the ideological elements of the Battle of Ideas also aimed to distract the population from daily challenges in an environment of shortage.

The most significant external factor that contributed to the reform reversal was the economic support to Cuba from Venezuela under Hugo Chávez. During this period, Venezuela replaced the Soviet Union as the great subsidizer of the Cuban economy: US$4 billion in credits, investment, and economic assistance in 2001–2007; an unpaid oil import bill of some US$2.5 billion; payments for over 20,000 Cuban medical doctors and other professionals providing services in Venezuela estimated at about US$5 billion in 2006; and two-way goods trade between Cuba and Venezuela amounting to US$2.6 billion, which made the latter Cuba's most important trading partner. China also increased trade with Cuba, becoming the island's second most important trading partner, and also granted credits and entered into investment agreements, although not as significant compared to Venezuela's investments. Finally, although the number of foreign-invested projects declined, key investors such as Canadian firm Sherritt International and Spanish hospitality chain Meliá expanded their holdings in the areas of mining and tourism, respectively, and other multinational corporations entered into arrangements for oil exploration.[6] The combination of these three positive foreign sector developments gave Fidel confidence to dismantle elements of the reforms that ran counter to his ideology.

The return of centralization, coupled with shortages of foreign exchange, brought about a reduction in the operational flexibility of state enterprises, delays in the purchase of imported raw materials, and forfeiture of commitment to pay CUC incentives to the sugar industry, basic industry, and transportation workers. Hotel managers complained that required weekly budgets forced them to estimate even how many rolls of toilet paper, light bulbs, or pounds of tomatoes would be needed for the following week, creating red tape and taking them away from their duty of providing quality service to customers. The de-dollarization policy generated a significant flow of dollars into the government's coffers in the short term, but had adverse results in the medium term: the restrictions on the use of the dollar, the 10 percent surtax on its exchange, the "appreciation" in the value of the CUC by 8 percent, and the general increase in prices in TRD-incentivized black markets for goods and currencies. Prices of goods on the black market, fed by theft from the state, were lower than those at the TRDs. The revaluation of the CUC made black market currency exchanges more lucrative and Cuban tourism offerings less competitive internationally, contributing to the stagnation in the number of tourists in 2006–2007 and in gross revenue until 2010.

To summarize, the economic results of the fourth idealist cycle were overwhelmingly negative: sharp decline in fixed capital formation, from 12.8 percent to 9 percent of GDP between 2001 and 2005; increase in the inflation rate from −1.4 percent to 5.7 percent between 2001 and 2006; record rise in monetary liquidity to over 20 billion pesos in 2006, 49 percent higher than the level in 2003; growth of the fiscal deficit from 2.8 percent of the budget to 4.6 percent; jump of 70 percent in the goods trade deficit between 2003 and 2006, reaching a new historical high of US$6.6 billion; increase in the external debt over the same period of 36 percent, setting a new record of US$15.4 billion in 2006; and decline by 31 percent in the number of foreign-invested enterprises (joint ventures or other arrangements) in Cuba.

Two indicators showed positive performance: a further decline in open unemployment, from 2.3 percent to 1.9 percent of the labor force between 2003 and 2006, and a miraculous jump in GDP growth, from 5.4 percent in 2004 to 11.8 percent in 2005 and 12.5 percent in 2006. The GDP growth rates in 2005–2006 were among the highest in the world—which would suggest that the reversal of the reforms had been wildly successful—but in fact resulted from two statistical manipulations: first, beginning in 2001, the base year for national accounts calculations "at constant prices" was shifted from 1981 to 1997, which resulted in an average increase of 56 percent in the growth rate for each year from 1989 to 2000 (the period for which the two series at constant prices, for 1981 and 1997, are available); and second, beginning in 2003, Cuban statisticians added to the conventional calculation of GDP the value of free social services consumed by the population plus the value of price subsidies to products sold through the rationing system, thereby overvaluating GDP. In contrast to the rosy picture painted by the official GDP statistics, production levels of thirteen out of nineteen key products in mining, manufacturing, and agriculture (sugar, steel, fertilizers, cement, shoes, soap, citrus fruits, rice, milk, eggs, fish and shellfish, raw tobacco, and cattle) were from 19 to 94 percent lower in 2006 than in 1989;

electricity production was unchanged in 2006 from 1989, but lower on a per capita basis, since population had grown over the period by 7 percent; and production was higher in 2006 than in 1989 for only five key products (oil, natural gas, nickel, root crops, and cigars). The previous analysis of underestimation of unemployment is also applicable to this cycle and will be elaborated in Chapter 4.

Raúl's Structural Reforms, 2007–present

The dreadful economic results accumulated over the several idealist cycles, worsened by the global financial crisis, brought about a slowdown of Cuban GDP growth in 2007–2009 and a contraction in mining production, segments of manufacturing, and most of agriculture; a significant rise in the budget deficit; and new historical heights in monetary liquidity, deficit in the goods trade balance, and external debt. To confront these challenges, in 2007 Raúl promised structural reforms that gave rise to the third pragmatist cycle, the strongest under the revolution. Following his call for a national economic policy debate, reforms started slowly and modestly. Since 2010, however, there has been an acceleration of reforms, many of which were approved by the Sixth Congress of the PCC in April 2011, and were still in the process of being implemented at the time we completed writing this book.

Raúl has dismantled to a large extent the Battle of Ideas programs, which previously were assigned a larger budget than some ministries. While Raúl has maintained the economic socialist model (central planning and predominance of state enterprises), he has proclaimed that such model must be "updated" to account for the market and private enterprise. The principal measures taken to date confirm the robustness of the current pragmatist cycle: (a) de-collectivization (for example, transformation of some ministries into state enterprises, dismissal of redundant workers from the state sector, expansion of the private sector, distribution to individuals of idle state lands in usufruct, greater flexibility for enterprises in setting prices, authorization for sale of homes and automobiles); (b) decentralization of decisionmaking (for example, allowing self-financing of state enterprises and cooperatives, allowing cooperatives to set the sale price of their output, and allowing agricultural producers to sell directly to state and to tourism enterprises); (c) larger role for the budget and its relation with fiscal and monetary policies, with tax reform aimed at increasing government revenues; (d) eradication of voluntary work and of construction brigades because of their inefficiency; (e) gradual elimination of the rationing system and increased role of market prices in resource allocation; (f) expansion of self-employment to cover 181 occupations, permission for private transportation service providers—including taxis—to operate, and creation of cooperatives in production and services; (g) permission for producers to sell their output directly at free agricultural markets; (h) criticism of egalitarianism, virtual elimination of moral incentives, and predominance of material incentives; and (i) reduction in social expenditures, which must be based on economic criteria and availability of fiscal resources. Meanwhile, the open unemployment rate has increased and so has income inequality. These measures and their effects will be analyzed in Chapters 4 and 5.

Conclusion: Failure of Idealist Cycles and Structural Reform

For more than five decades, socialist Cuba's policies followed a recurring pattern of idealist and pragmatist cycles, successively moving away from or toward the market. These cycles have lasted, on average, four to five years each. The frequent swings in the economic-ideological pendulum brought about contrasting policy prescriptions that created instability and uncertainty and had adverse effects on economic performance (it is worth noting that the longest cycle, the first pragmatist cycle, 1971–1985, which lasted fifteen years, is the one that achieved the most favorable and stable results). Fidel was the key internal factor in the generation of the cycles until his illness and transfer of power to Raúl in 2006.

The evolution of the sugar sector can be used to illustrate the effects of the policy zigzags: out of favor and perceived as an instrument of underdevelopment in 1959–1966; favored greatly and showered with resources diverted from other sectors of the economy in 1967–1970; provided with investment resources and subsidized by Soviet prices in 1971–1989, which resulted in high and stable levels of production; left to its own devices and shrinking when price subsidies ended in 1990–2003; and restructured through sharp reductions in capacity and production in 2004–2011 (at the time of this writing, Raúl may be attempting to revive it). The restructuring of the sugar industry (sharp agricultural and industrial capacity cuts) was carried out with a short-term perspective, at a time when world sugar prices were low; more recently, world sugar prices have risen substantially, putting into question earlier decisions. Moreover, a portion of the sugarcane fields that were demolished could have been used to produce cane for biofuels, as has been done in Brazil.

The first two clearly delineated idealist cycles (the Fidel-Guevarista cycle and the Rectification Process) brought about crises in the economic organization model and the development strategy, leading to economic and social deterioration and threatening the stability of the regime. On both occasions, Fidel shifted gears and reluctantly accepted the introduction of market-oriented reforms. The first two pragmatist cycles improved economic and living conditions, but accentuated inequalities and, in the first case, also increased open unemployment. The exaggerated egalitarianism associated with the idealist cycles was one of the factors responsible for weak economic performance through its adverse impact on incentives. It should be noted that the sharp decline in open unemployment was accompanied by large increases in underemployment or disguised unemployment with a reduction in labor productivity and real salaries; moreover, from the end of the 1990s to 2010, open unemployment was understated by ignoring the growing hidden unemployment. The fourth idealist cycle also had negative economic impacts masked by statistical manipulation of GDP.

Fidel played a key role in launching and ending each of the cycles, although other contributing factors were also at play. Beyond Fidel's ideological preferences, the decisions to slow, halt, or reverse pragmatist cycles and return to idealist cycles that were destined to fail were driven, in our opinion, by fear on the part of Fidel and the political leadership of losing political control. Political logic, therefore, prevailed over economic logic, even if it resulted in deterioration of economic and living standards. The political leadership has not been harmed by the negative effects of its actions, since it is protected against such through the perks of power; the political leadership is also not subject to public transparency and accountability processes, as currently there is no possibility that these leaders would be removed from their posts through true democratic elections.

Idealist cycles prevailed over pragmatist cycles, compounding and deepening economic challenges, and making them more difficult to solve, including a massive bureaucracy, at all levels of government, plagued by corruption. In November 2005, Fidel warned that while enemies from abroad had plotted unsuccessfully to destroy the revolution, the revolution itself could self-destruct. At the time Raúl assumed power in 2006, the economic and social situation was unsustainable. Thus in 2007 he publicly announced that structural reforms (pragmatic policies) were the only way to tackle the nation's problems. While by the end of 2012 the Cuban government had implemented numerous positive measures, the road ahead was long and winding. Broadening and deepening of reforms was essential for achieving a high and sustained rate of economic growth, higher labor productivity, reduction in excess monetary liquidity, elimination of monetary duality, decrease in the goods trade deficit, creation of private sector productive employment to absorb excess workers dismissed from the state sector, increases in real salaries and pensions, and improvement in the quality of social services. At the time of this writing, the possibility that Cuba will return to an idealist policy cycle does not seem feasible.

Notes

1. This typology was originally presented in Mesa-Lago, 1994, and expanded, systematized, and updated in Mesa-Lago, 2000, 2003, and 2009b. This chapter updates

it through 2012. The statistics used herein originate from Cuban official sources or from the above-cited works by Mesa-Lago, or are presented in other chapters of this book. For other interpretations of cycles or stages of Cuban economic history, see Pérez Villanueva, 2010c; Santamaría, 2011. For a comparison of Cuba's socioeconomic situation in 1958 and 2008, see Mesa-Lago, 2009a.

2. An econometric analysis for the period 1980–2005 conducted by a Cuban economist supports Mesa-Lago's hypothesis (although the author does not cite his work): during cycles associated with centralization policies (idealist), Cuban productivity and GDP declined, while both rose during cycles associated with decentralization policies (pragmatist) (Doimeadios, 2007).

3. The director of JUCEPLAN, Humberto Pérez, who also led the economic reforms, was dismissed and tried on charges that he had mechanically reproduced in Cuba a reform model not suitable for the island. Years earlier, Raúl had sent Pérez to Moscow to study economics and planning and later supported him as director of JUCEPLAN. Fidel assigned Raúl to preside over the tribunal that tried and dismissed Pérez.

4. Just as he had derailed détente efforts by Presidents Gerald Ford and Jimmy Carter, in 1996 Fidel ordered his air force to shoot down, over international waters, two small unarmed aircraft piloted by Cuban Americans. This action reversed the congressional support that President Bill Clinton had generated to defeat the Helms-Burton Act, thereby clearing the way for its passage.

5. Julio Carranza, Luis Gutiérrez, and Pedro Monreal, *Cuba, la restructuración de la economía: una propuesta para el debate* (Havana: Editorial Ciencias Sociales, 1995). The first and third authors were residing outside the island as of 2012.

6. Since 2001, a change in the US embargo has permitted the exportation of food and medicines to Cuba.

2

The Domestic Economy, 2006–2012

This chapter focuses on domestic economic performance in Cuba during Raúl Castro's era (2006–2012), although, when appropriate, it also refers to earlier periods in order to provide a longer perspective. The chapter compares the most recent economic indicators with those of 1989, the year of best economic performance before the crisis of the 1990s, and with regional averages for Latin America. The chapter covers trends and problems of Cuban economic statistics, macroeconomic indicators, and physical production trends.

Trends and Problems of Cuban Economic Statistics

In recent years, Cuban economic statistics have improved with respect to availability and timeliness, supporting the expansion of economic analysis on the island. The National Statistical Office (ONE) has shortened the time lags in the release of statistics on its website (www.one.cu): in January it posts preliminary statistics for the previous year for selected series, and in the May–June time frame it does the same with respect to most of the contents of the principal annual statistical publication, the *Anuario Estadístico de Cuba*. However, statistics pertaining to macroeconomic and external sector performance tend to lag in publication; at the time of this writing (end of November 2012), national accounts and external sector statistics in the *Anuario* were not yet available for 2011; highly aggregated foreign trade statistics were available in another ONE publication, the *Panorama Económico y Social de Cuba*.

A dozen Cuban economists affiliated with the Center for the Study of the Cuban Economy (CEEC) at the University of Havana, currently headed by Omar Everleny Pérez Villanueva, have increased notably the number and quality of academic analyses they have produced based on official statistics, often advancing constructive criticisms of the domestic situation.[1] Their works are frequently published in the *Boletín Cuatrimestral* of the CEEC and by the Economic Press Service, both accessible on the Internet, as well as in books, conference proceedings, and international journals. *Revista Temas* often publishes articles by academics regarding economic policy and reforms and organizes symposiums around specific topics. Journals published by the Catholic Church, such as *Vitral,* whose influence has waned, and more recently *Espacio Laical, Palabra Nueva,* and *Convivencia,* do the same. Dissident economists continue to carry out critical evaluations of the situation; among dissident economists, one of the loudest voices is that of Oscar Espinosa Chepe, who has published a stream of articles and two recent books. All of these works have been valuable sources of information for this book.

Despite the mentioned improvements in Cuban statistics, serious analysis of economic and social issues is hampered by the relatively few statistics that are available compared to other countries in the region as well as by concerns about their reliability and lack of comparability over time. First, Cuban statistics are generally absent from publications of international organizations. For example, in its annual report for 2011 (ECLAC 2011a), the Economic Commission for Latin America and the Caribbean only includes Cuban statistics for three of twenty-four comparative tables: gross domestic product (GDP) growth rate, GDP per capita growth rate, and central government finances. Most of the tables exclude Cuba altogether, leave blank the cells corresponding to Cuba, or provide Cuban data through 2007, the latest year for which the information is reported.[2] Thus, no information for 2011 is included for Cuba regarding gross capital formation, balance of payments, exports and imports of goods, terms of trade, external transfers, foreign direct investment, gross external debt, international monetary reserves, labor force participation rate, employment, open unemployment, real average salary, monetary indicators, consumer prices, and public debt. As a consequence, the text of ECLAC's report—which is based on the comparative statistics—hardly mentions Cuba at all. Cuban labor market statistics are also sparse in publications of the International Labour Organization (ILO), including the LABORSTA database as well as publications of the ILO's Regional Office for Latin America and the Caribbean (Pérez-López, 2012).

Second, for a number of years the Central Bank of Cuba (BCC) published an annual report, prepared to meet the information demands of foreign creditors, that analyzed the performance of the domestic economy and the external sector and provided some financial statistics not available elsewhere. The report was last published in 2008 (with statistical information through 2007). There are no published statistics on international monetary reserves and on the banking sector. ONE does not publish full statistics on the balance of payments, and statistics on nickel exports, oil and refined oil products imports, production of sugar and nickel, and so on, have become more scarce in recent years.

Third, the credibility of some Cuban statistics has diminished recently, for example regarding some macroeconomic indicators such as GDP, capital formation, inflation, and open unemployment. The next section discusses challenges in analyzing Cuban GDP growth rates in an international comparative framework as a result of a different estimation methodology developed by Cuba. In Chapter 4 we describe the underestimation of the open unemployment rate.

Domestic Macroeconomic Indicators

GDP Growth Rates

According to official statistics, Cuban GDP at constant 1997 prices grew steadily between 2004 and 2006, with the growth rate peaking at 12.1 percent in 2006 (see Table 2.1), the highest for that year in the region and even higher than China's growth rate of 10.7 percent. Since 2007, there has been a steady decline in the growth rate, which was 1.4 percent in 2009 (compared to the projected growth rate of 6 percent for that year).[3] The global financial crisis that began at the end of 2007—at a time when the Cuban economy was already experiencing external sector stress—sharply reduced the availability of international financing and also affected the demand for Cuban commodity exports (nickel, sugar, cigars) and world market prices, overall trade in goods and services (including tourism and exports of professional services), and most likely the level of remittances, thereby deepening the external sector imbalances. As Cuba is not a member of the International Monetary Fund, the World Bank, or the Inter-American Development Bank, these institutions were not available to offer Cuba balance of payments support and credits.[4] The combination of deficits in the balance of trade, slower growth, diminished access to international financing, and a fixed exchange rate (that overvalues the convertible peso [CUC]) brought on a liquidity crisis that prompted the Cuban government to freeze bank accounts in hard currency and suspend external payments (see Chapter 3). Government authorities did not have the domestic resources or the international support necessary to launch countercyclical policies, thus requiring the adoption of stringent adjustment measures that had long-term adverse impact on growth performance (Mesa-Lago and Vidal Alejandro, 2010).

**Table 2.1 Domestic Macroeconomic Indicators, 1989 and 2005–2011
(percentages)**

Indicators	1989	2005	2006	2007	2008	2009	2010	2011	Regional Average, 2011
GDP growth rate	1.2	11.2	12.1	7.3	4.1	1.4	2.1	2.7	4.3
Capital formation[a]	25.6	9.0	11.5	11.0	11.4	9.5	8.0	7.0[b]	22.9
Inflation rate	0.5	3.7	5.7	2.8	–0.1	–0.1	1.4	1.7	6.9
Monetary liquidity (M2)[a]	21.6	46.6	38.1	36.8	41.5	41.3	40.6	40.2	
Fiscal balance[a]	–7.2	–4.6	–3.2	–3.2	–6.9	–4.8	–3.8	–3.8	–1.5

Sources: Data for 1989 from CEE, 1991; data for 2005–2011 from ONE, 2009, 2010a, 2011a, 2012b; Pedraza, 2011. Gross capital formation data for 2005–2011, inflation for 2011, and regional averages from ECLAC, 2011a.
Notes: Data for 1989 are at 1981 prices; data for 2005–2011 are at 1997 prices.
a. Percentage of GDP.
b. Authors' estimate based on official estimate of 26 percent underfulfillment of the investment plan (R. Castro Ruz, 2011g).

Again, according to official statistics, GDP grew by 2.1 percent in 2010, a growth performance at odds with other domestic macroeconomic indicators, and considerably slower than the 6 percent average rate of growth for Latin America and the Caribbean. In 2011, the official growth rate was reported as 2.7 percent, compared to the projected growth rate of 3 percent, with the underperformance attributed largely to the failure to meet targets regarding construction and completion of investment projects (R. Castro Ruz, 2011g). The reported 2.7 percent growth rate for 2011 is questionable: government sources reported 1.9 percent growth during the first half of the year, the high season for tourism as well as the most active time period for production of sugar and of principal food crops; thus, to average 2.7 percent for the year as a whole, performance during the usually-less-dynamic second half of the year would have had to be on the order of 3.5 percent.[5] In any case, the official growth rate for 2011 was the second lowest in the region, roughly two-thirds of the Latin American average growth rate of 4.3 percent (see Table 2.1). The official average growth rate of the Cuban economy during 2010–2011 was 2.4 percent, less than half of the 5.1 percent achieved by Latin America as a whole.

The rapid GDP growth rate during 2004–2007 is in part the result of an "adaptation" of the internationally accepted national accounts methodology, introduced in 2003 by Cuban statisticians, that added to GDP the value of free social services[6] and of price subsidies for rationed goods. This manipulation of the data inflated the value of GDP. Thus, for 2003, Cuba released two GDP growth rates: 2.6 percent based on the internationally accepted national income accounting methodology and 3.8 percent (46 percent higher) based on the "new" locally developed methodology. In 2004, Cuba released a single GDP growth figure of 5.4 percent based on the new methodology, with Cuban officials stating at the time that it still did not reflect fully the value of GDP. ECLAC initially estimated the GDP growth rate for 2004 following the conventional methodology at 3 percent (80 percent lower than the official rate), and later revised it to 4.5 percent (still 20 percent lower). In 2005, ECLAC stopped publishing the official Cuban growth rates altogether, stating that it was in the process of reviewing the new methodology, and in 2006–2007 it published the official Cuban estimates but did not provide its own estimate and repeated the cautionary note.[7] At the end of 2008, ECLAC accepted the Cuban calculation methodology, asserting that now it had been aligned with international standards, but as we have shown elsewhere, Cuban statistics do not support this assertion (Pérez-López and Mesa-Lago, 2009). Raúl has commented on this problem: "we are particularly interested in having [the growth of GDP] reflect as much as possible what is happening in the domestic economy, where there are daily shortages of products" (R. Castro Ruz, 2007b). Rafael Hernández, director of the journal *Temas,* has stated that the Cuban people read about the growth of the economy in statistical terms, but do not feel such economic growth within their homes (Davies, 2007).

The growth target for 2012 was 3.4 percent, higher than the 2.7 percent official growth rate in 2011, but lower than the average growth rate of 4.4 percent contemplated in the 2012–2016 plan (Yzquierdo Rodríguez, 2011). Raúl observed that "in 2012, the economy will continue to be affected by the global economic crisis and very high international prices for food . . . prices of oil and of other raw materials will also continue to be high and there will continue to be restrictions on the availability of new financing" (R. Castro Ruz, 2011f).

GDP Composition

The composition of Cuban GDP has changed significantly over the past two decades, with the share contributed by the goods sector declining markedly, and that contributed by the services sector gaining in importance. The share of GDP contributed by the goods sector (agriculture, livestock, fishing, mining, and manufacturing) fell from 37.7 percent in 1989 to 19.1 percent in 2011, while the share contributed by the services sector climbed from 62.3 percent to 80.9 percent over the same period. With respect to the services sector, the contribution to GDP of basic services (electricity, gas, water, construction, transportation, and communications) was basically stagnant from 1989 to 2011, while that of other services (commerce, hotels, restaurants, financial services, administration, and public health and social services) expanded rapidly, from 48.5 to 65.3 over the same period. The contribution of the services sector to GDP peaked in 2006 (at 83 percent of GDP) and declined (to 81 percent of GDP) in 2011 (see Figure 2.1).

A declining share of employment in the primary sector of the economy (agriculture, mining) and an increasing share of employment in secondary (manufacturing) and tertiary (services) sectors is normally associated with economic development in developed and developing nations. In the case of Cuba, the rise in services' share of GDP is associated with a sharp decline in goods production (agriculture and manufacturing). Several Cuban economists have analyzed the basis and implications of the rapid growth of the services sector. Pedro Monreal (2007) has expressed concerns about a "dysfunctional tertiarization of the economic structure" of the country, caused by the mushrooming of the services sector. Jorge Sánchez-Egozcue and Juan Triana (Sánchez-Egozcue and Triana, 2010; Triana, 2011) have pointed

**Figure 2.1 Distribution of GDP by Goods, Basic Services, and
Other Services, 1989, 2006, and 2011**

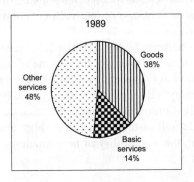
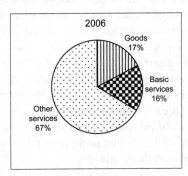
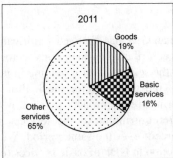

Sources: Authors' estimates based on BNC, 1995, for 1989; and ONE, 2011a, 2011b, 2012h, for 2006 and 2011.

Notes: "Goods" include agriculture, livestock, fishing, forestry, mining, and manufacturing (for 1989 it also includes electricity, gas, and water). "Basic services" include electricity, gas, water, construction, transportation, and communications. "Other services" include commerce, hotels, restaurants, financial services, administration, and public health and social services.

out that the services industries that have led GDP growth (e.g., education, administration) tend to be labor-intensive, have low productivity, and contribute little to the external sector, as their outputs are consumed domestically. Pavel Vidal Alejandro (2009) has observed that there are "signs of exhaustion of the growth of the services sector, as it has been principally based on exports of medical services to Venezuela" (2009). Finally, the rapid growth of the services sector has led to overestimation of GDP.[8] Armando Nova (2007) posits that the change to the methodology of calculation of national accounts not only overestimates GDP but also does the same with respect to the services sector, and therefore reduces the relative share provided by the goods sector.

Capital Formation

Robust capital formation is critical for future economic growth. The higher the share of GDP devoted to investment, the higher the likelihood of economic growth in the medium and long term. This indicator is also difficult to measure because of data limitations, especially the several inconsistent series published by Cuba and ECLAC (Mesa-Lago, 2005a). Gross fixed capital formation fell by 73 percent from 1989 to 2011, from 25.6 percent of GDP to 7 percent; in 2011 it was less than a third of the regional average of 22.9 percent of GDP (see Table 2.1).

Minister of Economy Marino Murillo (2009b) reported that, as a result of economic challenges, the economic plan for 2009 had to be adjusted midyear and investment declined 16 percent compared to 2008. With regard to 2010, Murillo (2010) stated that the investment plan had been cut back initially by 950 million CUP and later by 1.2–1.4 billion CUP, actions that threatened projected growth. In 2011, Murillo's successor, Adel Yzquierdo Rodríguez (2011), reported that the investment plan had been underfulfilled, by 26 percent, and so had the construction and new investment plan, by 12 percent. Investments by state-owned enterprises and joint ventures in mining, cement production, and port modernization were behind schedule because of the lack of financing and delays in the arrival of components (ECLAC, 2011b). According to Omar Everleny Pérez Villanueva (2006), capital stock obsolescence threatens future growth; he considers that investment has been insufficient to promote sustainable growth, stating that long-term economic recovery requires investment at the rate of about 25 percent of GDP, the rate that prevailed from 1975 to 1989.

Price Stability

Cuban official sources reported inflation at 0.5 percent in 1989 and 5.7 percent in 2006, declining and then turning negative (deflation) in 2008–2009, and reaching 1.4 percent in 2010 and 1.7 percent in 2011. The Economist

Intelligence Unit (EIU, 2011) estimated the 2011 inflation rate at 4.7 percent, almost three times the official figure. The EIU estimate seems to be supported by a report from ONE (2012i) indicating a 24 percent average increase in prices in agricultural markets. The official inflation rate for 2011 is roughly one-quarter of the 6.9 percent average inflation rate for the region, while the EIU estimate is roughly two-thirds of the regional average. In any event, it is important to keep in mind that the Cuban government sets the majority of prices, and therefore, to a large extent, prices on the island do not reflect the interplay of supply and demand; that the consumer price index (CPI) refers only to products sold in pesos and excludes those sold in convertible pesos, so that the rising prices of products sold at foreign-currency stores (TRDs) are excluded; and that Cuba has not released information on the methodology of calculation of the CPI, for example the basket of goods and the weighting scheme.

Vidal Alejandro (2008a, 2011b) argues that the Central Bank of Cuba's financing of the deficit through money creation expands the money supply and fuels inflation while reducing real wages, a pattern that was observed during the crisis of the 1990s. The BCC's policy of fixing the exchange rate of the convertible peso contributes to controlling inflation, but it is not certain that the BCC will be able to maintain this policy indefinitely and avoid a future devaluation (see Chapter 3).

Monetary liquidity (as measured by M2, currency plus demand deposits) as a share of GDP almost doubled between 1989 and 2010, from 21.6 to 40.6 percent, followed by a slight decrease to 40.2 percent in 2011. As M2 only relates to the CUP and excludes the CUC, these percentages underestimate monetary liquidity as a share of GDP (ONE has the statistics to make these adjustments, but does not publish such information). In absolute terms, the M2 money supply reached a historical peak in 2009, at 25,846 million CUP, eight times its level in 1989. Vidal Alejandro (2007) argues that salary increases without an expansion in the availability of goods and services add to the cumulative excess monetary liquidity.

The fiscal deficit contracted in 2006–2007, rose to reach 6.9 percent of GDP in 2008, and then contracted in 2009–2011. The fiscal deficit in 2011 was 3.8 percent of GDP, higher than the projected 3.6 percent of GDP, and more than twice the average fiscal deficit in Latin America of 1.5 percent of GDP (see Table 2.1).

Physical Production

Table 2.2 presents time series of physical production for twenty-two products, including products consumed domestically as well as exported products;

Table 2.2 Physical Production in Mining, Manufacturing, and Agriculture, 1989 and 2005–2011 (thousand metric tons)

	1989	2005–2006[a]	2007	2008	2009	2010	2011	Change Between 1989 and 2010–2011 (%)
Mining								
Oil	718	2,900[j]	2,905	3,003	2,731	3,025		321
Natural gas[b]	34	1,091	1,218	1,161	1,155	1,072	1,020	3,000
Nickel	47	76[k]	73	70	70	68[n]		45
Manufacturing								
Sugar	8,121	1,348	1,193	1,445	1,379	1,185	1,157	−86
Steel	314	257	262	274	266	278	282	−10
Cement	3,759	1,705	1,805	1,707	1,625	1,641	1,731	−54
Electricity[c]	15.4	16.4	17.6	17.7	17.7	17.4	17.8	16
Textiles[d]	220	27	24	29	28	26	25	−89
Fertilizers	898	41	22	40	9	22	40	−96
Cigars[e]	308	418	412	386	375	375	392	27
Shoes[f]	12	5	2	4	3	2	2	−83
Soap[e]	37	14	15	17	13	14	11	−70
Agriculture								
Citrus	981[i]	555	469	392	418	345	265	−73
Rice	536	434	440	436	563	454	566	6
Milk (cow)	1,131	415	485	545	600	629	600	−47
Eggs[e]	2,673	2,341	2,352	2,328	2,426	2,430	2,620	−2
Tobacco leaf	42.0	30.0	26.0	22.0	25.0	20.5	19.9	−53
Tubers	681	1,801[l]	1,378	1,392	1,565	1,515	1,445	112
Vegetables	610	3,206[m]	2,603	2,439	2,548	2,141	2,200	260
Coffee	29	2	1	1	1	2	2	−93
Cattle[g]	4,920	3,737	3,787	3,821	3,893	3,992	4,059	−18
Fish and shellfish[h]	192	55	61	61	65	55	49	−74

Sources: Data for 1989 from CEE, 1991; data for 2005–2011 from ONE, 2009, 2010a, 2011a, 2012a; sugar quantity for 2011 based on Yzquierdo Rodríguez, 2011.
Notes: a. Highest production year between 2005 and 2006.
b. Million cubic meters.
c. Thousand gigawatt hours.
d. Million square meters.
e. Million units.
f. Million pairs.
g. Thousand heads; peak of 7,172,000 heads in 1967.
h. Peak of 244,000 thousand metric tons in 1986.
i. 1988.
j. Peak of 3,609,000 thousand metric tons in 2003.
k. Peak of 76,500 thousand metric tons in 2001.
l. Peak of 1,946,400 thousand metric tons in 2004.
m. Peak of 4,014,000 thousand metric tons in 2004.
n. Authors' estimate.

the behavior of eight of these products is also shown in Figure 2.2. For four-teen of the twenty-two products, output in 2011 (or in 2010 when informa-tion for 2011 was not available) was below the 1989 level, in most cases by a substantial percentage. Generally speaking, the mining sector has had the

Figure 2.2 Physical Production of Selected Products, 1989 and 2005–2006 to 2010–2011 (thousand metric tons, except million units for cigars, and thousand heads for cattle)

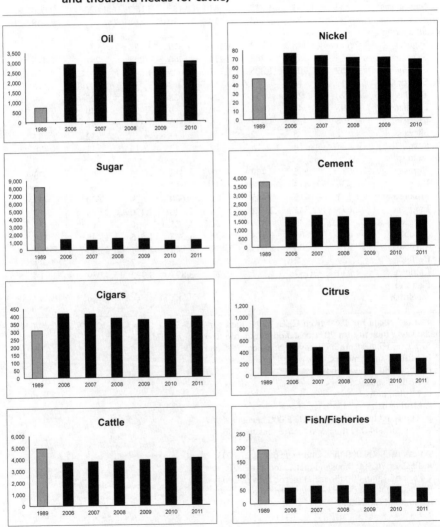

Sources: Data for 1989 from CEE, 1991; data for 2006–2010 from ONE, 2009, 2010a, 2011a, 2012a.

best growth performance and agriculture the worst, with manufacturing also performing poorly.

Mining

As mentioned, mining was the best-performing sector over the reference period, with output growing impressively. Output of natural gas, for example, grew over thirtyfold from 1989 to 2011 (albeit from a tiny production level in 1989), and oil output grew over fourfold and nickel output by 45 percent over the same period.

Oil and natural gas. The bulk of Cuba's current oil extraction is from deposits located off the island's northern coast, between Corralillo and Havana. Production wells operate in relatively shallow waters, two to eight kilometers from shore, well within Cuba's territorial waters. Cuba's crude oil is heavy (has high specific gravity) and high in sulfur content, which make it a relatively low-quality crude not well suited for refining into high-value-added products such as gasoline. Cuba's oil is mainly used domestically (a small amount is exported to Asia) by thermoelectric plants that have been retrofitted to use it as fuel. Crude oil production peaked at 3.6 million tons in 2003 and declined to 2.7 million tons in 2009, as production from existing oil fields matured and addition of new fields slackened.

In 2009 the Cuban government canceled oil exploration and production concessions granted to Canadian corporations Pebercan and Sherritt;[9] Sherritt continues to operate through a production-sharing agreement with the state company Cubapetróleo (CUPET), but its production declined by 39 percent from 2006 to 2009; in 2010, Sherritt extracted 25 percent of the nation's crude oil. Crude oil production rebounded to 3 million tons in 2010 (47,000 barrels per day), still 14 percent below peak output, but four times the 1989 level (see Table 2.2).[10] The increase in crude oil production has raised the share of consumption accounted for by domestic production, from 12 percent in 1989 to 38 percent in 2010; although a significant improvement, this still means that Cuba needs to import 62 percent of the oil it consumes, primarily from Venezuela. Production of refined oil products—fuel oil, diesel, naphtha, kerosene, lubricants, and other products—peaked in 1990 at 6.8 million tons, fell sharply to 1.1 million in 1999, rose to 5.2 million in 2008, and fell to 5 million in 2010, 27 percent below the peak. Statistics are not yet available for 2011, except for fragmentary information stating that production of refined oil products decreased by 4.2 percent, gasoline by 11.8 percent, and natural gas by 9 percent (ONE, 2011a; *Reuters,* June 13, 2010, May 13, 2012; Piñón, 2011, 2012).

In 2000, CUPET opened up for bidding by international oil companies the rights for exploration and joint production in deep-water areas in the

Florida Straits and the Gulf of Mexico, within Cuba's Exclusive Economic Zone. The areas consisted of 112,000 square kilometers, divided into sixty-three blocks. According to Cuban experts, these areas could contain between 5 and 20 billion barrels of oil, based on geological studies. A study from the US Geological Survey that estimated a mean of 4.6 billion barrels of undiscovered oil plus natural gas in the North Cuba Basin bolstered the interest of multinational oil companies in exploring in Cuban waters (USGS, 2005). By January 2012, twenty-two of the blocks had been leased, generating more than US$1 billion for the Cuban state, to companies from Angola, China, India, Norway, Russia, Spain, Venezuela, and Vietnam.[11]

In 2012, several of the multinational oil companies holding offshore leases contracted with Saipem, a subsidiary of Italian oil company Eni, for the use of the state-of-the-art semisubmersible rig *Scarabeo 9* to drill several offshore exploratory wells.[12] Completion of each exploratory well was planned to take about ninety days, at a cost of US$100–175 million per well; should oil in commercial quantity and quality be found during the exploration, a production infrastructure would have to be built, which would take three to five years. The total cost to develop the anticipated offshore oil deposits has been estimated at US$20 billion, for a projected production volume of 700,000 barrels per day (fourteen times current production levels). Exploration is being conducted at the risk of the foreign companies; once the oil is commercialized, foreign companies would be reimbursed for their investment first and subsequently proceeds would be distributed between the Cuban state (60 percent) and the foreign companies (40 percent) (Piñón, 2008, 2011, 2012; *Associated Press,* March 23, 2009).

Scarabeo 9 arrived in Cuban waters in January 2012 and began drilling its first exploratory well for Repsol. The initial exploratory well was located about 45 kilometers north of Havana and 140 kilometers from the Florida coast, a location that raised concerns about damage to the US shores in the case of an accidental oil spill, and led to discussions regarding possible emergencies between Cuban and US experts. An agreement was been reached whereby the US Coast Guard and an oil spill response organization in southern Florida would work jointly to address potential emergencies (Piñón, 2012; Whitefield, 2012; *Reuters,* May 18, 2012, May 20, 2012).

In May 2012, Repsol announced that *Scarabeo 9*'s exploration had resulted in a dry hole. The second well, drilled for Malaysian oil company Petronas and Russia's Gazpromneft (June–July), found oil so thick that it could not be economically extracted; the third, for Venezuela's PDVSA (August–November), found hydrocarbons in geological formations that did not offer the possibility of commercial development. After completing the PDVSA well, *Scarabeo 9* left Cuban waters in late November to drill off Brazil, bringing to an end the first round of Cuban deep-water offshore oil exploration. Meanwhile, Russian oil company Zarubezhneft is planning to drill in shallow waters about 200 miles east of Havana, an area not as promising as the deep waters, using a Norwegian rig (Krauss and Cave, 2012). To summarize, promising geological studies raised expectations of significant oil deposits in Cuba's waters. The first round of exploratory drilling in 2012 was disappointing, with no confirmation of deep-water oil deposits of commercial quantity and quality and extractable at competitive costs. As oil industry analyst Jorge Piñón opined in November 2012, "the Cuban oil dream is over and done with, at least for the next five years" (Krauss and Cave, 2012). Despite these results, industry analysts continue to assess positively the eventual discovery and production of oil in the North Cuba Basin.

Venezuela financed the completion and startup of a large oil refinery in Cienfuegos that was unfinished at the time of the end of relations with the Soviet Union; the refinery started operations at the end of 2007, processing some 65,000 barrels per day of a blend of Venezuelan and Cuban crudes;[13] the Cuban-Venezuelan joint venture oil company CUVENPEQ is planning to expand the refinery's capacity to 150,000 barrels per day by 2015, relying on Chinese technology.[14] The Nico López refinery in Regla-Havana, a combination of the refineries built by Esso and Shell in the 1950s, is obsolete; its capacity has dwindled to 25,000 barrels per day and there are plans to shut it down. The similarly obsolete Hermanos Díaz refinery in Santiago de Cuba, successor to the Texaco refinery built in the 1950s, is being modernized and expanded in capacity from 22,000 to 50,000 barrels per day through another initiative of CUVENPEQ. Finally, a joint project between Venezuela and Russia foresees the construction of a new oil refinery in Matanzas, which would start operations in 2015, with refining capacity of 150,000 barrels per day. Should all of these plans materialize, investments in the oil refinery industry would amount to about US$12 billion, increasing refining capacity from 114,000 to 350,000 barrels per day, which would allow Cuba to process crude oil not only from Venezuela, but also from Angola, Brazil, Colombia, Mexico, Russia, and other oil-producing countries that lack sufficient refinery capacity. Further, should the enlarged Cienfuegos refinery start operations in 2015, Cuba could refine its crude oil domestically to meet local consumption, reduce its dependence on Venezuela for refined products, and avoid potential conflicts with the US embargo that might arise if Cuba were to sell its crude oil in international markets (Cancio, 2009a; *Reuters,* March 7, 2011; *El Universal,* December 6, 2011; Arreola, 2012; Piñón, 2012).

Natural gas, a co-product of oil extraction in the Varadero, Boca de Jaruco, and Puerto Escondido fields, is gathered and distributed through a plant built by Sherritt as a joint venture with CUPET and ERGAS, the state gas company. Natural gas production increased by thirty-two times from 1989 to 2010, reaching 1,072 million cubic meters in 2010, lower than the peak level of 1,218 million cubic meters reached in 2007. In 2010, natural gas contributed 12.8 percent of national production of primary energy. Natural gas is used for residential consumption and also to fuel electricity generation plants (ONE, 2011a; Piñón, 2011).

Sugarcane bagasse represented about 36 percent of national primary energy production in 2010, roughly the same share contributed by crude oil, despite the 73 percent decline in bagasse production from 1989 to 2010 as a result of the sharp decline in the sugar industry. The first electricity generation plant fueled by bagasse is being built by a joint venture between British company Havana Energy and Cuban enterprise Zerus in Ciego de Avila, adjoining the sugar mill Ciro Redondo; up to five such thirty-megawatt plants are envisaged (*Big Pond News*, December 24, 2011; *Reuters*, November 8, 2012). The contribution of hydroelectricity to national primary energy production is tiny, at under 1 percent (ONE, 2011a).

Nickel. The province of Holguín, on the Eastern portion of the island, is estimated to contain more than 30 percent of the world's known reserves of nickel, the third largest such reserve in the world. There are three nickel plants with the following annual production capacities of unrefined nickel: Pedro Sotto, 33,000 tons; Che Guevara, 30,000 tons; and René Ramos Latour, 10,000 to 15,000 tons. In the first half of 2002, the René Ramos Latour plant was temporarily shut down for repairs; current rumors are that the plant will be permanently closed as current world nickel prices make it economically unfeasible to operate (Leyva Martínez, 2012). Production of unrefined nickel reached a peak of 76,500 tons in 2001 (benefiting from an investment of US$350 million by Canadian company Sherritt to modernize and expand the Pedro Sotto plant), and subsequently declined to 70,100 tons in 2009 and to an estimated 68,000 tons in 2010.[15] Despite the 17 percent fall in Cuban nickel production between 2001 and 2010, output in the latter year was still 45 percent higher than in 1989 (see Table 2.2). In mid-2011, the Che Guevara plant was shut down temporarily because of mechanical failure, but the Pedro Sotto plant set a new output record, producing 37,700 tons (in part because of an additional investment by Sherritt); production by the other two plants has not been reported.

Recently announced investments to expand installed nickel production capacity include a US$410 million investment by Sherritt to expand capacity of the Pedro Sotto plant by 16,000 tons between 2008 and 2011; a US$1.2 billion investment by China to develop a nickel deposit in San Felipe, Camagüey, that would produce 50,000 tons per annum (the project apparently has been abandoned); and a US$465 million investment by China to complete a ferronickel plant in Las Camariocas that was left unfinished by the Soviet Union (the project apparently was canceled in 2007). CUVENPEQ has signed an agreement to complete the latter plant by the end of 2013 or early 2014 through a combination of investments from Venezuela (US$521 million) and Cuba (US$700 million); capacity of the plant would be 68,000 tons per annum, of which 21,000 tons would be nickel (Mesa-Lago, 2009c; Frank, 2010b; *Reuters,* January 16, 2012; Arreola, 2012).

The newest of the nickel plants in operation on the island, the Che Guevara plant, was built with obsolete Soviet technology and is a prodigious consumer of energy; reportedly it consumes three times more oil per ton of nickel than does the most energy-efficient producer, the Pedro Sotto plant, built in 1957 by US companies and since then modernized by Sherritt's joint venture with the Cuban government. The Las Camariocas plant was designed using similar obsolete technology and therefore is likely to be a large energy consumer as well; this plant might have been commercially viable when the Soviet Union subsidized nickel and oil prices, and probably would require Venezuelan subsidies to operate. In 2007 the price of nickel in the world market averaged US$37,134 per ton, six times its level in 2001, as a result of strong world demand associated with economic expansion. In 2009 the average nickel price fell to US$14,672 per ton as a result of the global economic slowdown; Cuban vice president José Ramón Machado Ventura stated at that time that, should prices fall below US$9,000 per ton, it would not be feasible to continue to produce the mineral (Frank, 2009). The world economic recovery brought prices back up to an average of US$22,909 per ton in 2011, still 38 percent below 2007 levels, but they weakened again in 2012 to an average of about US$18,000 per ton for the first nine months of the year (International Monetary Fund, 2012). An innovation that threatens the price of nickel is the development by China of nickel pig iron; this product, which has already captured about 10 percent of the world nickel market, can be used to produce stainless steel at a much lower price than using common nickel. Should some of the technical problems regarding nickel pig iron be resolved, it is quite possible that this product would continue to take market share from nickel and in effect set a world market price ceiling for nickel (Hoffman, 2010).

The nickel industry was the subject of an internal investigation in 2010 by the Cuban government that resulted in the arrest of several managers and government officials and led to the dismissal of the minister of basic industries, Yadira García, on charges of mismanagement (Frank, 2007, 2011b). In August 2012, Cuba announced the conviction of a dozen people found guilty of corruption in negotiating and executing contracts related to the expansion of the nickel joint venture with Sherritt; among those sentenced were two officials of the joint venture and several employees of the Cuban enterprise Cubaníquel, including a former vice minister (Tamayo, 2012b).

Manufacturing

Since the crisis of the 1990s, Cuba's manufacturing sector has experienced obsolescence of its capital stock, inability to keep up with technological changes, and shortages of raw materials that have prevented it from returning to the rates of capacity utilization of the 1980s (Pérez Villanueva, 2006). The weak performance of manufacturing is evident from official index numbers of annual physical production compiled by ONE based on production of 126 manufactured products (see Table 2.3).

Using as base the level of physical production in 1989 (equal to 100), the manufacturing sector in 2011 had an index value of 45 (output was 55 percent lower than in 1989), while the sugar industry recorded an index value of 16 (84 percent lower) and nonsugar manufacturing an index value of 51 (49 percent lower). Out of the twenty-four nonsugar manufacturing lines listed in Table 2.3, output level in 2011 exceeded that of 1989 for only four; for two, output was 25 percent lower than in 1989, and for another

Table 2.3 Index Numbers of Physical Production in the Manufacturing Sector, 2006–2011 (1989 output = 100)

	2006	2007	2008	2009	2010	2011
Total	38.7	40.2	46.1	44.9	43.6	45.1
Sugar manufacturing	15.8	15.3	18.7	18.1	15.7	16.4
Nonsugar manufacturing	43.6	45.5	52.0	50.6	49.6	51.2
Foodstuffs	59.0	63.5	65.6	67.8	64.9	67.7
Beverages	95.2	102.2	108.3	104.8	106.0	110.7
Tobacco	108.7	102.9	99.0	95.8	95.6	97.0
Textiles	7.7	6.8	8.2	7.8	7.0	6.8
Clothing	18.1	20.6	20.2	23.7	23.2	30.7
Leather and leather products	14.1	8.7	18.8	15.7	13.5	17.1
Wood and wood products	10.4	10.5	16.9	13.3	11.9	10.9
Paper and paper products	5.4	5.6	6.0	6.4	6.5	7.3
Publishing, printing, recording	19.5	19.9	20.1	19.2	18.7	18.0
Oil-refining products	24.7	26.4	60.6	53.4	52.7	50.3
Pharmaceutical products	477.9	537.7	822.0	865.1		
Fertilizers	7.8	6.0	7.6	3.3	5.3	8.0
Chemical products	79.7	80.9	85.9	80.8	87.0	86.1
Rubber and plastic products	13.6	15.8	15.1	11.4	16.9	19.6
Nonmetal mineral products	11.2	6.6	8.8	10.5	10.6	9.7
Construction materials	28.8	28.8	28.0	26.8	26.7	28.5
Common metals	100.8	103.3	100.6	99.6	99.4	103.9
Metal products (except metal machinery and equipment)	29.1	29.7	24.9	22.5	20.2	22.8
Metal machinery and equipment	2.0	0.0	0.6	0.5	0.4	0.4
Electrical machinery and equipment	30.7	25.3	30.1	23.2	26.9	34.6
Radio, television, and communications equipment	107.5	84.6	65.9	56.8	33.3	40.9
Medical and optical instruments	1.4	13.6	33.0	32.8	31.2	42.9
Transportation equipment	2.0	11.0	22.6	7.6	1.8	3.0
Furniture	82.1	90.4	112.7	129.9	136.9	134.1

Sources: ONE, 2011a, 2012a.
Note: Empty cells indicate that data are not available.

two it was between 25 and 50 percent lower. Production in the remaining sixteen lines in 2011 was less than half that of 1989; in eleven of them, output was 75 percent lower or more.

Causes of the deterioration of manufacturing. Several reasons explain the weak performance of the manufacturing sector (see Ritter, 2011a). The collapse of the Soviet Union and of the socialist bloc ended price subsidies for oil, forcing Cuba to turn to the world market for energy imports, increasing the oil import bill, and rendering uncompetitive several industries that were based on inexpensive oil imports. Because of hard-currency availability constraints, this also had the effect of forcing a sharp reduction in imports of raw materials and essential inputs for manufacturing, including machinery and spare parts. Further, as a significant share of Cuba's capital stock originated from the Soviet Union and former socialist countries, the disappearance of certain industries in these countries meant that Cuba was no longer able to secure spare parts and equipment to keep its machinery operating. Finally, the technology embodied in the capital stock imported from the Soviet Union and Eastern Europe was less energy-efficient and less advanced than that from industrialized countries, making Cuban manufactured exports uncompetitive in international markets.

The sharp contraction of the economy (a 35 percent drop in GDP) in the early 1990s paralyzed investment for several years; investment has recovered slowly but has not returned to the high rates of capital formation of the late 1980s. During the depth of the economic crisis, priority was given to imports of essential consumer goods, to the detriment of machinery and equipment imports. Maintenance of capital goods was also deferred, reducing productivity and in many instances rendering capital goods unusable. The massive return to their home countries of technicians and experts from the Soviet Union and the socialist countries also affected maintenance. The overvalued exchange rate of the convertible peso acted as a disincentive to exports while stimulating imports of manufactured goods, particularly from China, at the same time that the lack of market-determined prices made it difficult for Cuba to identify products that were internationally competitive. The massive dismantling of the sugar industry resulted in huge cutbacks in production and meant that Cuba missed out in profiting from high prices of sugar on the world market and in developing an ethanol production industry.

Sugar. Compared to an average production level of about 8 million tons per annum in the 1980s, sugar output averaged 1.3 million tons per annum in the 2005–2011 period, 16 percent of the annual average in the 1980s.[16] This was in large part the result of a decision taken in 2002 to sharply downsize the industry, allegedly because of the low world market price of sugar,[17] but also perhaps a reflection of Fidel Castro's disdain for the industry (according to Fidel, sugar was ruinous for the country and belonged to the era of slavery; F. Castro Ruz, 2005a). In accord with the downsizing plan, production would concentrate on a small number of the most modern mills, sugarcane would be grown in the most productive fields, and the labor force would be reduced to retain the most experienced and skilled workers; these changes would increase efficiency, reduce costs, and boost profits. After a sharp reduction in output at the outset of the restructuring process, the plan called for stabilization of sugar output at about 4 million tons per annum, with the possibility of increasing output if world market conditions demanded it. The land withdrawn from sugarcane production would be devoted to other food crops. In a short time, Cuba shut down 46 percent of the mills, shifted 60 percent of sugarcane lands to other crops, and dismissed some 100,000 workers, about a quarter of former industry employees (Pérez-López and Álvarez, 2005; Pollitt, 2010).

Contrary to the short-term objectives of the restructuring plan, sugar production and yields fell sharply, while nonsugar agricultural production contracted as well.[18] Sugar production plummeted to an estimated 1.16 million tons in 2011, 20 percent lower than the goal of 1.45 million tons, 86 percent lower than the 1989 harvest, and one of the lowest production levels in more than a century. Sugar agro-industry efficiency indicators (see Table 2.4 and Figure 2.3) uniformly show the lack of success of the restructuring efforts: while land devoted to sugarcane was reduced from 1.35 million hectares in 1989 to 431,000 hectares in 2010, agricultural yield fell from 60 to 26.7 tons per hectare over the same period; the agricultural yield in 2010

Table 2.4 Sugar Agro-Industry Indicators, 1989 and 2001–2010

	Land Under Cultivation (thousand hectares)	Yield per Hectare (harvested tons)	Sugarcane Ground per Day (thousand tons)	Industrial Yield (%)[a]	Harvest Days	Lost Time (%)
1989	1,350	60.0	518.8	12.0[b]	128[c]	23.1
2001	1,001	31.4	292.7	11.0	100	29.4
2002	1,041	33.3	279.1	10.4	124	34.9
2003	649	34.3	192.0	9.9	120	42.5
2004	661	36.0	190.6	10.6	127	67.7
2005	517	22.4	129.5	10.4	92	22.5
2006	397	28.0	96.1	10.6	117	39.9
2007	330	36.1	112.1	10.0	113	41.4
2008	380	41.3	87.8	11.1	180	44.5
2009	434	34.3	80.5	10.0	186	42.4
2010	431	26.7	78.5	10.4	148	43.1

Sources: Authors' estimates based on CEE, 1991; ONE, 2006, 2008a, 2011a, 2012a.
Notes: a. 96 degrees polarization basis.
b. 1985.
c. 1988.

Figure 2.3 Sugar Agro-Industry Indicators, 1989 and 2001–2010

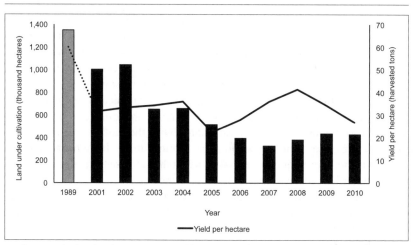

Sources: Authors' estimates based on CEE, 1991; ONE, 2006, 2008a, 2011a, 2012a.

was 37 percent of the world average of 70.7 tons per hectare and 33 percent of the yield in Brazil (79.2 tons per hectare), the largest-producing country. The gap between Cuba's sugarcane agricultural yield and that of other countries widened significantly between 2000 and 2010 (FAO, 2011); according to reports, agricultural yield rose to 32.5 tons per hectare in 2011, still half of the yield in 1989. Average sugarcane ground per harvest day fell from 519 tons in 1989 to 79 tons in 2010; industrial yield declined from 12 percent to 10.4 percent over the same period; the number of harvest days meanwhile increased from 128 to 148, the latter an improvement over the over 180 days in 2008 and 2009, but still a lengthy period (as harvest days extend beyond April, the sucrose content of sugarcane drops and rainfall affects harvesting, leading to lower industrial and agricultural yields). Finally, lost time because of lack of sugarcane supplies for grinding, breakdown of equipment, and so on, jumped from 23.1 percent of harvest days in 1989 to 67.7 percent in 2004, and fell to 43.1 percent in 2010 . The number of sugar mills in operation declined steadily: 156 in 1989, 104 in 2002, 71 in 2003, 54 in 2009, 44 in 2010, and 39 in 2011.

The downsizing of the sugar industry has had a significant impact on Cuba's external sector. Focusing on the low international sugar prices that prevailed at the beginning of the twenty-first century, Cuba dismantled the industry precipitously. Because of the inability of the industry to respond to favorable changes in prices by increasing supply, Cuba lost medium- and long-term opportunities to capitalize on favorable prices for sugar. World market sugar prices climbed significantly beginning in 2005, and in 2011 the world price of sugar was US$0.26 per pound, more than four times the price in 2002 (IMF, 2011; FAO, 2012). This was the highest price in thirty years—fueled by high consumption in China, India, and other Asian countries, the elimination by the European Union of price subsidies for beet sugar, and the diversion of sugar to produce ethanol in Brazil.[19] Moreover, Cuba would have been able to offset somewhat the adverse impacts associated with high oil prices if it had converted some of its sugar agro-industrial complex into ethanol production, as sugarcane is technically and economically superior to corn as a feedstock for ethanol. According to an expert, Cuba's lost revenue opportunity associated with the inability of the sugar industry to react to changing world market prices might have been as large as US$3 billion per annum, with half attributable to potential sugar exports and the other half to the opportunity cost of not producing ethanol (Piñón, 2012). Sugarcane also generated other products, such as alcohol, molasses, rum, aguardiente, and cattle feed, whose production also declined with the downsizing. Finally, sugar was also used as collateral to guarantee short- and medium-term loans; with the inability to use sugar for this purpose, it became more difficult and costly for Cuba to obtain external financing (Sánchez-Egozcue, 2011b).

Cuban agriculture expert Armando Nova (2006, 2010a) argues that the future of the sugar industry has been compromised by the serious strategic error of allowing the obsolescence of the industry's capital stock. Compounding the former are a centralized resource allocation process that delays the assignment of funds for maintenance, investment, and supplies; sugarcane varieties not suited to land being cultivated; planting scheduled during a time of year that is not ideal for this task; invasion of sugarcane lands by grass and invasive pests (one particularly damaging species is marabú, a thorny shrub that grows quickly and is difficult to eradicate); insufficient irrigation; significant loss of sugarcane because it arrives at the mills late or in bad condition; and an unstable labor force.

After the 2006 harvest (total production of 1.2 million tons of sugar), and in light of the jump in the world price of sugar, Fidel and then–sugar minister Ulises Rosales drew plans to triple sugar production, exports, and revenues in two years, by increasing investment, planting an additional 120,000 hectares with sugarcane, bringing back into operation nine sugar mills (to make a total of fifty-one), increasing imports of replacement parts, fertilizers, and herbicides, and creating a state agency to seek cooperative agreements with foreign investors (*Granma,* March 4, 2006; *Agence France-Presse,* August 27, 2006). These changes did not bring the anticipated supply rebound, however, and production goals were subsequently missed (10 percent fall in sugar production in 2008 and 2009, 15 percent fall in 2010, and 20 percent fall in 2011) and coincided with the dismissal of two sugar ministers over a two-and-a-half-year span. At the end of 2011, the Cuban government abolished the Ministry of Sugar and distributed its duties among the Ministries of Agriculture, Economy, and Foreign Trade; Cuba also established the AZCUBA Sugar Group, composed of thirteen companies at the provincial level that took over the mills, equipment, and other facilities of the Ministry of Sugar, as well as a trading company and other entities (Decretos-Leyes nos. 287 and 294, 2011).

Cuban government officials have offered numerous explanations for the poor performance of the sugar industry in the 2007–2011 period, blaming exogenous factors (e.g., weather) but also accepting flaws in organization and management of the sugar industry and of the economy at large. *Weather:* Excessive rainfall hampered sugarcane transportation and caused the shutdown of several mills because of the lack of raw material; hurricanes harmed or destroyed several mills and sugarcane plantations and damaged 40,000 tons of sugar in warehouses (see Box 2.1); and a drought adversely affected sugarcane production. *Flaws in planting and cutting:* Of the land slated for sugarcane, 16 percent was not planted; of the overall plan, only 25 percent of planting was met; sugarcane land was shifted to other, more profitable crops; excessive cutting of sugarcane during the previous harvest reduced ratoons; the harvest started late because of delays in the preparation of fields; there was heavy marabú, infestation; 20 percent of mechanization targets were not met; there were frequent breakdowns of mechanical harvesters and a lack of spare parts; and agricultural yield declined. *Problems with the operation of sugar mills and equipment:* Mills started operations late because repairs were not completed on-time; frequent equipment breakdowns halted production; only 66 percent of potential grinding capacity was utilized; the number of tractors was reduced by 58 percent and they were replaced by animal traction; machetes and gloves were low-quality; less than 15 percent of the provinces and either 23 percent or 66 percent of the mills met their production goals; and the largest sugar mill operated at half of its rated capacity and the third largest mill was closed for ten days because of boiler failure. *Lack of imported inputs:* Seven Brazilian harvesters, 160 trucks, 360 trailers, and 54 percent of purchased lubricants failed to arrive on time. *Infrastructure deficiencies:* Roads and bridges were in bad condition and needed to be rebuilt; there was a 59 percent reduction in the number of trucks; there were difficulties with railroad and surface transportation; and maintenance was poor. *Labor incentives:* Worker discipline was poor because of lax supervision; the new system of pay based on performance was poorly operated; and technicians were inadequately trained.

Domestic consumption of sugar is roughly 700,000 tons annually. In 2011, with production of some 1.2 million tons, only about 500,000 tons were available for export after meeting domestic consumption: 400,000 to China and 100,000 to the rest of the world. In 1989, Cuba was the world's

Box 2.1 Damages Caused by Hurricanes in 2008

The four hurricanes that struck Cuba in 2008 (Fay, Gustav, Ike, and Paloma) caused combined losses estimated at US$9.7 billion, or roughly 15–20 percent of gross domestic product. They damaged or destroyed 30 percent of crops and 53,000 tons of food; leveled 156,000 hectares of sugarcane, flooded an additional 518,847 hectares of sugarcane (90 percent of total plantings), and damaged or destroyed sugar mills, warehouses, and railways; uprooted 350,000 banana trees in Guantánamo and Granma provinces and over 80 percent of such trees in Villa Clara; ruined 135,000 tons of citrus fruits (29 percent of the harvest) and several juice-processing plants, a portion of the rice crop, and 25 percent of the rice stored in Pinar del Río, a large portion of the tobacco crop and drying barns in Pinar del Río, and 85 percent of the coffee harvest; killed half a million barnyard birds (including 80 percent of all barnyard birds in Isla de la Juventud) and millions of eggs; and destroyed 375,000 hectares of forest.

Ike struck the eastern part of the island, where the nickel plants are located; it caused serious damage to the Che Guevara plant and minor damage to the Nicaro plant; six weeks after the hurricane's strike, the two plants were still not in operation and nickel output was 20 percent below level sought by the production plan. Gustav struck the western end of the island, taking down 150 high-voltage electricity distribution towers in Pinar del Río, leaving 80 percent of the population without electricity, and nearly destroyed the electric grid of Isla de la Juventud. A month after these two hurricanes, 250,000 citizens in five provinces were still without electricity. Some 530,758 dwellings were damaged or destroyed by all four hurricanes (80 percent of dwellings in Isla de la Juventud and 45 percent in the province of Pinar del Rio were destroyed). Considering that 70,000 dwellings had been affected by earlier hurricanes, 77 percent of the affected dwellings (462,583) had not been repaired or rebuilt by the end of 2008 and it was predicted that it would take between three and six years to do so. Thus the national housing deficit probably rose to about 1 million units. Also damaged were the telephone communication system, roads, highways, bridges, factories, healthcare facilities, and schools.

In part because of the hurricanes, in 2008 there were production declines of bananas (23 percent), citrus fruits and raw tobacco (16 percent each), corn (12 percent), sugar (7 percent), vegetables (6 percent),

(continues)

Box 2.1 Cont.

poultry meat (5 percent), and eggs and rice (1 percent each). Despite these production declines, the National Statistical Office reported an increase of 0.6 percent in agricultural output in 2008. The Cuban government attributed the economic slowdown in 2008 in large part to the hurricanes, but some Cuban economists had predicted a slowdown well before the storms struck (Vidal and Fundora, 2008).

The crop losses created a severe shortage of goods at farmers' markets, made worse by the government's decision to freeze prices in those markets at the levels that prevailed prior to the hurricanes (in order to prevent farmers from raising prices and to prevent the potential for speculation, including trafficking in the black market); this led to hoarding and diversion of supplies from legal to illegal markets. Pavel Vidal Alejandro (2008b) had warned that this would occur if incentives to stimulate recovery of food production were not imposed. Meanwhile, the government increased the price of fuel by 68–86 percent during the year, which contributed to price increases by increasing the cost of mechanical harvesting and transportation and virtually eliminating profits from the sale of foodstuffs in legal markets. Food supplies declined by 80 percent between August and October 2008, with food imports climbing as a result. By the end of 2008, food supply had increased, although it was still lower than a year earlier, and some products, such as bananas, which had been unavailable at any price, began to reappear in agricultural markets.

Cuba received humanitarian aid from the World Food Programme and other United Nations agencies, as well as from Venezuela, China, Russia, Vietnam, Argentina, Brazil, Mexico, and other countries, but refused aid from the United States and countries of the European Union, except for Spain and Belgium. Received aid, as officially reported, amounted to about 5–10 percent of total losses.

Sources: R. Castro Ruz, 2008c; Messina et al., 2008; J. L. Rodríguez, 2008; ONE, 2009; and 2008 press stories from *Granma, Tribuna de la Habana, Cuban TV, Reuters, EFE, Associated Press, El País,* and *El Nuevo Herald.*

largest sugar exporter, and sugar accounted for 73 percent of the total value of exports; in 2010, Cuba had to import sugar from Colombia and Brazil to meet domestic consumption and export commitments, and sugar accounted for 5 percent of the value of exports. The monthly allocation of sugar to citizens under the rationing system was cut in 2010 from five to four pounds per month per person, thereby reducing internal consumption to 600,000 tons. Current plans are to increase production of sugar and derivatives, including by allowing foreign investors to participate in the sugar production sector, consistent with Raúl's opening to foreign investment (see Chapters 5 and 6). Brazilian company Odendrecht signed a contract in January 2012 to manage the "5 de Septiembre" sugar mill, built by the Cuban government, near Cienfuegos, in the 1980s (Frank, 2008a, 2010b; Mesa-Lago, 2008a, 2009c; ONE, 2011a; *Financial Times,* January 30, 2012).[20]

Sugar production was projected to increase to 1.45 million tons in 2012 (*Reuters,* February 6, 2012); the goal for 2015 is 2.5 million tons, similar to the production level in 2004. The plan for the 2012 harvest involved maintaining sixty-one mills in operational condition and actually operating forty-six; reaching a yield of 37 tons of sugarcane per hectare (4.5 higher than in 2011, but still significantly below the 60 tons per hectare reached in 1989 and the world average of 70 tons per hectare); bringing sugarcane fields closer to the mills in order to reduce transportation costs, providing the mills with fresher cane, and reducing waste; operating sugar mills at 80 percent of installed capacity versus 71 percent in 2011; doubling the price paid per ton of cut sugarcane to farmers and increasing the distribution of idle lands in usufruct to private farmers (see Chapter 5); and ensuring the delivery of 98 percent of imports of fertilizers, herbicides, and machinery.

A pilot program conducted at the "Jesús Rabí" sugar mill in Matanzas province used CASE harvesters, heavy-duty trucks, and trailers imported from Brazil instead of obsolete equipment, which reduced transportation time of harvested sugarcane to mills and increased industrial yield. The pilot program also included application of the system of worker compensation based on performance, which led to significant increases in salaries (for example, the operator of a harvester reported earning a monthly salary of 4,590 pesos, ten times the average salary). Agricultural yield was 60 tons per hectare, almost twice the 2011 average, and reached 120 tons in irrigated areas. There was also a reduction in the work force and in fuel consumption. But the experiment required an investment of US$6.3 million, and funds were not available to replicate it in other sugar mills in the nation. Other potential obstacles to modernization of the industry include the advanced age of the sugar mills (only eight of the mills were built after the revolution) and their overall poor maintenance, which has given rise to long histories of breakdowns and interruptions (with lost time averaging 42 percent over the 2006–2010 period, the goal of reducing lost time by 10 percentage points in a single year was perhaps unrealistic); and the poor condition of the roads for transporting sugarcane (implementing the idea of locating sugarcane fields closer to mills would be a colossal task). In February 2012, only two of the thirteen sugar-producing provinces were operating and the press was reporting on problems with equipment in sugar mills, transportation of harvested sugarcane, and utilization of capacity. At the end of May, however, production was estimated at 1.38 million tons, a 16 percent increase over 2011 and only 4 percent below the target (*Bohemia,* July 15, 2011; *Granma,* August 6, 2011, December 23, 2011, May 18, 2012; Espinosa Chepe, 2011a; *Reuters,* June 2, 2011, July 14, 2011, September 16, 2011, February 6, 2012, May 29, 2012). More recently, Orlando Celso García, president of the AZCUBA Sugar Group, has stated that sugar production in 2012 was 1.68 million tons, 20 percent higher than the 1.24 million tons reached in 2011, and that the target for 2014 is 2.4 million tons (*Diario de Cuba,* September 25, 2012).

Electricity. Throughout 2005, electricity blackouts, particularly in Havana, became so frequent and so extended that residents began to refer to the times when electricity was flowing as "alumbrones" (unexpected and short-lived bursts of light). Fidel declared 2006 as the "Year of the Energy Revolution" and predicted that Cuba would set an example for the world with respect to energy production and efficiency and save 1 billion pesos annually. The plan centered on gradually replacing six large thermoelectric plants, all over sixty years old and wasteful consumers of hydrocarbons, with 265 diesel electricity generation plants and 4,518 "electricity generation groups" to be located throughout the country. The latter are assemblies of small generators coupled together and synchronized with the national electricity grid; should the grid fail, these reserve groups would kick in to restore electric service. To conserve electricity, household appliances, incandescent light bulbs, and kerosene stoves were mandatorily replaced by "energy saving" devices. This plan required the replacement of 2 million electric plugs, 1.5 million electric cords, 12,400 transformers, and 16,000 electric poles. Fidel initially estimated the cost of the program at US$1.7 billion, but later reduced it to US$262 million (*Granma,* December 24, 2005, December 30, 2005, January 22, 2006). In early 2006, he complained that "the strategists at the Ministry of Basic Industry and at the Electricity Union, operating from dogmatic positions and with mistaken views, had judged that synchronization [of the electricity generation groups with the national grid] was impossible and the electricity problem would only be resolved by the acquisition of new thermoelectric plants. What a crazy idea!" Fidel also argued that for the amount of money that would be needed to acquire a thermoelectric plant (US$490 million), Cuba could obtain electricity generation groups capable of generating nearly three and a half times as much electricity as a thermoelectric plant (F. Castro Ruz, 2006b).

Production of electricity reached the historical high of 17,727 million kilowatt hours in 2009, thereby substantially easing the problem of electricity blackouts. Several problems associated with the energy plan have been pointed out: (a) the electricity generation groups are a short-run fix rather than a long-term solution, because the existing thermoelectric plants (eroded by the use of domestic, heavy, high-sulfur crude) continue to deteriorate and will break down in the future, thereby putting more pressure on the electricity generation groups; (b) the electricity generation groups require frequent and expensive maintenance; (c) supplying diesel to the numerous electricity generation groups located throughout the island requires a distribution system and a fleet of tank cars, and diesel fuel is more expensive than crude oil and its demand has been growing as a result of the operation of the electricity generation groups; (d) stoves, refrigerators,[21] and other electric appliances that have been distributed to the population will increase electricity demand, and it is unlikely that the government will be able to collect fully on US$400 million in loans made to households to support sales of such products; (e) and theft of electricity distribution equipment is common and it would not be surprising if equipment from electricity generation groups were also to be stolen (*Trabajadores,* May 15, 2007; Mesa-Lago, 2007).

Speaking in 2007, eighteen months into the "energy revolution," then–vice president Carlos Lage acknowledged that the electricity generation groups had consumed 1.2 million tons of costly diesel fuel, that Cuba continued to be vulnerable to disruptions in fuel supplies, and that savings from energy consumption programs had been insufficient (*Juventud Rebelde,* April 4, 2007). An article in the official newspaper *Granma* stated that it was premature to assess the impact of the program. Service interruptions continued to be frequent, with 91 percent of blackouts affecting secondary circuits and homes subject to the energy plan. Still pending was the rewiring of 2.3 million homes, the replacement of several thousand kilometers of distribution lines, the construction of 45 percent of projected new substations and 63 percent of secondary circuits, and the installation of 41 percent of transformers, 48 percent of electric poles, 53 percent of breakers, and 50 percent of electricity consumption meters. Low-voltage zones had increased as a result of the aging and deterioration of the national grid and the installation of new appliances in state enterprises and homes; and energy shortages had become more serious, given increased dependence on electricity for cooking in homes (Mayoral, 2007).

In 2010, electricity production fell by 2 percent to 17,396 million kilowatt hours, 13 percent higher than the production level in 1989, although nearly the same on a per capita basis: 1,440 kilowatt hours in 1989 compared to 1,540 kilowatt hours in 2010 (based on CEE, 1991; ONE, 2011a). For 2012, Canadian firm Sherritt projected a decline of 11 percent in electricity generation due to declining supplies of natural gas (CubaStandard.com, February 23, 2012).

Five years after the launching of the energy plan, three of these problems have been confirmed: (a) real fuel consumption by the electricity generation groups of 337 tons per gigawatt hour was 60 percent higher than the 210 tons per gigawatt hour estimated when the plan was announced; (b) electricity generation by such groups increased from 1 percent to 25 percent of total electricity generation between 2004 and 2009, but dropped to 22 percent in 2010 (the decline in absolute terms was 10.5 percent); and (c) residential consumption of electricity increased by 34 percent between 2004 and 2010 as a result of the mandatory use of new "energy saving" appliances. Former minister of economy Marino Murillo (2010) told the ANPP that electricity consumption by households was extremely high; Raúl confirmed that electricity consumption by households had been growing at a higher rate than anticipated (R. Castro Ruz 2010c). Other problems that have been reported include lack of replacement parts, deficient maintenance of electricity-generating groups that use sophisticated technologies, and transmission and distribution losses (14.3 percent in 2009 and 15.9 percent in 2010) because of deterioration of the systems (Espinosa, 2010a).

Although blackouts have been reduced substantially, they still occurred in Havana, Matanzas, and other provinces in 2009, requiring "scheduled blackouts" and a reduction in electricity of 12 percent in such provinces (Murillo, 2009a). In 2011–2012 there were service interruptions, some of them lasting as long as eight hours, allegedly resulting from repairs or trimming of trees. In early September 2012, a massive electricity outage that lasted several hours cut service to ten of the fifteen provinces in the nation and affected half of the island's population, including in the capital city; the outage, which reportedly resulted from a failure in a high-voltage transmission line, illustrated the flaws in the electrical grid and its aging infrastructure (*Diario de Cuba,* September 10, 2012; *United Press International,* September 12, 2012).

Other manufacturing. In 2011, production levels of four key manufactured products that played a key role in industrialization and import substitution were below their 1989 levels: 54 percent for cement, 89 percent for textiles, 96 percent for fertilizers, and 10 percent for steel. Production of shoes and laundry soap were 83 percent and 70 percent lower, respectively, than in 1989 (see Table 2.2).

In contrast, manufacturing of cigars, a traditional export, expanded and peaked in 2005 at a level 21 percent above its 1989 production, declined over the period 2005–2010, and recovered in 2011; production in 2011 was higher than in 1989 by 27 percent. The downward trend in cigar production is a function of the drop in demand for tobacco products resulting from the global campaign to curb tobacco consumption for health reasons and the decrease in tobacco leaf production on the island. Meanwhile, Chinese demand for Cuban cigars has been growing, with China becoming the third largest importer after Spain and France (*EFE,* February 22, 2010; *Reuters,* June 14,

2010).[22] Production of medicines, which is not reported in physical quantities (units, tons) but rather in value (pesos), doubled between 2005 and 2008, but statistics for 2009–2010 have not been reported, probably because production of medicines declined (ONE, 2011a).

Transportation and Communications

Transportation. Between 1989 and 2011, the total number of passengers transported by public vehicles fell by 47 percent, from 3 million to 1.6 million (see Table 2.5). Over 40 percent of passengers were transported through "alternative means," such as animal and human traction vehicles (*bicitaxis,* or rickshaws), whose number jumped by 238 percent between 2000 and 2011, and the share of passengers transported by those means rose from 24 percent to 40 percent over that period. There are no statistics on the number of buses that existed in 1989, but the number of passengers transported through this means declined by 68 percent between 1989 and 2010.[23] After dropping off sharply during the crisis of the 1990s, the number of buses grew by 61 percent between 2000 and 2010 because of bus imports from China. The number of locomotives fell by 26 percent between 1989 and 2010 (despite imports of locomotives from China) and the number of passengers traveling via railroad by 63 percent.[24] The number of ships fell by 77 percent (no statistics are available beyond 2008) and the number of passengers using maritime transportation by 57 percent. The number of passengers using air transportation was flat between 1989 and 2011. Between 2000 and 2011, the overall volume of freight transported (in million tons) declined by 65 percent; freight transported by road bus fell by 49 percent between 1989 and 2011, by railroad by 57 percent, and by ship by 90 percent.

Between 1988 and 2005, the number of passenger buses in the city of Havana (2.2 million inhabitants according to the 2002 census) fell by 74 percent, from 2,700 to 700 (*Trabajadores,* October 11, 2005). The passenger capacity of the stock of buses in 2006 was 490,000, or about 11 percent of demand; in 2008, plans were under way to expand service to some 1.4 million passengers, to meet about 37 percent of demand (Terrero, 2007).[25]

In early 2006, the Cuban government announced the purchase of 8,000 Chinese Yutong buses (China's news agency reported the number at 5,348 buses, however), at a cost of US$37.5 million, for delivery by 2009; purchases of buses from Germany and Russia were also reported (*Granma,* February 16, 2006; *Xinhua,* September 25, 2007). However, in mid-2007 the minister of transportation, Jorge Luis Sierra, stated that the new equipment would not be sufficient to meet accumulated demand and that, despite the additions to the fleet, passenger transportation would continue to be a critical

Table 2.5 Transportation Indicators, 1989, 2000, and 2005–2011

	1989	2000	2005	2006	2007	2008	2009	2010	2011	Change Between 1989 and 2011 (%)
Number of vehicles[a]										
Buses		4,284	3,952	4,565	4,181	6,073	5,372	8,922		
Urban		980	854	810	896	1,253	1,477	1,489		
Locomotives	384	212	202	273	261	283	272	283		–26[e]
Ships	117	78	32	33	32	27				–77[f]
Passengers transported[b]	3,036	802	1,292	1,454	1,669	1,782	1,796	1,601	1,610	–47
Bus	2,803	549	680	698	755	898	923	900	902	–68
Railroad	26.4	16.1	11.0	10.5	10.3	7.9	7.5	8.3	9.7	–63
Water	0.7	0.4	0.3	0.3	0.2	0.3	0.3	0.3	0.3	–57
Air	1.1	1.4	1.8	1.7	1.6	1.5	1.2	1.2	1.1	0
Alternative means[c]		191	553	700	854	826	814	642	645	238[g]
Share of total (%)		23.8	42.9	48.1	51.2	46.2	45.3	40.4	40.1	
Freight carried[d]										
Road	18.3	8.4	9.4	14.0	11.3	11.4	15.6	9.9	9.4	–49
Railroad	13.0	4.0	4.0	4.3	4.2	4.7	4.6	4.4	5.6	–57
Water (international)	5.2	5.5	1.8	2.4	2.4	1.1	0.5	1.1	0.5	–90

Sources: CEE, 1991; ONE, 2006, 2011a, 2012a.
Notes: Empty cells indicate that data are not available.
a. Public use.
b. Millions.
c. Animal and human traction.
d. Public use, million tons.
e. Change between 1989 and 2010.
f. Change between 1989 and 2008.
g. Change between 2000 and 2011.

problem because of labor indiscipline, severe reduction in the number of technicians and skilled workers, deficient training in the operation and maintenance of the new vehicles, underutilization of equipment, lack of spare parts, and waste of fuel; of the purported 8,000 recently acquired buses, only 1,000 were in operation, resulting in only a modest improvement in service (*Agence France-Press,* March 17, 2007; *Associated Press,* June 29, 2007). Reports circulated in late 2007 about buses that were missing doors, windshields, lights, and so on, and about many units being out of service and waiting to be repaired (*Granma,* September 22, 2007; del Valle, 2008). At the end of 2007, Minister Sierra announced a new investment of US$83 million over five years to purchase 1,500 buses, mostly from China and some from Russia, and again made the point that the de-capitalization of the public transportation system, undertaken over a period of fifteen years, would take a lengthy period of time to reverse (*Associated Press,* December 16, 2007).

According to press reports, in 2009 Havana had 1,072 new buses in operation and the public transportation service was meeting 40 percent of demand; the uncomfortable "camellos" (a homegrown vehicle consisting of a humpback trailer outfitted to carry passengers and pulled by a semi-truck) had been totally removed from service; it was forecasted that by 2012 there would be 2,300 buses in operation, which would address about 85 percent of demand (*Associated Press,* June 12, 2009).[26] But in September 2012 it was reported that Havana had only 900 buses and that only half of them were in operation due to paralyzed equipment caused by lack of repairs and scarcity of spare parts (*Café Fuerte,* August 18, 2012).

A report to the ANPP delivered in 2011 recognized that Ministry of Transportation services provided to the population were far from meeting customer expectations. The railroads were unable to meet demand, with the aged fleet of railroad wagons requiring urgent replacement. The road passenger transportation fleet was in poor condition and imports were 15 percent below projections as a result of difficulties in attaining external financing (*Bohemia,* July 29, 2011). The plan for public transportation of passengers by land in 2011 was not met as a result of lack of equipment (Yzquierdo Rodríguez, 2011).

In 2007, 70 percent of freight trucks in the state's fleet were used for purposes other than those for which they were intended; an audit by the Ministry of Economy found that most of the 200 enterprises subject to the audit did not properly control for gasoline consumption and drivers did not regularly report points of departure and arrival and distance traveled because they used the vehicles for personal use (*Reuters,* April 19, 2007).

Five Ilyushin aircraft (for passengers and freight) were bought from Russia in 2007 (*Novosti,* August 22, 2007). ONE does not report the number of civilian aircraft in the national fleet. A new commercial port and container terminal is being built at Mariel at a cost of US$800 million, with the expectation that it will replace the existing container terminal at the port of Havana; the project, financed by Brazil, will be operated by a company from Singapore (*Reuters,* July 13, 2011).

Communications. Between 2006 and 2010, the number of cellular phones increased by six and a half times, from 153,000 to 1 million, after the Cuban government authorized access to such devices by the population; the number of fixed (land) lines increased by 21 percent, from 962,000 to 1.2 million; the share of persons using the Internet climbed from 11.2 percent to 15.9 percent (but only 0.5 percent of homes had Internet access, and only 3.3 had a computer, as of 2008); and broadband Internet access jumped from nil to 3,700 subscriptions (see Table 2.6).

In 2010, Cuba ranked at or near the bottom within Latin America with respect to communications sector indicators: last on cellular telephony, households with telephone service, and access to the Internet; next to last on subscriptions to broadband Internet services; and in fourteen or fifteenth place on households with land lines and persons using the Internet (ITU, 2010).[27] Cellular telephones and services are sold at TRDs in convertible pesos (sending a tweet in Cuba costs more than a worker's minimum daily salary); cellular telephones are also received as gifts or sent by relatives or

Table 2.6 Telecommunications Indicators, 2006–2010

	2006	2007	2008	2009	2010	Latin America, 2010 Average	Cuba's Ranking[a]
Cellular telephones (thousands)	153	198	330	621	1,003	28,386	
Per thousand inhabitants	1.4	1.7	2.9	5.5	8.9	98.1	20
Land lines (thousands)	962	1,055	1,088	1,120	1,163	5,243	
Per thousand inhabitants	8.5	9.4	9.7	9.9	10.3	15.0	14
Persons using the Internet (%)	11.2	11.7	12.9	14.3	15.9	28.3	15
Broadband subscriptions (thousands)	0	1.9	2.2	2.9	3.7	1,556	18
Homes with Internet access (%)			0.5				16
Homes with computers (%)			3.3				16

Sources: Authors' estimates based on ITU, 2010; ONE, 2011a.
Notes: Empty cells indicate that data are not available.
    a. Out of twenty countries, except for broadband subscriptions (nineteen countries) and homes with Internet access and homes with computers (sixteen each), with 1 indicating best performance and 20 indicating worst performance.

friends who live abroad. Access to the Internet requires a special permit issued by the government and is mostly limited to workplaces and computer
clubs. Users typically face long waits to receive and send electronic mes-
sages and even longer to view a photo or a video.

A 1,630-kilometer submarine fiber-optic cable linking Venezuela and
Cuba reached Cuba in February 2011. The cable, laid by the French-Chinese
company Alcatel Shanghai Bell, was financed by Venezuela at a cost of
US$70 million. The new cable link was anticipated to greatly improve
voice, data, and image transmission; it was to start operations in July 2011.
In November 2011, the press reported that the cable had been tested and
was "operational," but had not been made generally available to users. Although there has been no formal announcement of the completion of the
project, it was reported in November 2012 that the link was providing services to selected entities of the Cuban and Venezuelan governments. The
lack of transparency about the project may be related to accusations of
shoddy work and corruption: reportedly, low-quality materials were used in
the project; two vice ministers and several executives from the companies
involved were arrested on fraud charges, and the Cuban minister of communications was dismissed (*El Universal,* February 9, 2011; *Cuba Times,*
November 14, 2011; Frank, 2011a; *El Universal,* July 9, 2012; Arreola,
2012; *Reuters,* June 14, 2012; Remón, 2012).

Nonsugar Agriculture, Livestock, and Fishing

Cuba does not publish agricultural output indexes. There are contradictions
between statistics on agricultural output given by ONE in the *Anuario* and
in its quarterly reports: the former include an "estimate of output from self-
consumption plots . . . in cooperatives and in private farms" (ECLAC,
2007), making these figures higher than those in the latter series, which excludes such production (Hagelberg, 2011). ONE's (2012f) annual report on
agricultural production for 2011 shows higher percentage growth rates
compared to 2010 than those estimated based on *Anuario* data for 2010
(ONE, 2011a). There are also discrepancies among three statistical series in
the *Anuario* related to land use (ONE, 2011a).

Agriculture has been the worst-performing sector of the Cuban economy. Agriculture has been the Achilles' heel of socialist economies, given
their concentration of land in the hands of the state, centralized decisionmaking, and, in the Cuban case, a state procurement system (*acopio*) that
dictated production decisions and obliged producers to sell agricultural output at predetermined prices. Agriculture's share of GDP fell from 10 percent to 3.5 percent between 1989 and 2010, as a result of "the collapse of
sugar agriculture, the systematic decline of the livestock sector, and the
stagnation of non-sugar agriculture" (Pérez Villanueva, 2008b). Agricultural

production fell by 12.4 percent in 2005 and 7.5 percent in 2006; after a jump of 19.6 percent in 2007 (in large part explained by the sharp declines of the two previous years), output stagnated in 2008, grew by 3.3 percent in 2009, and declined by 5.1 percent in 2010 (preliminary statistics for 2011 indicate an increase in most products; see Chapter 6). In 2010, 18.5 percent of the labor force was employed in agriculture and fishing, industries that generated 3.5 percent of GDP, clearly indicating that labor productivity is very low in these sectors (ONE, 2011c).

In 2011, output levels of seven key agricultural products were well below their 1989 levels: 18 percent for cattle, 2 percent for eggs, 53 percent for tobacco leaf, 47 percent for milk, 74 percent for fish and shellfish, 73 percent for citrus fruits, and 93 percent for coffee (a decade earlier, citrus fruits and fish and shellfish were important exports). In contrast, production of vegetables increased 260 percent above their 1989 level, whereas tubers rose 112 percent and rice 6 percent (see Table 2.2). Between 2001 and 2010, agriculture had the lowest productivity across all sectors of the economy (one-twelfth that of finance, insurance, and business services in 2010).

With the poor record of the agricultural sector, food self-sufficiency has fallen sharply, which has required substantial import of foodstuffs (see Chapter 3). Raúl has acknowledged that the island is unable to meet the population's food needs (*Granma*, February 26, 2007; Nova, 2007; R. Castro Ruz, 2011g). The situation has improved somewhat with the implementation of reforms that have distributed idle state lands in usufruct to individual farmers and given more autonomy to cooperatives; these reforms and their effects will be analyzed in Chapters 5 and 6.

Land tenure and production by the state and nonstate sectors. Data on cultivated and uncultivated agricultural land (including idle land), by state and nonstate sectors, are presented in Table 2.7.

The nonstate sector consists of three different entities, basic units of cooperative production (UBPCs), agricultural production cooperatives (CPAs), and credit and services cooperatives (CCSs), the latter combined in Table 2.7 with small private farmers.

The UBPCs, created out of state farms, inherited debts and obsolete equipment upon their inception. Their members, former state employees, were neither consulted about the shift into the new entities nor trained about the implications of work in cooperatives. UBPC members continue to behave as state employees rather than cooperative shareholders, as they do not feel ownership entitlement. UBPCs have no decisionmaking autonomy; the state directs them, seeking little input on what to plant and how much to sell to the state (at fixed, below-market prices) and to agricultural markets. Only about 44 percent of the UBPCs are commercially viable, with the rest requiring state subsidies. Between 2006 and 2009, the number of UBPCs

Table 2.7 Distribution of Agricultural Land, Cultivated and Uncultivated, by State and Nonstate Sectors, 1989, 2005, 2007, and 2010 (percentages)

			Nonstate			
Year and Land	Total	State	Total	UBPCs	CPAs	CCSs + Small Private Farmers
1989						
Agricultural land	100.0	74.3	25.7	11.4	3.4	10.9
Cultivated	65.1	50.8	14.3	6.6	2.2	5.5
Uncultivated	34.9	23.5	11.4	4.7	1.2	5.4
Idle	7.0	5.2	1.8	0.7	0.3	0.8
2005						
Agricultural land	100.0	40.3	59.7	33.0	9.0	17.7
Cultivated	48.9	13.8	35.1	17.9	5.2	11.9
Uncultivated	51.1	26.5	24.6	15.1	3.8	5.7
Idle	16.7	10.2	6.5	4.8	0.8	0.9
2007						
Agricultural land	100.0	35.8	64.2	37.0	8.9	18.3
Cultivated	45.2	10.5	34.7	18.0	4.6	12.1
Uncultivated	54.8	25.3	29.5	19.0	4.2	6.3
Idle	18.6	9.5	9.1	7.0	1.1	1.0
2010						
Agricultural land	100.0	26.0	74.0	29.9	8.8	35.3

Sources: Authors' estimates based on CEE, 1991, for 1989; ONE, 2006, 2011a, for 2005 and 2007; and Nova, 2010b, for 2010.

Note: Percentages estimated on the basis of total agricultural land: 6,772,000 hectares in 1989, 6,597,100 hectares in 2005, and 6,619,500 hectares in 2007; there is no data on cultivated and uncultivated land for 2010. UBPCs = basic units of cooperative production, CPAs = agricultural production cooperatives, CCSs = credit and services cooperatives.

fell from 1,541 to 1,403, because of poor economic performance, inability to pay debts, labor shortages, falling yields, and corruption. CPAs are composed of former private farmers who combined their land, machinery, and equipment, and face strong state interference, although less so compared to UBPCs. The number of CPAs has also declined due to poor financial performance. Between 2007 and 2010, the number of CPAs fell from 3,612 to 3,162, and their members from 242,100 to 217,000, as a result of the same problems that affected the UBPCs. In the CSSs, farmers do not cede their land, machinery, and equipment to the cooperative, but retain ownership and join together to negotiate credits, purchase inputs at wholesale terms, and share machinery and equipment. Out of the three types of cooperatives, the CSSs have the highest degree of independence from the state (Mesa-Lago and Pérez-López, 2005; Nova, 2006, 2007; A. Pérez, 2006; Martín and Pérez, 2007; *Granma,* December 4, 2009; Hagelberg, 2011). According to Armando Nova (2011): "The forms of land tenure that show the highest efficiency are the CSS and private farmers; currently, these two land tenure forms grow 57 percent of total food production while controlling only 24.4 percent of cultivated land; they have only 3.7 percent and 1.7 percent, respectively, of land reported as idle."

Agricultural land declined from 6.77 million hectares in 1989 to 6.62 million hectares in 2007. The state's share of agricultural land declined from 74.3 percent in 1989 to 35.8 percent in 2007 and to 26 percent in 2010, while the nonstate sector's share grew from 25.7 percent to 64.2 percent and to 74 percent, respectively (see Table 2.7). Since 2008, about 1 million hectares of idle state lands in usufruct have been transferred primarily to individuals (see Chapter 5). As these landowners are likely associated in CCSs or farm privately, the share of agricultural land accounted for by these two forms of tenure increased from 17.7 percent in 2005 to 35.3 percent in 2010. The state's share of cultivated land fell from 50.8 percent to 10.5 percent between 1989 and 2007 (more recent data are not available), whereas that of the nonstate sector rose from 14.3 percent to 34.7 percent. Uncultivated land as a share of all agricultural land increased from 34.9 percent to 54.8 percent between 1989 and 2007, and the share of uncultivated land that is idle expanded from 7 percent to 18.6 percent over the same period.[28] State idle lands are overrun with marabú.

In 2011 the nonstate sector comprised between 79 percent and 97 percent of harvested agricultural land for most key products (except citrus fruits) and similarly contributed most of production (between 86 percent and 99 percent, except citrus fruits, barnyard birds, and hogs). In addition, the nonstate sector accounted for 86 percent of the births of calves and for 89 percent of the milk, 68 percent of hogs, and 57 percent of barnyard birds (see Table 2.8).

When comparing the shares of land under cultivation and of production for the state and nonstate sectors in Table 2.8, it is evident that in 2011 the nonstate sector attained higher yields (tons per hectare) than the state sector in six of ten agricultural products (rice, tobacco, corn, beans, banana plantains, and other fruits), while the state sector attained superior yields with respect to four (sugarcane, vegetables, citrus fruits, and tubers). But because the notoriously inefficient UBPCs and CPAs are included in the nonstate sector, they probably depress average yields in that sector. We suspect that statistics for the noncooperative private sector are available, although they have not been published to date. These data are essential for measuring the productivity of the private sector and its potential improvement under Raúl's reforms (see Chapter 6).

Nonsugar agriculture. In this section we describe trends in a number of key agricultural products for domestic consumption and export, identify the reasons for their lackluster performance, and discuss some of actions taken

**Table 2.8 Distribution of Harvested Land and Agricultural Production,
by State and Nonstate Sectors, 2011 (percentages)**

	Land		Production	
	State	Nonstate	State	Nonstate
Sugarcane	2.6	97.4	3.2	96.8
Tubers	7.4	92.6	8.6	91.4
Bananas (fruit and plantains)	12.5	87.5	11.4	88.6
Vegetables	11.1	88.9	15.4	84.6
Rice	21.5	78.5	13.5	86.5
Corn	4.8	95.2	3.6	96.4
Beans	5.7	94.3	3.4	96.6
Tobacco	3.7	96.3	1.1	98.9
Citrus fruits	45.4	54.6	60.0	40.0
Other fruits	12.0	88.0	6.0	94.0
Cattle[a]			14.5	85.5
Milk (cow)			11.2	88.8
Hogs			31.7	68.3
Barnyard birds			43.2	56.8

Source: Authors' estimates based on ONE, 2012a.
Notes: Empty cells indicate that data are not available.
a. Data on state vs. nonstate production distribution for cattle are not available, and are estimated here (14.5% state, 85.5% nonstate) based on births of calves; if based on stock of milk cows, the distribution would be 10% state and 90% nonstate.

to confront certain challenges, although reform measures will be discussed fully in Chapter 5.

The citrus harvest peaked at 981,000 tons in 1988, when Cuba was the world's largest exporter; production subsequently declined to around 400,000 tons in 2007–2009 and to 265,000 in 2011, for several reasons: the end of commercial relations with the Soviet Union, which until then had purchased most of the crop and provided the bulk of fertilizers and pesticides; the aging of groves and failure to replace trees; uncontrolled plagues because of the lack of pesticides (including for the insects that carry the bacteria that causes Huanglongbing, or yellow dragon disease, which can devastate orchards); destruction of many orchards by the 2008 hurricanes; and low prices paid for products of the nonstate sector. About 80 percent of the citrus harvest is processed as juice, 15 percent is consumed domestically, and 5 percent is exported or supplied to the tourism industry. It has been estimated that an investment of US$200 million would be required for citrus production to recover (*Reuters,* January 7, 2011; *Diario de Cuba,* August 16, 2011; ONE, 2011a).

The amount of land devoted to tobacco production fell by 25 percent between 2006 and 2010, while tobacco output fell by 31 percent and yield by 21 percent (the decline in yield was higher in the state sector than in the nonstate sector); in 2011, 96 percent of tobacco land was cultivated by the nonstate sector, which generated 99 percent of production (see Table 2.7). Low prices paid by the state to nonstate producers, lack of agricultural inputs, and contraction in world consumption of tobacco were responsible for the poor performance of the sector. The fall in production of tobacco leaf (53 percent lower in 2011 compared to 1989) contributed to a decline of 10 percent in the output of cigars between 2006 and 2010, concentrated in cigars for export, which decreased hard-currency income from exports, although production recovered in 2011.

Rice is a basic staple in the daily diet of Cubans; more than 900,000 tons of rice are distributed to consumers annually through the rationing system (the monthly quota is seven pounds per person per month), and additional quantities are sold through the TRDs. After a sharp drop in the 1990s, rice production began to climb in 2001 and reached a peak in 2003 at 716,000 tons, but then later declined to 434,200 tons in 2006, and stagnated in the subsequent years, climbing to 566,400 tons in 2011, at 21 percent below the 2003 peak and about 6 percent above the 1989 level. In 2010, domestic rice production met about half of national demand and 413,910 tons were imported from Vietnam at a cost of US$219 million (CEE, 1991; ONE, 2006, 2011a; Murillo, 2010). In 2011, 79 percent of land devoted to rice was in the hands of the nonstate sector, which provided 87 percent of production (see Table 2.8). Official explanations for the poor production included degraded soils and damaged irrigation systems; lack of delivery of equipment, such as rice dryers; and infrastructure deterioration during the "Special Period in Time of Peace," such as roads, machinery, tractors, transportation equipment, and mills (*Juventud Rebelde,* August 17, 2008; *Bohemia,* December 12, 2008). The production decline in 2010 was attributed to low yields because of lack of inputs, breakdowns of tractors and dryers, poor equipment maintenance, and waste of about half of water delivered through irrigation. Cuba's cost of producing rice is seven times that of Vietnam's (*Trabajadores,* December 13, 2010). Recently, the Cuban government has begun to pay higher prices to rice producers and to allow them to hire outside workers, which is likely to increase future production (*Reuters,* March 2, 2012).

The coffee harvest amounted to 28,920 tons in 1989, roughly half of the average annual production of 60,000 tons prior to the revolution (*Trabajadores,* May 24, 2010),[29] and subsequently fell to about 2,000 tons in 2010 and 2011, 93 percent lower than in 1989. The goal for 2011 was 6,400 tons, but only 2,000 tons were harvested, which casts doubt on whether the ambitious goal of 22,000 tons in 2015 is achievable. Cuba exports nearly all of the coffee it produces, uses a portion for sale at TRDs, and imports low-quality beans from Brazil and other countries (at a cost of US$50 million per annum), which it mixes with green peas for distribution to consumers through the rationing system. The official reasons of the poor performance of coffee production are low production prices paid by the state's *acopio* procurement system to some 35,000 private farmers; labor shortages, which require the mobilization of students and inexperienced workers for the harvest; chronic delays in conducting the harvest, leading to spoilage of beans; "diversion" of 10–20 percent of production by private farmers to sell illegally on the black market; and the hurricanes of 2008, which destroyed some of the plantations. Since 2006, the Cuban government has doubled and even tripled the price it pays to coffee producers without a corresponding output reaction; more recently, the government has granted hundreds of abandoned state coffee farms to private farmers (CEE, 1991; *Granma,* November 11, 2007, August 5, 2010, September 7, 2010, September 29, 2010, February 10, 2011, March 25, 2011; *Reuters,* February 10, 2011, September 19, 2011, January 23, 2012; *Radio Rebelde,* September 16, 2011; see Chapter 5).

Production of four crops peaked in 2004–2006 and then declined steady through 2010–2011: vegetables, which peaked at 4 million tons and declined to 1.5 million tons (–45 percent with respect to peak production); tubers, which peaked at 1.8 million tons and declined to 1.4 million (–22 percent); corn, which peaked at 399,000 tons and declined to 248,900 tons (–38 percent); and beans, which peaked at 133,000 tons and declined to 72,900 tons (–45 percent). The private sector provided the largest share of production of all four crops in 2011: 85 percent of vegetables, 91 percent of tubers, 96 percent of corn, and 97 percent of beans (see Table 2.8). In 2010, Cuba imported corn valued at US$179.4 million and beans at US$40 million (ONE, 2006, 2011a).

Livestock. The cattle herd peaked at 7.1 million heads in 1967, declined steadily to 3.7 million in 2006, and recovered to 4 million in 2011; in the latter year, the cattle herd was 18 percent smaller than its 1989 size and 44 percent smaller than its 1967 peak; the number of cattle per capita fell from 0.83 to 0.36 between 1989 and 2011. Imports of beef amounted to US$300 million in 2010 (CEE, 1991; ONE, 2011a). The poor performance of the livestock sector was the outcome of several factors: a drop in the import of cattle feed as well as a reduction in the supply of fodder from sugarcane; the infestation of marabú, affecting 70 percent of grazing lands; and the loss of pastures as a result of lack of seed, irrigation, and fertilizer. The size of the cattle herd in Camagüey province—the province with the largest concentration of cattle and producer of 28 percent of the nation's milk—fell by half. Most of the cattle are underfed and lack proper water supply during the dry season (half of the year), which affects milk production. The mortality rate of calves jumped from 8.8 per 1,000 live births in 1989 to 40.8 in

2005, but then fell to 22.3 by 2010, though this was still two and a half times the 1989 rate. There is a scarcity of the fencing necessary to divide pasture lands, and a lack of funding to build and maintain milking barns and equipment and refrigerated storage tanks. Private farmers control 53.6 percent of cattle[30] and sell to the state 66 percent of production at fixed prices that are quite low, which incentivizes theft and illegal slaughtering of cattle. In Camagüey, 1,448 kilometers of roads are in very poor condition and deficiencies in the transportation system delay the movement of milk to processing facilities and ultimately to consumers, with the result that a significant share of the product is spoiled (14 million liters of milk and a similar amount of fresh cheese spoiled in 2006); lack of containers and poor quality control also affect milk. Private farmers and cooperatives underreport milk production and sell artisanal cheese under the table (*Granma, May 3, 2007; Carrobello and Terrero, 2008; Nova, 2010a*).

The increase in cattle supported a rise in milk production of 24 percent between 2007 and 2011 (see Table 2.2). Contributing to higher milk production were the practice of fattening cows with fodder (fodder imports rose in 2010), an increase of 21 percent in the number of cows producing milk, and a 47 percent higher yield per cow (higher in the nonstate sector compared to the state sector, in part because of higher prices paid by the government to private farmers and cooperatives since 2008). Despite this, Cuba still imported US$117 million in powdered and condensed milk in 2010 (ONE, 2011a). In 2011, milk production fell again and Raúl mobilized the police and the Ministry of Interior to take steps to combat theft and illegal slaughter of cattle by farmers, members of cooperatives, butchers, managers of state enterprises, local officials, and employees of the Livestock Control Center seeking to sell meat on the black market. Raúl warned that this time "it is not just one more campaign, as has occurred in the past. . . . [T]his time we will eliminate the cattle rustlers" (R. Castro Ruz, 2011g).

There are no statistics for 1989 on the number of hogs and barnyard birds for the state and nonstate sectors. The number of hogs in 1965 was 1.8 million, roughly the same level as in 2008 (68 percent were owned by the nonstate sector in the latter year); the number of hogs fell to 1.4 million in 2011, 22 percent lower than in 1965. The number of barnyard birds was 21.4 million in 1965 and rose to 31 million in 2010, an increase of 45 percent.[31] Production of eggs fell from 2.5 to 2.1 billion between 1989 and 2005, and later climbed to 2.6 billion in 2001, only 2 percent below the 1989 level. In 2010, Cuba imported poultry meat valued at US$135 million (CEE, 1991; Mesa-Lago, 2000; ONE, 2011a).

Fishing. Fish and shellfish catch peaked at 244,000 tons in 1986, declined to 192,000 tons in 1989, and subsequently followed a downward trend, reaching 49,000 tons in 2010, 74 percent below the 1989 figure and 80 percent below the 1986 peak (see Table 2.2). Reasons behind the poor performance of the industry include an aged fishing fleet that has not been properly maintained and whose equipment has not been modernized; heavy debt and debt service associated with purchase of vessels many years ago, inability to obtain credit, lack of liquidity, and creditors' concern about likelihood of repayment; technological problems; climate change; lack of quality control over catch;[32] high oil prices that raise the cost of fishing, particularly on the high seas away from the Cuban insular platform; and serious administrative deficiencies and corruption (Mesa-Lago, 2008a, 2009c).

Other reasons behind the deterioration of the agricultural sector. Traditionally, the Cuban government has blamed two external factors—weather (hurricanes, excessive rainfall, drought) and the US economic embargo—for the poor performance of the agricultural sector. The first factor is analyzed in Box 2.1. Concerning the embargo, US imports of forage and foodstuffs have been permitted since 2001 and have increased substantially since then (see Chapter 3). Raúl has stated on several occasions that the embargo is not the principal reason for Cuba's poor economic performance, which is rooted in domestic issues. In what follows we discuss the main reasons behind the poor performance of the agricultural sector based on several articles published in Cuba in the 2006–2011 period (Borrego, 2006; González, 2006; *Granma,* March 24, 2006, September 29, 2007, February 21, 2009, December 4, 2009; Nova, 2006, 2007, 2010b; Pagés and Castaño, 2006; *Juventud Rebelde,* January 21, 2007, September 23, 2007, July 30, 2010; Martín and Pérez, 2007; *Bohemia,* December 12, 2008; *Trabajadores,* October 12, 2009; "Controversia," 2010; Carrobello and Rubio, 2011).

Cuban sociologist Juan Valdés Paz, a former official of the Ministry of Agriculture, asserts that no socialist regime has been able to overcome the challenges of the agricultural sector ("Controversia," 2010). Armando Nova (2011) points to several key problems that have not been solved: the failure to accept the real and objective existence of markets; the lack of recognition of property rights and of the right of the producer to decide what to produce, to whom to sell it, and at what price and under what conditions; and the inability of producers to access markets to purchase needed inputs. Although more detailed and disaggregated statistics are needed, private farmers are more productive than state enterprises and UBPCs and this is why Raúl has begun to transfer idle state lands in usufruct to private farmers.

Under the *acopio* procurement system, mandatory sales by cooperatives and private farmers to the state monopoly—the Agricultural Procurement Agency—mean that the government buys about 75 percent of agricultural production, and the *acopio* system functions as an intermediary that buys low from farmers and sells high to retailers.[33] The *acopio* system suffers from several grave deficiencies: (a) its two key institutions (the Ministry of Domestic Trade and the Ministry of Agriculture) have set contradictory criteria with respect to quality and destination of products; (b) it extracts an average profit of 29 percent, as high as 41 percent in some instances; (c) it is chronically late in paying producers, resulting in the accumulation of huge debts and creating disincentives for farmers; (d) it fixes monthly prices rigidly based on inadequate information on levels of inventories and of demand, and even when quality of produce is poor and products are not selling well, it does not lower prices and instead the produce spoils (there is a procedure to lower prices if an expert deems that low quality of the product deserves it, but often there is no expert available, there is no telephone to call the expert, and by the time the expert arrives, the produce has spoiled); (e) it stores produce in warehouses for up to forty-eight hours without refrigeration; (f) it relies on defective equipment to weigh produce purchased from farmers; (g) its transportation equipment is obsolete and poorly maintained, with much of it nonfunctional because of lack of batteries, tires, replacement parts, and so on; and (h) it does not provide adequate inputs to farmers (fertilizers, seeds, fuels, machetes, boots, gloves) for them to meet their production goals.

Organizational flaws provoke substantial losses in agricultural production. For example, in 2007, millions of liters of milk spoiled because of delays in the collection of raw milk, shortage of bottles, lack of controls, and exit from the sector of experienced workers. In 2009, a significant portion of an unexpectedly large tomato crop was spoiled because of the lack of containers for collection and transportation. There is also a national shortage of warehouses and refrigerated facilities to store produce. The government has not met commitments regarding the supply of inputs to the nonstate agricultural sector and has also delayed payments for produce bought. Thus, state entities fail to deliver committed amounts of food to consumers as a result of "lack of foresight, lack of consideration of demand, infrequent use of contracts, and other factors, which demonstrate severe deficiencies in the planning process" (R. Castro Ruz, 2010c).

An estimated 75 percent of soils are degraded and most of water resources are contaminated by the use of chemical fertilizers; 80 percent of cattle-grazing lands in the province of Matanzas and half of the agricultural lands in the province of Camagüey are infested with marabú; the application of agro-chemicals and the indiscriminate burning of marabú have caused irreparable harm to soils. Cuba is ranked 105th among 182 countries on availability of water per capita for all uses: 1,222 cubic liters below the hydric stress limit established by the Food and Agriculture Organization. An estimated 600 million cubic meters of water per annum are lost due to leaks and breaks in the water distribution system. Ninety-three reservoirs holding

1.3 million cubic meters of water are not usable, as the necessary investments have not been made. Irrigation systems have deteriorated because of lack of maintenance and repair.

There is a severe shortage of agricultural machinery and equipment because of financial limitations to imports, idleness due to lack of spare parts, and poor maintenance. Despite the dire need for agricultural machinery and equipment imports, large stocks of such (six-disc plows, universal multiplows, multidisc harrows, and so on) and frequently used spare parts (axles, bearings) are stored in warehouses, as customers lack the needed funds to pay for them. *Acopio* entities owe millions of pesos to the factories that manufacture agricultural machinery and equipment.

The Agricultural Polytechnic Institute of Havana has trained more than 40,000 agricultural technicians, but these professionals have not been used to generate change in the sector.[34] According to Raúl (R. Castro Ruz, 2010c), only 20 percent of the agricultural experts trained under the revolution are working in the field: more than 75 percent of agricultural enterprises lack agronomists, nearly half of the cooperatives lack agricultural technicians, and only 20 percent have veterinarians and accountants. One of the reasons for the shortage of agricultural technicians is that low salaries have induced many trained professionals to leave the country or to shift to more lucrative occupations; for example, the management team of a hotel in Varadero was composed of veterinarians. Several of these problems are being addressed by Raúl's reforms, as discussed in Chapter 5.

Summary of Findings

Since 2006, the timeliness and availability of Cuban economic statistics have improved, but there are still important gaps, credibility problems, and contradictions, particularly with respect to the calculation of GDP, capital formation, inflation, and agricultural production. Meanwhile, publications by Cuban academic economists have increased in quantity, quality, and objectivity.

The official growth rate of GDP (overestimated because of a methodology that differs from international norms) rose to 12 percent in 2006, slowed to 1.4 percent in 2009, and rebounded to 2.7 percent in 2011, lower than the average rate of growth for Latin America, which was 4.3 percent; Cuba's recovery is the slowest in the region. The contribution of goods to GDP fell from 38 percent in 1989 to 19 percent in 2011, while that of basic services was basically stable at 14–16 percent, and that of other services jumped from 48 percent to 65 percent. This shift is not an indicator of economic development, but rather of a process of de-industrialization, the overvaluation of domestic services, and the tremendous expansion of exports of professional services. Capital formation fell from 25.6 percent in 1989 to 7 percent of GDP in 2011, a third of the regional average in 2011 and a quarter of the 25 percent rate recorded by Cuba in 1989, which is roughly the rate economists consider necessary for sustainable long-term growth. The official inflation rate was 1.7 percent in 2011, a quarter of the regional average; the calculation of inflation is questionable, as it excludes transactions in convertible pesos. Monetary liquidity rose to over 40 percent of GDP in 2011, almost twice the 1989 level. The fiscal deficit fell to 6.9 percent in 2008 and continued to fall to 3.8 percent in 2011, two and a half times the regional average.

In 2011, out of twenty key products for domestic consumption and export, output was well below (11–96 percent) the 1989 level for fourteen, and above for only six. Mining, supported by foreign investment, had the best performance: production of national gas increased thirtyfold (from a very low base in 1989), oil production fourfold, and production of nickel by 45 percent, but in all three cases, peak production levels were reached between 2001 and 2007. Two of the plants that produce raw nickel date from the 1940s and 1950s; Sherritt upgraded the largest nickel plant (Pedro Sotto in Moa) and a capacity expansion is planned, but the oldest of the plants is rumored to be shutting down permanently. The completion of a new nickel plant at Las Camariocas is projected for 2014.

Although the first round of deep-water offshore exploratory drilling conducted in 2012 was disappointing, Cuba still has high hopes that there will be a significant discovery of oil deposits in deep waters off the northern coast of the island. Should oil in commercial quantities be discovered, it will take three to five years to start commercial exploitation. Cuba currently produces 38 percent of the crude oil and oil products it consumes, and imports the rest, principally from Venezuela. The Cienfuegos refinery is being expanded to double its capacity, a new refinery is being planned in Matanzas, and there are plans to modernize the Santiago de Cuba refinery. Should all of these plans materialize, Cuba's refining capacity would rise to 350,000 barrels per day by 2015, and its dependence on Venezuelan supplies would ease.

Manufacturing's share of GDP fell from 28 percent in 1989 to 16 percent in 2010, and the index of manufacturing output in 2011 was 55 percent below the 1989 level. Between 1989 and 2011, output in twenty of twenty-four nonsugar manufacturing industries declined, evidencing of generalized de-industrialization process. In 2002, Cuban launched an aggressive program to downsize the sugar industry, justifying the decision on low world market prices and high production costs: land devoted to sugarcane, the number of mills, and the size of the work force were cut back; Fidel also opposed the conversion of sugar into ethanol. Sugar production in 2010–2011 was slightly over 1 million tons, 86 percent lower than in 1989, and agricultural and industrial yields fell sharply. In 2011–2012, international sugar prices reached their highest level in thirty years; the low level of production and the inability to engineer a supply response prevented Cuba from capitalizing on the high prices, potentially costing the island US$3 billion. Raúl's recent strategy to stimulate sugar production could prove successful if it can be applied at the national level, but will require substantial resources.

The "energy revolution," launched by Fidel in 2006, aimed at shoring up the aging and unreliable electricity generation system with small, diesel-powered electricity generation units coupled with an energy conservation program that replaced incandescent light bulbs and highly energy-consuming appliances with "energy saving" alternatives. Rather than a long-term solution, the energy plan was a short-term fix, with several of the predicted problems eventually materializing. In 2010–2011, blackouts were less frequent but had not been totally eliminated (they reappeared in 2012), residential electricity consumption was higher, and electricity generation lower, although generation was 19 percent above the level in 1989 (it was flat on a per capita basis compared to 1989, however). Raúl has announced plans to invest in the construction of a new and large thermoelectric plant, an indication of the limitations of the small-capacity electricity generation units.

The number of passengers transported by the public system fell by half, and 40 percent of passengers were transported using alternative means, such as animal or human traction. Despite the import of buses from China—which substituted for the reviled "camellos"—the number of passenger buses fell by 68 percent, the weight of freight transported by 65 percent, and the number of ships by 77 percent; only 65 percent of locomotives were operational. Lack of maintenance of transportation equipment and shortage of spare parts are serious issues. As a result of Raúl's authorization for citizens to own and use cell phones and increased availability of such equipment as gifts from friends and relatives abroad, the number of cell phones rose more than sixfold between 2006 and 2010, while the number of telephone land lines rose by 21 percent; and the percentage of the population using the Internet rose to 15.9 percent. Nevertheless, Cuba still ranks near the bottom within Latin America on these indicators.

The worst-performing sector has been agriculture, whose contribution to GDP fell from 10 percent to 3.5 percent between 1989 and 2011. Production of citrus fruits, rice, milk, eggs, raw tobacco, and coffee was from 2 percent to 93 percent lower in 2011 than in 1989; the number of cattle was 18 percent lower (on a per capita basis, it fell from 0.83 to 0.36), and fish and shellfish catch was 74 percent lower. However, production of vegetables and tubers exceeded 1989 output by considerable margins. The value of food imports grew to US$1.7 billion in 2012 (84 percent of the products in the basic family consumption basket are imported), although remaining roughly the same volume as in 2011, because of increases in world market food prices.

The nonstate agricultural sector (credit and services cooperatives and private farmers) controlled 35 percent of land in 2010 (up from 12 percent in 2007), but generated 40–97 percent of agricultural production and 68–89 percent of livestock animal products, depending on the product. Among the factors behind the poor performance of agriculture are the inefficiency of the state sector, weak incentives for the nonstate sector associated with low procurement prices and excessive controls, scarcity of fodder for cattle, failure to replant citrus trees, and the deterioration of the fishing fleet. It has been common practice to blame the poor agricultural performance on external factors (hurricanes, drought, excessive rainfall, the US embargo), but Raúl has highlighted the primacy of internal factors, and scholars and journalists have begun to discuss publicly some of them: the concentration of land in the state sector and in the basic units of cooperative production and the agricultural production cooperatives; the notoriously inefficient *acopio* procurement system, which pays producers low prices and does not make such payments on time, fixes prices centrally and rigidly and does not adjust them when products are not sold because of low demand or spoilage of produce, lacks adequate storage facilities and transportation services, does not meet contractual obligations on inputs to farmers, and prohibits intermediaries; organization and planning problems that often lead to high levels of waste; the overall degradation of soils, expansion of marabú infestation, shortage of water for irrigation, and water distribution losses and contamination; shortage of agricultural machinery, equipment, and spare parts; and the exit of skilled workers to better-compensated occupations.

These are the serious problems confronting Cuba's domestic economy, particularly in agriculture and manufacturing, that have prompted Raúl's reforms, which are analyzed in Chapters 5 and 6. In the next chapter we examine Cuba's international economic relations from 2006 to 2011.

Notes

1. Members of the CEEC include the following scholars: Anicia García, Hiram Marquetti Nodarse, Armando Nova González, Jorge Mario Sánchez-Egozcue, Ricardo Torres Pérez, Juan Triana Cordoví, and Pavel Vidal Alejandro.
2. Nine tables do include statistics for 2010, but many of them add a footnote cautioning that the statistics are preliminary, or not comparable with those for the rest of the region or with earlier Cuban statistics.
3. The slowdown in the growth rate in 2009 was partly the result of four damaging hurricanes in 2008 (see Box 2.1).
4. See Feinberg, 2011 (sec. 4), for a discussion of Cuba's current relations with the international financial institutions.
5. ECLAC (2011a) estimated growth in 2011 at 2.5 percent and the Economist Intelligence Unit (EIU, 2011) at 2.4 percent.
6. Resolution no. 355 of 2006 of the Ministry of Finance and Prices estimated rates (prices) of education, public health, and other services in order to "eliminate

the undervaluation of such services for purposes of calculating GDP." Some experts have suggested that costs of services in developed countries have been used for this purpose.

7. In 2007, then–minister of economy José Luis Rodríguez (2007b) stated: "Cuba's current GDP is perfectly compatible with any country in the world and [the Cuban government] reiterates its right to demand that its accomplishments be reflected, without conditions or questioning, . . . in the publications of international organizations."

8. The slight reduction in the relative value of services compared to GDP since 2007 might have contributed to lower the degree of overestimation.

9. Pebercan and Sherritt were responsible for 60 percent of national oil production in 2009; the companies alleged that Cuba owed them US$900 million for their share of oil production. Cuba paid a lump-sum settlement to Pebercan of US$140 million to end the contractual arrangement.

10. The recovery rate of Cuba's heavy oil is 7 percent of proven reserves because of its high density and geological conditions; work is ongoing to improve on such recovery rate.

11. The distribution of oil leases by company is as follows: seven to Spanish company Repsol in partnership with Indian company ONGC Videsh and Norwegian company Statoil; four to Malaysian state company Petronas in partnership with Russian company Gazprom; four to Venezuelan state company PDVSA; four to Vietnamese state company PetroVietnam; two to Angolan company Sonangol; and one to ONGC Videsh alone. Brasil's Petrobras relinquished a concession that it had been granted and Canada's Sherritt did the same with respect to four others because of financial difficulties, the high cost of deep-water offshore drilling, and the inability to enter into a partnership with another company (*Reuters,* July 30, 2008; *Associated Press,* March 23, 2009). In 2012, Mexico's PEMEX was reportedly seeking a concession.

12. *Scarabeo 9,* built in Chinese and Singaporean shipyards, had less than 10 percent US content in order to meet US embargo requirements. A key safety device in deep-water exploration rigs, the blowout preventer, was manufactured in the United States.

13. According to Guaicaipuro Lameda, former president of Venezuelan state oil company PDVSA, feasibility studies conducted in 2000–2001 concluded that the Cienfuegos refinery was not commercially viable and therefore PEMEX and PETROBRAS did not participate in the project (F. Sánchez, 2006). Expert Eduardo del Valle agrees with this evaluation and argues that it would be commercially more sound to allocate resources to increase the capacity of the existing refineries to produce light refined products (Cancio, 2009a). Juan Triana Cordoví (2007) posits that high world market oil prices make the Cienfuegos refinery commercially viable.

14. CUVENPEQ is also planning a petrochemical complex in Cienfuegos, including urea and ammonia factories, using Japanese and Chinese technology.

15. Cuba has not provided official figures on 2010 production. The estimate is based on a statement by a Cuban official that production in 2010 was 6,700 tons below the projected level (Murillo, 2010), which we have conservatively estimated at 75,000 tons; if the target had been lower, for example 73,000 tons, the estimate of production would be lower accordingly.

16. The sugarcane harvest (*zafra*) starts in December and generally ends in April of the following year (when severe rains make it difficult to cut the sugarcane); to simplify matters, we refer to the year in which the harvest ends.

17. The world market price of sugar fell to about US$0.6 cents per pound in 2002, the lowest in at least a decade (IMF, 2011).

18. Brian Pollitt (2010) attributes the drop in nonsugar agriculture to the unfeasibility of transferring specialized sugar-industry machinery to other agricultural crops, the lack of incentives for workers dismissed from the sugar industry to shift to manual labor in other crops, the poor quality of some of the released lands, which were only suitable for raising cattle and remained under the control of the Ministry of Sugar, and the lack of experience with other crops in the sugarcane state farms and the basic units of cooperative production (UBPCs).

19. In October 2012 the world market price for sugar was still high, at over US$0.20 per pound.

20. The significance of this fact is that the "5 de Septiembre" is not one of the mills that was nationalized by the Cuban government and therefore it may be less vulnerable under the US Helms-Burton Act to claims by former owners of expropriated properties.

21. A significant portion of the population owned US-made refrigerators that were more than sixty years old, but still functioning; the government pressured the owners to swap such units for energy-saving Chinese refrigerators. The latter break frequently and repairing them demands that the case be torn apart and replaced with a new one, at a cost of 1,200 CUP plus labor. Consolidado la Cubana, a repair shop, has a backlog of hundreds of refrigerators that are awaiting the arrival of the cases in order to repair them.

22. Between 2005 and 2010, production of other manufactured products also declined: radios (–90 percent), water pumps (–85 percent), television sets (–64 percent), gas stoves (–51 percent), pharmaceutical products (–48 percent), sewn wood (–28 percent), roasted and packaged coffee (–14 percent), canned fruits and vegetables (–8 percent), and toothpaste (–3 percent). Production of bread and crackers, construction materials, and paper stagnated, while production of condensed and evaporated milk ceased entirely. There were increases in the production of fuel oil (183 percent), electric fans (82 percent), rum (37 percent), wheat flour (25 percent), and beer (14 percent) (ONE, 2011a).

23. Number of bus passengers per 1,000 inhabitants fell from 255 to 79 between 1989 and 2010 (CEE, 1991; ONE, 2011a).

24. The number of railroad cars for cargo fell by 37 percent and the length (kilometers) of railways declined by 26 percent between 2000 and 2010; in the latter year, 94 percent of rail tracks were in bad condition and needed repair (ONE, 2011a; Espinosa Chepe, 2010a).

25. In Havana city in 2006, 20 percent of passengers were transported by 3,500 buses from state enterprises, while the remaining 80 percent relied on 330 municipal buses; 9 percent of drivers did not even stop at bus stops, where customer lines exceeded 100 meters, and failed to pick up some 500,000 persons who were waiting for service (F. García, 2007).

26. According to ONE (2010a, 2011a), between 2006 and 2010 Cuba imported 29,096 passenger motor vehicles valued at US$283 million, and 6,312 passenger vehicles for public transportation valued at US$318 million.

27. When Cuba was not in last place, the countries below it were Bolivia, Haiti, Honduras, Nicaragua, and Paraguay (ITU, 2012).

28. Another official statistical series reports that idle state sector land rose from 18.6 percent to 26.4 percent between 1997 and 2007 (Raúl has stated that it was 30 percent in 2009), while idle nonstate sector land increased from 7.8 percent to 14.2 percent (ONE, 2011a).

29. Cocoa production declined by a third between 1989 and 2010, from 2,566 to 1,709 tons (CEE, 1991; ONE, 2011a).

30. There are no statistics on the distribution of cattle between the state and nonstate sectors; in 2010 the number of calf births in the nonstate sector was 84 percent of total calf births, and the number of cows being milked in the nonstate sector was 90 percent of the total (ONE, 2011a).

31. The number of hogs in the state sector fell 61 percent between 1989 and 2010, from 1.3 million to 504,900, while the number of barnyard birds fell 52 percent, from 27.9 million to 13.4 million (CEE, 1991; ONE, 2011a).

32. In 2006 the EU Commission found insufficient food safety oversight of Cuban fish and shellfish catch concerning contaminants, and requested that Cuba improve its sanitary controls over such products (*EFE,* November 24, 2006).

33. Leonel Valdivia, director of the *acopio* agency, when asked by a reporter to comment on the possibility of phasing out *acopio* as an intermediary in agricultural sales, responded as follows: "No, it will not disappear because if it did, marketing of agricultural products would fall in the hands of private intermediaries and prices would shoot up." The journalist countered that "agricultural producers earn more when they sell their output to private intermediaries and get payment right away," and Valdivia accepted this point (González, 2006). Agricultural producers generally are not able to leave their farms, travel long distances, and spend the day selling their output at farmers' markets, and therefore the role of the intermediary is key; the challenge is to regulate intermediaries, not eliminate them (Martín and Pérez, 2008).

34. According to the 2002 census, the number of graduates is much higher: 41,724 in agricultural sciences, 171,993 mid-level technicians, and 8,762 skilled workers.

3

International Economic Relations, 2006–2012

This chapter reviews the performance of Cuba's external sector, possibly the most critical sector of its economy, from 2006 to 2012. It follows the same structure as the previous chapter, covering statistical trends and problems; external sector indicators (foreign trade, merchandise and services balance of trade, composition of trade by commodity, external debt, foreign investment, monetary duality and exchange rate, and international tourism); and international economic relations with principal partners.

Statistical Trends and Problems

As is the case with other economic statistics for Cuba, external sector data have become available more timely since the National Statistical Office (ONE) began to publish them electronically on its website; still, the corresponding section of its 2011 yearbook, *Anuario Estadístico de Cuba,* was not available until mid-December 2012, when the writing of this book was completed.[1] Official external sector statistics suffer from gaps, methodological opacity, and contradictions not unlike those that afflict macroeconomic statistics in general, although to a lesser degree. Two local currencies are used on the island: the Cuban peso (CUP), the currency in which most Cuban workers are paid their salaries and that they use to purchase basic consumer goods; and the convertible Cuban peso (CUC), a currency created in 1994 with a value then at par with the US dollar, which is used in transactions of goods that are typically not available through normal distribution channels. The official exchange rate of one CUP to one US dollar is used in national accounts and in commercial transactions between domestic enterprises. Cuban citizens can sell and buy convertible pesos at government-operated hard-currency exchange houses (CADECAs) at the rate of one CUC to twenty-four or twenty-five CUP (depending on whether convertible pesos are being sold or purchased, respectively). The CUC is overvalued with respect to the US dollar; since 2011 the two currencies exchange at par, but several discounts are applied (as discussed later in the chapter). Foreign trade statistics are reported in "pesos," without any further elaboration. According to the judgment of experts on the subject, Cuba uses the exchange rate of one CUC to one US dollar, which is used in this book and therefore external trade statistics are reported in US dollars.

Cuba discontinued publication of full statistics on the balance of payments in 2001; only partial statistics have been reported for 2004–2009 (excluding statistics on the balance of the capital account and on the overall balance) and none for 2010–2011. There are contradictions in external sector data published within the same issue of the ONE yearbook, for example among foreign trade data provided in three tables in the *Anuario* (as discussed later). One of the *Anuario*'s tables presents export statistics according to the UN's Standard International Trade Classification, but excludes "fuels, lubricants, and minerals," and therefore does not disaggregate their share (43 percent) of the value of exports. No statistics on the value of nickel exports have been published since 2006 and the same is the case for the value of imports of oil and refined products, although statistics on the quantity of such imports have been released. Data on foreign direct investment (stock) have not been published, while the most recent annual investment (flows) statistics are for 2006 and data on the number of foreign companies in different forms of association with the government were last published for 2007. Statistics on the overall foreign debt are not available; the *Anuario* does have statistics on the "active" foreign debt through 2008, but not on the debt that is in arrears (this was reported in a footnote in the *Anuario* through 2009, but was not included in the 2010 and 2011 yearbooks). There are no official statistics on international monetary reserves (ONE, 2007, 2010a, 2011a). The most recent balance of payments statistics from the Economic Commission for Latin America and the Caribbean (ECLAC, 2011b) cover only the period 2004–2007, exclude the capital account and the overall balance, and differ from those in the 2010 *Anuario;* the statistics provided by ECLAC about the Cuban foreign debt repeat those in the *Anuario,* but end with 2007.

External Sector Indicators

Imports, Exports, Balance of Goods and Services,
and Balance of Payments

The value of Cuban goods exports plummeted during the crisis of the 1990s, stagnated, and later recovered; in 2010 their value was still 25 percent below their 1989 value (value as a percentage of gross domestic product [GDP] fell from 27.5 percent to 7 percent between 1989 and 2010), but the value of exports rose in 2011 to reach 11 percent above their 1989 value (for the first time in twenty-two years). Meanwhile, the value of goods imports rose steadily after the crisis, and in 2011 their value was 73 percent higher than in 1989.[2] Thus, the deficit in the goods balance of trade rose rapidly and peaked at US$10.6 billion in 2008, when the Cuban economy began to slow as a result of the global financial crisis, weaker world market prices for nickel exports, and high import prices for oil and foodstuffs. Although the goods trade deficit contracted to US$8 billion between 2009 and 2011, in the latter year its level was still twice as high as in 1989 (see Table 3.1) and "the factors responsible for the tendency for ever-rising imports" remain at play (Sánchez-Egozcue, 2011b).

This performance confirms the tendency of the Cuban economy during the revolution to run deficits in the goods balance of trade (this has been the case every year except for one) and the failure of export promotion policies implemented over the past two decades aimed at closing the gap between goods exports and imports. Hiram Marquetti (2006a) has estimated that in order to reach their 1989 level, goods exports would have to increase at an annual rate of 20 to 30 percent for five years, which he believes is improbable given historical performance, growth projections through 2010, and difficult-to-correct structural factors.

There are no official statistics on Cuba's services trade in 1989. In that year, Cuba's services exports probably consisted mostly of tourism expenditures (see below). Between 2005 and 2010, however, services exports rose from US$6.8 billion to US$9.6 billion (see Table 3.1). In 2010, services exports accounted for 68 percent of the value of goods and services exports. Services imports were about US$200 million in 2005 and rose to about US$700 million in 2010. In the latter year, services imports represented about 6.2 percent of total goods and services imports.

Since 2005 the deficit in the goods balance of trade has been offset by a surplus in the services balance of trade in each year with the exception of 2008, when goods imports reached an exceptionally high level (see Figure 3.1). The principal driver of the surplus in the services trade balance and in the combined goods and services trade balance has been exports of professional services, principally to Venezuela (discussed later), coupled with exports of tourism services. The goods and services trade balance, which averaged an annual surplus of US$326 million in 2005–2009, skyrocketed to US$2.8 billion in 2010 for two principal reasons: an exceptional increase of 61 percent in the value of goods exports (despite the deterioration in the terms of trade) and an increase of 25 percent in the surplus in the services balance of trade, which reached a record-high level of US$8.9 billion (see Table 3.1). No information was available for 2011 at the time we completed writing this book.

Table 3.1 Foreign Trade Indicators, 1989 and 2005–2011 (US$ billions)

	1989	2005	2006	2007	2008	2009	2010	2011	Change Between 1989 and 2010 (%)[a]
Goods									
Exports (fob)	5.4	2.2	2.9	3.7	3.7	2.9	4.5	6.0	11
Imports	8.1	7.6	9.5	10.1	14.2	8.9	10.6	14.0	73
Balance	-2.7	-5.4	-6.6	-6.4	-10.6	-6.0	-6.1	-8.0	196
Services									
Exports		6.8	6.9	8.2	8.8	7.8	9.6		41
Imports		0.2	0.2	0.2	0.6	0.7	0.7		250
Balance		6.6	6.7	8.0	8.2	7.1	8.9		35
Balance of goods and services		1.2	0.1	1.6	-2.4	1.1	2.8		133
Current account balance		0.1	-0.2	0.4	-2.3	-0.2			-23
Terms of trade[b]		100.0	126.2	132.9	87.0	79.3	76.7		

Sources: Authors' estimates based on CEE, 1991, for 1989; ONE, 2011a, 2012a, for 2005–2010 (ONE revised its statistics on exports, trade balance, and current account balance in 2012); and ECLAC, 2011a, for 2011. For terms of trade (from ECLAC, 2011a), we have switched the base year from 2000 to 2005.

Notes: Empty cells indicate that data are not available. Fob is free on board.
a. Where data for 1989 are not available, data for 2005 are used in this calculation instead, as are data for 2011 instead of 2010 where available.
b. Index: 2005 = 100.

Figure 3.1 Balance of Foreign Trade in Goods and Services, 2005–2010

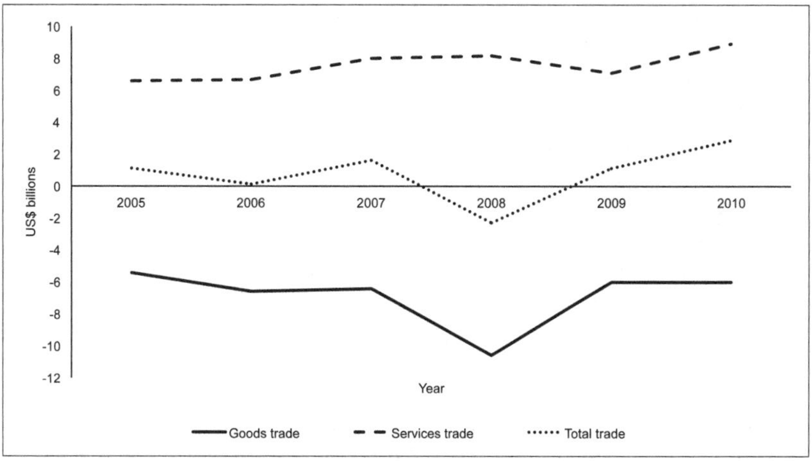

Sources: Authors' estimates based on ONE, 2011a, 2012a.

As noted, Cuba discontinued publication of full statistics on the balance of payments in 2001; while it has published summary statistics on the current account, it has not done the same with regard to the capital account or the global balance. Fragmentary information on components of the balance of payments is available, but this tends to be inconsistent and even contradictory.[3] Our efforts to reconcile the different statistics on components of the current account—trade in goods and services, rents or factor income, and transfers—to construct the current account were unsuccessful for the reasons stated earlier. Cuba has reported the overall balance of the current account as follows: US$140 million in 2005, –US$214 million in 2006, US$401 million in 2007, –US$2,309 million in 2008, and –US$162 million in 2009 (ONE, 2010a, 2011a, 2012a).[4] The huge deficit in 2008 reflected the global fiscal crisis and the record-negative goods and services trade balance (see Table 3.1). Rents or factor income (interest payments on foreign debt, repatriation of profits) increased slightly, because Cuba suspended debt service payments and other payments to foreign creditors (discussed later). There are no statistics for 2010–2011.

The main components of current transfers are remittances and donations. Remittances sent by migrants to their home countries have increased tremendously in recent years, and account for a significant share of the inflow of resources for many developing countries. In the case of Cuba, the bulk of remittances are sent by Cuban Americans to relatives and friends on the island. ECLAC estimated such remittances in the late 1990s to early 2000s at about US$1 billion per annum, the Inter-American Development

Bank at US$983 million, and Manuel Orozco of the Inter-American Dialogue at US$830–985 million. Other analysts have estimated them at US$400–500 million (Pérez-López and Díaz-Briquets, 2005; ECLAC, 2008b, 2009b, 2010b; Ravsberg, 2010a). Remittances may have contracted between 2005 and 2008 because of the global financial crisis, which affected the economies of remittances-sending countries, and because of restrictions imposed by President George W. Bush on remittances sent from the United States (discussed later). They likely grew between 2009 and 2011 for several reasons: the relaxation by President Barack Obama of the restrictions imposed by his predecessor, which allowed Western Union to pay remittances on the island in convertible pesos instead of US dollars (thereby avoiding the 10 percent surcharge on exchanges of US dollars and increasing the amount actually delivered to remittances recipients), and increased the amount that could be remitted by wire transfer from US$5,000 to US$10,000; the commencement of global economic recovery beginning in 2009; and the devaluation of the CUC with respect to the US dollar in 2011 (Morales and Sacarpaci, 2011). ECLAC (2011b) estimated that the value of remittances grew by 14 percent in 2010 to US$2 billion, and analysts have estimated their value in 2011 at about US$2.3 billion (Morales and Scarpaci, 2012). Donations in Cuba are relatively small compared with remittances, accounting for about 14 percent of transfers between 1995 and 2001 (Pérez-López, 2009), and their size as a share of transfers has probably since contracted. Cuba's transfers balance was US$974 million in 2004 (near the amount reported for remittances by ECLAC), –US$367 million in 2005, US$278 million in 2006, –US$199 million in 2007, US$482 million in 2008, and US$235 million in 2009, one-fourth of the value recorded in 2004 (ECLAC, 2011b; ONE, 2011a, 2012a); more recent statistics were not available at the time we completed writing this book.

Goods Terms of Trade

On the basis of unit value indexes of Cuban goods exports and imports (2005 = 100) computed by ECLAC (2011b), Cuba's terms of trade improved in 2006 and 2007 but declined in subsequent years to 76.7 in 2010 (see Table 3.1). The improvement in the terms of trade in 2006–2007 was largely attributable to high world market prices for nickel, which reached an all-time high in 2007 of US$37,229 per ton (mineral exports, principally nickel, accounted for 57 percent of the island's exports in that year),[5] as well as improvement in the price of sugar (US$0.10 per pound). As discussed in Chapter 2, however, Cuba was not able to capitalize on this favorable commodity price scenario, because of its inability to increase output of nickel and sugar. The subsequent deterioration in the terms of trade was due to a 60 percent decline in the price of nickel, to US$14,672 per ton in 2009, and a 20 percent increase in the price of food imports, which boosted the food import bill to US$1.5 billion in 2009; the world market price of oil, after peaking in 2008 (at US$97 per barrel), fell in 2009 (to US$62 per barrel) and rose again in 2010 (to US$79 per barrel) (IMF, 2011). Although world market prices for nickel and sugar rebounded strongly in 2010, poor output performance again did not allow Cuba to capitalize on those high prices, bringing about a loss of potential export revenue of US$120 million and US$65 million respectively (Murillo, 2010).

With the recovery of the global economy, oil world market prices again rose above US$100 per barrel for several months in 2011 and 2012, with an adverse effect on Cuba's balance of payments: oil imports from Venezuela were more costly, and payments by Cuba to Canadian firm Sherritt for oil that this company extracted from Cuba also rose (in 2010, the total of both accounts combined was US$2,894 million). Meanwhile, world market food prices also increased, driving up the food import bill from US$1.5 billion 2010 to US$1.7 billion in 2011. On the export side, the world market price of nickel rose to an average of US$23,909 per ton in 2011, although it fell to US$21,350 in January 2012, 42 percent lower than the peak price reached in 2007 (IMF, 2011; R. Castro Ruz, 2011g; Piñón, 2011; Yzquierdo Rodríguez, 2011).

Composition of Goods Trade

The composition of goods trade has changed significantly since 1989. Sugar's share of exports shrunk from 73 percent in 1989 to 5.6 percent in 2010 (see Table 3.2) as a result of the severe contraction of sugar production, notwithstanding the high world market prices of sugar in recent years. Although there are no statistics on nickel exports since 2006, the share of exports of ores and scrap metals (which included nickel exports in 2006, when they accounted for 53 percent of value of exports within this category) increased from 9 percent in 1989 to 58 percent in 2007, and fell back to 27 percent in 2010. Tobacco's share of exports rose from 1.6 percent in 1989 to a high of 8.4 percent in 2006, boosted by a recovery in the production of cigars and high prices of cigars on international markets, but subsequently declined partly because of the global decline in tobacco consumption due to health reasons. Other traditional exports that were once important have also seen their shares decline significantly: citrus fruits from 5.6 percent to nil between 1989 and 2010; fish and shellfish from 2.4 percent to 1.3 percent; and vegetables and fruits from 3 percent to 0.5 percent. In contrast, the share of alcoholic beverages (principally rum) grew from 0.3 percent to 1.8 percent during this period.

Among nontraditional export products, the share of medicines and pharmaceuticals climbed from 1 percent in 1989 to a peak of 17.6 percent

Table 3.2 Distribution of the Value of Goods Exports and Imports, 1989 and 2006–2010 (percentages)

	1989	2006	2007	2008	2009	2010
Exports						
Ores and scrap metal[a]	9.2	48.0	58.0	40.4	30.4	26.9
Medicines and pharmaceuticals	1.0	10.4	7.8	8.1	17.6	10.7
Sugar	72.6	7.4	5.2	6.1	7.5	5.6
Tobacco (cigars and leaf)	1.6	8.4	6.4	6.3	7.3	4.3
Machinery and transportation equipment	0.8	7.8	4.6	4.5	5.9	2.4
Alcoholic beverages	0.3	0.9	1.4	2.3	2.4	1.8
Fish and shellfish (fresh and frozen)	2.4	2.2	2.2	2.0	1.6	1.3
Iron and steel	0.2	1.5	1.5	2.1	1.5	1.3
Miscellaneous manufactures	1.0	4.7	3.6	1.6	2.1	1.0
Cement	0.1	1.3	1.2	1.3	1.5	0.7
Vegetables and fruits	3.1	0.8	0.8	0.7	1.0	0.5
Citrus	5.6	0.2	0.1	0.0	0.0	0.0
Other products	2.1	6.4	7.2	24.6	21.2	43.5
Total exports	100.0	100.0	100.0	100.0	100.0	100.0
Imports[b]						
Consumer goods	12.5	14.0	16.3	17.0	18.1	15.3
Food	11.4	13.2	15.3	15.6	16.8	13.8
Others	1.1	0.8	1.0	1.4	1.3	1.5
Intermediate goods	56.4	53.4	53.9	60.8	61.9	69.0
Fuels, lubricants, and minerals	32.4	24.1	23.6	32.0	29.7	42.5
Manufactures	13.7	20.4	19.8	17.9	20.0	15.9
Chemical products	6.5	7.0	8.2	8.3	9.2	9.1
Raw materials, inedible	3.8	1.9	2.3	2.6	3.0	1.5
Capital goods	31.1	32.6	29.8	22.2	20.0	15.7
Machinery	23.6	28.5	24.1	17.4	15.5	11.9
Transportation equipment	7.5	4.1	5.7	4.8	4.5	3.8
Total imports	100.0	100.0	100.0	100.0	100.0	100.0

Sources: Authors' calculations based on CEE, 1991; ONE, 2010a, 2011a.
Notes: Goods exports are ranked according to their relative importance in 2010.
a. Includes nickel products.
b. We recalculated the distribution of imports across the three categories in order to correct an erroneous calculation in the Anuario.

in 2009, and declined to 10.7 percent in 2010, still eleven times their share in 1989.[6] Meanwhile, the share of machinery and transportation equipment rose from 0.8 percent to 2.4 percent, the share of cement from 0.1 percent to 0.7 percent, and the share of miscellaneous manufactures remained essentially unchanged. For "other products," the share of this category rose steadily, from 2 percent in 1989 to 43.5 percent in 2010; a careful review of goods exports in the *Anuario* does not identify which products fall into this category. Answering this question is crucial to explaining the impressive jump of such exports in 2010. It is possible that this category might include re-exports to other countries of oil supplied by Venezuela to Cuba or exports to Venezuela of refined products from the Cienfuegos refinery, but neither of these two potential export goods are detailed in the *Anuario*.[7]

The *Anuario* and other Cuban statistical publications do not contain data on exports of products of the biotechnology industry, one of the industries in which Cuba has made significant investments and which reportedly has grown in recent years. Thus it is not possible to validate the substantial increases in biotechnology exports that have been reported in the press, although it is possible that they are included within the category of medicines and pharmaceuticals, which accounted for 11 percent of goods exports in 2010. According to Pedro Monreal (2006), at the start of the 1990s, Cuban officials forecasted that the biotechnology industry would become an export leader, but those expectations have been tamped down in recent years. Omar Everleny Pérez Villanueva (2006) asserts that exports of chemical pharmaceuticals have fallen since 1995, and that they are still far from their level in 1989, with the exception of vaccines, while Jorge Sánchez-Egozcue (2011b) assesses production of medicines and pharmaceuticals, after a strong start and some diversification, has shifted into a slow-growth phase.

Consumer goods' share of imports rose from 12.5 percent in 1989 to 15.3 percent in 2010, with food imports rising from 11.4 percent to 13.8 percent over the same period (peaking at 16.8 percent in 2009; see Table 3.2); the import shares of seven basic foods in the diet of the average Cuban increased during the period, except for vegetables, fruits, and beans, whose shares remained essentially unchanged.[8] While certain foodstuffs cannot be produced on the island because of climatic reasons, for example wheat, others that are imported in large quantities, like rice and beans, can be produced domestically (L. Pérez, 2008). The poor performance of the agricultural sector has required massive imports of foodstuffs (US$1.8 billion in 2012) and worsened the goods trade deficit. Cuba imports 84 percent of foodstuffs distributed through the rationing system: 58 percent of calories, 62 percent of proteins, and an even higher percentage of fats (*Granma,* February 26, 2007; Nova, 2007). According to Pérez Villanueva (2006), foodstuffs, fuels, and medicines have consistently accounted for over 60 percent of the total value of imports and use over 80 percent of hard-currency revenues, with no possibility in the short term of altering this situation.

Intermediate goods' share of imports jumped from 56 percent in 1989 to 69 percent in 2010; the share accounted for by fuels, lubricants, and minerals grew at the fastest rate, climbing from 32.4 percent to 42.5 percent over the same period, despite an increase in domestic oil production, because of the sharp rise in the world price of oil. Within intermediate goods imports, the *Anuario* does not disaggregate the value of oil and oil products, although elsewhere it reports the physical volume (metric tons) of both; as we lack information on the price paid by Cuba for oil imports, it is not possible to make an estimate of their value.[9] Imports of manufactured products grew from 13.7 percent to 15.9 percent between 1989 and 2010, reflecting in part the decline in domestic production of manufactures discussed in Chapter 2; imports of chemical products also grew, from 6.5 percent to 9.1 percent (including imports of medicines and pharmaceuticals, which accounted for 2.5 percent of imports in 2010).

Capital goods' share of imports fell by half, from 31 percent to 15.7 percent between 1989 and 2010; among capital goods, the share of machinery imports fell from 23.6 percent to 11.9 percent and the share of transportation equipment imports from 7.5 percent to 3.8 percent, despite the aforementioned purchase of buses and locomotives.[10] This pattern is consistent with the observation in Chapter 2 that gross capital formation as a share of GDP has been declining in Cuba and is insufficient to support future growth.

Cuban economists have identified other key issues affecting the balance of trade of goods and services: import substitution initiatives have not been effective; linkages between internal production and exports are weak; services exports have a multiplier effect much lower than that of sugar and of the manufacturing sector; and while tourism potentially has strong linkages to the domestic economy, such linkages have not been fully developed and in fact there has been some regression (Vidal Alejandro and Fundora, 2008). Unlike sugar and tourism, nickel has a low multiplier effect, because although it is mined domestically, it is refined abroad (Monreal, 2007). There are domestic barriers to the promotion of exports: excessive centralization, restrictions on access to financing, overvaluation of the CUC, and lack of capacity for supply to react to higher international prices (such as of sugar and nickel) (Sánchez-Egozcue, 2011b).

Cuba swapped a disproportionate concentration on sugar exports for an excessive dependence on exports of professional services (principally to Venezuela, as discussed later), which contribute more than half of total income from exports of goods and services. While some Cuban economists note the success of these exports in generating hard currency, others question their sustainability and low impact on the economy at large. The majority of economists concur that "Cuba should not repeat the historical mistake of making its economy dependent on one sector and one country" (Sánchez-Egozcue and Triana, 2010). Growth of GDP, growth of exports, and growth of investment are positively correlated, and all three indicators slowed in 2007–2009, and therefore the availability of hard currencies declined, limiting the growth of most sectors of the economy (Vidal Alejandro, 2009).

Foreign Debt

In 1989, Cuba's hard-currency debt amounted to $6.2 billion, excluding debt owed to the Soviet Union and other socialist countries, estimated at

US$16.2 billion to US$32.9 billion, depending on the exchange rate for the ruble (Mesa-Lago, 2000). The *Anuario* has reported that Cuba's "total debt" was US$10.96 billion in 2000 and US$10.89 billion in 2001, excluding unpaid debt to the former socialist countries (ONE, 2005). Beginning with the 2006 yearbook, the *Anuario* has reported only the "active debt," meaning debt that has been subject to renegotiation, and has provided this information only for 2004–2007; the rest of the foreign debt is considered "inactive" and is reported in a footnote as US$7.6 billion, disregarding interest accrued over twenty-five years (ONE, 2007, 2011a). This explanatory footnote was deleted in the 2010 and 2011 *Anuario* yearbooks, hence making it impossible to know Cuba's officially reported total debt (ONE, 2011a, 2012a). The Economist Intelligence Unit (EIU) estimates that Cuba's foreign debt is higher than reported by Cuban statistical publications (even when considering active and inactive debt; see Table 3.3). In 2007, the most recent year for which such statistics are available, the total debt was reported at US$16.5 billion, of which 54 percent was considered active and 46 percent inactive, excluding debt owed to the Soviet Union and Venezuela. The EIU meanwhile estimated Cuba's total debt in 2007 (excluding debt owed to Russia and most likely Venezuela) at US$17.8 billion, 8 percent higher than the Cuban estimate, and at US$21 billion in 2011. Total debt rose 241 percent between 1989 and 2011 as a result of the accumulation of unpaid interest, the depreciation of the US dollar, and new debt from China and other countries.

According to Cuban sources, 60 percent of the inactive debt (about US$4.6 billion) was incurred with members of the Paris Club, an organization of representatives of the largest creditor governments. In 1986, Cuba suspended repayment of debt owed to Paris Club member countries and requested its rescheduling; negotiations started in 1999 and ended in 2001

Table 3.3 Foreign Debt Estimates, 1989 and 2004–2011 (US$ millions)

	1989	2004	2005	2006	2007	2008	2009	2010	2011
Debt as reported by Cuba									
Active debt		5,806	5,898	7,794	8,908	11,591	12,310		
Inactive debt		7,592	7,592	7,592	7,592				
Total		13,398	13,490	15,386	16,500				
Debt as reported by the EIU	6,165	13,789	14,485	16,616	17,829	19,041	19,420	19,750	21,025

Sources: Data for Cuba's reporting are authors' estimates based on ONE, 2006, 2007, 2011a, 2012a; data for the Economist Intelligence Unit's reporting are from EIU, 2008, 2011, except that the 1989 estimate is from Mesa-Lago, 2000.

Note: Cuba's statistical debt series ends in 2009 for active debt and 2007 for inactive debt.

without an agreement.[11] The Paris Club estimated Cuba's foreign debt in mid-2010 at about US$30.5 billion (50 percent larger than the EIU's estimate), in part because of accumulated unpaid interest but possibly also because it might include an estimated US$21 billion of debt to the former Soviet Union that is now claimed by Russia, a current member of the Paris Club. In 2011, the Paris Club proposed to Cuba the resumption of negotiations—interrupted for a decade—to resolve the issue of unpaid debts, but there is no information on a formal response by Cuban authorities (*EFE*, June 29, 2011; *Reuters*, November 7, 2011). Cuba's debt at the end of 2010, including sums owed to Paris Club members, the former socialist countries, Venezuela, China, and other nations, has been estimated at nearly US$72 billion, of which US$28.1 billion was owed to Russia, US$15.6 billion to Venezuela, US$9.1 billion to China, US$3.4 billion to Japan, US$3.3 billion to Spain, and US$2.4 billion to Argentina (ICCAS, 2011). While some of these estimates are questionable—for example, the estimate of debt to Russia in dollars is based on a high exchange rate for the ruble and the estimate of debt to Venezuela assumes that Cuba has not paid at all for the oil Venezuela has supplied—they are indicative of the large magnitude of Cuba's foreign debt.

For 2010, the EIU estimated Cuba's total external debt (probably a conservative estimate in view of the preceding analyses) as being equivalent to 34 percent of Cuba's GDP, compared with an average of 20 percent for Latin America as a whole, and to 298 percent of Cuba's exports, compared with a regional average of 96 percent. Annual debt service (payment of principal and interest) grew from 7 percent of the owed principal in 2007 to 9.9 percent in 2010.[12] At the end of 2011, the financial rating agency Moody's Investors Service (2011) assigned a rating of "Caaa1" (poor quality and very high credit risk) to Cuba's foreign debt because of a moratorium on repayment lasting for more than twenty years and accumulation of unpaid interest, very weak domestic economic performance, lack of information and transparency, extreme dependence on imports, and restricted access to external financing.

In 2008, Cuba experienced its worst economic moment since the collapse of the Soviet Union: the deficit in the goods balance of trade reached a record high of US$11 billion; four hurricanes caused damages estimated at US$10 billion (see Box 2.1); the global financial crisis further restricted access to credit; world market prices of oil and foodstuffs continued to rise; and the world market price of nickel fell sharply. This created an acute hard-currency liquidity scarcity, which made it impossible to meet debt service obligations, pay foreign companies operating on the island for goods provided or services rendered, and allow foreign joint ventures to repatriate their share of profits. Among the outstanding debts was US$129 million owed by Cuban national oil company CUPET to Canadian oil company

Pebercan. Cuba defaulted on payments to Pebercan in May 2008 and in December suspended payments to businesses from Belgium, Canada, Chile, France, Germany, Japan, Mexico, South Africa, and the United Kingdom. In January 2009, Cuba froze the accounts in domestic banks of about 600 foreign suppliers, with combined holdings of about US$1 billion, and suspended the payment of dividends to foreign joint venture partners; in May, Cuba postponed a range of imports. As discussed later, Cuba has progressively removed some restrictions on the accounts of foreign enterprises.

On July 26, 2008, Raúl warned that the nation could not spend more resources than it had, and therefore that it was necessary to make sharp reductions in expenditures and in imports. In December he restated that "the accounts are not balancing [and we have to] align dreams with reality. . . . [T]he country does not have the luxury of indefinitely spending more that it receives from the sale of its goods and services." Thus it was essential to align hard-currency expenditures to revenues, he added (R. Castro Ruz, 2008c). In early 2009, Raúl dismissed the entire economic cabinet and in August announced a set of adjustment measures, "painful and unpleasant measures that simply were unavoidable" (R. Castro Ruz, 2009c).

According to Pavel Vidal Alejandro (2010b), the liquidity crisis arose in part because Cuban banks issued an excessive amount of convertible pesos, far beyond what could be backed up by hard-currency reserves, and the banks feared not being able to meet payment demands. This was compounded by the fact that Cuba could not call on international financial institutions for assistance (because Cuba is not a member), and because its lender of last resort, Venezuela, at the time was experiencing financial problems of its own, triggered by a 36 percent fall in the world price of oil, and had actually cut back on payments for Cuban professionals. The serious financial situation created uncertainty among foreign investors and joint venture partners, and reduced confidence in the CUC and in the solvency of domestic banks (foreign entities changed their practices and since then conduct their operations through foreign banks operating on the island), and further limited access to new credit in international markets (Frank, 2008b; Vidal Alejandro, 2008a, 2010c; *Reuters,* March 14, 2011).

The Central Bank of Cuba (BCC), through its Regulation no. 1 of March 2009, made two important changes to the system of domestic payments in hard currency. First, since 2005, the BCC had established a single account to collect all holdings in hard currency and convertible pesos (either from internal resources of the state or arising from international transactions), approved all hard-currency operations of state enterprises and state entities (over US$10,000), and prioritized which payments to make to creditors and when. The new regulation authorizes ministries and their enterprises to make purchases exceeding $10,000 without involvement from the BCC, which implies a certain amount of autonomy. Second, new control measures were put in place: a ban on cash deposits or withdrawals from the accounts of foreign enterprises or joint ventures; a directive mandating that accounts of foreign enterprises may only be established and used by foreign citizens; cancellation of credit cards issued to foreign firms not officially established on the island and a ban on the issuance of such cards in the future; a requirement that foreign companies not formally established in Cuba are to update every two years the roster of foreign citizens authorized to open and close accounts; and a requirement that Cuban banks are to track unusual or suspicious financial transactions and report them to the Ministry of Interior (Arreola, 2009; Cancio, 2009b).

In 2009, imports contracted by 37 percent and the deficit in goods trade by 43 percent, which provided temporary relief to the external imbalances. In mid-2010, state banks offered to make payments on the frozen accounts over a five-year period at 2 percent annual interest, provided the account holder continued to do business in Cuba. This proposal was not applicable to joint ventures and hotel management companies, which were directed to negotiate their cases directly with government officials. Foreign business-people and diplomats reported in mid-2010 that although Cuba had signed payment agreements with several entities, no action had been taken with respect to half of the frozen deposits, and that payments had been delayed for up to one year (Frank, 2010a). According to other analysts, Cuba has made good on the bulk of the repayment delays, with only one-third of the frozen accounts remaining in that condition, and Cuban banks have been gradually regaining deposits from foreign companies (Sánchez-Egozcue, 2011b). Statistics from the Bank for International Settlements show that Cuban banks held deposits in international banks amounting to about US$5.7 billion in September 2011, compared with US$2.6 billion at the end of 2008, more than doubling their liquidity and their ability to tackle debt servicing and financing of imports; this has been possible because of surpluses in the goods and services trade accounts (Luis, 2012). In 2010, Raúl reported a reduction by two-thirds of frozen accounts and increases in deposits by foreign companies in Cuban banks; in mid-2011, before the National Assembly of People's Power (ANPP), he committed Cuba to meeting all repayment agreements and settling all frozen accounts by the end of the year (R. Castro Ruz, 2010b, 2011d). Also speaking before the ANPP, the minister of economy stated that in 2012, Cuba would "continue the rescheduling of debts incurred in previous years" (Yzquierdo Rodríguez, 2011).

Foreign Direct Investment

Foreign investment in Cuba takes one of three forms: joint ventures between a foreign investor and the government, with the government typically owning at least 51 percent of assets; international economic association contracts for the production of goods or services; and enterprises wholly owned by foreign investors (which are very few). Foreign investors cannot hire or fire employees directly and must pay them in the national currency (CUP) rather than hard currencies (sometimes foreign investors informally make some hard-currency payments to workers). The annual flow of foreign direct investment (FDI) has not been made public since 2006, when a record high of US$981 million was reported, originating primarily from Venezuela (Pérez-López, 2008, 2009). The number of joint ventures with foreign investors fell by 41 percent between 2002 and 2006, from 403 to 237, while the number of international associations fell by 87 percent between 2003 and 2006, from 441 to 57; more recent statistics have not been published.[13] Since 2008, the Cuban government has shut down several joint ventures and canceled the operating licenses of at least fourteen foreign firms, many of them accused of illicit activities. Other foreign investors have left for other reasons, among them British company Unilever and Israeli citrus producer BM Group (*Reuters,* May 5, 2012). FDI is concentrated in activities that have short production chains, lack potential for sustainable growth because of natural resource constraints (except tourism), and have had very limited impact in fully using the installed industrial capacity and skilled labor force (Pérez Villanueva, 2006, 2007; Cancio, 2008).

Marta Lomas, former minister of foreign investment and economic cooperation, stated in 2007 that Cuba was not interested in having many joint ventures, but rather joint ventures with the ability to have an impact on the economy. She added that the reduction in the number of joint ventures came about because Cuba no longer needed small investors and was prioritizing strategic sectors such as energy, mining, and tourism (*Reuters,* January 29, 2007; *Granma,* June 26, 2007). Pérez Villanueva (2007, 2012) added that the joint ventures that were terminated were not significant for the overall performance of the economy, that the remaining joint ventures are capable of raising output and productivity, and that the reduction in number of joint ventures has resulted in increased sales, exports, and incomes. Francesc Bayo (2010) argues that by closing a number of the joint ventures, Cuba reinforced oligopolistic behavior favoring multinational conglomerates, making more difficult the creation and growth of small and medium-sized enterprises that are labor-intensive and could promote competition. Raúl stated that Cuba was willing to increase foreign investment "without repeating the errors of the past . . . [by] working with serious entrepreneurs and preserving the predominance of socialist property" (R. Castro Ruz, 2007a). The Sixth Congress of the Cuban Communist Party (PCC) essentially confirmed this strategy (see Chapter 5).

The economic sectors that have performed best are those in which foreign investment has played an important role (tourism, oil, nickel). Foreign-invested enterprises have also been key in generating hard currency and creating productive employment, and in opening markets for Cuban exports of goods and services. A concern in recent years has been that private foreign investment from market economies is being replaced by investment by state enterprises from Venezuela and China, which neither contribute state-of-the-art technologies nor base their investments on rigorous economic feasibility criteria (Pérez-López, 2008, 2009).

Monetary Duality and Exchange Rate

Monetary duality—the simultaneous circulation within Cuba of both the CUP and the CUC—began in 1994 when the latter was created as a currency valued at par with the US dollar. Strictly speaking, the CUC is not convertible internationally and its value is determined by the Cuban government rather than by market forces; the CUP and the CUC are exchangeable only within the country. The existence of the two currencies has segmented the economy into two portions: one that functions with the CUC (for example, transactions among large entities, purchases at foreign-currency stores [TRDs]) and one that functions with the CUP (state sector salaries, prices of goods subject to the rationing system, prices for public services). The artificial overvaluation of the CUC distorts costs (it was one of the reasons for the demise of the sugar industry) and makes it difficult to measure accurately the level of efficiency and productivity of enterprises, the competitiveness of exports, and the real value of imports. Finally, monetary duality masks subsidies and taxes that affect certain sectors of the economy (Vidal Alejandro, 2008b, 2010a, 2010c, 2011b; Sánchez-Egozcue, 2011b; on reforms that propose to eliminate the monetary duality, see Chapters 5 and 6).

In 2004, Cuba banned use of the US dollar in transactions, reversing a decision made in 1993 during the economic crisis that ensued from the loss of Soviet trade and aid; the population still may hold dollars, but to be accepted by TRDs, hotels, restaurants, and other entities that operate with hard currencies, the dollars must be exchanged for convertible pesos at CADECA houses. Until 2005, the exchange rate set by the government was one CUC to one US dollar. After that, a 10 percent surcharge was added when exchanging US dollars for convertible pesos, but the surcharge was not applied to exchanges of other currencies such as Canadian dollars, British pounds, or Swiss francs; the official explanation for the surcharge is that it compensates Cuba for the risk it incurs in exchanging US dollars in foreign countries. Since March 2005, the CUC has been sold at CADECA exchange houses for twenty-four CUP, and purchased for twenty-five CUP. Meanwhile, in transactions among state enterprises, one CUC is equivalent to one CUP (ECLAC, 2011b). In April 2005, the value of the CUC vis-à-vis the US dollar, the euro, and other currencies was raised by 8 percent.[14] In addition, a commission of about 3.5 percent was also instituted (Acuerdo no. 15, 2005).[15] In March 2011, the CUC was devalued, eliminating the 8 percent premium that had been added in 2005, so that the CUC and the US dollar returned to par, although the 3.5 percent exchange commission and the 10 percent surcharge (only applicable to US dollars) remained (Acuerdo no. 30, 2011; *Granma,* March 14, 2011).[16]

The reasons given by the BCC for the devaluation of the CUC included the global economic and financial crisis; the volatility of international currency markets; the gradual elimination of restrictions on foreign-currency accounts held by foreign entities; and the desire to improve the nation's hard-currency balances and strengthen international financial relations. But there were other reasons as well: a desire to reduce prices in hard currency of tourism offerings (prices had been affected by the 8 percent appreciation of the CUC in 2008) and attract more foreign tourists; reduce debts of foreign companies whose deposits had been frozen since the end of 2008; stimulate remittances; promote import substitution and promote exports; and close the breach between the value of the CUC and the CUP (*La Jornada,* March 14, 2011; *Reuters,* March 14, 2011). Despite the devaluation, the CUC continues to be overvalued and it is likely that other devaluations will follow. There is a lively internal discussion of ways and means to eliminate the monetary duality gradually, as promised by Raúl, but little in the way of concrete actions (see Chapter 5).

International Tourism

International tourism is one of Cuba's economic success stories: tourism is the second largest source of hard-currency revenue and a significant contributor to offsetting the deficit in the goods trade. A key factor in the development of Cuban tourism has been foreign investment and management agreements with hospitality companies from Spain, Canada, France, Italy, and the Netherlands (Pérez-López and Díaz-Briquets, 2011). The share of hotel rooms managed by foreign companies grew from 27 percent in 2000 to 56 percent in 2010 (Espino, 2011b).

The number of foreign tourists visiting Cuba jumped from 270,000 in 1989 to 2.3 million in 2005, declined in 2006–2007, and reached a record high of 2.7 million in 2011, ten times the 1989 level although only 18 percent over the 2005 level (see Table 3.4 and Figure 3.2). The top ten countries of origin of Cuban tourists in 2011 were Canada (36.9 percent), the United Kingdom (6.5 percent), Italy (4.1 percent), Spain (3.8 percent), Germany (3.5 percent), France (3.5 percent), Russia (2.9 percent), Mexico (2.8 percent), Argentina (2.8 percent), and the United States (2.7 percent, excluding Cuban Americans, addressed separately later). In 2011, visitors from Canada, the United Kingdom, Germany, France, Russia, Mexico, Argentina,

Table 3.4 International Tourism Indicators, 1989 and 2005–2011

	1989	2005	2006	2007	2008	2009	2010	2011	Change Between 1989 and 2010–2011 (%)
Visitors (thousands)[a]	270	2,319	2,221	2,152	2,348	2,430	2,532	2,716	906
Gross income (million CUC)[b]	168	2,399	2,235	2,236	2,347	2,080	2,218	2,503	1,389
Rooms (thousands)[c]	21.4	43.6	44.9	47.3	49.1	52.7	56.9		166
Average stay (days)		7.0[d]	7.1	7.1	7.0	6.8	6.6		−6[f]
Occupancy rate (%)		63.6	61.3	60.9	60.1	59.8	57.1	53.2	−16[f]
Average daily income (US$)		175[e]	147	149	144	129	143		−18f

Sources: Authors' estimates based on ONE, 2011a, 2012a; numbers of rooms and daily income from ECLAC, 2009b, 2011b; days of stay from Espino, 2011a.

Notes: Empty cells indicate that data are not available.

a. Approximately 98% of visitors to Cuba are tourists.

b. The current official exchange rate is 1 CUC = 1 US$; Cuba reported income in dollars until 2004 and then in CUC beginning in 2005, but the data are the same (Cuba reports this information in dollars to the International Tourism Organization).

c. ECLAC reports these as rooms for international tourism, while ONE describes them as rooms in hotels and other establishments. María Dolores Espino (2012) considers them as rooms in principal state tourism facilities, not necessarily devoted to international tourism; the number of rooms that are apt for international tourism is estimated at 51,000 as of 2010.

d. 2004.

e. 2003 (peak).

f. Change between 2005 and 2010–2011.

Figure 3.2 International Tourism Indicators, 1989 and 2005–2011

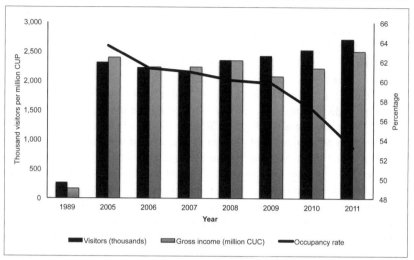

Sources: Authors' estimates based on ONE, 2011a, 2012a.

and the United States increased, while visitors from Italy and Spain declined (ONE, 2012a).

Gross income from tourism includes the costs of imported inputs supplying the tourism industry (between 28 and 39 percent, although there are no reliable statistics), which must be subtracted to calculate *net* income. Gross income grew from US$168 million in 1989 to a peak of nearly US$2.4 billion in 2005, but subsequently stagnated, declining to US$2.2 billion in 2010 and growing to US$2.5 billion in 2011, below the target of US$2.6 billion that had been set for 2002.[17] The number of rooms suitable for international tourism nearly tripled between 1989 and 2010 (from 21,400 to 56,900), but between 2005 and 2010 the average stay fell from 7 to 6.6 days, the occupancy rate from 63.6 percent to 57.1 percent (and to 53.2 percent for 2011), and the average daily income per tourist from US$175 to US$143 (see Table 3.4).[18]

An issue that affects the industry's performance is the cyclical nature of tourist arrivals, and therefore the different rates of utilization of facilities throughout the year: peak demand occurs over a roughly hundred-day period from the end of December to the beginning of April, when large contingents of Canadian and European tourists travel to the island because of the hard winters in their home countries and the attraction of Cuba's tropical climate. Low demand occurs during the hurricane season and periods of hot weather in the Caribbean (Pérez-López and Díaz-Briquets, 2011).

The moderate rate of growth of gross income from tourism since 2005 (17 percent over the period 2005–2011) is a function of several variables, among them increased competition from other tourism destinations in the region, deterioration in the quality of Cuban facilities and services as a result of underinvestment and low priority assigned to the sector, the scarcity of tourism services outside of hotels, overvaluation of the CUC, and expensive lodging rates (Pérez Villanueva, 2010c; Sánchez-Egozcue and Triana, 2010). Cuba's tourism packages carry a higher price than those from other comparable destinations in the Caribbean, for example the Dominican Republic.[19] Moreover, the quality of Cuban tourism services is poor, particularly because of unmotivated personnel, uninspired cuisine, and costly automobile rental rates. Many of the hotels were built before the revolution or in the 1990s and maintenance has been lackluster; alongside these average or poorly maintained hotels, there are boutique hotels and properties managed by foreign hospitality chains that provide high-quality lodging and other services. Cuba has one of the lowest return rates among important global tourism destinations (*Reuters,* January 25, 2007; *El Economista,* April 7, 2007). The Canadian Association of Tour Operators complained to the Cuban Ministry of Tourism in 2006 about poor services, theft in hotels and airports, rising costs, and high rates of airline cancellations (*Encuentro en la Red,* April 26, 2006). The appreciation of the value of the CUC in 2005 raised the price of tourism offerings, particularly for tourists using dollars, but also for those using euros; the devaluation of the CUC in 2011 lowered costs for tourists and probably will stimulate an increase in number of visitors and level of revenue.

The global economic crisis affected the tourism industry in 2007–2009. Minister of Tourism Manuel Marrero confirmed that the number of tourists declined and that visitors were spending less (*Agence France-Press,* May 6, 2009). Due to the effects of the financial crisis in Europe, the share of tourists originating from this region declined from 32.7 percent in 2007 to 23.6 percent in 2010. However, official data on international visitors for 2005–2011 show that, for virtually all European countries, the number of tourists traveling to Cuba peaked in 2005–2006, before the crisis, and there has been a steady decline since then in the number of tourists from the United Kingdom, Italy, Spain, Germany, France, the Netherlands, Portugal, Switzerland, and Belgium. The same can be seen with respect to several Latin American countries, such as Mexico and Venezuela. In contrast, at the same time, the number of tourists from Canada increased steadily, as did the number of tourists from Russia, Argentina, the United States, Chile, Colombia, and Peru, offsetting the decrease in the number of tourists from other, more established sources (ONE, 2012a). The global economic crisis, therefore, does not explain the decline in tourists from traditional sources; possible reasons for the decline might be the aforementioned quality issues and high costs, coupled with saturation of the demand for Cuban tourism in tourist-originating countries. The behavior of Canadian tourists may be explained by country-specific conditions: severe winters, proximity to Cuba, abundance of airline flights to the island, competitively priced tourism packages, and less demanding tourist expectations.

Restrictions on travel to the island by Cuban Americans imposed by President George W. Bush in 2004, which reduced the number of visits per individual to three per year, established a limit of forty-four pounds for luggage, and reduced the daily amount that Cuban Americans could spend while on the island from US$164 to US$50, reduced the number of Cuban American visitors from 100,000 in 2005 to 30,000 in 2008. Moreover, the US administration reduced academic, religious, and professional travel to Cuba by US citizens and increased penalties against those who violated the rules, resulting in a decrease in the number of US citizens traveling to the island of 57 percent (*Reuters*, June 22, 2011; *Associated Press*, June 23, 2011).[20] In 2009, President Obama substantially relaxed the restrictions on travel by Cuban Americans imposed by his predecessor: there are no longer limits on the number of visits per person, the number of pieces and weight of luggage (thereby allowing passengers to carry an unlimited number of suitcases, packages, and so on, for their family or friends), and the amount of dollars that can be spent in Cuba (it is now the same as for other, non–Cuban American travelers). In 2011, President Obama liberalized rules regarding travel to Cuba by US citizens (not of Cuban origin) for academic, religious, and professional reasons, issued licenses to additional travel agents to organize travel to the island, and allowed more international US airports to offer direct air travel to the island (previously, only Miami, New York, and Los Angeles were authorized to do so), with a consequent large increase in the number of daily flights to Cuba.[21] The reelection of President Obama augurs well for the continuation, or even further relaxation, of US policies regarding visits to the island by Cuban Americans.

Official statistics regarding travel to the island by US citizens do not fully reflect these changes: they show an increase from 41,904 visitors in 2008 to 73,566 in 2011; it should be clear that these are US citizens who are not of Cuban origin, who travel to the island either legally or illegally through third countries. Separately, the number of Cuban Americans traveling to Cuba has been estimated at 296,000 in 2009, 375,500 in 2010, and over 400,000 in 2011 (*Agence France-Press*, July 22, 2009; *New York Times*, June 11, 2011; *Reuters*, July 29, 2011; *La Jornada*, July 5, 2011).[22] ONE (2012g) reports a category of visitors from "other" countries that accounted for 668,030 visitors in 2010 and 714,000 in 2011. This category is likely primarily composed of Cuban Americans, who constitute the second largest group of visitors to the island (about 15 percent) after Canadians (Espino, 2011b). Cuban tourism, then, is concentrated on visitors from

Canada (a steady source of tourists over a number of years) and Cuban Americans (a cohort whose magnitude has fluctuated over time depending on political winds). Taken together, Canadian and Cuban American visitors were responsible for 52 percent of visitors in 2011, and the trends for these cohorts explain the growth in the number of tourists since 2009 and the peaks in 2010 and 2011.

To boost the tourism sector, in 2011–2012 the Cuban government announced an investment of 185 million CUP to modernize and upgrade hotels and airports, a 20 percent reduction in landing fees paid by airlines, and the purchase of ten new aircraft for national carriers. Some of Raúl's reforms support the tourism sector: for example, the liberalization of small private restaurants (*paladares*) that provide better-quality dining compared to offerings in the state sector, the possibility of renting homes to tourists, the liberalization of private taxis, and the passage in August 2010 of legislation that allowed foreigners to lease land for up to ninety-nine years for tourism development projects (see Chapter 5). Cuban authorities have been in negotiations with foreign investors over the development of up to sixteen luxury golf courses and marinas subject to ninety-nine-year land leases, but these plans had not materialized as of the end of November 2012 (*El País,* June 9, 2011; *Reuters,* September 20, 2010, May 15, 2012). It is unlikely that the steep rise in customs duties on items carried by travelers to the island, effective as of September 2012, will have a discernible impact on tourism flows, as the duties increase—which government officials have justified as intended to bring order to airports overcrowded with excess baggage and looking like cargo terminals—will most directly affect Cuban American travelers bringing goods to family and associates. These travelers are unlikely to be deterred by the higher duties, and likely will continue bringing goods to their families; and to the extent they are "professional travelers" (*mulas*) who bring goods to the island for transformation and resale, the higher duties will be passed on to the ultimate consumers (*Reuters,* July 19, 2012; *Associated Press,* September 3, 2012).

International Economic Relations with Principal Partners

Trends in the Distribution of Foreign Trade

Between 2005 and 2010, Cuba's goods trade increasingly concentrated in Venezuela and China. Trade turnover (sum of exports and imports) between Cuba and the two countries grew from 33.4 percent to 52 percent; with Venezuela it jumped from 23 percent to 40 percent (and to 42 percent in 2011) and with China from 10 percent to 12.5 percent (and fell to 10.3 percent in 2011) (ONE, 2012a). In contrast, Cuba's trade with the other eleven of its top thirteen most significant trade partners, as shown in Table 3.5, fell over the period, particularly in 2010. Notable were the declines in Cuba's trade with European nations (from 31 percent in 2005 to 19.8 percent in 2010) and Canada (from 8 percent to 6.4 percent) (ONE, 2011a). Trade with the rest of the world fell from 19 percent to 14 percent.

Cuba's bilateral goods trade with nearly all trading partners during this period was in deficit—meaning that Cuba exported considerably less than it imported—with the exception of Canada and the Netherlands, because these two countries are the main markets for Cuba's raw nickel exports for processing or for sale to other customers (Pérez-López, 2009). The growth in Cuba's goods trade deficit with Venezuela between 2006 and 2010 is particularly significant, as it grew from 27 percent to 42 percent (and to 44 percent in 2011) of the overall goods trade deficit, while with China it declined from 20 percent to 9 percent (and to 6 percent in 2011), and it also did the same with respect to other countries (ONE, 2012a). Cuba's relationship with three important trading partners, Venezuela, China, and the United States, is based on "special" circumstances: intergovernmental agreements, tied credits, or ad hoc licensing of exports to the island (Sánchez-Egozcue, 2011b).

Table 3.5 Distribution of the Value of Goods Trade and of the Balance of Goods Trade, by Principal Partners, 2005–2010 (in percentages)

	Total Goods Trade						Balance of Goods[a]	
Trade Partner	2005	2006	2007	2008	2009	2010	2006	2010
Venezuela	23.2	21.3	19.5	27.3	26.6	39.5	–27	–42
China	10.2	14.6	17.8	12.0	14.3	12.5	–20	–9
Canada	8.0	7.2	10.2	7.9	6.3	6.4	+3	+5
Spain	8.5	8.2	8.4	8.0	7.7	6.2	–11	–10
Brazil	3.6	3.6	3.2	3.6	4.8	3.3	–6	–6
Netherlands	6.6	6.9	3.8	2.2	2.6	2.8	+11	+5
United States	4.9	3.9	4.2	5.4	5.1	2.7	–7	–7
Mexico	3.0	2.3	1.6	2.1	2.9	2.5	+2	–7
Italy	3.1	3.5	3.0	3.1	3.0	2.2	–6	–4
France	2.2	2.0	1.7	1.5	1.6	2.0	–2	–2
Germany	3.4	5.2	2.9	2.3	2.6	1.9	–9	–4
Russia	1.9	2.3	2.6	1.8	2.4	1.9	0	–3
Vietnam	2.6	2.0	2.1	2.9	2.4	1.9	–3	–4
Rest of world	18.8	17.0	19.0	19.9	17.7	14.2	–25	–12
Total	100.0	100.0	100.0	100.0	100.0	100.0		

Sources: Authors' calculations based on ONE, 2011a.
Notes: Countries are listed by decreasing order of value of goods trade with Cuba in 2010.
   a. A negative sign means that the country had a deficit in the bilateral trade; a plus sign means that the country had a surplus.

Dependence on Venezuela

Chapter 1 discussed the growing economic support Cuba has received from Venezuela since Hugo Chávez came to power in 1999, and particularly since 2001. This support permitted Fidel to reverse the modest reform process of the 1990s and to return to centralization of decisionmaking and central planning. Jorge Domínguez and colleagues (2012) posit that the favorable relationship with Venezuela created the illusion that economic changes could be postponed indefinitely. In 2008, Raúl stated that the island enjoyed "privileged relations with Venezuela" (R. Castro Ruz, 2008b). Fidel, Raúl, and Chávez have stated several times that there exists an economic-political union between the two countries.[23] But Vice Minister of Foreign Relations Rogelio Sierra acknowledged: "We would be foolish to fall into the same economic dependence that we had with the Soviet Union and the United States" (*Reuters,* November 7, 2009). As evidence of the ephemeral nature of some relations, Pérez Villanueva (2010c) notes that Cuban exports of professional services to Venezuela show evidence of exhaustion and depend on unpredictable circumstances.

Trade, oil supplies, investment, credits, and subsidies from Venezuela are of crucial importance to Cuba. In 2010, goods trade between the two countries reached a record high US$6 billion, representing 40 percent of Cuba's total goods trade, primarily because of the increase in the price of oil. The goods trade deficit with Venezuela was US$2.6 billion in 2010, 42 percent of the overall deficit, and substantially higher than the 27 percent it represented in 2006. Cuba has not reported how it finances such deficit, but it is probably through surpluses in services trade.[24] Cuba's services trade surplus in 2010, excluding tourism, was US$7.4 billion, most likely for payments to professionals working abroad (physicians, nurses, teachers, sports trainers, security personnel), mostly stationed in Venezuela. The services trade surplus exceeded by more than US$1 billion the deficit in the goods trade balance of US$6 billion (ONE, 2011a). Not all of Cuba's services exports go to Venezuela; according to statistics from Venezuela's Foreign Trade Bank, Cuba's services exports to Venezuela constituted roughly 73 percent of Cuba's total services exports in 2007–2009, valued at US$5.4 billion out of a total of US$7.4 billion (Romero, 2011). But as these are Venezuelan government statistics, it is possible that they might understate the importance of Venezuela in Cuba's services exports.

There are very few statistics on the number of Cuban professionals in Venezuela and none on the amount that Cuba receives in return for the work of its professionals in that country. The most recent information refers to some 40,000 professionals, of which 30,000 work in public health (*La Jornada,* November 11, 2010). Based on Cuban statistics on the total value of services exports (US$6.5 billion in 2008) and from Venezuela on the number of Cuban public health professionals working in Venezuela (29,296 in 2008), analyst Rolando Castañeda (2010) has estimated an average annual compensation of US$200,508 per Cuban public health professional, or US$16,709 per month, forty-four times the salary received by a Venezuelan counterpart. This estimate probably overstates Cuba's revenue per professional posted abroad for the following reasons: (a) as discussed earlier, the value of Cuban services exported to Venezuela is about 73 percent of the overall value of Cuban services exports, and the number of Cuban public health professionals posted to that country represents about 75 percent of Cuba's total professionals posted abroad (*El Universal,* November 11, 2010); (b) the value of Cuban services exported to Venezuela should be divided by the total number of Cuban professionals posted abroad, not just by the number of public health professionals; and (c) there are considerable differences between the compensation commanded by a physician and that by a nurse or some other professional. Using the estimate of 40,000 Cuban professionals in Venezuela in 2010 and adjusting the value of Cuba's services exports to Venezuela to US$5.4 billion, an average compensation per Cuban professional of US$135,000 annually, or US$11,250 monthly, can be estimated. Although these estimates are lower than Castañeda's, the huge disparity in compensation between Cuban and domestic Venezuelan professionals still holds, as the alternative estimate is twenty-seven times the salary of a Venezuelan physician and, obviously, many more times larger than that of a nurse or a teacher. The conclusion is that Venezuela grants Cuba a subsidy through the employment of professionals that Cuba could not easily duplicate by exporting its professionals to other countries. As a point of reference, an African newspaper reported in September 2012 that the Namibian government was negotiating a new agreement with Cuba to extend the services of Cuban medical personnel in the country for 2013 and beyond; according to the report, Cuba received an average of approximately US$36,600 annually for each of the fifty-two Cuban medical personnel in Namibia in 2012, and under the new agreement would receive nearly double that amount, US$73,092 annually, in 2013 (Kisting, 2012).

Pursuant to the comprehensive cooperation agreement signed in 2000 between Fidel and Chávez, Cuba provides professional services and goods to Venezuela in return for Venezuelan oil and oil products. A subsequent 2004 agreement added that services provided by Cuba would be paid with Venezuelan products priced in domestic currency (the bolivar) or some other mutually agreeable currency; the agreement has been extended several times and currently covers the period 2010 to 2020; information is not available on the terms of the exchanges or on the methodology for setting prices for services exports (Pérez-López, 2009). According to ECLAC (2011b), the price of Cuban services is indexed to the price of Venezuelan oil. The value of Venezuelan oil imported to Cuba in 2010 was US$2.7 billion

(105,000 barrels per day × 365 days × US$72 per barrel)[25] and the value of Cuba's professional services, as noted earlier, has been estimated conservatively at US$5.4 billion annually, resulting in a surplus of US$2.6 billion, which Cuba uses to offset the deficit in the goods trade balance with Venezuela and the rest of the world.

Venezuela supplies Cuba with 105,000 barrels of crude oil and oil products per day (up from 53,000 barrels per day in 2001), of which 92,000 are destined for domestic consumption (covering 62 percent of Cuba's demand) and 13,000 for processing at the Cienfuegos refinery. These oil supplies are supposedly paid for with Cuban professional services, but as has been shown, the value of services exports is approximately twice the oil import bill. Cuban oil imports from Venezuela are subject to a preferential payment scheme: Cuba is required to pay a portion of the oil bill within ninety days and payment for the remainder is deferred for twenty-five years, with a two-year grace period, at an interest rate of 1 percent; the share of the oil bill subject to the special financing terms is on a sliding scale, increasing if the world price of oil rises,[26] thereby offering Cuba some protection from fluctuating oil market prices (Castañeda, 2010). There are no reliable statistics on Cuba's payments for Venezuelan oil: the *Anuario* no longer reports the total volume and value of imported crude oil by supplying country. A Venezuelan academic has reported that Cuba accumulated a debt with Venezuela of US$4.9 billion between 2001 and 2009, with 24 percent owed to Venezuela's state oil company, PDVSA (Romero, 2011). A much higher debt estimate of US$13.8 billion has also been reported (*El Nacional,* November 14, 2010). Cuba is exporting oil to the world market; this was confirmed in 2009 by Vice Minister of Economy and Planning Julio Vázquez, who referred to such exports as originating from domestic production (*La Jornada,* October 6, 2009).

Since it was created in 2001 and through 2011, the Cuba-Venezuela Intergovernmental Cooperation Commission has approved 370 investment projects in Cuba with an estimated value of US$11 billion. Of these, 76 investment projects valued at US$1.4 billion were approved in 2008; 173 projects valued at US$2 billion were approved in 2009, including doubling the refining capacity of the Cienfuegos refinery through an investment of US$1.4 billion; and 116 projects valued at between US$1.2 billion and US$1.6 billion were approved in 2011, among them the construction of a gas liquefaction plant, a 320-kilometer gas pipeline, and an oil refinery in Matanzas, and the expansion of an oil refinery in Santiago de Cuba (Castañeda, 2010; *Granma,* July 20, 2010; *El Nuevo Herald,* December 19, 2011; Romero, 2011). Venezuela's Economic and Social Development Bank (BANDES) allocated US$1.5 billion to finance projects in Cuba in 2007–2010, and 88 percent of all of Venezuela's investments in Cuba were backed by BANDES during this period. Moreover, through its Autonomous International Cooperation Fund (FACI), the bank granted credits amounting to US$890 million to 100 Cuban enterprises; other credits amounting to US$193 million were granted to finance upgrading of railroads and of the international airports in Havana and Varadero (*El Nuevo Herald,* October 14, 2011). At the Intergovernmental Cooperation Commission's meeting in 2011, its Cuban vice president, Ricardo Cabrisas, urged the elimination of unnecessary and inappropriate expenditures and achievement of maximum efficiency in all projects (*El Universal,* December 19, 2011).

Despite the existence of a program to stimulate Venezuelan tourism to Cuba, the number of Venezuelan tourists is very small, and fell from 185,157 to 34,096 between 2005 and 2011, with Venezuela's share of tourists to Cuba falling from 8 percent to 1.3 percent (ONE, 2012a).

To summarize, Cuba's international economic relations with Venezuela can be gauged conservatively at US$12.9 billion as of 2010: goods trade of US$6 billion, services trade of US$5.4 billion, and investments of US$1.5 billion. This figure excludes the oil debt on which Cuba should be paying interest. It also excludes credits from BANDES and FACI. Taken together, these international economic transactions equate to 20.8–22.5 percent of Cuban GDP in 2010 (based on two different GDP estimates from EIU, 2011). Venezuela's Center for Economic Research estimated the value of Venezuelan economic relations with Cuba at a cumulative US$25.8 billion for the period 2005–2009 and at US$34.4 billion for 2005–2010 (CIECA, 2009; Theis, 2010). Regarding the economic relationship between Cuba and the Soviet Union, it is difficult to estimate trade, subsidies, credits, and investments because the data are not available and the relationship was conducted in different currencies—rubles, dollars, pesos; however, the value of this relationship in 1989 was estimated at US$12.7 billion (Mesa-Lago, 2000). This figure would have to be adjusted for inflation to compare it with the magnitude of the current economic relationship with Venezuela. It is clear, however, that the economic relationship with Venezuela is as fundamental to Cuba as the one that existed with the Soviet Union.

The Venezuelan economy has deteriorated in recent years. The 77 percent drop in the world market price of oil (from US$147 per barrel in July 2008 to US$34 in February 2009) dealt a heavy blow to the economy, as oil sales represent 90 percent of Venezuela's exports and contribute half of its national budget. The partial recovery of the world price of oil (to US$100 per barrel in 2011) mitigated the problem but did not reverse the decline in a wide range of economic indicators (ECLAC, 2011b, 2011c; *The Economist,* January 9, 2012). Moreover, the Venezuelan oil industry faces serious challenges that have adversely affected output, exports, profits, and financial sustainability. Crude oil output has declined from over 3 million barrels per day to about 2.5 million as a result of poor maintenance, the dismissal of some 18,000 PDVSA employees (about half of the state oil company's technical staff), and the lack of new investment. Government controls on prices of foodstuffs led to generalized shortages, expansion of black markets, and inflation, the latter also spurred by expansion of the money supply and a negative real interest rate. To control inflation and counteract declining government revenue, the Venezuelan government imposed adjustment measures: it reduced expenditures by 6.7 percent, increased the value-added tax from 9 percent to 12 percent, increased the foreign debt by 183 percent, cut in half the permitted amount of hard-currency expenditures and credit card purchases of Venezuelans traveling abroad, cut by 40 percent expenditures of PDVSA, and also reduced salaries of highly paid public officials. Controlling inflation and addressing severe external sector imbalances will require drastic measures such as imposition of new taxes, cuts to nonpriority social programs and price subsidies, reductions in foreign aid, and most probably a new devaluation of the currency (Castañeda, 2010, 2012; *El Nacional*, July 26, 2011).

In addition to Venezuela's economic problems, the situation is also uncertain in the political realm. In June 2011, Chávez underwent emergency surgery in Havana and later a second surgical procedure to treat an undisclosed cancer. The Venezuelan president initially stated that the surgery had been successful in eliminating his cancer but later changed his message and traveled to Cuba in July and August for chemotherapy. In February 2012, Chávez reported the recurrence of a tumor and returned to Cuba for another operation followed by additional chemotherapy (*Reuters,* July 8, 2011; *ABC News,* January 23, 2012; *Miami Herald,* February 22, 2012, March 27, 2012). Although Chávez handily defeated opposition candidate Henrique Capriles Radonski in Venezuela's October 2012 presidential election, winning an additional six-year term, the deterioration of his health was a serious concern for Cuba. On December 8, 2012, Chávez said on television that his cancer had reappeared and that he had to undergo another operation in Cuba, for the first time stating that Vice President Nicolás Maduro should replace him if his health were to worsen. The fourth surgical intervention, performed on December 12, was officially reported to have been "complex, difficult, and delicate." Chávez died in March 2013 and his appointed successor, Nicolás Maduro, violated the Venezuelan Constitution that stipulated that in the case of the death or incapacitation of the elected president, the president of the National Assembly would be the successor. According to the constitution, presidential elections were held and the opposition again chose Henrique Capriles as its candidate. Capitalizing on Chávez's death and exercising the power of incumbency to impose many restrictions on Capriles's campaign, Maduro built up a double-digit advantage over his opponent, which gradually eroded as the time of the election neared. Maduro was proclaimed president with only 1 percentage point difference over Capriles, amidst accusations of fraud and significant political instability (*El Nuevo Herald,* December 9, 2012; *CNN News,* December 9, 2012; *Miami Herald,* December 13, 2012, March 6 and April 12, 2013; *Reuters,* April 16, 2013).

China

Cuba's goods trade with China—currently the island's second most important trading partner—grew from 10.2 percent of trade turnover in 2005 to a peak of 17.8 percent in 2007, and receded to 12.5 percent in 2010 (see Table 3.5). China's trade with Cuba is small compared with the huge size and dynamism of the Chinese economy, and relatively modest compared with China's trade with Latin America: China is the number two trading partner (after the United States) of large-economy Latin American countries such as Argentina, Brazil, Mexico, and Venezuela, as well as of economies more like Cuba's in size, such as the Dominican Republic and Panama.

Cuba's principal export to China is sugar (400,000 tons in 2010, 72 percent of total exports); Cuba has maintained sugar exports to China even by purchasing sugar from Brazil and Colombia. The second most significant Cuban export to China is nickel (15,000 tons in 2010, 21 percent of total exports), followed by other relatively minor exports such as shellfish, citrus fruits, biotechnology products, tobacco, and rum. China has become the largest supplier of transportation equipment to the island pursuant to a US$1.8 billion credit it granted Cuba in 2004 to purchase buses, locomotives, trucks, and tractors; the pace of such sales has slowed recently, perhaps because the credit has been exhausted. Between 2001 and 2004, China granted Cuba credits and made a donation of US$375 million to finance purchase of domestic electric appliances—refrigerators, television sets, rice cookers—as well as goods for education, public health, and telecommunications (Díaz Vázquez, 2008; Pérez-López, 2009). China has designated Cuba as "a government tourist destination" and thus the number of Chinese tourists to Cuba grew from 8,700 in 2005 to 14,749 in 2011; China's share of tourists to Cuba (around 0.5 percent) is similar to Belgium's, a tiny number of tourists considering the size of China's population and its emergence as a source of global tourism.

There are a dozen Sino-Cuban joint ventures in the areas of light industry, machinery, telecommunications, agriculture, and assembly of television sets. Investment projects financed by China and announced in 2007 included completion of a nickel processing plant in Las Camariocas partially built by Council for Mutual Economic Assistance (CMEA) countries (investment of US$500 million) and development of a large nickel deposit at San Felipe (investment of US$1.3 billion). These investments did not materialize and were eventually taken over by Venezuela (Mesa-Lago, 2009c). Cuba's debt with China is estimated at US$4–5 billion.[27]

During a visit to Cuba in November 2008, Chinese president Hu Jintao announced a Chinese donation of US$8 million to assist Cuba in dealing with the aftermath of hurricanes, released the second tranche of an already granted US$78 million credit, and postponed for five to ten years the repayment of loans given in 1994–1998 (repayment of the Cuban debt accumulated during 1990–1994 had previously been postponed for ten years). Also in 2008, Chinese oil company SINOPEC and its Cuban counterpart signed an agreement for oil and gas exploration in Cuba (*Agence France-Press,* November 22, 2008). In 2011, China postponed for ten years the payment of the trade debt and grated a US$600 million credit to Cuba (ECLAC, 2010c). In June 2011, then–vice president Xi Jinping, the recently elected general secretary of the Communist Party of China and presumptive president to succeed Hu Jintao beginning in 2013, visited Cuba and signed thirteen cooperation agreements and announced several credits; among the projects being developed with Chinese assistance are expansion of the Cienfuegos refinery, construction of a gas liquefaction plant (also involving Venezuela), oil exploration (China is already extracting oil from several wells along Cuba's northern coast), renovation of the port of Havana, and modernization of banking supervision, public health, and digital television (*EFE,* June 6, 2011; *El País,* June 9, 2011; *United Press International,* June 23, 2011). As mentioned in Chapter 2, the deep-water oil-drilling rig *Scarabeo 9,* which operated in Cuban waters in 2012, was built in Chinese shipyards; Chinese companies also hold exploration and development rights for several offshore blocks in Cuba's exclusive economic zone (*EFE,* October 27, 2008; *Associated Press,* November 19, 2008; *Agence France-Press,* November 22, 2008).

There are challenges for the further development of economic relations between China and Cuba. About 40 percent of Chinese enterprises are privately owned, are independent from the state, compete with each other, seek to maximize profits, and are judicious about foreign investments. Therefore, the Chinese state does not have a free hand to direct them to act even if Sino-Cuban government-to-government relations are strong (Fornés, 2007; Díaz Vázquez, 2008). Sea transportation from China to Cuba takes approximately forty-five days, and suppliers demand advance notice of sixty to ninety days to process orders; delays in the arrival of goods from China and postponement of orders are frequent, with disruptive impact on the Cuban economy (Murillo, 2010). Prices of Chinese goods in Cuba are sometimes higher than those of goods from other countries; there are also intermediaries that charge commissions and slow transactions and thus Cuba needs to penetrate more deeply into the Chinese market and build direct ties with producers; interest rates applied by Chinese enterprises to Cuban trade are the same as are applied in domestic trade, although Cuba has been seeking preferential rates (Fornés, 2007). A Cuban expert has stated that since 2003, "Cuba has rigorously met all contractual and repayment commitments with China" (Díaz Vázquez, 2008). However, Chinese businessmen have expressed concerns about inefficiencies in the execution of investment projects on the island, delays in payments, and repeated requests to restructure debts, and have offered Cuba assistance in modernizing business management. At a meeting in 2010 attended by 500 high-level officials from the Cuban government and from the Cuban Communist Party, then–minister of economy Marino Murillo urged strict compliance with all contractual obligations with China and on-time payments in order not to jeopardize credits from that nation (Frank, 2010c).

Canada

Canada is Cuba's third largest trading partner. That nation's share of goods trade turnover rose as high as 10.2 percent in 2007, although it slipped to 6.4 percent in 2010 because of the global economic crisis and Cuba's liquidity problems. Canada is one of two trading partners with whom Cuba shows a surplus in the goods trade balance (see Table 3.5), as a result of significant Cuban exports of raw nickel from the Pedro Sotto plant (a joint venture with Canadian corporation Sherritt International) to be further processed at a refinery in Alberta, Canada, also owned by Sherritt. Cuban exports to Canada peaked in 2007 when the world price of nickel reached a historical high.

Canadians are by far the largest group of tourists to the island, almost six times as numerous as the second largest group (British) and twice as numerous as Cuban Americans. The number of Canadian tourists to Cuba has increased steadily over the past decade, surpassing the milestone of 1 million in 2011 (ONE, 2012a). In 2010 Cuba was the preferred destination of 36 percent of Canadians traveling to the Caribbean, compared to 25.3 percent who chose the Dominican Republic, and Cuba's share of Canadian tourism has been on the rise except for a brief decline during the global financial crisis. Based on Cuba's share of Canadian tourism and Cuba's overall gross income from tourism, we can estimate that Cuba's income from Canadian tourists was US$827 million in 2010; daily expenditures per Canadian tourist grew from US$61 to US$97 between 2000 and 2009 (Espino, 2011b).

Canadian companies have invested around US$2 billion in projects in Cuba's nickel, oil and gas, and tourism industries. The largest Canadian investor, Sherritt, suspended an investment of US$29 million in the Pedro Sotto nickel plant in 2008, because of slack world demand for nickel as a result of the global crisis, but recorded strong earnings in 2007 and again in 2011 when world market nickel prices soared. Sherritt, also a significant domestic oil producer in Cuba under a production-sharing agreement (Sherritt accounted for 25 percent of Cuba's domestic crude oil extraction), withdrew from four oil exploration concessions in the exclusive economic zone in 2008 because of low world market oil prices (at the time) and the high cost of deep-water offshore drilling. The second largest Canadian investor in Cuba is oil company Pebercan, which produced 8 percent of Cuban domestic crude oil, also under a production-sharing agreement. Leisure Canada is planning to build three hotels as well as a golf course and a marina on the island; it has also secured a ninety-nine-year lease for valuable seafront property in the prestigious area of Miramar. Another Canadian entity on the island, Standing Feather International, is planning to build a hotel with a golf course and villas for sale to foreigners (Ritter, 2011d).

The economic relationship between the two countries cooled in 2008–2009 largely because of Cuba's liquidity crisis. Cuba ran up debts of US$126 million to Pebercan and of US$393 million to Sherritt, and canceled the production-sharing contract with Pebercan in early 2009, bringing to an end a relationship that had spanned sixteen years. Sherritt continued its operations, but oil production fell by 39 percent between 2006 and 2009. Cuba promised to repay Sherritt over a five-year period (*Reuters,* August 27, 2008; *Nuevo Herald,* January 24, 2009; *Associated Press,* February 26, 2009).

The year 2011 was a difficult one for Canadian businessmen operating in Cuba. In July 2011, Cuban authorities shut down Canadian trading company Tri-Star Caribbean and arrested its local management staff, ostensibly because of financial irregularities. The same actions were repeated in September 2011 regarding the Tokmakjian Group, one of the largest Western trading companies operating on the island. As of November 2012, executives of the two companies were in government custody awaiting legal action and the businesses had been shut down (*Reuters,* October 9, 2012).

European Union

Goods trade between Cuba and the members of the European Union as a group fell from 29.4 percent of Cuba's total trade in 2005 to 19.6 percent in 2010. Several EU member states are significant investors in Cuba. Although the number of EU tourists to Cuba declined from 923,000 to 668,000 (from 39.8 percent to 26.4 percent of Cuba's total tourist visits) over the same period, in 2010 EU countries were still the second largest source of tourists visiting the island.

Cuba's relations with the EU were "frozen" in 2003. In the aftermath of Cuba's "Black Spring" government crackdown, which resulted in the jailing of seventy-five dissidents, the EU imposed a range of sanctions on the island: among them termination of cultural cooperation and exchanges, and adoption of a policy of inviting Cuban dissidents to attend diplomatic receptions hosted by EU countries (to which Cuba responded by not allowing government officials to attend such functions). Spurred by Spain's president of government, José Luis Rodríguez Zapatero, and his minister of foreign relations, Miguel Moratinos, in June 2008 the EU Council ratified its "Common Position" on Cuba, adopted in 1996, but reinstated "without any conditions" its cooperation with Cuba, and suspended the recently established sanctions, while encouraging Cuba to free all political prisoners, improve human rights, and continue a dialogue with representatives of civil society and dissidents (see Farber, 2011). Fidel, in one of his "Reflections," described the EU's decisions as "hugely hypocritical," and Raúl criticized the Common Position, stating that Cuba would not accept pressure or blackmail. However, then–foreign minister Felipe Pérez Roque stated that the EU's decisions were "a step in the right direction," a statement that provoked comments in the international press about a schism within the Cuban leadership, which was quickly denied by Fidel in another Reflection. Falling in line with his superiors, Pérez Roque said that Cuba had defeated the EU's sanctions policy and demanded the repeal of the Common Position, a change in stance that did not prevent his being sacked shortly after (*El País,* June 23, 2008, June 25, 2008). The results of the EU's new policies were reviewed by member states in Brussels in June 2009, under the presidency of the Czech Republic—which had opposed the reinstatement of cooperation with Cuba but had ultimately accepted it subject to an annual review (Leiva, 2008a, 2008b). During a visit to Cuba in October 2009, EU commissioner for development and humanitarian assistance Louis Michel met with Raúl (but avoided meeting with dissidents) to celebrate the reinstatement of bilateral cooperation and announced a donation of US$38 million for hurricane relief. Although an announcement was made of a visit to Cuba by Rodríguez Zapatero in 2009, it did not materialize (Leiva, 2009). Evaluations conducted by the EU in 2010 and 2011 did not result in changes to its Common Position on Cuba. In December 2011 in Spain, opposition leader Mariano Rajoy was elected president of government; Rajoy and his minister of foreign relations have stated that Spain will not support a change to the Common Position until Cuba demonstrates progress in human rights and political pluralism (*EFE,* January 24, 2012). According to an analyst specializing in EU affairs, in November 2012 the EU Foreign Affairs Council had begun a review of the Common Position, which has not been rigorously implemented and has been deemed as ineffective and anachronistic by many member states (Roy, 2012).

Within the EU, Spain has played a key role in the Cuban economy. Spain is Cuba's fourth largest trading partner, although its participation in Cuban trade turnover declined from 8.5 percent in 2005 to 6.2 percent in 2010 (see Table 3.5). About 75 percent of Cuba's exports to Spain consist of tobacco, fish and shellfish, and rum, while Cuba imports Spanish machinery and equipment (30 percent), foodstuffs, and other consumer goods. Cuba's systematic deficit in the goods trade balance with Spain is difficult to sustain; prior to 1990, Spain granted credits to partly offset the deficit, but the growth of the debt and the lack of repayment marked an end to this policy. Thus, trade turnover has declined substantially (Bayo, 2010). As a result of Spain's economic crisis, overall commercial relations between the two countries likely declined in 2012 and probably beyond.

Although Spain is one of Cuba's principal foreign investors, it has no economic cooperation agreement with the island along the lines of those signed with several Latin American countries and with China. The focal point of Spanish investment has been tourism: numerous hotels in Cuba have been built by joint ventures with Spanish companies and even more hotels are managed by Spanish hospitality companies, whose professionals have trained Cuban counterparts. A second area of Spanish investment is oil exploration, specifically by Repsol, which was responsible for the first deep-water exploratory well drilled in 2012, which turned out to be dry. Other areas of Spanish investments include tobacco, foodstuffs, and finance (Bayo, 2010). Spain is the fourth largest source of tourists traveling to Cuba (representing 4 percent of total tourist visits to the island) (ONE, 2011a).

There are several estimates of Cuba's debt to Spain, ranging from US$1.4 billion to US$4 billion, depending on whether total debt or debt to the government or to private businesses are considered. There have been several efforts to reschedule the debt; Rodríguez Zapatero's government considered, but did not approve, partial or full forgiveness. Cuba has not accepted Spain's proposals to convert outstanding commercial debt into private investment. Repayment problems have led to the closing of several credit lines (Bayo, 2010).

United States

The United States fell in standing among Cuba's trading partners from fifth in 2007–2009 to seventh in 2010, as its share of Cuba's goods trade shank from 4.2 percent to 2.7 percent (see Table 3.5). Since 2001, US-Cuba trade consists essentially of US food exports to Cuba permitted by legislation passed in 2000 (the Trade Sanctions Reform and Export Enhancement Act, approved under President George W. Bush) that provided an exception to the US embargo by allowing some forms of exports to the island.[28] Initially under this legislation, Cuba was required to pay in cash prior to the shipment of goods to the island; since 2009, payment in cash needs to be made when the shipment arrives at a Cuban port, but before the vessel is unloaded.

The United States is the principal supplier of the following foodstuffs to Cuba: beverages, soybeans, frozen chicken, corn, frozen pork, wheat, and beans (García, Amaya, and Piñeiro, 2010). The rationale for Cuba purchasing foodstuffs from the United States rather than from other countries is lower transportation and insurance costs because of proximity, and lower prices (Sánchez-Egozcue, 2011b). The cumulative value of Cuban imports of US foodstuffs in the period 2001–2011 was US$3.8 billion; imports peaked in 2008 at US$710 million (when several hurricanes battered the island and devastated domestic food production, as discussed in Chapter 2) and have been steadily declining since, falling to US$347 million in 2011. The reasons for the fall in imports are lack of convertible currency to make cash purchases for US products; credits from Venezuela and China with attractive terms to support their food exports to Cuba; credits and special access agreements negotiated with Argentina, Brazil, Canada, France, Iran, Mexico, Russia, and Vietnam; and lower likelihood that US farmers and food companies will be able to influence the US government to ease or eliminate the embargo (US-Cuba Trade and Economic Council, 2012). Hurricane Sandy, which battered the eastern end of the island in late October 2012, inflicted heavy damage on Cuban agriculture, affecting some 100,000 hectares of land under cultivation as well as cattle and poultry farms (*Diario de Cuba,* October 29, 2012, November 1, 2012), which may result in Cuba boosting imports of US agricultural products.

Approximately 463,000 US and Cuban American tourists traveled to Cuba in 2010, representing 18 percent of the total number of tourists who visited the island that year, and constituting the second largest group from any country. This tourist flow contributed nearly US$400 million in gross revenue to the Cuban economy. In addition, it has been roughly estimated that Cuban Americans annually remitted about US$1 billion to the island in the late 1990s, and probably more in 2010 and 2011.

The US commercial embargo on Cuba (the Cuban government calls it "blockade") has been repeatedly and nearly unanimously repudiated by the United Nations, most recently in November 2012;[29] actions taken by President George W. Bush to strengthen the embargo were criticized even by many Cuban Americans who were affected by the rules limiting further travel to the island and the sending of remittances. This policy was ineffective and was used by the Cuban government to justify errors and the poor results of its economic policies. Unquestionably, the US embargo has economic costs for Cuba,[30] but it no longer is as serious an obstacle as it once was, since the island currently trades with the United States (foodstuffs under special conditions) and has access to international financial markets. The key issue affecting economic performance is Cuban economic policies, a point acknowledged on several occasions by Raúl.

As discussed earlier, President Barack Obama relaxed the restrictions on travel and remittances by Cuban Americans that had been imposed by his predecessor; raised the limit on remittances that can be sent to Cuba by wire transfer and distributed to recipients in convertible pesos; authorized US citizens to travel to the island for cultural, religious, and professional reasons; postponed payment for US food imports until the arrival of shipments at a Cuban port; and reinstated migration discussions. The Obama administration continued to condition the lifting of the embargo on Cuban government actions, including the freeing of additional political prisoners. It should be noted that ending the embargo will require the repeal or amendment of several laws that are currently in place, including the Helms-Burton

Act, which will not be an easy task. Even though President Obama has been reelected, his party does not control the House of Representatives, and there is a significant group of senators who would be opposed to ending the embargo. Fidel refused to condition the lifting of the embargo on an improvement of human rights and freedoms on the island, deeming it an intervention into the internal affairs of the nation. Raúl has made several offers to enter into negotiations with the United States and to meet in a neutral location to discuss all issues, including freeing of political prisoners (he has already freed some and would probably seek reciprocity for five Cuban citizens who have been tried and sentenced as spies by US courts), but within a framework of equality, and without negotiating Cuba's political system or diminishing its sovereignty (R. Castro Ruz, 2009c, 2010c). In 2011, Raúl admitted that Obama had taken a number of positive yet limited measures and that Cuba was open to negotiations, but emphasized that the embargo continued to remain in place and that it had actually been strengthened with respect to banking transactions (R. Castro Ruz, 2011a).

According to a Cuban analyst, full reestablishment of commercial relations between the United States and Cuba would result in trade turnover of US$2.6 billion in the first year (Sánchez-Egozcue, 2011b). Lifting of the embargo would result in significant benefits to Cuba and few disadvantages. The United States would not subsidize commodity prices in trade with Cuba, as was done by the Soviet Union and as is now done by Venezuela. Thus, in order to promote prosperous and stable relations in the future, it is crucial that Cuba improve its economic performance and production levels in order to generate exports to in turn finance imports from the United States.[31]

Latin America

Brazil is Cuba's fifth largest trading partner. Its share of Cuban trade turnover rose from 3.6 percent in 2005 to 4.8 percent in 2009, but tapered off to 3.3 percent in 2010 (see Table 3.5); according to press reports, trade turnover increased 28 percent in 2011, returning to its 2008 level. In 2008, Brazil granted Cuba credits to finance imports of foodstuffs, modernize a nickel processing plant, and develop transportation and tourism infrastructure; former president Luiz Inácio Lula da Silva traveled to Cuba and signed ten cooperation agreements, including financing of an expansion of the port of Mariel, and Brazilian state oil company Petrobras committed to investment in oil and natural gas exploration (*Reuters,* January 15, 2008; *El Nuevo Herald,* December 17, 2008). Current Brazilian president Dilma Roussef visited Cuba in January 2012, and announced a new credit of US$600 million to finance Cuban purchases of Brazilian foodstuffs and agricultural equipment and a contract between private conglomerate Odebrecht and

Cuban entities to produce sugar on the island and later ethanol from sugar-cane (*Miami Herald*, January 31, 2012). Cuba owes Brazil about US$1.2 billion.

Mexico, Cuba's eighth largest trading partner, has seen its share of trade turnover decline, from 3 percent in 2005 to 2.5 percent in 2010 (see Table 3.5). Mexico was the source of 2.9 percent of tourists traveling to the island in 2011 and is owed US$400 million by Cuba. Another important economic partner is Argentina, whose share of trade turnover declined from 3.4 percent in 2005 to 1.6 percent in 2010; Argentina is owed about US$2.4 billion by Cuba. Argentina's tourists increasingly have been traveling to Cuba, accounting for 2.8 percent of total tourists to Cuba in 2011. Cuba's trade with other countries in Latin America is small (ONE, 2011a; ICCAS, 2011).

Cuba is not a member of the principal multilateral trade arrangements in the region among market-oriented economies: the North American Free Trade Agreement, the Central American Common Market, and the Southern Common Market. Cuba also did not participate in the stalled negotiations toward the Free Trade Area of the Americas. However, alongside Venezuela, Bolivia, and Ecuador, Cuba became a founding member in 2004 of the Bolivarian Alliance for the Americas[32] and has benefited from the alliance's bank, established with an initial capital of US$2 billion, through credits and project investment. In 2008, Raúl participated in the Latin American and Caribbean Summit, the first time that hemispheric leaders met without the presence of US and EU representatives, which opened the way for Cuba to join the Rio Group. In 2009, the thirty-four member countries of the Organization of American States, including the United States, lifted Cuba's suspension from the organization since 1962, and invited the island to request readmission; the Cuban government rejected the invitation. In 2011 in Caracas, Cuba became one of the founding countries of the Community of Latin American and Caribbean Countries, an organization that excludes the United States and Canada, and whose presidency Cuba will hold in 2013 (Romero, 2011; *Miami Herald*, February 6, 2012). Cuba is also a member of the Caribbean Common Market, but its trade with Caribbean countries is small, representing only 0.8 percent of Cuba's total trade turnover in 2006 (ONE, 2007).

Russia

Russia was Cuba's principal trading partner in 1989, accounting for 65 percent of Cuba's total trade turnover in 1989, but fell to twelfth place in 2010, accounting for 1.9 percent of total trade turnover. Russia's importance as a source of tourists to Cuba has been growing, with Russian tourists accounting for nearly 2.9 percent of the island's tourists in 2011. In 2008, President Dmitry

Medvedev visited Cuba and announced a new credit line of US$350 million to finance Cuban imports from Russia of agricultural and construction equipment and some investment projects. Raúl followed up with a visit to Moscow in 2009, at which time some thirty-three agreements were announced, including the purchase of a cargo aircraft, projects aimed at exploration for oil and gas as well as nickel deposits, and donation of foodstuffs (*BBC Mundo*, November 10, 2008; *EFE*, March 2, 2009). In July 2011, the two countries signed a new agreement seeking to stimulate two-way trade; reportedly thirty Russian firms were considering investment projects on the island (*EFE*, July 13, 2011).

In September 2008, the International Commercial Arbitration Court of the Russian Chamber of Commerce and Industry upheld a claim of the International Investment Bank (in which Russia controls 58 percent) against the Central Bank of Cuba for about US$330 million in unpaid loans. Also in 2008, however, Russia rescheduled repayment of some US$870 million owed by Cuba in 2006–2007 over ten years, with a four-year grace period. Not solved to date is the debt Cuba incurred with the Soviet Union over the 1961–1990 period, estimated at US$21 billion, which will require an agreement on the value of the exchange rate of the ruble (*Novosti*, April 1, 2008; *Kommersant*, September 4, 2008). In late September 2012, Russia's vice minister of finance stated that after a hiatus of ten years, Russia and Cuba would soon be engaging in bilateral negotiations to address Cuba's US$25 billion debt to Russia, but there is no additional information on the results of this negotiation (*Diario de Cuba*, September 25, 2012).

Summary of Findings

Limitations in economic statistics do not permit a thorough analysis of Cuba's international economic relations. Cuban balance of payments statistics are incomplete and out-of-date; the same is true regarding statistics on investment and foreign debt. There are no official statistics on international monetary reserves.

Although Cuban goods exports have recovered in recent years, particularly in 2011, when for the first time in twenty-two years the value of goods exports exceed their 1989 level. Meanwhile, imports rose steadily, reaching historical highs in 2008 and 2011; the value of imports in 2011 was 73 percent higher than in 1989. The goods trade deficit has been substantial in every year, peaking in 2008, declining in 2009–2010, but rising again in 2011, when the deficit was twice as high as in 1989.

Sugar's share of total exports fell from 73 percent in 1989 to 5 percent in 2010, while nickel's rose to 58 percent in 2007 and later retreated to 27 percent in 2010, with both trends reflecting world market price fluctuations and also output declines. The shares of other traditional products in the goods exports basket declined, except for pharmaceuticals and alcoholic beverages. Fuels' share of imports rose steadily to 42 percent in 2010 and that of foodstuffs to 14 percent. In contrast, machinery's share of imports fell by half between 1989 and 2010 (to 12 percent), one of the reasons behind the serious de-capitalization and de-industrialization that has occurred. Cuba continues to be essentially an exporter of raw materials and an importer of value-added products.

The number of tourists to Cuba jumped tenfold and gross income from tourism jumped fourteenfold between 1989 and 2011; the number of rooms for international tourists tripled, but the occupancy rate fell to 53 percent and average hotel income fell by 18 percent as a result of the poor quality of facilities and services, their high cost in comparison with the offerings of other countries, and the global financial crisis. The steady increase of Canadian tourists to Cuba and the recent increased flows of Cuban American travelers to the island (accounting for a combined 55 percent of Cuba's total tourists) explain the growth of the tourism sector despite the fall in tourists from Europe and from most Latin American nations.

Cuba's deficit in the goods balance of trade was initially partly offset and then exceeded by the surplus in the services balance of trade. The principal components of services exports are professional services (principally exported to Venezuela) and tourism the former's share in services exports grew rapidly, whereas the latter's share declined as the tourism industry matured and growth slowed. Professional services exports contribute a large amount of hard-currency revenue, but do not have significant linkages to the rest of the economy. Cuba has succeeded in ending its long-term dependence on sugar exports, but has traded it for an even deeper dependence on professional services exports concentrated in one market (Venezuela). There are not sufficient statistics to reconstruct the balance of payments accounts, but a key component is remittances sent to the island primarily from Cuban Americans; the volume of these remittances has expanded since the US government liberalized rules governing them in 2009.

The favorable performance of certain key sectors of the Cuban economy—oil, tourism, nickel—has been heavily influenced by foreign investment. The number of joint ventures with foreign investors fell by 41 percent between 2002 and 2006, and that of cooperative production arrangements by 87 percent, reinforcing an oligopolistic model that favors multinational corporations and limits entry of small and medium-sized enterprises. Cuba's foreign debt grew by nearly three and half times between 1989 and 2011 (excluding debt with Russia and Venezuela), equivalent to 34 percent of GDP in 2010, compared to a 20 percent average for Latin America, and equivalent to 298 percent of the value of exports in 2010, compared to a 90 percent average for the region. The record-high deficits in the goods balance of trade in 2008, the excessive issuance of convertible pesos, the global financial crisis, the lack of access to support from international financial institutions, and a cutback in assistance from Venezuela, all combined in 2009 to create a liquidity crisis that resulted in the freezing of accounts of foreign enterprises operating on the island and the suspension of repayment of credits. In response, Raúl cut back on imports and domestic expenditures and instituted other measures that improved liquidity and reduced the number of frozen accounts by about two-thirds. The process of adjustment to the liquidity crisis of 2009 was still progressing in 2012.

Monetary duality—the circulation of both the CUC and the CUP—has given rise to market segmentation and serious distortions in the economy. The CUC is overvalued: until 2005 it was exchanged at par with the US dollar; later it "appreciated" vis-à-vis hard currencies and a 10 percent surcharge was imposed when exchanging convertible pesos for US dollars, which worsened the overall liquidity situation because it affected remittances and tourism. In 2011 the CUC was devalued (returning to its 2005 level). Although this latter measure is positive, the CUC continues to be overvalued; there is a lively debate within Cuba on how to eliminate the monetary duality (see Chapters 5 and 6).

The Cuban economy has hobbled along on the strength of investment, trade, credits, and subsidies from Venezuela; foreign investment by private businesses in strategic sectors such as oil, gas, and nickel; and trade, credits, and investment from China. Two-way goods trade with Venezuela grew from 23 percent to 42 percent of Cuba's total trade turnover between 2005 and 2011, but with China it fell from 17.8 percent to 9.7 percent between 2007 and 2011, and it also declined with other trading partners. Other important Cuban trading partners are Canada, the European Union, Brazil, and the United States (which under the Obama presidency took several steps to ease relations with Cuba, but still maintains the embargo). Cuba's current dependence on Venezuela is substantial, estimated at US$12.9 billion in 2010 (21–22 percent of Cuban GDP): 42 percent of Cuba's goods trade turnover and 44 percent of Cuba's goods trade deficit, the focal point for professional services exports and significant source of investment. In addition, Venezuela provides Cuba with 105,000 barrels of crude oil per day (valued at about US$2.8 billion in 2010 and covering 62 percent of Cuban demand) at generous terms. The value of Cuban professional services paid by Venezuela amply exceeds that of oil imports. The disappointing results of the first stage of deep-water drilling off Cuba's northern coast constitute a negative development, as it moots, at least in the short to medium term, the possibility of oil production significant enough to reduce Cuba's dependence on oil imports from Venezuela or elsewhere.

The deterioration of the Venezuelan economy, Chavez's death, and the political instability caused by the opposition's contestation of the controversial presidential election of Nicolás Maduro are risks for Cuba. Recall that in 2007, when confronting the possibility of Chávez losing a referendum for reelection, Fidel warned about the devastating consequences that such an outcome would bring for Cuba. Analysts believe that severe policy adjustments to control inflation and reduce government expenditures in Venezuela are inevitable. Maduro has to make a difficult choice between three key goals: investing in the economy in order to strengthen it, continuing Chávez's populist social programs essential for domestic political support, and maintaining costly economic aid to Cuba and other countries in the region. If foreign assistance is cut, the economic lifeline to Cuba would be threatened and a crisis would ensue albeit somewhat less acute than those experienced in the 1990s when the Soviet Union collapsed, as in the interim Cuba has developed other economic options, such as tourism, remittances, domestic oil production, and nickel production, and also has diversified somewhat its export basket, but still the blow would be devastating. Raúl has been active in seeking alternative trade and investment partners, but these efforts have so far not panned out and Cuba depends heavily on Venezuela. For all of these reasons and considerations, faster and deeper structural economic reforms in Cuba become more imperative.

Notes

1. Because the release of the external sector section of the 2011 *Anuario* occurred after we completed writing this book, the tables and text in this chapter have only been partially updated through 2011.

2. The 2010 *Anuario* devotes twenty-one pages to imports and only six to exports (ONE, 2012a).

3. For example, the 2010 *Anuario* contains three tables with information on elements of the balance of payments that show inconsistencies and contradictions: tab. 5.2, on global supply and demand for 2005–2010, gives statistics on goods exports and imports; tab. 8.1, on the 2006–2008 balance of payments, provides statistics on the balance of goods trade that are inconsistent with those in tab. 5.2; and tab. 8.3 shows historical statistics (1950–2010) of goods exports and imports and of the goods trade balance that are consistent with those of tab. 5.2, but not with those of tab. 8.1 (ONE, 2011a).

4. ECLAC (2011b) reproduces Cuban statistics. For an effort to reconstruct the Cuban balance of payments for 1998–2007, see Pérez-López, 2011.

5. The value of nickel exports rose by 26 percent in 2007 as a result of the high world market price, but there was no increase in production.

6. Output of medicines rose between 2005 and 2009, with a significant slowdown in the growth rate in 2009, and no statistics were released for 2010 and 2011 (ONE, 2011a, 2012a). Marino Murillo (2010) reported that production in 2010 was adversely affected by the lack of inputs.

7. The *Anuario* reports the overall value of exports of "fuels and lubricants, minerals, and related products" but omits this category in the subsequent disaggregation by specific exports, hence making impossible to estimate fuels alone.

8. The corresponding shares in 1989 and 2010 were: meats, 0.7 and 2.5 percent; rice, 0.8 and 2.1 percent; wheat, 1.8 and 1.9 percent; corn, 1.3 and 1.7 percent; dairy, 1 and 1.3 percent; vegetables and fruits, 0.9 percent (both years); and beans, 0.6 (both years) (CEE, 1991; ONE, 2010a, 2011a).

9. In 2010, Cuba imported 4,848,500 metric tons of crude oil and 1,328,600 metric tons of refined oil products (ONE, 2011a).

10. In 2007, 3.4 percent of total imports, and 11 percent of machinery imports, were imports of "electricity generation groups," principally electricity generators destined to the "energy revolution."

11. Members of the Paris Club are Australia, Austria, Belgium, Canada, Denmark, Finland, France, Germany, Ireland, Italy, Japan, the Netherlands, Norway, Russia, Spain, Sweden, Switzerland, the United Kingdom, and the United States.

12. Authors' calculations based on EIU, 2011; regional comparisons from ECLAC, 2011a. Lorenzo Pérez (2008) estimated that Cuba's external debt in 2006 was 173 percent of the value of exports of goods and services, the third highest among twenty-six countries in Asia, Eastern Europe, and Central America and the Caribbean. Servicing of the debt—if it were paid—would require the equivalent of 80 percent of government income and would be unsustainable.

13. In 2009, Minister of Trade and Foreign Investment Rodrigo Malmierca stated that there were 258 FDI projects on the island; in 2012 the number had fallen to 240 (*Reuters,* May 15, 2012).

14. The exchange rate became 1 CUC to 1.08 US dollars, excluding surcharge and commission.

15. In 2010 the commission was waived for dollars sent via Western Union, but it remained in place for dollars exchanged at CADECA houses.

16. ECLAC and Cuban economists had recommended devaluation.

17. For January–September 2012, ONE (2012h) reported an increase of 7.7 percent in gross revenue compared to a like period in 2011.

18. ECLAC's estimates of average daily income are based on gross income rather than on average expenditures per tourist, which fell by 30 percent between 2006 and 2010. They also omit transactions involving Cuban Americans, who usually stay with relatives rather than in hotels and would therefore bring down the average (Espino, 2011b, 2012).

19. In 2011 the Dominican Republic attracted nearly 60 percent more tourists than Cuba, whose share of the world tourist market was 1.7 percent that year, compared to 2.7 percent for the Dominican Republic (UNWTO, 2012).

20. There was also a decline in the number of cruise ship visitors (from 102,000 in 2005 to 11,000 in 2008) as a result of criticism by Fidel of cruise ship tourism and the acquisition of a Spanish cruise company by Royal Caribbean that led to the cancellation of stops in Cuba (*Associated Press,* January 23, 2008).

21. Several efforts in the US Congress to modify the US embargo to permit US citizens to travel to the island free from any restrictions have failed.

22. Jorge Pérez-López and Sergio Díaz-Briquets (2011) have suggested promoting travel by Cuban Americans during the time of the year when demand from international tourists is low, which would lead to better use of installed capacity.

23. In 2005, then–vice president Carlos Lage stated publicly that Cuba had two presidents: Fidel and Chávez.

24. The value of Cuban exports to Venezuela jumped by 354 percent between 2009 and 2011 (from US$528 million to US$2.4 billion), without explanation of what products Cuba exported (the *Anuario* does not provide details).

25. Venezuelan crude oil streams tend to be heavy and have a high sulfur content; as such they command lower world market prices than light crudes; the average

export price for a basket of Venezuelan medium and heavy crudes in 2010 was US$72 per barrel, compared to US$77 per barrel for a basket of crude oils exported by members of the Organization of Petroleum Exporting Countries (OPEC), and US$80 per barrel for the lighter Brent-blend crude from the North Sea. In 2011 the corresponding prices per barrel were US$101 for the Venezuelan basket, US$107 for the OPEC basket, and US$111 for the Brent blend. Data from the website of Venezuela's Ministry of Energy, Petroleum, and Minerals, www.menpet.gob.ve.

26. That is, 30 percent is subject to special financing when the oil market price exceeds US$40 per barrel, 40 percent when it exceeds US$50 per barrel, 50 percent when it exceeds US$80 per barrel, and 60 percent when it exceeds US$100 per barrel.

27. China's credits to Cuba are markedly smaller than those it has granted to other Latin American countries, for example US$10 billion to Argentina and to Brazil, and US$20 billion to Venezuela (*New York Times,* April 16, 2009; *La Vanguardia,* November 28, 2010).

28. The Cuban Democracy Act of 1992 codified various elements of the broad US commercial, economic, and financial embargo in place since the early 1960s; the Helms-Burton Act of 1996 further restricted the ability of US citizens to do business with Cuba.

29. The result of the vote, taken on November 13, 2012, was 188 countries against the embargo and 3 in favor, with 2 abstaining, making 2012 the twenty-first year in a row that the UN General Assembly voted against the embargo.

30. Among the remaining problems with the embargo: it bans imports into the United States of products from third countries that have certain content of Cuban inputs; sanctions international banks for accepting Cuban government deposit in dollars unless previously notified to US authorities; results in higher costs for imports into Cuba of US products obtained through third countries; and forces imports to Cuba from other countries to travel longer distances at higher freight costs to avoid passage through the United States. Cuba estimates—questionably—that the cumulative loss to Cuba (since 1961) associated with the embargo has been US$100 billion. Also, US citizens receive lower compensation than Cubans for properties confiscated by the Cuban government.

31. For an analysis of the benefits and disadvantages of the reestablishment of relations between Cuba and the United States, as well as the positions of Fidel and Raúl with respect to President Obama, see Mesa-Lago, 2009a, 2009d. For a Cuban point of view, see Sánchez-Egozcue, 2011a.

32. The alliance includes Bolivia, Cuba, Ecuador, Nicaragua, and Venezuela, plus Antigua, Barbuda, Dominica, and the Grenadines. It excludes most Latin American countries and those with the largest economies.

4

Social Welfare,
2006–2012

This chapter describes and evaluates the social situation in Cuba from 2006 to 2012, following the methodology of previous chapters. It covers unemployment, salaries, and inequality; and social services (education, public health, social security pensions, social welfare, and housing).

Cuban social statistics vary widely with respect to comprehensiveness and reliability. Educational statistics are probably the most complete and reliable; housing statistics are scarcer and those on the housing deficit are questionable. Pension and social welfare statistics seem to be trustworthy but are not as reliable as those regarding education. Open unemployment is systematically underestimated due to the huge size of underemployment in the state sector, which began to decrease in 2010. There is no reliable information on the consumer basket of basic commodities or on the purchasing power of salaries, and little information regarding income differences between the state and nonstate sectors, and on income by gender. With regard to health, the statistical series on maternal mortality rate has been the subject of changes and there are significant contradictions regarding the number of physicians abroad. There are no official statistics on the incidence of poverty, income distribution, or race; the same is the case with respect to the quality of social services.

Unemployment, Salaries, and Inequality

Open and Hidden Unemployment

The Cuban revolution achieved full employment, one of its most significant social accomplishments, and tried to maintain it even during the economic crisis of the 1990s. But the elimination of open unemployment was attained to a large extent and at a high cost through the creation of unproductive employment in the state sector: a factory, a farm, or a service provider that required 100 employees would employ 200, thereby pushing down open unemployment but also adversely affecting productivity, eroding work incentives, and generating hidden unemployment. During idealist cycles, priority was given to achieving full employment at the expense of driving down productivity, while during pragmatist cycles more attention was devoted to productivity, but without implementing a substantial reduction in redundant state employment.

During the economic crisis of the 1990s, in order to avoid an increase in open unemployment, the state subsidized unprofitable enterprises, keeping them technically operating and workers on their payrolls even if necessary inputs were not available. Actually, open unemployment fell in 1992–1993 at the trough of the crisis (see Table 4.1).[1] While positive from a social standpoint, this policy had negative economic effects: increased absenteeism, decreased labor discipline, inefficiency, poor utilization of the labor force, and a severe decline in labor productivity (the historical part of this section draws from Mesa-Lago, 2010b).

Reliability of open and hidden unemployment statistics. The Economic Commission for Latin America and the Caribbean (ECLAC, 2000) estimated that "equivalent unemployment" (underutilization of the labor force,

Table 4.1 Open and Hidden Unemployment, 1989–2011 (percentage of labor force)

	Open	Hidden[a]	Total		Open
1989	7.9	7.9	15.8	1999	6.3
1990	7.3	10.3	17.6	2000	5.4
1991	7.7	19.0	26.7	2001	4.1
1992	6.1	24.2	31.7	2002	3.3
1993	6.2	34.0	40.2	2003	2.3
1994	6.7	32.5	39.2	2004	1.9
1995	7.9	32.1	40.0	2005	1.9
1996	7.6	26.6	34.2	2006	1.9
1997	7.0	25.7	32.7	2007	1.8
1998	6.6	25.1	31.7	2008	1.6
				2009	1.7
				2010	2.5
				2011	3.2

Sources: Mesa-Lago, 2010b, updated with ONE, 2011a, 2012a.
Note: a. "Equivalent" unemployment or underutilization of labor force estimated by ECLAC, 2000.

underemployment, or hidden unemployment) in Cuba rose from 7.9 percent to 34 percent between 1989 and 1993, and later fell to 25 percent in 1998, the last year for which ECLAC published such estimates. The official open unemployment rate in Cuba rose from 6.2 percent in 1993 to 7.9 percent in 1995, and later fell to 6.6 percent in 1998. Combining the two measures, total unemployment jumped from 15.8 percent in 1989 to 40 percent in 1995 and subsequently declined, but in 1998 it was 31.7 percent, higher than the 30.2 percent rate before the revolution (see Table 4.1). With the economic recovery in the second half of the 1990s, 435,000 jobs were created, absorbing some of the "available" workers (who had been retrenched when their workplaces closed down), and productivity improved, but in 1996 productivity was still 22 percentage points below the 1989 level. "This improvement in productivity is not a result of the full employment of the labor force, but rather [due to] the exploitation of human and technical capacities that were underutilized. . . . [T]he labor force that is potentially underemployed could be as high as 800,000 persons. . . . The excessive level of employment has resulted in expenditures that [are] unsustainable" (Togores, 1999).

Pavel Vidal Alejandro and Omar Everleny Pérez Villanueva (2010) argue that while the adjustment measures of the 1990s were inevitable, to prevent open unemployment from rising the government chose not to reduce employment levels and fiscal expenditures and not to close unprofitable state enterprises; instead it increased subsidies to state enterprises. The resulting deficit, which rose beyond 30 percent of gross domestic product (GDP), was financed by money creation, triggering a ninefold increase in prices and reducing salaries and real pensions by 70 percent. Wage earners and pensioners suffered the consequences of the fiscal deficit, the inflated payrolls of state enterprises undermined productivity growth, and thus began the vicious circle of low salaries and low productivity, which continues today and is extremely difficult to break.

In 2002, Fidel predicted that unemployment in Cuba would disappear and guaranteed jobs to all youth. The "Battle of Ideas" propelled the concept of higher education for all, which delayed the entry into the labor market of enrolled students (discussed later); the government also created "study as work" programs to absorb displaced workers as well as programs to train social workers, and encouraged workers to seek employment in urban agriculture. According to official figures, open unemployment fell steadily, from 7.9 percent in 1989 to 1.7 percent in 2009 (see Table 4.1), at the expense of increasing hidden unemployment. The open unemployment rate in 2009, at a time when Cuba was in the throes of a liquidity crisis, was the lowest in Latin America—where open unemployment averaged 8 percent (ECLAC, 2009a)—and was one of the lowest in the world.

The official open unemployment rate severely underestimated real unemployment because it considered the following categories of people as being employed: dismissed workers undertaking training, students receiving a payment even if they were not enrolled in schools, part-time farmers producing food for own consumption in their homes or in urban gardens, and so on. If the official statistics were adjusted to subtract these workers, the rate would climb significantly. Moreover, many unemployed people did not seek employment through municipal job-placement offices, because they did not want to be assigned to work in agriculture. Newspaper *Juventud Rebelde* questioned the official unemployment figures: "The data on unemployment are not real"; provinces such as Granma proclaimed "to have reached full employment"; if this were the case, "why do we see so many people in the streets not working?" A survey showed that the number of unemployed workers was eighteen times the official figure (37,000 versus 2,000), which "shot up the unemployment rate to 9 percent," and "if Granma was one of the examples of low unemployment, what would be the situation in other provinces that showed higher unemployment?" The director of employment at the Ministry of Labor and Social Security claimed that there were 210,797 working-age persons nationwide (4.3 percent of the economically active population) who had no interest or motivation to work (Ortiz et al., 2007). At the start of 2008, some 300,000 people were deemed "disconnected from work" (6 percent of the economically active population, versus the official rate of 1.6 percent); 20 percent of the working-age population in Havana did not work, 45 percent of whomwere seeking employment but were not interested in state jobs because of low salaries compared to the private sector; and 17 percent of 2007's technical school graduates had not claimed the jobs offered to them (ONE, 2008a, 2008c; *Granma,* March 9, 2008, March 21, 2008).

Adverse economic effects of the full employment policy. Pérez Villanueva (2008c) has explained how, in many instances, the full employment policy engendered underemployment; the jobs created were predominantly in the services sector, particularly social programs associated with the Battle of Ideas, whereas the share of employment in the productive sector (e.g., agriculture and manufacturing) actually declined. Pedro Monreal (2009) estimated that 30–40 percent of the employed Cuban labor force was unnecessary, while Anicia García and colleagues (2011) calculated the figure at 30–50 percent. A survey by Cuba's Center for Psychological and Sociological Research found that "employment has become the fifth—or even lower—preferred alternative of youth that were interviewed" (*Granma,* January 12, 2009). Jorge Sánchez-Egozcue and Juan Triana (2010) argued that hidden unemployment remained and questioned the feasibility of continuing to create jobs that lowered average labor productivity. Ariel Terrero (2010) recognized the magnitude of the problem and its perverse economic implications:

Unemployment [has not] been an option contemplated by the government to reduce costs during the crisis. But it has been costly. . . . Hidden unemployment prevents growth in worker productivity, [as the government pays] hundreds of thousands of workers who are not making a solid contribution to society and discourages industrious workers who see unproductive workers around them. . . . Inflated payrolls adversely affect the relationship between productivity and salaries and become . . . a barrier to raise salaries. . . . The state cannot continue to pursue the ambition of full employment at the expense of economic efficiency, as the national economy is not able to support it.

The dismissal plan, compensatory measures, and selection criteria. In his report to the National Assembly of People's Power (ANPP) at the close of 2009, then–minister of economy Marino Murillo (2009b) announced that productivity had declined by 1 percent because of "underemployment and inflated payrolls in the majority of the nation's enterprises." In April 2010, Raúl warned that inflated payrolls would increase the amount of currency in circulation and prices would rise: "Some analysts estimate that the number of redundant jobs exceeds 1 million persons. . . . Continuing to spend beyond our means would . . . put into question the very survival of the revolution" (R. Castro Ruz, 2010a). In July, Raúl revised the number of redundant state workers to 1.3 million and warned: "Without increases in efficiency and productivity, it will be impossible to raise salaries, increase exports and substitute imports, expand food production, and maintain our very high level of social expenditures" (R. Castro Ruz, 2010b). A communiqué issued in September by the country's labor confederation, the Workers' Central Union of Cuba (CTC), announced that 500,000 state workers would be dismissed between October 2010 and March 2011, and 1 million in total by the end of 2011 (*Granma,* September 13, 2010).[2]

The open unemployment rate for 2010 was first reported as 1.6 percent and later as 2.5 percent; it is not clear whether the higher rate reflected the dismissals in that year or an adjustment to reflect a more realistic assessment of the unemployment situation (ONE, 2011a, 2011c). Table 4.2 presents three alternative open unemployment rates for 2010 calculated based on different estimates of hidden unemployment: 12.3 percent based on 500,000 redundant workers, 22.1 percent based on 1 million, and 27.9 percent based on 1.3 million. The open unemployment rate increased to 3.2 percent in 2011 and to 3.8 percent in 2012 (ONE, 2012a; Martínez, 2012).

In April 2010, Raúl promised: "The Revolution will not leave anyone unprotected; it will fight to create the conditions so that all Cuban citizens will have dignified jobs. But the state cannot place each worker in a job after making several offers; instead the workers themselves should find their own jobs" (R. Castro Ruz, 2010a). To absorb the workers dismissed from the state sector, the plan was to create 465,000 private sector jobs (see

Table 4.2 Alternative Estimates of Hidden Unemployment, 2010

	Open Unemployment		+ 500,000 Redundant Workers		+ 1,000,000 Redundant Workers		+ 1,300,000 Redundant Workers	
	Thousands	%	Thousands	%	Thousands	%	Thousands	%
Labor Force	5,112	100.0	5,112	100.0	5,112	100.0	5,112	100.0
Employed	4,984	97.5	4,484	87.7	3,984	77.9	3,684	72.1
Unemployed	128	2.5	628	12.3	1,128	22.1	1,428	27.9

Sources: Authors' estimates based on ONE, 2011a, and official goals of Cuba's plan to dismiss redundant state workers.
Note: a. The original plan foresaw dismissal of 500,000 workers in March 2010, 1 million in December, and 1.3 million in 2014.

Chapter 5). Dismissed workers would receive their basic salary for one month and, if not reemployed within the month, an additional 60 percent of the basic salary for one to five months depending on how long they had been employed prior to dismissal (one month for 19 years, two months for 20–25 years, three months for 26–30 years, and a maximum of five months for over 31 years). For those unable to find employment who were the sole means of support for their families, the state would provide support through the social welfare system.

Vidal and Pérez Villanueva (2010) observed that the vast majority of state workers who are candidates for dismissal were hired in the 1990s, when the government postponed the needed adjustment. The current dilemma is similar to the one faced then, but the circumstances and constraints are different: there are no reserves to implement anti-inflationary policies, the impoverished population is incapable to again finance a high fiscal deficit with its meager salaries and pensions, the economy is besieged by low productivity and high unemployment, and unless this vicious circle is broken, sustained economic growth is untenable. Terrero (2010) has posited that the speed in implementation of retrenchment will be based on the answer to the following question: "Where will one million dismissed workers be placed?"

Employment in the state sector grew from 81.8 percent to 83.8 percent between 2006 and 2010, but decreased to 77.3 percent in 2011, while employment in the nonstate sector contracted from 18.2 percent to 16.2 percent and then expanded to 22.7 percent (see Table 4.3). Thus, the 500,000 workers to be dismissed would represent 12 percent of state sector employment in 2010, and the firing of 1 million workers would represent 24 percent.[3]

Table 4.3 Distribution of Employed Persons, by Sector, 2006–2011

	2006		2007		2008		2009		2010		2011	
	Thousands	%	Thousands	%	Thousands	%	Thousands	%	Thousands	%	Thousands	%
Total employed	4,755	100.0	4,868	100.0	4,948	100.0	5,072	100.0	4,984	100.0	5,010	100.0
State	3,889	81.8	4,036	82.9	4,112	83.1	4,249	83.8	4,178	83.8	3,873	77.3
Nonstate	866	18.2	832	17.1	836	16.9	823	16.2	806	16.2	1,137	22.7
Cooperatives	257	5.4	242	5.0	234	4.7	232	4.6	217	4.4	652	13.0
Private	609	12.8	590	12.1	602	12.2	591	11.6	589	11.8	485	9.7

Sources: Authors' estimates based on ONE, 2010a, 2011a, 2012a.

The secretary-general of the CTC, alluding to the many thousands of university graduates, stated that job offers would not necessarily have to match the qualifications of the applicants, and urged the labor movement to get behind the dismissal policies (*Granma,* September 13, 2010; *Trabajadores,* September 19, 2010, September 20, 2010). The selection of workers to be dismissed would be "strictly based on the principle of suitability" (*idoneidad*)—that is, qualifications, productivity, efficiency, meeting of production goals rather than tenure, and avoidance of any possible "favoritism of any form based on gender or any other criterion" (R. Castro Ruz, 2010b). Suitability was to be judged by a committee of experts, one member designated by management, one by the union, and three to five selected by assemblies of workers. The manager of the enterprise would convene the committee and propose which workers were to be evaluated; the final decision on which workers to dismiss would be made by top-level supervisors. The union would need to be vigilant to ensure that the norms were observed and the process was properly applied. Sources of new job opportunities identified included nonstate employment, self-employment, work in cooperatives (agriculture, food production, construction, transportation, services), as well as state employment in growth areas such as oil exploration, construction, biotechnology, pharmaceuticals, tourism, and export of services (*Proceso de reducción,* 2010; *Trabajadores,* June 11, 2010).

Causes for postponement of the dismissal plan. Initially scheduled to start in October 2010, the dismissal plan was delayed by three months and then rescheduled to begin in January 2011 and end by March 31, 2011. At the close of February, only 10 percent of the dismissal goals had been reached in the provinces of Camagüey, Granma, and Santiago de Cuba (*EFE,* March 1, 2011). Raúl warned that it was important to act cautiously, as implementation of such a complex plan could not be restricted by inflexible deadlines; the speed in the implementation would depend on the ability of the government to guarantee its success, and at least three to five years would be required, meaning 2011–2015 (*Granma,* February 1, 2011). In May 2011 a new timeline for the dismissals was approved, and a freeze on employment in state enterprises was imposed (*Granma,* May 17, 2011). The new plan called for dismissing 170,000 state workers and expanding nonstate employment by 240,000 workers in 2012 (Yzquierdo Rodríguez, 2011), representing 17 percent and 51 percent, respectively, of the goals originally set for 2011 (eliminating 1 million state jobs and creating 465,000 nonstate jobs).

The dismissal plan was postponed because of several reasons: the original plan was drafted in a rush and its implementation period was too short (six months for dismissing 500,000 workers and fourteen months for 1 million workers); the impossibility of generating 465,000 nonstate jobs to absorb dismissed workers, in part because of red tape, excessive regulations and taxes, and lack of credit and inputs (see Chapter 5); the lack of a technical study on the organization of state sector employment; opposition by managers of enterprises and by workers, the former concerned about having an adequate number of workers to meet plan goals, and the latter preoccupied by the loss of income due to dismissal and the meager compensation plan; conflicts among workers, who accused each other of poor labor performance or corruption to avoid dismissal; lack of confidence in the impartiality of the process and in the unions' defense of the interests of workers; concern that despite the promise that selection would be based on suitability, there would be discrimination against women, Afro-Cubans, and youth, who would be the first to be dismissed; and the possibility that the process would result in chaos, massive discontent, and social-political destabilization. Terrero stated: "the Ministry of Labor has not been sufficiently transparent with the dismissals. . . . We do not know if women have been affected more severely than men . . . [nor do we know] the ages of those dismissed" (Cuban TV, April 26, 2012).

Salary and Purchasing Power

Decline of real salaries. Real salaries in Cuba (adjusted for inflation) reached their lowest point in 1993, the trough of the economic crisis, at 90 percent below their level in 1989 (see Table 4.4 and Figure 4.1). Since then, nominal wages (not adjusted for inflation) have risen, but in 2011 real salary was still 73 percent below the 1989 level, roughly the same as in 1992.[4] It should be noted that inflation measures do not take into account transactions in convertible pesos (CUC), and therefore the inflation rate should have been higher and the fall in the real salary more pronounced. Vidal Alejandro (2008b, 2009) has posited that the rise in the fiscal deficit, inflation, and the monetary surplus could lead to situation like that of the 1990s, when there was "a very sharp reduction in real salaries" and workers "were forced to pay an inflation tax in order to finance the deficit."

In 2007, Raúl admitted that "salaries are clearly insufficient to satisfy needs" and had essentially ceased to play the role of ensuring the socialist principle of "from each according to his capacity and to each according to his work." He argued for a closer link between salaries and prices (R. Castro Ruz, 2007a). The increases in nominal wages after 2005 had pushed real salaries up by about 10 percentage points by 2011, but as mentioned they were still 73 percent below their 1989 level. Osvaldo Martínez (2007) advised that the issue of low salaries should be approached in a gradual and sustainable manner, setting aside spectacular and immediate solutions "that are based on ignorance, fraud, or deliberate confusion." Raúl added: "We would all like to move quickly, but we must act realistically" (R. Castro Ruz, 2008b). Should salaries increase too quickly, without underlying increases in production, the outcome would be escalating inflation and lower purchasing power (*Associated Press,* October 20, 2008).

Table 4.4 Average Real Salary and Pension, 1989–2011

	Inflation Rate (%)	Consumer Price Index (1989 = 100)	Average Salary per Month			Average Pension per Month		
			Nominal (current CUP)	Real (CUP 1989)	Real Index (1989 = 100)	Nominal (current CUP)	Real (CUP 1989)	Real Index (1989 = 100)
1989		100	188	188	100.0	56	56	100.0
1990	2.6	103	187	182	96.8	57	55	98.2
1991	91.5	196	185	94	50.0	85	43	76.8
1992	76.0	346	182	53	28.2	91	26	46.4
1993	183.0	978	182	19	10.1	92	9	16.1
1994	-8.5	895	185	21	11.2	93	10	17.8
1995	-11.5	792	194	24	12.7	95	12	23.2
1996	-4.9	754	202	27	14.4	96	13	23.2
1997	1.9	768	206	27	14.4	97	13	32.2
1998	2.9	790	207	26	13.8	98	12	21.4
1999	-2.9	767	222	29	15.4	103	13	23.2
2000	-2.3	750	238	32	17.0	105	14	25.0
2001	-1.4	739	252	34	18.1	107	14	25.0
2002	7.3	793	261	33	17.6	113	14	25.0
2003	-3.8	763	273	36	19.1	119	16	28.6
2004	2.9	785	284	36	19.1	121	15	26.7
2005	4.2	818	330	40	19.3	179	22	39.3
2006	5.5	863	387	45	23.9	192	22	39.3
2007	2.8	887	408	46	24.5	194	22	39.3
2008	-0.1	877	415	47	25.0	236	27	48.2
2009	-0.1	867	429	49	26.0	241	28	50.0
2010	1.4	879	448	51	27.1	245	28	50.0
2011	1.1	889	455	51	27.1	250	28	50.0

Sources: Data for the first four columns (inflation rate, consumer price index, and nominal and real average salary per month), through 2006, from Vidal Alejandro, 2007; all other data are authors' estimates based on CEE, 1991; ONE, 2007, 2008a, 2009, 2010a, 2011a, 2012a, 2012b.

Figure 4.1 Average Real Salary and Pension, 1989–2011

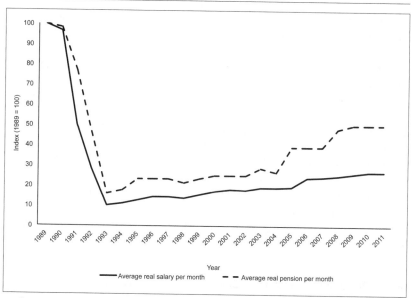

Sources: Authors' estimates based on CEE, 1991; ONE, 2007, 2008a, 2009, 2010a, 2011a, 2012a, 2012b.

In 2007, then–minister of economy José Luis Rodríguez (2007b) argued that nominal salaries had grown at a higher rate than labor productivity, "a negative tendency for the economy that must be definitively reversed." The relationship between average salary and labor productivity remained negative through 2009; according to official sources, the deterioration in this relationship stopped in 2010, and in 2011 productivity rose by 2.8 percent, slightly higher than the 2.7 percent increase in nominal salaries (Martínez, 2011a; Yzquierdo Rodríguez, 2011).[5]

Policies to raise salaries. The Cuban government took four measures in 2008 to increase salaries: it authorized payment of part of workers' salary in joint ventures or foreign enterprises in convertible pesos or in hard currencies; lifted the ban on multi-employment (*pluriempleo*), meaning that workers could hold more than one job and earn more than one salary, after they met all requirements of the main job; eliminated caps on salaries of production workers, thereby permitting those who worked more to earn more; and established payment based on performance, connecting the level of salaries with the level of effort expended by workers. These measures will be analyzed in Chapters 5 and 6.

Rationing, prices, and purchasing power. Nowhere else in the world has a rationing system been in place as long as in Cuba, since 1961. The two principal reasons for rationing have been poor domestic production of consumer goods and egalitarian policies that seek to guarantee minimum levels of consumption—even if insufficient—to all citizens. The scope of the rationing system has been progressively reduced by removing some items from the rationing card altogether and offering them for sale without restriction through the "parallel market" at much higher prices.[6] From 2005 to 2008, beef, root crops, and lard were removed from the rationing card, followed in 2009 by potatoes, chickpeas, instant cocoa, and cigarettes,[7] while the quota allocations of salt and beans were cut to half and one-fifth respectively of the previous quota levels; in 2010, hand and laundry soap, toothpaste, and detergent were removed, and the sugar quota was reduced from five to four pounds per month. In 2012, of about sixty products as shown in Table 4.5, only 17 percent were still being offered through the rationing system, with the remaining 83 percent offered through agricultural markets and at foreign-currency stores (TRDs).

Table 4.5 Rationing, Unrestricted Sales, and Prices in Havana, February 2012 (prices per pound unless otherwise specified)

Monthly rations per person (CUP)

Fish:[a] 0.70 lb[b] at 1.40	Sugar:[c] 3 lbs white and 1 lb brown at 0.10–0.15
Ground soy or chicken: ½ lb at 0.70	Powdered milk:[d] 4.4 lbs at 2.50
Rice: 5 lbs at 0.25, and another 2 lbs at 0.90	Evaporated milk: for children up to one year of age, 0.20 per can
Black beans: ½ lb at 1.20	Eggs: 5 eggs at 0.15 each, and another
Bread: 1 roll daily for 0.05	5 at 0.90 each
Cooking oil: ½ lb at 0.20	

Unrestricted (free) sale in agricultural markets (CUP)

Rice: 3.50–4.00	Beets: 3.00
Beans: 8.00–15.00	Eggplant: 2.50
Plantain: 2.00–3.0	Lettuce: 4.00
Sweet potato: 2.50	Bananas: 4.00
Yuca: 3.00	Orange: 1.43 per fruit
Malanga: 3.00–6.00	Lemon: 1.00 per fruit
Peas: 3.50	Pineapple: 15.00–20.00 per fruit
Corn flour: 10.00	Papaya: 12.00 per fruit
Pumpkin: 2.00–2.50	Guayaba: 3.00–5.00
Tomato: 4.00–10.00	Mango: 10.00 per pound or 5.00–15.00 per fruit
Onions: 7.00–10.00	Pork: 20.00–35.00
Garlic: 2.00–4.00 per bulb	Pork leg or loin: 40.00–45.00
Green peppers: 8.00	Liver: 23.00
Carrots: 3.00–12.00	Ribs: 20.00
Green beans: 3.00	Pigs' feet: 5.00
Cabbage: 2.00	Lard: 15.00

(continues)

Table 4.5 Cont.

Unrestricted (free) sale in TRDs (prices converted to CUP[e] from CUC prices shown in parentheses)

Ground beef: 2.50 CUP (60 CUC)	Cigarettes: 0.50–0.65 (12–16) per pack
Ground turkey or chicken: 1.25 (30)	Bath or laundry soap: 0.30–0.40 (7–10) per bar
Beef steak: 24.00 (576)	Toilet paper: 0.25 (6) per roll
Ham, sliced: 20.00 (480)	Toothpaste: 1.20–2.00 (29–48) per tube
Hake: 15.00–20.00 (360–480)[f]	Detergent: ½ lb for 0.50 (12)
Snapper: 6.60 (158)[f]	Deodorant: 1.00–2.00 (24–48) per stick
Rice: 4.40 (105)	Hand basin: from 40 (960)
Lard: 4.40–6.60 (105–158)	Toilet bowl: from 80 (1,920)
Grains: 1.75–2.00 (42–48)	Mattress: 100–200 (2,400–4,800)
Coffee: ½ lb at 3.45–3.75 (83–90)	Microwave oven: from 200 (4,800)
Sugar: 4.40 (105)	Gas stove: from 250 (6,000)
Cooking oil: 1 liter for 2.20–2.40 (53–58)	Television (Chinese): 250–350 (6,000–8,400)
Powdered milk: 2.40 (58)	Washing machine: 250–500 (6,000–12,000)
Hot dogs: 8 hot dogs for 1.25 (30)	Refrigerator: from 500 (12,000)
Domestic beer: 1.00 (24) per bottle	Gasoline: 1 liter for 1.20–1.70 (29–41)[g]

Sources: Rationing card, and information gathered by informants in Havana on February 24, 2012.
Notes: a. For several months in 2012, fish was not available and 11 ounces of chicken at 0.70 CUP was substituted.
   b. 1 pound = 0.454 kilogram.
   c. Sugar can also be purchased without restrictions at 8 CUP per pound for white and 5 CUP per pound for brown.
   d. The 4.4-pound ration is only available for children up to two years of age (from ages two to seven, the ration is 2.2 pounds at 1.25 CUP), for ill persons, and for people who require special diets.
   e. Conversion rate: 1 CUC = 24 CUP.
   f. Fish is sold at special stores, rather than at TRDs.
   g. Gasoline is sold at the state's Cubapetróleo (CUPET) stations, rather than at TRDs.

According to the government, price subsidies to consumer products amounted to US$900 million in 2010, and in 2011 the state subsidized 88 percent of the price of rationed foodstuffs (*La Vanguardia,* December 30, 2010; *Inter Press Service,* November 1, 2011). Former BCC president Francisco Soberón (2006) argued that since Cuban citizens with nonwage income—such as remittances—benefit from the rationing system in the same manner as do wage earners, this creates an ethically unacceptable and catastrophic situation for the national economy that is "leading us to the elimination of the rationing card." Raúl has also criticized the rationing system: "I am convinced that several problems that we face today have their roots in this distribution measure [which had a reason at the beginning of the revolution but not now] that represents an egalitarianism that benefits equally those who work as those who do not work or do not need such benefits, and enables barter and resale in underground markets" (R. Castro Ruz, 2010c). Those individuals who need help, Raúl said, would receive it through the social assistance system. In the future, "subsidies would not be granted to products, but rather to individuals who really need them" (social assistance is discussed in further detail later in this chapter; for discussion on measures to end the rationing system, see Chapter 5).

There is no reliable measure of inflation in Cuba. Based on statistics in Table 2.1, it can be estimated that prices rose by 16 percent between 2005 and 2011, or at an annual average rate of 2.2 percent. But recall that in the calculation of the consumer price index (CPI), transactions in convertible pesos are excluded. Moreover, fragmentary information suggests that increases in prices of most commodities over this period went beyond the average rate of 2.2 percent. Leaving aside rationed goods, whose share of total consumption has declined, prices of goods transacted in Cuban pesos (CUP) increased by more than eight and a half times between 1989 and 2006; in the latter year, interprovincial transportation fares rose threefold and electricity rates between 50 percent and 333 percent (Espinosa, 2007d). Prices in informal markets—agricultural and self-employed, legal and illegal—grew 4.3 percent between February 2007 and February 2008 (ONE, 2008e). According to ECLAC (2011b), out of nineteen products sold in agricultural markets during the 2006–2010 period, prices of thirteen rose; the unweighted average of all price changes over the period was 3.6 percent. Sales prices of all goods sold in agricultural markets were 11.8 percent higher in 2011 compared to a year earlier (ONE, 2012i).[8]

The retail price of gasoline rose by 69 percent in September 2008, but in December it fell by 28 percent; in September 2010, at the very time that the opposition parties in Venezuela won a third of the seats in the National Assembly, the price of gasoline rose by 18 percent. In February 2012, the price of gasoline ranged from 1.20 to 1.70 CUC per liter, depending on the grade, equivalent to US$4.80 to US$6.80 per gallon (*Reuters*, September 8, 2008, December 8, 2008; *Granma*, September 27, 2010; information gathered by informants in Havana, February 24, 2012). Residential electricity consumption rates rose between 15 percent and 284 percent in January 2010; this was followed by another increase of between 15 percent and 248 percent in January 2011; monthly electric bills fluctuated between 40 and 659 CUP (*La Jornada*, January 4, 2010; Espinosa, 2011c). Bus transportation fares in Havana doubled, from 0.20 CUP in the old "camellos" to 0.40 CUP in the new Chinese buses; interprovincial transportation fares jumped fourfold in 2007 and airline passenger transportation fares by up to 300 percent in that same year (Resolución 32, 2007; *Encuentro en la Red*, March 23, 2007). A collective taxi (*almendrón*) charges 10–15 CUP for a short ride, while a hard-currency taxi charges 2 CUC, equivalent to 48 CUP (information gathered by informants in Havana, February 24, 2012).

A study on the purchasing power of Cubans based on information available at the end of 2008 estimated the average number of days required by a household and by a worker to purchase a pound of different food items: for example, powdered milk, 4 household and 7.2 worker; butter, 3 and 5.3; pork ribs, 1.4 and 2.6; chicken meat, 1 and 2; potatoes, 0.6 and 1.1; and black beans, 0.4 and 0.7 (González-Corzo and Pérez, 2009).

Based on the average monthly salary of 448 CUP (US$18) in 2010, workers would have to labor for the following lengths of time to purchase the following items at TRDs: 1 month for a pound of ham or beef steak, 11 months for a microwave oven, 13 months for a gas stove, 13–19 months for a Chinese television set, and 27 months—over two years—for a small refrigerator (authors' calculations based on Table 4.5). Purchasing a gallon of gasoline in 2010 cost one-third of the average worker's monthly salary, and purchasing a one-way bus trip from Havana to Santiago de Cuba cost 39 percent of that average monthly salary.

These calculations show clearly that the average salary in the state sector is insufficient for workers to satisfy basic needs. Cubans have been able to make ends meet despite low and declining salaries, reductions to the rationing quotas at subsidized prices, and increases in prices of basic goods, because the majority of households have other sources of income: remittances, which reportedly are received by about 65 percent of households; lunches at workplaces and schools (the former were recently eliminated and the latter scaled back); payment of salaries in hard currency by foreign-invested enterprises; legal or under-the-table income earned by self-employed workers; and theft of state goods to sell or put to personal use (de la Fuente, 2011; Ritter, 2010). Moreover, most Cubans do not pay rent, and education and healthcare are free (although their quality has declined, as discussed later).

Inequality

The Cuban revolution mitigated the marked inequalities that existed in income, in access to education and health services, and between urban and rural areas. Egalitarianism prevailed during idealist cycles, when salary differentials were greatly reduced, while it declined in importance during pragmatist cycles. In 1989, Cuba was probably the most egalitarian country in Latin America, but at the cost of significantly reduced individual incentives, effort, and labor productivity and high absenteeism, with adverse impacts on production and services. Raúl urged citizens to prepare for a "realist" form of socialism, economically viable, that would eliminate excessive government subsidies to promote equality: "Socialism means social justice . . . equality of rights and of opportunities, not of income. . . . Equality is not egalitarianism" (R. Castro Ruz, 2008b). This section examines several forms of inequality that still remain and have been accentuated by the reforms, related to income, provinces, race, and gender.

Income. There are several sources of income: salaries paid by the state sector; partial salary payments in hard currencies; pension and social assistance transfer payments; nonstate sector income from cooperatives, private farmers, self-employed workers, and speculators in the black market; and remittances. The National Statistical Office (ONE) publishes statistics for state sector average salaries and average pensions only. In 2010, 52.6 percent of the population's total income was in the form of salaries, 12.5 percent in earnings of private farmers, 4.5 percent in earnings of nonagricultural private workers (e.g., self-employed), 3.5 percent in earnings of cooperatives (of which 2.5 percent came from basic units of cooperative production [UBPCs]), and 26.9 percent in other forms of income; this latter high figure probably includes remittances. The average monthly pension in 2010 was 245 CUP (US$10), equivalent to 54 percent of the average monthly state salary. The salary scale was narrow: the ratio of the highest monthly salary (550 CUP, in mining) to the lowest (366 CUP, in commerce, restaurants, and hotels) was 1.5 to 1. The situation changes if highly remunerated private activities are considered. For example, 589,000 private farmers earned 4.9 billion CUP, for an average monthly income of 700 CUP, roughly 1.56 times the average monthly state salary, while 147,000 self-employed workers earned 1.8 billion CUP, for an average of 1,023 CUP per month, or 2.28 times the average state monthly salary (based on ONE, 2011a, 2011d). Anicia García and colleagues (2011) show that average monthly income in the state sector in the period 1993–2009, at 1997 prices, was nearly stagnant, while it increased steadily in the cooperative and private sectors, so that by 2009 the latter was about 2.5 times higher than the former. In 2004, 15 percent of high-income earners received part of their pay in hard currency, another 21 percent received tips in hard currency, and 39 percent received remittances. According to Pérez Villanueva, 13 percent of the bank accounts in 2011 gathered 90 percent of total deposits, and some had balances of between 160,000 and 200,000 CUP (*Associated Press,* November 10, 2011).

The Cuban government does not publish statistics on income distribution and neither do ECLAC or the United Nations Development Programme (UNDP). It has been estimated that in 2000, the ratio of highest to lowest income was 375 to 1; the ratio between the income of a *paladar* owner and a pensioner receiving the smallest pension was 3,125 to 1, and the ratio between the incomes of a *paladar* owner and a teacher was 1,041 to 1 (Mesa-Lago, 2003). The Gini income inequality coefficient, estimated by foreign researchers based only on CUP, rose 64 percent between 1989 and 1999 (from 0.250 to 0.407); if CUC earnings and remittances were included, the coefficient would be even higher (Mesa-Lago, 2005b; Espina, 2008). Although recent figures have not been published, there is consensus that inequality has deepened and that it will rise as a result of structural reforms

(González-Corzo, 2009, 2010). Mayra Espina and Viviana Togores (2012) have noted that the upward mobility that tended to exist has been reversed by several factors: growing employment and income in the nonstate sector, the rising role of the market, a decline in income, an increase in poverty, and deterioration in the standard of living. Case studies of upward and downward mobility in the population show a perception of unfairness in the distribution of opportunities, and a general sense of being worse off today compared to the 1980s.

The tax reform of 1994 created a regressive system, although there were some improvements over time. In 2006, 64 percent of total fiscal revenue came from indirect taxes to sales of goods and services, which have a regressive effect, whereas only 36 percent was generated by direct taxes (income tax, profit tax), with progressive effects. In 2010 the percentages had changed to 51 percent and 49 percent respectively; still, only 2.3 percent of fiscal revenue came from personal income and 12.6 percent from profits (ONE, 2011a). A tax reform law approved in 2012 superseded the previous law and introduced additional elements of direct taxation (see Chapter 5).

Provinces. There are important differences across Cuba's provinces with respect to many economic and social development indicators (Íñiguez Rojas, 2006). Between 1999 and 2003, Human Development Index (HDI) scores for the City of Havana and two other provinces rose, while for others they fell. Provinces with high HDI scores were City of Havana, Cienfuegos, Havana province, Ciego de Ávila, and Matanzas; those with medium HDI scores were Sancti Spíritus, Villa Clara, Las Tunas, Pinar del Río, Isla de la Juventud, and Camagüey; those with low scores were Holguín, Granma, Santiago de Cuba, and Guantánamo. The score for City of Havana was 31 percent higher than for Granma on six indicators: infant mortality, maternal mortality, occupation, investment per capita, schooling, and average salary (Mesa-Lago and Pérez-López, 2005). In 2006, infant mortality ranged between 1.4 and 9.0 deaths per 1,000 live births across provinces, while maternal mortality ranged between 16.9 and 96.6 deaths per 100,000 live births; with respect to remittances in US dollars, City of Havana received forty-four times the amount received by Guantánamo (ONE, 2007; Sánchez-Egozcue, 2007). In 2011, the regional gap regarding infant mortality had narrowed to 3.9 to 7.9 deaths per 1,000 live births, and the gap with respect to maternal mortality to 11.9 to 85.5 deaths per 100,000 live births (ONE, 2012a).

Race. At the start of the revolution, Afro-Cubans were incorporated gradually into the mainstream economy and society in regard to universal free education and healthcare, full employment, homeownership, and access to beaches, hotels, and clubs that formerly were segregated, but important socioeconomic differences persisted between Afro-Cubans and white citizens: 36 percent of the economically active population of Afro-Cubans held jobs, versus 64 percent for whites; unemployment for Afro-Cubans was 3.0–3.3 percent, versus 2.9 percent for whites; participation of Afro-Cubans in managerial, administrative, and technical jobs was 4–5 percentage points below the average for whites; Afro-Cubans were underrepresented with regard to graduation from higher education institutions and self-employment compared to whites; and Afro-Cubans still experienced worse housing conditions compared to whites. These inequalities repeat themselves from generation to generation (Espina, 2010). In addition, Afro-Cubans remain overrepresented in jails and prostitution, and underrepresented on television, and still suffer derogatory stereotypes and racist jokes. At the beginning of the 1960s, the government proclaimed that discrimination had ended and that any remaining vestiges would be eliminated with time, and proscribed an open debate on race (de la Fuente, 2001). Afro-Cuban anthropologist María Faguaga (2008) lamented that in the past five decades there has been no institutional struggle against racism in Cuba and that authorities are not competent to eliminate the old exclusionary practices, such that "we continue to be victims and perpetrators of racism" (see also Morales, 2007).

Alejandro de la Fuente (2001, 2011) and Cuban researchers Rodrigo Espina Prieto and Pablo Rodríguez (2006) have shown that the reforms that began in the 1990s have expanded racial inequality because of four factors: access to foreign remittances, employment in tourism and joint ventures, demographics of poor neighborhoods, and reduction in state employment alongside expansion of nonstate employment. Because 86 percent of Cuban Americans are white and only 14 percent are nonwhite, remittances tend to go primarily to white households, 44 percent of which received remittances in 2000 compared with 23 percent of Afro-Cuban households. Although the educational achievement of Afro-Cubans is similar to that of whites,[9] they are underrepresented in jobs in the tourism industry, especially as managers and technicians, as well as in joint ventures with foreign investors; both of these sectors pay higher salaries (including a portion in hard currencies) compared to the rest of the economy. In 2005, 58 percent of whites in three provinces lived in neighborhoods with marginal housing, compared to 69 percent of mulattoes and 96 percent of blacks; only 9 percent of blacks lived in "residential" neighborhoods (with good-quality housing), despite the urban-reform law, because the severe shortage of housing has resulted in lack of residential mobility. Between 81 and 84 percent of Afro-Cubans hold state sector jobs, with Afro-Cubans tending to be overrepresented at the lower salary end, and only a small percentage of Afro-Cubans are self-employed, which tends to be higher-paying that state employment. In 2000,

34 percent of blacks were at the bottom of the income scale versus 27 percent for whites, while only 6 percent of blacks were at the top of the income scale compared with 11 percent for whites. These adverse conditions lead Afro-Cubans to speculation activities such as trafficking in the black market and even crime. The income gap will increase as state employment declines and is supplanted by private employment.

Positive developments in terms of racial equality include an increasing number of Cuban intellectuals, including Afro-Cubans, as well as of foreign scholars who study and denounce racial discrimination; the organization of Afro-Cubans into ethnic societies; the recognition of inequality by the National Union of Writers and Artists of Cuba (UNEAC);[10] higher representation of Afro-Cubans in the Central Committee of the Cuban Communist Party (PCC), among delegates to the First National Conference of the PCC (38 percent), and in the ANPP (35 percent); and some openness from officials to discuss the topic of race (de la Fuente, 2011; *Granma,* January 29, 2012). Two collections of essays recently published on the island address different aspects of discrimination (Dossier, 2009; Núñez et al., 2011).

Gender. Women's access to education, contraception, abortion (among the highest rate in the world; see Farber, 2011), and childcare facilities has improved. Nevertheless, Table 4.6 and Figure 4.2 show that Cuban women continue to trail men in all labor force indicators, with very few exceptions. In 2011, women represented 49.9 percent of the total population, but only 37.5 percent of total employment (versus 62.5 percent for men); the employment gap was narrower in the state sector, but it was still significant, with women holding 44 percent of jobs. Women represented only 15 percent of employment in the nonstate sector (16.5 percent in cooperatives and 24.5 percent in self-employment). In terms of employment by economic sector, participation by women ranged from 16.7 percent to 24.7 percent, except in services: 41.9 percent in commerce, restaurants, and hotels; and 51.6 percent in finance, insurance, and business services, as well as in community, social, and personal services. Although working women had higher educational achievement than working men (54.3 percent of working women had pursued higher education), they held only 34.4 percent of leadership positions and were a small minority within the ANPP and the Council of State (Espina, 2010; ONE, 2011a). Finally, women had a slightly higher unemployment rate than men, 3.5 percent versus 3 percent.

ONE's *Anuario Estadístico de Cuba* does not provide statistics on women's and men's salaries. However, female's wages are likely lower than male's since women concentrate in the state sector, where salaries are lower; in services, whose salaries are inferior than in other sectors (e.g., the average salary in commerce, restaurants, and hotels is 65 percent of the average salary in mining; ONE, 2012a); and in administrative jobs, rather

Table 4.6 Labor Force Differentials, by Gender, 2011 (percentage distribution)

Category	Women	Men
Total population	49.9	50.1
Total employment	37.5	62.5
State sector	44.0	56.0
Nonstate sector	15.0	85.0
Cooperatives	16.5	83.5
Self-employment	24.5	75.5
Employment by sector		
Agriculture	16.7	83.3
Mining	19.4	80.6
Manufacturing		
Electricity, gas, and water	24.7	75.3
Construction	16.8	83.2
Transportation	24.5	75.5
Commerce, restaurants, and hotels	41.9	58.1
Finance, insurance, and business services	51.6	48.4
Community, social, and personal services	51.6	48.4
Education level		
Higher	54.3	45.7
Type of job		
Leadership role	34.4	65.6
Unemployment rate[a]	3.5	3.0

Source: Authors' calculations based on ONE, 2012a.
Note: a. Percentage of economically active population.

than in leadership positions, which comparatively pay much higher salaries. Moreover, women's tenure is often interrupted by childrearing or by taking care of elder parents or sick relatives. The projected dismissals in state employment are likely to hit women disproportionately harder than they will men, and unless women are able to find employment in the private sector, their unemployment will rise and their salary gap compared with men's will widen. Analyzing the reemergence of the gender gap, sociologist Mayra Espina (2010) has observed that women are more broadly affected than men by poverty, particularly single mothers, heads of households, and those who dropped out of school.

Raúl recalled that during the First Congress of the PCC, held in 1975, a resolution regarding racial and gender discrimination was adopted, but "its implementation was left in limbo and not properly controlled; now we cannot afford back tracking" (R. Castro Ruz, 2010b). He recognized the importance of this issue at the Sixth Congress, in 2011, and called for higher representation by Afro-Cubans, women, and youth in leadership of the PCC and of the government. "Not to have resolved the problem of race in more than half a century is shameful" (R. Castro Ruz, 2011a). The First National

Figure 4.2 Labor Force Differentials, by Gender, 2011

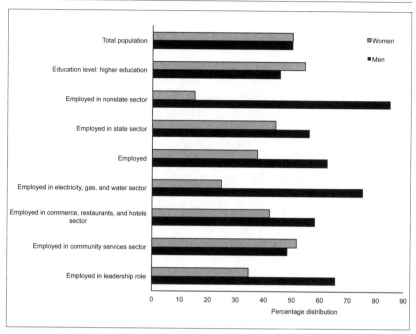

Source: Authors' calculations based on ONE, 2012a.

Conference of the PCC, in 2012, stipulated the elimination of discrimination based on race, gender, and religion, and the broader inclusion of members of these groups and of youth in society (PCC, 2012). Women's participation in the PCC's Central Committee rose; in 2012, women's participation in the First National Conference was 43 percent, and in the National Assembly it was 45.2 percent (R. Castro Ruz, 2011b; *Granma,* January 29, 2012, August 23, 2012).

Social Services

Rising Cost of Social Services

During the crisis of the 1990s, Cuba protected expenditures in education and public health despite contracting fiscal revenues, but the cost was born by the population at large through a large budget deficit and lower real wages and pensions (Vidal Alejandro, 2008b).[11] At the turn of the century, Carmelo Mesa-Lago (2000, 2005a) showed that social services were financially

unsustainable and recommended reforms to improve their resource allocation and efficiency and to reduce costs; these issues have recently been confirmed by Cuban academics and high-level government officials.

For example, the former minister of finance said in 2007: "To maintain
high levels of social justice, the nation requires more production of goods
and services produced with greater efficiency and quality, including social
services. . . . [T]o accomplish this it is essential to apply measures to eliminate waste and increase controls" (Barreiro, 2007). Espina (2008) identified the following weaknesses: excessive emphasis on social expenditures,
irrational allocation of resources, massive increase in higher education enrollment, unsustainability of social policies, excessive administrative centralization, and universal distribution of free social services without regard
to the income of recipients. Raúl asserted: "Expenditures in the social
sphere should be in accord with real possibilities and [we have to] eliminate
those that we can do without. . . . [E]xpenditures on public health and education are unsustainable and they must be trimmed" (R. Castro Ruz, 2009b).

Raúl's measures have reduced somewhat the share of social services in
total expenditures, which had increased steadily through 2007. Social expenditures as a percentage of the state budget fell from 55.3 percent to 53.1
percent between 2007 and 2010, and as a percentage of GDP they peaked at
36.4 percent in 2009 and fell to 34 percent in 2010 (see Table 4.7). In 2008,
Cuba's share of social expenditures within its state budget, 58 percent, was
sixth in Latin America, behind Argentina (58.8 percent), Chile (66.3 percent), Colombia (70.9 percent), Uruguay (73.4 percent), and Brazil (80.5
percent) (ECLAC, 2010c; ONE 2012a).[12]

In absolute terms (million CUP), social expenditures peaked in 2009;
expenditures for education, housing, and social assistance peaked in 2008,

**Table 4.7 Expenditures on Social Services as a Percentage of the
State Budget and of GDP, 2007–2010 (at current prices)**

	Spending as Percentage of State Budget			Spending as Percentage of GDP		
	2007	2009	2010	2007	2009	2010
Education	20.2	19.5	20.1	12.1	13.2	12.9
Public health	16.5	16.8	15.2	9.9	11.3	9.7
Social security pensions	10.6	11.4	11.9	6.4	7.6	7.6
Housing	4.6	4.1	4.2	2.8	2.8	2.7
Social assistance	3.4	2.2	1.7	2.0	1.5	1.1
Total	55.3	54.0	53.1	33.2	36.4	34.0

Source: Authors' calculations based on ONE, 2011a. As of the end of November 2012,
ONE's 2011 *Anuario* had not published budget data for 2011.

and for public health in 2010, while expenditures in social security continued to rise in the latter year (ONE, 2011a). In view of the aging of the population, the two areas with the largest potential for expansion are pensions and public health (in that order), and social assistance expenditures should also increase in light of the reforms.

Education

General indicators. The illiteracy rate in Cuba was 2.7 percent in 2010, the second lowest in the region (ECLAC, 2011d). The net enrollment rate in primary education (ages six to eleven) was 99.4 percent in 2005–2006 and 99.3 percent in 2009–2010, while it rose from 85.6 percent to 90.2 percent in secondary education (ages twelve to seventeen) and fell from 65.4 percent to 52.1 percent in higher education (ages eighteen to twenty-four) over the same period. Cuba ranked fifth in the region in 2009 on gross enrollment in primary education, fourth on secondary education, and first on tertiary education (ONE, 2011a; ECLAC, 2010c, 2011b; UNESCO, 2011). As a result of the decline in the birth rate and of the aging of the population (discussed below), there has been a decline in enrollment in primary education since the 2000–2001 school year and in secondary education since 2004–2005; enrollment in higher education has also dwindled, since 2007–2008, on the heels of an enormous rise in enrollment in 2005–2007 (ONE, 2008a, 2012a). It is projected that by 2025, enrollment in primary education will fall by 20–69 percent, in secondary education by 59–76 percent, and in tertiary education by 34–65 percent (based on ONE, 2008b).

The explosion in enrollment in higher education and its effects. As part of the Battle of Ideas, there was a huge rise in enrollment in higher education. In 2003–2004, the number of university-level institutions grew from 17 national universities to 732 in municipalities (later rising to 3,150); 44,000 new professors were hired (an increase of 83 percent); and 300,000 graduates per annum were projected. Half of the new students consisted of distance learners in disciplines such as sociocultural studies and social work, as well as retirees enrolled in adult education courses. Questions were raised about the rapid increase in the number of municipal universities, the qualifications of instructors and students, and the capacity of the nation to employ such a large number of university graduates (Mesa-Lago, 2005b).

University enrollment jumped by 207 percent between the 1989–1990 and 2007–2008 school years. As Table 4.8 shows, however, the bulk of the new enrollment was in the humanities and social sciences (27.7 percent of total enrollment in 2007–2008, an increase of 3,943 percent during the

Table 4.8 University Enrollment by Discipline, 1989–1990, 2007–2008, and 2011–2012 (number of students)

	School Year			Percentage of Total		Change Between 1989–1990 and 2007–2008 (%)	Change Between 2007–2008 and 2011–2012 (%)
	1989–1990	2007–2008	2011–2012	2007–2008	2011–2012		
Humanities and social sciences	5,095	205,992	77,243	27.7	22.0	3,943	-62
Medicine	37,305	187,690	118,914[a]	25.2	33.9	403	-37
Pedagogy	115,529	125,095	43,700[a]	16.8	12.4	8	-65
Economics	18,789	93,162	36,121	12.5	10.3	396	-61
Physical education	14,052	67,578	23,792	9.1	6.8	381	-65
Technical sciences	29,819	42,741	36,100	5.8	10.3	43	-16
Agronomy	11,606	16,034	9,378	2.2	2.6	38	-42
Natural sciences, mathematics	6,399	3,922	4,500	0.5	1.3	-39	14
Art and others	2,863	1,765	1,368	0.2	0.4	-38	-22
Total	241,453	743,979	351,116	100.0	100.0	207	-53

Sources: Authors' calculations based on CEE, 1991; ONE 2011a, 2012a.
Notes: Disciplines are listed by size of enrollment in 2007–2008.
a. The *Anuario* must have inverted the enrollment numbers for medicine and pedagogy for the 2011–2012 school year. The table corrects the inversion.

period), medicine (25.2 percent and 403 percent), economics (12.5 percent and 396 percent), and physical education (9.1 percent and 381 percent); 16.8 percent of students were enrolled in education (pedagogy) in 2007–2008, but this represented an increase of 8 percent over 1989–1990. These five disciplines together accounted for 91 percent of total enrollment in 2007–2008, and a growth of 256 percent over the period.[13] The growth in enrollment in medicine can be attributed to the profitable export of Cuban health professionals, particularly to Venezuela, since 2002. In contrast, enrollment in agronomy only rose by 38 percent and in technical sciences by 43 percent, while enrollment in natural sciences and mathematics fell by 39 percent.[14] The huge investment in the aforementioned five disciplines (particularly the humanities and social sciences, and physical education) stands in stark contrast with the deficit in disciplines that are key to development (the natural sciences and mathematics, and agronomy) and suggests an important misallocation of scarce resources with negative repercussions for the future. Moreover, the enrollment of skilled workers in technical-vocational schools in 2008–2009 was 65 percent lower than in 1988–1989, particularly in the fields of energy, transportation, and construction (A. García et al., 2011).

Although there were 195,988 pedagogy graduates in 2002, and 125,095 students were enrolled in this discipline in 2007–2008, new minister of education, Elsa Velázquez, reported in 2008 that there was a shortage of 8,192 teachers in Havana, as many teachers had left the profession because of low salary (*EFE,* July 8, 2007). This forced the creation of a program of "emerging" primary school teachers, whereby 4,500 youth from the interior of the country were moved to Havana and given an eight-month tutored course to prepare them to be primary education teachers—sometimes the tutors themselves were "emerging" teachers (*Juventud Rebelde,* June 5, 2007, August 5, 2007; *Granma,* October 24, 2007).[15] Minister of Higher Education Miguel Díaz-Canel reported that a high percentage of students enrolled in municipal universities who took exams in May 2009 had serious deficiencies in spelling (*Granma,* July 22, 2009). Many physicians also left their profession and shifted to other occupations in search of higher salaries, and hence lost the return on the costly investment in their training. The high number of social-worker graduates (16,595 in 2005–2008) made it difficult to find employment for them; instead they were assigned to work at retail gas stations to oversee sales and prevent fraud (without success). Rather than the expected 300,000 higher education graduates initially projected for 2007–2008, only 71,745 students graduated, or 9.6 percent of enrolled students (ONE, 2009).

Raúl (2008b) asked the ANPP how many agronomists had been trained during the revolution; he was informed that 31,000, or roughly 534 per year, had graduated, but that only 20 percent were working in agriculture. A deficit of some 3,000 agronomists was reported by the Cuban press, as new graduates rejected job offers in agriculture because of low salaries, which contributed to the poor agricultural performance (*Trabajadores,* November 10, 2008; *Bohemia,* December 12, 2008). Former minister of higher education Juan Vela stated that "there are certain specialties for which we do not have sufficient skilled personnel . . . critical to the scientific development of the country" (*EFE,* July 17, 2008).

Measures to confront the challenges. In 2008, serious problems were identified in the educational system and in the emerging teachers program in particular, which led to the replacement of Minister of Education Luis Ignacio Gómez, who had held the position for eighteen years. In July, Raúl encouraged retired teachers to return to the classroom; Decree-Law no. 260 of 2008 allowed retired teachers to receive teacher salaries in addition to continuing to draw their pensions; according to press reports, some 9,900 retired teachers took this option in 2010 (*EFE,* September 17, 2010). In 2009, salaries of teachers and professors were raised. Enhanced training for primary and secondary school teachers was offered, and teachers were also encouraged to take specialized courses and pursue master's and doctorate degrees (Correa, 2011). Raúl has done away with several programs created under the Battle of Ideas and during previous idealist cycles: the student work brigades, the social-work university brigades, and the "pioneer action forces."[16] The education budget was cut by 4 percent between 2008 and 2010, and the number of municipal universities was reduced by 96 percent in 2010–2011 (from 3,150 to 119), as was the number of pre-university schools in the countryside (by 77 percent) and the number of rural basic secondary schools (by 45 percent). Eliminated were secondary adult peasant-worker schools, social-worker schools, integral education programs for youth, and retiree programs in popular universities (ONE, 2011a). Quotas were set for university enrollment, and high school graduates were required to pass tougher entrance examinations for municipal universities that tested for proficiency in mathematics, spelling, and history (*Granma,* July 22, 2009).

These measures have somewhat improved the balance in university enrollment by discipline. Overall enrollment fell by 53 percent between 2007–2008 and 2011–2012, but with differences across disciplines (see Table 4.8): from –61 percent to –65 percent in humanities and social sciences, physical education, pedagogy, and economics; –42 percent in agronomy; –37 percent in medicine; –22 percent in art; and –16 percent in technical sciences (the lowest reduction); enrollment in natural sciences and mathematics rose by 14 percent, the only discipline for which enrollment increased. The distribution of higher education enrollment in 2011–2012 was as follows: 33.9 percent in medicine, now the largest discipline in terms of enrollment, and justified on the basis of revenues earned abroad by

Cuban physicians; 22 percent in humanities and social sciences (probably still too high from an economic development perspective); 12.4 percent in pedagogy; 10.3 percent each in economics and technical sciences; 6.8 percent in physical education (probably too high as well); 2.6 percent in agronomy; and 1.3 percent in natural sciences and mathematics. In 2011–2012, enrollment in these last two disciplines combined was 23 percent below that in 2007–2008.

In 2011, Cuba had one of the most highly skilled labor forces in Latin America: 52 percent of the work force had attained mid-level technician skills and 19 percent held a university degree (ONE, 2012a). But a significant share of the skilled labor force were not employed in the field of their training and instead worked in more lucrative jobs that did not make use of their skills, for example as waiters in hotels and tourist restaurants, and as taxi drivers, thereby wasting the investment made in their education. As Jorge Máttar, deputy director of ECLAC's office in Mexico, said: "Cuba must be the country in Latin America with the highest underemployment rate; it has a very educated population—technicians, professionals—who are not well utilized [because they are] doing other types of jobs" (*Agence France-Press*, April 7, 2007). The idealist program of the Battle of Ideas, aimed at enrolling the maximum number of university students and technicians, failed not only because quality was sacrificed for quantity, but also because there were no productive jobs for those who graduated, thus wasting much of the investment in this program.

Public Health

There are three health systems on the island: one available to the population at large; a separate scheme for the leadership of the government, the PCC, and the armed forces, which offers higher-quality care than the general program; and a high-quality scheme available only to foreigners who pay in hard currency.[17] In 2007, US filmmaker Michael Moore, in his documentary *Sicko,* brought a number of ill Americans to a hospital in Havana, which admitted them solely upon providing their names and birth dates. Moore asked the hospital's director to provide the Americans with exactly the same care offered to Cuban citizens. Contrary to the hospital director's statement in the movie (and Moore's portrait) that all Cubans receive the same quality of care, the foreigners were treated on a floor in the best Cuban hospital reserved for foreigners who pay in hard currency and receive excellent quality healthcare, much better than that provided to Cubans.

General health indicators. Infant mortality is one of the health indicators that improved during the economic crisis of the 1990s, falling by 55 percent between 1989 and 2011 (from 11.1 to 4.9 deaths per 1,000 live births; see

Table 4.9), the lowest rate in the hemisphere after Canada.[18] As infant mortality reaches low levels, incremental reductions become more difficult and costly; all pregnant women are given a monthly sonogram and other tests to determine the health of the fetus, and if congenital abnormalities are identified, an abortion is recommended, a practice that contributes to reducing the infant mortality rate (Hirschfeld, 2007). Cuba's rate of induced abortions—the highest in the region—rose between 2005 and 2010 as follows: from 19.1 percent to 22.3 percent per 1,000 women aged twelve to forty-nine years; from 51.5 percent to 55.7 percent per 100 childbirths (more than 50 percent of childbirths ended as abortions); and from 33.8 percent to 35.6 percent per 100 pregnancies (MINSAP, 2011).

Maternal mortality rose from 29.2 to 49.4 deaths per 100,000 live births between 1989 and 2006, declined to 31.1 in 2007,[19] and rose to 40.6 in 2011, 39 percent higher than in 1989. In 2008, Cuba's maternal mortality rate (46.5) was the fourth lowest in the region, higher than in Chile and Costa Rica (18.2) and Argentina (43.7) (ECLAC, 2010c). Most of the maternal deaths in Cuba occur during childbirth or in the subsequent forty-eight hours due to uterine hemorrhages or postpartum infections (Garrett, 2010). Complications arising from abortions and their after effects increase the maternal mortality rate, which in part explains the discrepancy between the falling infant mortality rate and the rising maternal mortality rate. Cervical cancer, the fourth largest cause of death for females in Cuba, doubled between 1985 and 2009, even though it is detectable with an annual pap test. Between 1999 and 2010, this test, with reexamination after three years, reduced deaths due to cervical cancer from 257 to 197 per 1,000 women aged twenty-five years or older; through 1996, examinations were provided to women older than twenty years, with reexamination after two years (Garrett, 2010; MINSAP, 2011).

Life expectancy rose from 74.5 years in 1989 to 79.1 years in 2007 (maintained through 2011; see Table 4.9), the second highest in Latin America (ECLAC, 2011d). The overall mortality rate increased by 20 percent between 1989 and 2011, from 6.4 to 7.7 deaths per 1,000 inhabitants, in large part because of the overall aging of the population. Cuba's mortality rate, the second highest in the region (ECLAC, 2011d), will continue to rise because of demographic trends. The high mortality rate and the rise in life expectancy combine to put pressure on the public health system and increase costs associated with complex terminal illnesses. In 2011, the top two causes of death in Cuba (accounting for 60 percent of deaths) were heart illnesses and malignant tumors (ONE, 2012a).

The ratio of physicians per 10,000 inhabitants more than doubled between 1989 and 2011, from 33.1 to 69.8 (see Table 4.9), the highest in the region (ECLAC, 2011d). Nevertheless, in 2011, between 18,000 and 37,000 physicians (22 percent to 47 percent of the total stock of 78,622 physicians)

Table 4.9 Public Health Indicators, 1989 and 2005–2011

	1989	2005	2006	2007	2008	2009	2010	2011	Change Between 1989 and 2011 (%)
Infant mortality[a]	11.1	6.2	5.3	5.3	4.7	4.8	4.5	4.9	-55
Maternal mortality[b]	29.2	51.4	49.4	31.1[f]	46.5	46.9	43.1	40.6	39
General mortality[c]	6.4	7.5	7.2	7.3	7.7	7.7	8.1	7.7	20
Life expectancy[d]	74.5	77.0		78.0			78.3	79.1	6
Physicians[e]	33.1	62.8	63.6	64.0	66.3	66.6	68.0	69.8	110
Healthcare beds[e]	6.0	4.9	4.9	4.8	4.6	4.6	4.6	4.0	-33

Sources: Authors' calculations based on CEE, 1991; ONE, 2009, 2010a, 2011a, 2012a, 2012b.
Notes: Empty cells indicate that data are not available.
a. Per 1,000 live births.
b. Per 100,000 live births.
c. Per 1,000 inhabitants.
d. Years at birth.
e. Per 10,000 inhabitants.
f. The maternal mortality rate for 2007 would be 41.7 if corrected to account for understatement due to publication of a new statistical series beginning in 2006.

were working abroad, primarily in Venezuela,[20] plus an unknown number of physicians on the island were not practicing their career because of the low salary received (the director of a hospital earned 550–700 CUP per month, equivalent to US$23–29). Subtracting the number of physicians working abroad reduces the ratio of physicians per 10,000 inhabitants to 37–54 in 2011, between 4 percent to 21 percent higher than in 1989, but the ratio would be lower if the physicians who have abandoned their career were accounted for. The exodus of physicians has provoked a reduction in access to primary healthcare in Cuba, and long waiting lists for treatment by specialists and for surgery. In 2011, the number of family doctors fell by 63 percent; those who continue to practice must service the same previous number of patients (*Reuters,* April 8, 2008; ONE, 2012a). The 20 percent decrease in university enrollment in medicine in the 2011–2012 school year compared to the previous school year is likely to aggravate these problems. The number of dentists doubled between 1989 and 2011, but the ratio per 10,000 inhabitants was 11.4 in 2011, one-sixth of the ratio for physicians (ONE, 2012a). A team that visited twenty-two dental clinics in 2007 found that the majority of them did not have trained personnel and half lacked dentistry chairs, dentistry materials, and adequate water supply (*Juventud Rebelde,* October 28, 2007; *Agence France-Press,* December 6, 2007).

The number of healthcare beds per 1,000 inhabitants fell by 33 percent between 1989 and 2011, from 6 to 4 (see Table 4.9), while the number of "real" healthcare beds (those actually used) fell from 5.4 to 3.7, still the highest in the region (CEE, 1991; ONE, 2012a; ECLAC, 2011d). In January 2010, the Ministry of Public Health announced that twenty-six patients in the Mazorra psychiatric hospital had died from cold and malnourishment; fifteen hospital employees were accused of selling blankets and food intended for the use of patients and were subjected to a trial, at which sentences of six to twelve years were sought (*El Nuevo Herald,* January 29, 2010). Hospital patients commonly have to bring their own sheets, pillows, blankets, towels, soap, medicines, food, glasses, cutlery, buckets, and light bulbs. Although some hospitals have been remodeled, they generally are severely deteriorated, much of the equipment is obsolete or not in operating condition, and there is a severe shortage of medical utensils, materials for tests, and essentials for surgery, such as suture thread. Foreign medical teams who travel to Cuba to provide free services bring with them all equipment and materials for their own use and that of their patients. Cuban physicians are well trained but have few means to treat patients; there is a severe shortage of medicines, which are mostly sold at high prices in the TRDs (Garrett, 2010; *El País,* January 31, 2011).

Potable water and sewerage systems. In 2010, 94.5 percent of the Cuban population had access to potable water, the fifth highest access rate in the region (MINSAP, 2011; ECLAC, 2011d).[21] Most of the water and sewerage systems are 50 to 100 years old and are severely deteriorated because of lack of maintenance. According to the president of the National Institute of Hydraulic Resources, 80 percent of the potable water distribution system is in poor or average condition, as investments in water lines, pumping stations, and filtration plants have not been made for many years (*Bohemia,* September 11, 2007). *Granma* has reported that the most serious problems are in Santiago de Cuba and Havana; in the former, running water is not available for days at a time, while in several municipalities of the latter, running water is only available for three to four hours a day.[22] As a result of breaks in pipes, 50 percent of pumped water is wasted and more is lost within homes because of the poor condition of faucets, toilets, shower heads, and other fixtures (low rates of water flow and high repair costs are disincentives to fix leaky plumbing). Fixing an individual break in the underground water lines often increases pressure and provokes another break elsewhere; rehabilitation of the overall network is needed (there are some 2,500 kilometers of water pipes underground in the city of Havana alone), a task that would take ten to fifteen years (Arias and Pérez, 2010). Droughts have worsened the water distribution problem: in 2011, Havana had a deficit of 519,307 cubic meters of water per day, half of the population did not have running water, and 100,000 persons were supplied via tank trucks (*Granma,* January 21, 2011, April 12, 2011).

Serious deterioration has also occurred in the sewerage and wastewater treatment systems. In the 1990s, wastewaters were adequately treated, but the capacity to do so has been reduced, with only two plants operating in Havana as of 2012. Other wastewater treatment plants exist only in tourism areas such as Varadero; storm-sewer inlets are clogged and inoperable because of lack of maintenance (*Opciones,* January 2008). Garbage piles up in the streets due to lack of trucks to collect it (collection is mostly done by animal traction) and dumpers to deposit it; previously, solid waste was buried using bulldozers, but many of these have broken and now it is mainly done by hand in locations where rats and other insects proliferate and create health risks (*Granma,* January 9, 2010; *Bohemia,* August 23, 2012).

Morbidity. A number of communicable diseases, such as diphtheria, paratyphoid fever, poliomyelitis, measles, and pertussis, have been eradicated from Cuba. Table 4.10 shows morbidity rates for eight diseases from 1989 to 2011; such rates declined for five (viral hepatitis, gonorrhea, syphilis, acute diarrhea, and chicken pox) and rose for three (tuberculosis, acute respiratory diseases, and food poisoning). Even for those diseases for which the morbidity rate rose, Cuba's rates were among the lowest in the region. A public health risk is the decline in immunization of the population from 1989 to 2011, particularly the application of triple drug therapy (e.g., diphtheria,

Table 4.10 Morbidity and Immunized Population, by Type of Vaccine, 1989 and 2005–2011

	1989	2005	2011	Change Between 1989 and 2005 (%)	Change Between 1989 and 2011 (%)	Change Between 2005 and 2011 (%)
Morbidity (rate × 100,000 population)						
Acute respiratory diseases	36,804	42,081	53,650	14	45	35
Acute diarrheal diseases	8,842	7,794	5,830	-12	-34	-25
Chicken pox	365	225	282	-38	-22	25
Food poisoning	87[a]	124	209	42	140	68
Gonorrhea	381	64	46	-83	-88	-28
Syphilis	82	17	15	-79	-82	-12
Viral hepatitis	106	207	8	95	-92	-96
Tuberculosis	5	6	7	20	40	17
Immunized population (thousands)						
Double (DT)	157	137[b]	141	-13	-10	3
Triple (DPT)	354	211[b]	136	-40	-62	-36
Tuberculosis (BCG)	320	135b	131	-58	-59	-3

Sources: Authors' calculations based on CEE, 1991; ONE, 2007, 2012a.
Notes: Diseases are listed from highest to lowest morbidity in 2011. DT = diphtheria and tetanus; DPT = diphtheria, pertussis, and tetanus; BCG = *Bacille Calmette-Guérin.*
a. 2002.
b. 2003.

pertussis, and tetanus) and antituberculosis vaccines, although there was significant immunization improvement in 2011.

There is no information on dengue-related morbidity, although annual outbreaks of the virus were reported in 2006 and 2011, including the hemorrhagic strain, which causes high mortality. Municipal governments run periodic fumigation campaigns to eradicate the mosquito that transmits it (*Granma,* July 25, 2007, July 17, 2009, January 4, 2012; Ministry of Public Health, October 10, 2008). In 2011, 467 cases of AIDS were reported, a rate of 42 per 100,000 inhabitants, the lowest in the region but fifteen times the rate in 2005 (ONE, 2011a, 2012a). In July and November 2012, serious cholera outbreaks were reported in Manzanillo and Santiago de Cuba (*Granma,* July 3, 2012; *Miami Herald,* December 9, 2012). In addition, 11,200 persons were infected with HIV in 2011, of which 4,500 showed symptoms of illness; AIDS patients are treated in special facilities for eighteen to twenty-four months; in the summer of 2011, a government campaign attempted to detect the illness through tests conducted at beaches and recreational facilities (*El País,* January 31, 2011; *EFE,* July 11, 2011). The suicide rate was essentially unchanged between 2003 and 2009, decreasing only slightly, from 13.4 and 13.1 per 100,000 inhabitants; in 2009, Cuba's suicide rate was the highest in the region after Uruguay (OPS, 2010); the highest incidences are among the elderly, housewives, and unemployed youth (García Méndez, 2011).

Inefficiency of the public health system. Deficiencies in Cuba's public health system have forced those needing services to pursue two alternatives: bribing physicians, paramedics, and administrative personnel in order to gain faster access to specialists, surgery, hospitals, and tests; or using influence and connections (*sociolismo*) for the same purpose. The theft of medicines and other medical supplies and their sale on the black market is widespread; many state employees run medical practices under-the-table, charging in hard currency while using public equipment and facilities (Molina, 2005; Hirschfeld, 2007).

The irrational allocation of public health resources is illustrated by the continuing focus on the reduction of Cuba's infant mortality rate, already the second lowest in the hemisphere, while neglecting the potable water and sewerage infrastructure. The average occupancy rate of hospital beds fell from 83.9 percent in 1989 to 66.4 percent in 2010, and in gynecology and pediatric hospitals it hovered around 50 percent (CEE, 1991; MINSAP, 2011).[23] In March 2010, an audit of warehouses of medical supplies in the province of Villa Clara found hundreds of expired or nearly expired medicines. In May, First Vice President Machado Ventura denounced the theft of food intended for hospital patients, the purchase of useless equipment, the waste of investment in unusable structures, the sale by hospitals of construction materials intended for repairs, and the construction of an expensive new surgery wing in the Calixto García hospital, which has a leaky roof. Machado stated that half of the population was dissatisfied with the quality of public health services and encouraged physicians to avoid excessive tests and unnecessary prescriptions (*BBC Mundo,* May 6, 2010; *La Jornada,* October 6, 2010). The official press has discussed other instances of "irrationality": twenty-five maternal-care homes that have only three to five beds but twenty employees each (medical, nursing, kitchen, security, housekeeping), and are located nearby larger institutions that could offer the same services; nineteen medical transportation bases that have only one ambulance but thirty employees each; and a fully equipped polyclinic in San José de las Lajas staffed by seventy-five professionals who treat only fifteen patients per week (*El País,* June 13, 2011).

In 2010–2011 there were 27,062 foreign scholarship students enrolled in health careers in Cuban universities, 27 percent more than in 2006–2007 (ONE, 2012a). Cuba deploys—without repayment—public health personnel to poor countries where natural catastrophes have occurred, for example Haiti, but 45,174 Venezuelans also received free medical care in Cuba in 2003–2010, and more than 24,000 Venezuelans studied medicine on the island.[24] In 2004, Cuba and Venezuela established the "Misión Milagro" to provide free ophthalmology services to needy patients in Venezuela; by 2008 the program had been expanded to twenty-eight countries, with costs shared by Cuba and Venezuela; 1.5 million patients had been treated through 2009 (Pérez-López, 2009; Free Society Project, 2010; Romero, 2011). Meanwhile, there is a waiting list of several months to undergo cataract surgery in Cuba, and eye lenses are frequently unavailable. At a Communist Youth meeting at a hospital in Havana in 2007, participants asked how it was possible that there were no resources to treat Cuban patients when thousands of Cuban medical personnel were working abroad and generating substantial resources. Machado Ventura reiterated the need to use public health resources more efficiently, citing the expenses associated with foreign assistance in public health and stressing that the first priority should be to address the Cuba's domestic needs (*BBC Mundo,* September 25, 2007, May 6, 2010).

Measures to reduce costs. The health budget was cut 11 percent in 2010 and 7 percent in 2011; the number of hospitals decreased by 19 percent between 2005 and 2011 (mainly rural and infant-maternity facilities); the number of family doctor offices shrank by 18 percent and the number of maternal homes by half over the same period; health centers have been shut down; high-technology diagnosis and laboratory tests, when deemed unnecessary, have been replaced by "a good clinic examination"; maximum emphasis is placed on natural-traditional medicine and acupuncture, vis-à-vis science-based but more expensive medicine; and benefits to health personnel abroad have been reduced (MINSAP, 2010; *Granma,* February 18, 2011; *Juventud Rebelde,* July 29, 2011; ECLAC, 2011a; ONE, 2011a, 2012a; Resolución no. 321, 2011). In contrast, the number of fellowships for foreign students was cut by only 0.6 percent in 2011; there is no information on Cuban international aid (ONE, 2012a).

Social Security Pensions

Aging of the population. Cuba faces an advanced demographic transition that negatively affects the social security system, and has the oldest-aged population in Latin America after Uruguay. Between 1953 and 2010, the Cuban birth rate declined from 2.5 percent to 1.1 percent, the emigration rate rose from –0.06 percent (1970) to –0.34 percent,[25] and the rate of population growth fell from 2 percent to –0.02 percent (see Table 4.11). Population in absolute terms decreased over the period, though it increased slightly in 2010 and 2011. The share of the population in the "young tail" cohort (aged zero to fourteen years) peaked at 36.9 percent in 1970, fell to 17.3 percent in 2010, and is projected to fall to 14.3 percent in 2025; the productive age cohort (aged fifteen to fifty-nine), the cohort that sustains the young and old tails, peaked at 71.6 percent of the population in 2008, fell to 64.9 percent in 2010, and it is projected to fall to 59.6 percent in 2025, while the "old tail" cohort (aged sixty and older) grew steadily from 6.9 percent of the population in 1953 to 17.8 percent in 2010 (and to 18.1 percent in 2011) (larger than the young tail), and is projected to grow to 26.1 percent in 2025.[26] The projections for the three cohorts for 2035 are even more alarming: young, 13.9 percent of the population; productive, 52.2 percent; and old, 33.9 percent (*Granma Internacional,* September 15, 2011).

Table 4.11 Aging of the Population, 1953–2025 (percentages)

	1953	1970	1981	2002	2006	2008	2010	2025
Birth rate	2.50	2.20	1.40	1.26	0.99	1.09	1.14	
Emigration		0.06	0.15	0.13	0.31	0.33	0.34	
Population growth	2.11	2.16	1.14	0.28	–0.04	–0.01	–0.02	–0.03
Population by age cohort								
0–14 years (young tail)	36.2	36.9	30.3	20.1	18.4	11.4	17.3	14.3
15–59 years (productive age)	56.9	54.0	58.8	64.9	65.7	71.6	64.9	59.6
60+ years (old tail)	6.9	9.1	10.9	15.0	15.9	17.0	17.8	26.1

Sources: Authors' calculations based on Mesa-Lago, 2010c; ONE, 2008b, 2011a, 2011b.
Note: Empty cells indicate that data are not available.

Since 1978, Cuba has had the lowest fertility rate on the continent and one of the lowest in the world (even lower than China's). Several reasons are behind this: urbanization (75 percent of Cubans live in urban areas as of 2010); women's entry into the labor market (38 percent of workers are women); early education on reproduction and increased access to contraceptives (78 percent of married women aged fifteen to forty use contraceptives, the second highest rate in the region); universal, legal, and free access to abortions; and challenging socioeconomic conditions—insufficient salaries, a severe housing shortage, restricted access to food—that persuade women to have fewer children (71 percent of women in relationships do not want to have more children) (ONE, 2011a; UNDP, 2011).

By 2025, Cuba will have the oldest-aged population in the region: 59.6 percent of the working-age population will have to finance the 40.4 percent in the young and old tails, which will deepen the financial unsustainability of the social security system, with the number of pensioners overtaking the number of active workers by 2015 (ONE, 2010b). Financing the needs of the old tail is more expensive than financing those of the young tail, because of higher healthcare costs among the former (due to higher incidence of illness and expensive costs associated with more complex tests, surgery, and medications), combined with payment of pensions for a longer period as an outcome of increased life expectancy (Mesa-Lago, 2012). According to ECLAC (2009b), Cuba experiences an aging process similar to that of European countries, but without the resources and productivity that those countries have to assist the elderly.

Generous entitlement conditions for pensions. At the close of 2008, Cuba had the most liberal entitlement pension conditions in Latin America: among the lowest retirement ages (age fifty-five for women and age sixty for men), the second highest life expectancy, the longest pension-payment time span, the shorter work life needed to qualify for benefits (five years less than the regional average), a higher worker replacement rate compared to the regional average, and a low rate of contribution by workers to the system (Mesa-Lago, 2012). The lack of annual adjustment of pensions to inflation has held down costs somewhat, but has not solved the financial imbalance.

The armed forces and internal security personnel have their own pension schemes, which are more generous and costly than the general pension system. A male who joins the armed forces at age seventeen can retire after twenty-five years of service (at age forty-two, eighteen years before men enrolled in the general system) with a pension equivalent to the salary earned during his last year of service, whereas in the general system the pension is equivalent to the average salary of the last five years prior to retirement (Mesa-Lago, 2003).

High costs and growing deficit. Revenue from contributions, mainly paid by enterprises, is insufficient to cover pension expenses. Hence, as shown in Table 4.12, the ensuing deficit financed by the state rose from 38.2 percent to 41.5 percent of expenses between 1989 and 2009; it fell to 39.1 percent in 2010, but climbed back to 41.4 percent in 2011 and peaked at 43.8 percent in 2012 (ONE, 2012a). The cost of pensions increased from 5.8 percent to 7.6 percent of GDP between 1989 and 2009 due to the liberal entitlement conditions, the system maturity (expenses of the pension system are larger than revenue), and population aging. To balance the system financially (to match revenue and expenses in a given year) would have required increasing contributions from 12 percent to 20 percent of payroll in 2010, and this was not done; to achieve actuarial equilibrium (long-term balance between revenue and expenditures) would have required a further increase of somewhere between 29 percent and 86 percent of payroll (Mesa-Lago, 2010c). The number of active workers per pensioner shrunk from 3.6 to 3.1 between 1989 and 2010, and is projected to fall further to 1.5 in 2025.

Deterioration in the real value of pensions. The average nominal pension rose fourfold between 1989 and 2011 (from 56 to 250 CUP [US$2 to US$10] per month), particularly as a result of increases between 2005 and 2008, but its real value (adjusted for inflation) fell by half between 1989 and 2011 (from 56 to 28 CUP per month) hence lost its purchasing power

Table 4.12 Cost and Deficit of Social Security Pensions, 1989 and 2008–2010

	1989	2008	2009	2010	Change Between 1989 and 2010 (%)
Revenue (million CUP)	676	2,580	2,774	2,974	340
Expenses (million CUP)	1,094	4,342	4,747	4,885	346
Deficit (million CUP)	418	1,762	1,973	1,911	357
Deficit financed by the state (percentage of expenses)	38.2	40.5	41.5	39.1[a]	2
Deficit (percentage of GDP)	2.2	2.9	3.2	3.0	36
Costs of pensions (percentage of GDP)	5.8	7.1	7.6	7.6	31
Worker contribution (percentage of payroll)	10.0	10.0	12.0	12.0	20
Worker contribution needed to eliminate deficit (percentage of payroll)	16.2	20.2	20.5	19.7	22
Number of active workers per pensioner	3.6	3.1	3.1	3.1	−14

Sources: Authors' calculations based on CEE, 1991; ONE 2011a, 2012a; Pedraza, 2012.
Note: a. The percentage climbed back to 41.4 in 2011 and peaked at 43.8 in 2012.

and became insufficient to meet basic needs (see Table 4.4). According to a survey conducted in the city of Havana in 2000, 78 percent of senior citizens said that pensions were insufficient to cover their cost of living, and had to be supplemented with family help, additional income from work, or remittances.[27] Moreover, the social safety net deteriorated as a result of less access to and declining quality of public health services, as well as fewer subsidized goods sold through rationing. In another survey, conducted in 2000 in the municipality of Plaza de la Revolución, elderly citizens complained about difficulties they faced regarding transportation, housing, lack of credit, and shortage of assisted-living care facilities (ONE, 2008b).

Pension reform and its effects. Law no. 24 of 2008 confronted some but not all of the pension system's problems: it raised retirement ages by five years for both sexes (to sixty for women and sixty-five for men); toughened the formula to calculate the pension and added five years of required work; set a 5 percent payroll contribution for workers (to be reached gradually, tied to an increase in wages); allowed for a pension increase for each year that retirement is postponed; raised nominal pensions (particularly the minimum pension); and allowed pensioners to work without losing their pension. The reform should moderately contain expenses and increase revenue somewhat. But the deficit climbed back to 41.4 percent in 2011 and set a record high at 43.8 percent in 2012 (Pedraza, 2011, 2012; ONE, 2012a), and the reform is insufficient to secure the long-run financial sustainability of the pension system. As mentioned, despite the increase of the real pension between 2008 and 2011, in 2011 it still was half the 1989 level (see Table 4.4).

Poverty and Social Assistance

Poverty. There are no official statistics on poverty incidence in Cuba. It was estimated, based on surveys, that the urban population "at risk of poverty" rose from 6.3 percent in 1988 to 20 percent in 1999; preliminary estimates for 2001 showed no decline, and hence poverty risk stood at about 20 percent (Ferriol, 2003, 2004; Mesa-Lago, 2005b).[28] According to another survey, conducted in city of Havana, 23 percent of respondents self-identified themselves as being poor and an additional 23 percent as being "nearly poor," for a total of 46 percent. Respondents identified the following principal socioeconomic problems: insufficient salary, 75.5 percent; poor public transportation, 70 percent; and lack of adequate food consumption and lack or deterioration of housing, clothing, and footwear, 70 percent (ONE, 2001; Añé, 2007). Poverty is higher among Afro-Cubans, pensioners, children, women heads of household, single mothers, migrants from less developed areas of the country, residents of the eastern provinces and of marginal neighborhoods, unskilled workers, and those who lack access to hard currencies (Espina, 2008, 2010).[29]

An independent survey with a sample of 5,439 persons living in 1,157 households in the provinces of Santiago de Cuba and Guantánamo in 2007 measured rural poverty: monthly salary was 15 percent of the average family income; 4.5 percent of families received remittances (compared to 65 percent nationally); 26 percent owned their homes (compared to 85 percent nationally); 54 percent of housing units had earthen floor and 96 percent a rustic outhouse; they lacked furniture and adequate beds; and 2.4 percent of households had a family member who was in prison (V. Sánchez, 2007). Since 2001 there have been no statistics on poverty incidence at the national level, but it probably has increased due to the deterioration in economic and social indicators, and the reforms are likely to aggravate the situation.

Mario González-Corzo (2009, 2010) posits that the potential elimination of rationing, dismissals, and other structural reforms would have negative social effects. Salaries would likely rise at a slower pace compared to liberalized prices and therefore purchasing power would decline, disproportionately hurting low-income households, particularly those with limited or no access to remittances, payment supplements, or private sector earnings. Most affected would be Afro-Cubans, pensioners, and residents of the eastern provinces of the island. Dismissals are most likely to harm unskilled workers who lack any capital, those with scarce knowledge about how the market operates, those who lack initiative and would not be willing to undertake the risks associated with self-employment, and those closest to retirement age. The reforms would increase prices in the short term, as has happened with taxis and barber shops, although prices would likely moderate in the middle to long term, as a result of competition.

Social assistance changes. In 2010, Yusimi Campos, director of social assistance at the Ministry of Labor and Social Security, stated that although social assistance is a constitutional right in Cuba and although there is no intention to eliminate it, there would be a "rectification" of the criteria to grant assistance: "the economic situation of the household will be evaluated to determine if its members can pay for some or all of the services, according to their capacity to pay" (*ANSA y Clarín,* October 3, 2010). In 2010, expenditures amounting to 237 million CUP were cut as a result of purging the lists of recipients "based on their real needs and possibilities" (Martínez, 2011b; see Chapter 5).

Social assistance in Cuba eroded between 2005 and 2011 according to all indicators; social assistance beneficiaries and benefit levels peaked between 2005 and 2008, followed by reductions between 2009 and 2011. As shown in Table 4.13, from the peak of benefit levels to 2011, the number of social assistance beneficiaries fell by 70 percent (from 5.3 percent in 2006 to 1.6 percent of the population), elderly beneficiaries by 56 percent, disabled beneficiaries by 61 percent, mothers with disabled children by 30 percent, and beneficiaries receiving services at home by 74 percent. Social assistance expenditures fell by 67 percent between their peak and 2011, shrinking by 78 percent as a share of the national budget (from 4.2 percent in 2006 to 0.9 percent) and by 74 percent as a share of GDP (from 2.3 percent in 2005 to 0.6 percent). Although purging from the rolls those beneficiaries who are not in need is a rational policy, the statistics in Table 4.13 suggest that the cuts went deep at a time when the vulnerable population had increased as a result of the reforms.

A gross estimate of the share of the Cuban population who were poor and received social assistance benefits in 2009–2011 (see Table 4.14) suggests that coverage declined from 19 percent to 7.4 percent in the period. It should be noted that the poverty incidence used for this estimate is from 2001, but more current data do not exist and arguably the incidence of poverty probably rose after that, as previously discussed, due to the reforms. An adequate targeting method is needed to properly determine the number of poor and their needs.

The Catholic Church plays a growing role in Cuba in providing social assistance to persons in need. Large parishes serve meals for the needy and some have volunteers who deliver the meals to the homes of the elderly, sick, or handicapped; they also bathe them or wash their clothes. Religious orders own or manage homes for the elderly, the largest leprosarium, a home for children with Down syndrome, and a facility for patients suffering from AIDS. Most financing comes from abroad; Cáritas Cubana receives US$1.8 million annually from its counterparts in Germany, Spain, and Switzerland, and has helped over 300,000 persons affected by hurricanes and serves meals to 35,000 (Tamayo, 2012a; M. Sánchez, 2012). Protestant churches in the United States and in other nations are also active in providing humanitarian assistance and supporting entrepreneurship on the island (*CBN News,* June 22, 2011).

Housing

The urban reform law of 1960 confiscated all rental housing units and those that were not owner-occupied, prohibited selling and mortgaging of dwellings, and allowed renters to become owners of dwellings by paying rent to the state for twenty years.[30] Thus, 85 percent of Cubans own the homes where they live, probably the highest ownership rate in Latin America, but lack construction materials to repair and maintain them. Population doubled between 1959 and 2010, but not enough homes were built to offset the number that became unlivable due to lack of maintenance or that were destroyed by natural disasters. There is broad consensus in Cuba that housing is the most pressing social problem.

Table 4.13 Social Assistance Indicators, 2005–2011

	2005	2006	2007	2008	2009	2010	2011	Change Between Peak[a] and 2011 (%)
Beneficiaries (thousands)	535	600	595	582	426	235	182	−70
Total beneficiaries as percentage of total population	4.8	5.3	5.3	5.2	3.8	2.1	1.6	−70
Elderly	117	143	145	145	118	71	63	−56
Disabled	85	97	99	110	71	47	42	−61
Mothers with disabled children	6.7	6.7	7.8	7.6	7.6	6.3	5.4	−30
Recipients of services at home	9.8	13.5	16.1	17.3	13.1	5.7	4.5	−74
Expenditures (million CUP)	996	1,188	1,190	1,297	924	688[b]	431[c]	−67
Percentage of state budget	4.1	4.2	3.4	3.0	2.2	1.7	0.9[c]	−78
Percentage of GDP	2.3	2.2	2.0	2.1	1.5	1.1	0.6[c]	−74

Sources: Authors' calculations based on ONE, 2011a, 2012a, 2012b.

Notes: a. Percentage change between the peak year in the 2005–2008 period and 2011 (2010 for expenditures).
b. Expenditures in 2010 were distributed as follows: direct payments to individuals, 62%; allocations to homes for the elderly and the disabled, 28%; other expenditures, 10% (Martínez, 2011b).
c. Preliminary data.

Table 4.14 Gross Estimate of Share of the Poor Who Receive Social Assistance, 2009–2011

	2009	2010	2011
Total population	11,242,628	11,241,161	11,247,925
Number of poor (20% incidence)[a]	2,248,525	2,248,232	2,249,585
Social assistance beneficiaries	426,390	235,482	182,492
Percentage of poor covered	19.0	10.5	8.1

Sources: Authors' calculations based on ONE, 2011a, 2012a.
Note: a. The estimate that 20% of Cubans are poor refers to 2001.

The growing housing deficit. New construction of housing units per 1,000 inhabitants fell from 6.1 in 1989 to 3.6 in 2005 (see Table 4.15). In 2006, 111,400 new units were built and the construction rate climbed to 9.9, both historical highs, but the number of new units amounted to only 76 percent of the target of 150,000 units set for that year; 70 percent of the new dwellings consisted of those built by individuals (including already built dwellings that received "fit for occupancy" certification) together with completion of houses already under construction. Also unmet was the target of repair and maintenance of some 380,000 dwellings. Housing construction fell steadily after 2006: 52,660 units in 2007 (75 percent of the goal of 70,000) to 32,540 in 2011 for a construction rate of 2.8 units per 1,000 inhabitants, 53 percent below the 1989 rate. Between 2009 and 2012, 146,340 housing units were built, equivalent to 28 percent of the 530,758 units destroyed or damaged by the 2008 hurricanes (see Box 2.1).[31] Housing construction by individuals rose from 37 percent of the total in 2000 to 70 percent in 2006, and fell to 27 percent in 2011 (ECLAC, 2011b; ONE, 2012a).

There are numerous reasons for the low and declining housing construction by the state: budget allocations to housing consistently have been the lowest within social services (save for social assistance), falling from 4.6 percent to 4.2 percent between 2007 and 2010, despite the growing housing deficit; severe shortages of construction materials and allocation of some of them for export (such as cement) or for other government priorities; shortage of carpenters, bricklayers, stonemasons, plumbers, and electricians due to lack of training; insufficient budget and severe management problems at the state housing repair agency that contributed to the deterioration of housing stock; delays of up to eleven years in completing a five-story building; housing units that were started but not completed, lack of compliance with construction delivery schedules, and actual costs that far exceeded initial estimates; inefficiencies of the construction "microbrigades," composed mostly of workers without construction skills; and low quality of the dwellings built. The decline in the number of housing units

Table 4.15 Housing Construction, 1989 and 2005–2011

	1989	2005	2006	2007	2008	2009	2010	2011	Change Between 1989 and 2011 (%)
Number of units (thousands)	63.0[a]	39.9	111.4	52.6	44.8	35.1	33.9	32.5	–48
Units per 1,000 inhabitants	6.1[a]	3.6	9.9	4.6	4.0	3.1	3.0	2.8	–53

Sources: Authors' calculations based on CEE, 1991; ONE 2011a, 2012a.
Note: a. Annual average 1981–1989.

built by the private sector reflects red tape and state restrictions, low income of the population, and shortages of construction materials (*Granma,* May 21, 2010; R. Castro Ruz, 2011b). Raúl eliminated the construction microbrigades in 2011.

National Housing Institute (INV) president Víctor Ramírez reported in 2008 that 43 percent of housing units were in poor or mediocre condition; that 85 percent of units with more than three stories needed repair but that the lack of construction materials prevented this; that the housing deficit was estimated at 600,000 units[32] (with the damage done by the 2008 hurricanes, the deficit should probably exceed 1 million units)[33]; and that even if the construction goal for 2008 had been met, it would have only represented 5–7 percent of accumulated demand (*Juventud Rebelde,* July 9, 2008). City of Havana historian Eusebio Leal, who has spectacularly renovated part of the colonial area of Havana, stated on television in 2009 that 60 percent of the capital's housing stock was in poor shape; that there were on average three building collapses per day; and that had one of the 2008 hurricanes made a direct hit on the city, it would have been necessary to declare martial law and request US$1 billion in assistance to rehabilitate thousands of dwellings in the colonial area (*Hurón Azul,* February 11, 2009).

The municipalities of Old Havana, Center Havana, Cerro, Diez de Octubre, and San Miguel del Padrón have the most deteriorated housing within the city of Havana. In a single week in January 2012, three multistory buildings collapsed in Center Havana, resulting in several deaths and injuries, among them the Campoamor Theater, which had been shut down since 2005 but nevertheless was home for four families; a documentary made in 2006 by two German filmmakers, *The New Art of Making Ruins,* showed the deplorable condition of the theater (*Miami Herald,* January 18, 2012, January 26, 2012, January 28, 2012). In San Miguel del Padrón in 2008 there were forty-six poor neighborhoods consisting of hovels constructed from materials salvaged from garbage dumps; the hovels had earthen floors and the neighborhoods lacked streets and electricity, and potable water was supplied via containers (*Juventud Rebelde,* August 3, 2008). INV vice president Oris Silvia Fernández told the ANPP in 2010 that only 24 percent of family-occupied dwellings that lacked functional plumbing had been repaired, and that only 2.3 percent of 28,781 buildings that needed roofing work had been repaired (*Juventud Rebelde,* August 28, 2010). It is common for two or three generations of relatives to live in the same dwelling, and for divorced couples to continue sharing the same house; many houses have a *barbacoa,* or mezzanine, where relatives or another family reside. Fraudulent marriages arranged for the purpose of swapping houses (*permutas*) are common, and a recent practice is to move in with an elderly person to care for them and inherit the dwelling after their death.

Measures taken. Raúl's government has approved several measures to ease the severe housing shortage and deterioration. In 2010, former minister of economy Marino Murillo announced the end of subsidies for construction materials sold to individuals who were building houses, because those materials were being diverted to the black market (Murillo, 2010). In August 2011, Raúl eliminated restrictions on the sale of construction materials to the population, allowing the building or repair of a home without the need to resort to theft or bribes, which induced a construction boom.[34] To help the poor afford the high prices of construction materials, in January 2012 the government started a program of subsidies focused on low-income households, making available to them materials to repair their homes. The most significant step regarding housing and one of Raúl's key structural reforms was the authorization in 2011 for individuals to sell and buy homes, subject to regulations and restrictions, but nevertheless this has become a viable alternative to the inefficient, bureaucratic, and corrupted system of house-swapping, although the latter still persists (see Chapter 5).

Summary of Findings

Although Cuba has recovered since the economic crisis of the 1990s in several social indicators, in many others it has not. Full employment, one of the key social accomplishments, was achieved by padding government payrolls and increasing underemployment; in 2009, the open unemployment rate of 1.6 percent was one of the lowest in the world, but in 2010 the government announced that between 500,000 and 1.3 million workers (12 to 28 percent of the labor force) would be dismissed from state jobs because they were redundant. The dismissal plan was flawed: the implementation period was too short, bureaucratic opposition was underestimated, compensation was meager, and, most important, no realistic plan existed to generate the 465,000 private sector jobs necessary to absorb the dismissed state workers.

Despite increases in nominal salaries, the average real salary fell by 73 percent between 1989 and 2011, and has been officially recognized as insufficient to cover basic needs. The rationing system has been progressively phased out, and the rations it still provides currently cover a household's needs for about ten days of the month. Food and other necessities for the rest of the month have to be bought in agricultural markets and at foreign-currency stores at high and rising prices in convertible pesos.

Inequality has grown since the reforms of the 1990s and deepened with the structural reforms currently being implemented. As of 2012 the average income of self-employed workers is 2.3 times the average salary of a state worker; remittances and access to hard currency (through salary supplement for workers of joint ventures, tips from tourism) intensify the inequities. The tax system is regressive despite a small recent improvement (a new tax law was approved in July 2012 but will not come into effect until 2013 and beyond). Disparities across provinces have declined, but the provinces farthest away from the capital (particularly those in the eastern region) continue to lag behind. Racial inequality has grown, primarily because of the more limited access by Afro-Cubans to remittances and to jobs in the tourism industry, in joint ventures, and in the private sector, which pay better than the state sector jobs held by 83 percent of Afro-Cubans. Afro-Cubans also tend to concentrate in poor neighborhoods. There is a higher degree of recognition among the Cuban leadership of racial discrimination, and more studies and discussions are being held on the subject. Although women's education levels are equal to or even higher than those of men, labor force indicators show a gender gap with respect to occupation, type of job, unemployment, and representation in leadership positions; women probably also receive lower salaries than men for equal work and are more affected by poverty. Raúl has called for the complete eradication of racial and gender inequalities, and there has been an increase in women's participation in the Cuban Communist Party and the National Assembly.

The cost of social services, which constituted 53 percent of the state budget and 34 percent of GDP in 2010 (with a small decline in 2010 due to cuts in social expenditures), is unsustainable. Between 1989 and 2011, enrollment in higher education increased by 45 percent, but it grew twenty-two-fold in humanities and social sciences while falling by 30 percent in natural sciences and mathematics, the latter of which are key to future economic development. There is an acute shortage of teachers because of low state salaries; efforts to address the teacher gap by using "emerging teachers" failed. The government has encouraged retired teachers to return to classrooms, raised salaries, shut down inefficient programs (e.g., municipal universities, social-work programs, basic secondary schools, and pre-university schools in the countryside), trimmed university enrollment by half (a 62 percent reduction in humanities and social sciences, but a 14 percent increase in natural sciences and mathematics), established enrollment quotas for different disciplines, and toughened university entrance examinations.

Infant mortality has continued to decline (as of 2012 it was the second lowest in the hemisphere) but at an increasing marginal cost. Maternal mortality has increased, in part due to the widespread use of abortion, with Cuba having the highest abortion rate in Latin America. The general mortality rate has increased because of population aging, which also drives up the cost of healthcare. Life expectancy has increased and is the second highest in Latin America. The ratio of physicians per capita continues to rise and is the highest in the region, but a significant portion of doctors work abroad or in other, more lucrative occupations at home, reducing the number of physicians practicing domestically. The number of hospital beds has shrunk, but it is still the highest in the region on a per capita basis. There is a severe shortage of medications, with most of them sold at foreign-currency stores at high prices. Long waiting periods and lack of materials and equipment have forced citizens to resort to bribes and favors in order to hasten access to health services. Cuba devotes substantial resources to fellowships and health aid to other nations, despite scarcity domestically. The government has cut the health budget and shut down healthcare facilities, whose personnel have been dismissed.

Cuba has the second oldest–aged population in the region, the result of a combination of a low birth rate, the lowest fertility rate in the hemisphere, and a high emigration rate. The young cohort is shrinking, the productive cohort has begun to contract, and the older cohort is expanding rapidly (by 2035, the three cohorts will constitute 14 percent, 52 percent, and 34 percent of the total population, respectively). These demographic trends translate into higher future costs of social security pensions, compounded by the fact that Cuba's pension system has the most generous entitlement conditions in the hemisphere. Contributions, mainly from employers, are insufficient to cover expenses, and the state finances the deficit. Despite the rising costs of the pension system, the real value of the average pension fell by half between 1989 and 2011. The 2008 pension reform addressed some of the system's problems, but others remain: the deficit continues to increase (though after a moderate decrease in 2010), the reform cannot restore equilibrium in the long run, and real pensions continue to be low.

Although no recent statistics are available, poverty has probably risen as a result of the scaling back of the rationing system and quotas, falling real salaries and pensions, dismissals, and price increases; these factors particularly adversely affect Afro-Cubans, pensioners, single mothers and heads of households, residents of the eastern provinces and migrants, residents of poor neighborhoods, and individuals who do not have access to hard currency or remittances. At the same time that the number of Cubans who are at risk of poverty has increased, social assistance has declined according to all indicators.

Lack of adequate housing is probably the most challenging social problem. While 85 percent of Cubans own their homes, the housing stock has deteriorated severely as a result of lack of maintenance by the agency responsible for this task, state restrictions, and shortages of construction materials. The number of dwellings built annually has been insufficient to offset those destroyed by lack of maintenance and by hurricanes. The number of housing units built per 1,000 inhabitants decreased from 6.1 to 2.8 between 1989 and 2011. The housing deficit was officially estimated at 600,000 units in 2008, but probably exceeds 1 million. About 43 percent of dwellings were in poor or mediocre condition in 2008, and 85 percent of housing units with more or three stories were in need of repairs. Since 1960 and until 2011, sale of dwellings was prohibited, and the only legal way to exchange homes was through swaps, which are inefficient, bureaucratic, and prone to corruption. Positive recent steps are the liberalization of the sale of construction materials, subsidies to needy homeowners to assist them in repairing their homes, and the authorization of sales of homes.

Cuba made impressive advances in social welfare until 1989, but the crisis of the 1990s and subsequent problems led to the erosion of social welfare. In addition, after half a century of revolution, unresolved problems remain, including irrational policies and increasing costs of social programs (although most of the social programs have had positive social effects). These challenges will be difficult to address in the short term. The reforms being implemented to cope with these problems are pointed in the right direction, but deeper and faster changes are needed. Moreover, social policies will not be sustainable unless production and productivity rise, which will require successful structural reforms, as analyzed in Chapters 5 and 6.

Notes

1. Employment growth was primarily in services (with lower job-creation costs), which grew from 35 percent to 43 percent of total employment between 2003 and 2009, while employment shrank in other sectors (A. García et al., 2011).

2. The regulations underlying the retrenchment were contained in Resolution no. 35 of 2010 of the Ministry of Labor and Social Security; complementary regulations were published in the *Gaceta Oficial*, nos. 11–13, of November 2010.

3. According to projections by Anicia García and colleagues (2011), employment in the nonstate sector would represent the following percentages of total employment: 27 percent in 2011 (actual was 16 percent), 31 percent in 2012 (actual was 23 percent), 32 percent in 2013, 34 percent in 2014, and 35 percent in 2015.

4. Using 2000 as the base, ECLAC (2011b) estimated that the real salary in 2010 was 54 percent higher than in 2000, which is confirmed by statistics in Table 4.4, but it omitted the drastic fall since 1989.

5. Anicia García and colleagues (2011) show the relationship between real salary and productivity between 1990 and 2010.

6. There are six markets where different prices prevail: the rationing system; the parallel market (free sale of same products subject to rationing by the state at higher prices); the nonstate agricultural market (price determined by demand and supply); the state agricultural market, whose prices are capped; (e) the foreign-currency stores (TRDs, which have the highest prices, set by the state, in convertible currency); and the black market (whose prices are lower than those in the TRDs).

7. Elderly retirees would sell their cigarette quota acquired through the rationing system, earning a monthly net profit of 36 CUP (approximately US$1.50) (*Herald Tribune,* September 2, 2010).

8. Blanca Pampín, consultant to the National Association of Cuban Economists (ANEC), has reported that between 2010 and 2011, prices of basic consumption goods (rice, black beans, etc.) rose by 47 percent, as the price for seeds jumped by 67 percent, the price for fertilizers by 90 percent, and the price for pesticides by 50 percent (*Inter Press Service,* November 1, 2011).

9. This equality seems to be eroding; of the cohort of students who passed university entrance examinations in 2004, 68 percent were white and 32 percent were Afro-Cuban (Espina and Togores, 2012). With recent reductions in higher education enrollment and stricter entrance exams, it is likely that the gap has expanded.

10. Miguel Barnet, president of UNEAC and a member of the ANPP, promised that the latter would analyze the implementation of regulations to combat racial discrimination, after which the issue was delegated to a commission (*Diario de Cuba,* July 16, 2007). By the end of November 2012, neither the commission's study had been published nor the regulations approved.

11. For a historical perspective on social services under the revolution, see Mesa-Lago, 2010a.

12. The comparison underestimates Cuba's share, as the island's state budget is proportionally higher than in the other countries, and therefore Cuba's share should be higher. The distribution of social expenditures by sector in Cuba in 2010 was as follows: education, 20 percent of the budget and 13 percent of GDP, with shares stagnant as a trend; public health, 15 percent and 10 percent respectively, with shares declining; social security pensions, 12 percent and 7.6 percent, with shares increasing with respect to the budget and stagnant with respect to GDP; housing, 4.2 percent and 2.7 percent, with shares declining slightly downward; and social assistance, 1.7 percent and 1.1 percent, with shares decreasing.

13. Many students reportedly enrolled in university only to reduce the length of their compulsory military service and did not attend classes.

14. The ratio of enrollees to graduates varied widely across disciplines in 2007–2008: 1.4 in humanities and social sciences, 9.7 in technical careers, and 14.9 in natural sciences and mathematics (ONE, 2007).

15. Alfredo Guevara, former director of the Cuban Institute of Cinematographic Art and Industry (ICAIC) and an important intellectual, opined that Cuba's educational system "followed crazy criteria and practices disconnected from elementary principles of pedagogy . . . was dogmatic, [and showed] lack of knowledge about reality. . . . The emerging teachers program reflect improvisation and lack of proper design [and require] profound rectification" (Seventh Congress of UNEAC, April 2008).

16. Labor mobilization of students and voluntary work in general were abolished in August 2011 because they require expenditure of resources that exceeds economic impact and were used to cover up inefficiencies.

17. Facilities for political leaders and also for paying foreigners include modern and well-equipped areas of the Hermanos Ameijeiras and Frank País hospitals, the Center for Medical-Surgical Research (CIMEQ), the International Center for Neurological Rehabilitation (CIREN), the Cira García and Koly clinics, and the Retinitis Pigmentosa Clinic.

18. The infant mortality rate is published at the end of the year and is not usually revised. In developed countries, it takes a year or longer to publish final statistics. International and regional health organizations do not verify the accuracy of Cuban statistics (Dorschner, 2007).

19. Cuba began to publish a new statistical series from 2006 forward that eliminated maternal mortality "arising from other causes" and showed a reduction of the mortality rate of about 10.6 percentage points annually over the period 1996–2000 (Mesa-Lago, 2005b). Correcting to account for this understatement, the maternal mortality rate for 2007 would be 41.7.

20. There are different estimates of the number of Cuban physicians working in seventy-five foreign countries in 2007: 35,000 physicians (J. L. Rodríguez, 2007b); 30,000 healthcare professionals in Venezuela alone, of whom 13,020 were physicians (*Agence France-Press,* December 11, 2008); 38,544 healthcare professionals, of whom 17,697 were physicians (*Granma,* November 3, 2008); and 37,266 physicians, of whom 31,000 were working in Venezuela (Garrett, 2010). The salary earned by Cuban physicians who work outside the country is paid in CUP (although Cuba is compensated in hard currency), but they also receive a hard-currency supplement and relatives on the island receive a sum in CUC deposited into a Cuban bank account.

21. Potable water is distributed as follows: 75 percent of users receive it through household connections (39 percent in rural areas), 9 percent through tank trucks, and 16 percent through other means.

22. Modernization of the Santiago de Cuba aqueduct began in 2008, but several deficiencies slowed the construction: shoddy work, collapsing walls, a large leak, low quality of filters, and violation of testing protocols (*Granma Internacional,* July 15, 2010). The project was completed in 2011.

23. The average hospital stay fell from 9.9 to 8.5 days between 1989 and 2010, but this is still high by international standards.

24. The "Barrio Adentro" program, which deploys Cuban physicians and other public health personnel in Venezuela, is facing some challenges. In 2009, President Hugo Chávez declared a "public health emergency" because more than a thousand of its health offices had been abandoned by doctors (some of them left Venezuela for other countries). In 2011, the general auditor of Venezuela reported that US$723 million worth of medicines received from Cuba had not been ordered, had been received two years late, and were due to expire within nine months (*Reuters,* September 21, 2009; MPPS, 2011).

25. Between 1994 and 2010 a net total of 513,423 Cubans emigrated (4.6 percent of the total population in 2010), of whom 212,756 emigrated between 2004 and 2010; the number of emigrants in 2010 was the second highest after 1994. City of Havana is the oldest-aged province and the one with the largest number of emigrants: 114,900 in 2010, or 54 percent of the Cuba's total number of emigrants and 5.4 percent of the province's total population (ONE, 2007, 2010a, 2011a, 2011b).

26. Preliminary data from the 2012 census indicate that the young tail composed 18.4 percent of the population, the productive cohort 63.3 percent, and the old tail 18.3 percent (*Granma,* December 7, 2012).

27. The sources of income of retirees were: pensions, for 76 percent of retirees in 2008; help from family within the country, 26 percent; work they performed, 20 percent; and remittances, 15 percent (ONE, 2008b).

28. Poverty was defined as "insufficiency of monetary income that limits consumption of food and other essential goods and services, [as well as] lack of housing or deteriorating housing and furnishings, and lack of access to public transport" (Ferriol, 2003).

29. Mayra Espina examined six types of poverty studies conducted in Cuba between 1993 and 2004 and concluded that the HDI understates the seriousness of poverty in Cuba.

30. According to Salvador Gomila, adviser to the National Housing Institute (INV), in 2007 the state sold housing units for US$400, which were financed by bank loans with repayment terms linked to household income; lack of payment did not result in foreclosure, which meant subsidies of between 40 and 90 percent of the loan amounts (*BBC Mundo,* January 12, 2007).

31. INV president Víctor Ramírez estimated that more than 1 million housing units were affected by eight hurricanes between 2001 and 2008, or 29 percent of the housing stock in 2008 (*Granma International,* September 13, 2008).

32. The INV vice president at the time, Carlos Lage, reported that out of 600,032 dwellings that had suffered partial or complete collapses, only 26 percent had been repaired (*Granma,* February 2, 2009).

33. Sergio Díaz-Briquets (2009) estimated the housing deficit in 2009 at 1.6 million units based on official statistics (housing construction and figures from population and housing censuses) and the definition of "adequate housing," thus updating the housing deficit identified in the 1970 census.

34. In 2011, sales met only 15.6 percent of the target and prices were high (a metal window frame cost the equivalent of twice the average monthly salary), an issue recognized by Raúl (2011b).

5

The Reforms,
the National Debate,
and the Party Congress

In his July 26, 2007, address to the nation, Raúl spoke about the serious socioeconomic problems facing Cuba and promised to implement "structural and conceptual reforms," while warning that "we cannot fix everything immediately . . . [and] spectacular solutions should not be expected" (R. Castro Ruz, 2007a). His speech generated the widest and deepest national debate to date on potential reforms on the island and raised the population's expectations about change. This chapter covers the transfer of power to Raúl; the national debate about reforms; the reforms advanced by Raúl; and the agreements reached by the Sixth Congress of the Cuban Communist Party (PCC), including their limitations and subsequent adjustments.

The Institutionalization of Succession

Raúl has successfully accomplished four key political tasks: a rapid and peaceful succession of power from Fidel; the placement of cadres loyal to him in key positions in the government and the PCC; the reordering of the governing elite, consisting of "historical" revolutionaries, military men, PCC provincial secretaries, technocrats, and enterprise managers; and establishment of the basis for a new generation of leaders who will eventually institutionalize the succession process (see Mujal-León, 2011).

On February 18, 2008, Fidel stated in one of his "Reflections" that he neither aspired nor would accept the positions of President of the Council of State or of Commander in Chief (F. Castro Ruz, 2008). On February 24, the National Assembly of People's Power (ANPP) elected Raúl, at the time seventy-six years old, president of both the Council of State and the Council of Ministers; he resigned as minister of the armed forces and named as his successor General Julio Casas, then seventy-one years old, who had served as vice minister of the armed forces. Reputed reformist Carlos Lage, at the time vice president of the Council of State and executive secretary of the Council of Ministers, fifty-six years of age, and representative of a younger generation, was expected to be named as first vice president of the council, but instead the ANPP selected José Ramón Machado Ventura, seventy-seven years old, who had been a critic of Soviet perestroika and glasnost. The bulk of the key posts in the Council of Ministers continued to be held by "historicals": Juan Almeida (eighty-one years old) together with Ramiro Valdés, Abelardo Colomé, José Ramón Balaguer, and Julio Casas (between seventy-one and seventy-six years old; Casas died in September 2011). The average age among the top echelon of the Council of Ministers (president, vice presidents, and secretary) was seventy-six, and that among the top echelon of the Political Bureau of the PCC was sixty-seven, or seventy-five if three members aged forty-seven to fifty-one are excluded (authors' estimates based on the Cuban press; Chaguaceda, 2011). Fidel remained as first secretary of the PCC and Raúl as second secretary until 2011.

The ratification and even expansion of the orthodox old guard within the Council of State gave rise to two interpretations. The first was that the "historicals" would resist reforms; Fidel, although no longer president, remained as first secretary of the PCC, and through this post and his Reflections, he could obstruct a reform process. The second was that the ratification was a tactical move to render tribute to Fidel, who had retired but remained in the picture, while providing Raúl some space to promote a debate that would legitimate the necessary reforms to tackle the serious economic problems that prevailed. According to this view, it was imperative for Raúl to maintain unity among the leadership and it was preferable to have the old guard within the Council of State rather than outside, potentially blocking the changes. With the institutionalization of his power and the old guard in positions to which he appointed them, Raúl would be well placed to undertake the necessary reforms.

In 2008, Raúl replaced seven ministers responsible for the following portfolios: agriculture, sugar, foreign investment and economic cooperation, transportation, education, higher education, and public health. He also removed from key positions the so-called talibans, a group of young hardliners appointed by Fidel during the "Battle of Ideas," ended the group's programs, and dismissed its director. In March 2009, Raúl further restructured the cabinet, replacing twelve high-level officials, including the minister of foreign affairs, Felipe Pérez Roque, and Carlos Lage; the latter two, in simultaneous open letters, admitted committing "errors" and resigned their membership in the Council of State, the PCC's Central Committee, and the ANPP. Their letters were published in the official press (*Granma*,

May 3, 2009) together with a Reflection by Fidel about the two dismissed officials: "the honey of power . . . arose ambitions that led them to behave in an undignified manner."[1] Also replaced were the minister of economy, José Luis Rodríguez, and other key ministers in the economic arena: finance and prices, foreign trade, domestic trade, food industry, and steel and metalworking. In May 2009, Francisco Soberón, who had held the presidency of the Central Bank of Cuba (BCC) for twelve years, resigned from all of his official posts. These changes consolidated Raúl's political power and ensured him control over economic policymaking, sending the message to all officials that no matter their rank, their jobs were vulnerable. In another of his Reflections, Fidel denied rumors that were circulated regarding his men "being changed by Raúl," stating that he had been consulted on the changes and had approved them.

The changes removed from power a number of leaders, such as Lage and Rodríguez, who had played key roles in the economic reforms of the 1990s. Their replacements on the economic team have roots in the military or in the PCC: Lage and Rodríguez were replaced, respectively, by General José Amado Guerra, secretary of the Ministry of the Revolutionary Armed Forces under Raúl, and by Coronel Marino Murillo, former minister of domestic trade with a track record in combating financial indiscipline and corruption in state enterprises. "Historic" comandante Ramiro Valdés was named vice president of the Council of State. The new minister of steelmaking and metalworking, General Salvador Pardo, formerly managed military enterprises that supplied the Ministry of the Revolutionary Armed Forces. The new minister of finance and prices, Lina Pedraza, and the minister of food industry and fisheries, María del Carmen Concepción, are former officials of the secretariat of the Central Committee of the PCC and have a reputation for being demanding disciplinarians (Pedraza was also former minister of audit and control). Military officers composed 26 percent of the Council of State's membership.[2] Most of the new appointees have a history of upholding the law, supporting solid discipline, and observing fiscal control, characteristics akin with Raúl's style (Mesa-Lago, 2009c; Vidal Alejandro, 2010a). Since March 2010, Raúl has replaced the ministers of basic industry (twice), economics and planning, information and communications, culture, higher education, science, technology, and environment; he also replaced the head of the Institute of Physical Planning with General Samuel Rodiles (eighty years old) and named Gladys Bejarano to the new post of comptroller general. To sum up, since 2006, Raúl has replaced over thirty ministers in addition to other key officials.

In 2011, Fidel announced that he would retire as first secretary of the PCC; the Sixth Congress of the PCC, meeting in February, elected Raúl to that post and Machado Ventura as second secretary. The First National Conference of the PCC, in 2012, set a limit of two consecutive periods of five years of service each for individuals holding key posts in the PCC and the government, a move that would extend the period of service of the old guard through 2018. By then, Raúl would be eighty-six years old, and Machado Ventura eighty-seven, and the average age of Council of State members would be around eighty-seven, although it is highly probable that there would be changes before then and as part of the 2013 elections. Raúl said that "because of the law of life," it was quite likely that the Sixth Congress would be the last Congress led by the revolutionary "historic generation" and bemoaned the lack of a deep pool of young replacements with the necessary skills and experience to take over the leadership of the PCC and the government. He called for a "systematic rejuvenation of those serving in a chain of posts," reaching all the way to the highest levels. In announcing the composition of the new Central Committee, he highlighted the selection of young cadres (R. Castro Ruz, 2010c, 2011a, 2011b). The 2012 PCC conference reiterated the importance of promoting young cadres and removed 20 percent of the previous members in order to open up space for young members elected by the Sixth Congress (PCC, 2012). Four new members of the PCC's Political Bureau are considerably younger than average: Marino Murillo and Miguel Díaz-Canel, fifty-one years old, Mercedes López Acea, forty-seven, and Minister of Foreign Relations Bruno Rodríguez, fifty-four (appointed toward the end of 2012). In March 2012, the composition of the Council of State showed significant differences in age depending on the rank of the post: the overall average age was sixty-one, but for the top ten positions (president or vice president) the average age was seventy-five, while for ministers the average age dropped to fifty-six (authors' estimates based on Sitio del Gobierno, 2012). These changes have created a more viable way for succession by the new generation and their climb to higher positions (López-Levy, 2011). At the ANPP session in February 2013, there were important changes in the composition of the Councils of State and of Ministers that reduced their members' average ages: Díaz-Canel was elected first vice president of both councils and Machado Ventura was downgraded to the second vice presidency; López Acea was appointed to the Council of State. With these changes, the average age of the ANPP decreased to fifty-seven (*Granma*, February 25, 2013).

Debate About Reforms

Raúl directed the 3,000-plus state enterprises and agencies to submit, between August and September 2007, a list of the main problems they faced and suggestions to address them. Between October and December, 215,687 meetings were held, with the participation of some 5 million persons (40 percent of the total population) who made some 1.3 million suggestions.

According to Raúl, "the purpose of the meetings was not for us to learn about problems; we were already aware of most of them . . . [and] some of the suggestions reflect lack of information, particularly those in the economic sphere" (R. Castro Ruz, 2007b).

Rafael Hernández (2009) has argued that "there are not sufficient institutional spaces [in Cuba] for a critical debate," which he defines as a coming together of actors who have different viewpoints, with the objective of establishing a respectful dialogue and listening to each other, without preconceived positions, without imposing hierarchies, and with an open mind to opinions that might not be shared, in order to promote a culture of civilized discussion within civil society. The role of the economists in the debate called by Raúl, according to Pedro Monreal, was limited to providing statistics and analyses to inform public policies, but decisions were taken by the leadership (interview by F. García, 2007). Lage Cordoniú, a young economist, called for a more vigorous debate: "It is essential to have a true dialogue between social scientists and decision makers. What sense does it make to create institutions and ask comrades to devote time to study, and at the end . . . not even to ask them for their views? Policy errors have been committed despite the fact that trained experts were available. . . . This cannot be justified" ("Sobre la transición," 2007).

The following sections summarize the positions on the most important themes of the debate among economists, political scientists, lawyers, philosophers, sociologists, anthropologists, and other intellectuals (see Mesa-Lago, 2008a). The emphasis is on the period 2006–2008, but on certain topics the analysis is carried further in time to intertwine with previous opinions and provide unity and coherence to the arguments.

Economic Model

The debate over the economic model considered numerous points of view, but virtually all proposals were within "socialist parameters" and excluded the possibility of a system with predominant market-oriented features and low state regulation. The parameters of the model were not well defined, however, and the socialist spectrum was wide: from market socialism à la China and Vietnam, to the statist-collective approach pursued by North Korea and to the worker self-management approach followed decades ago by the former Yugoslavia. A number of participants in the debate argued that Cuba should develop and pursue its own model, without actually defining what such a model might be.

Political scientist Carlos Alzugaray (2009a) observed that Cuban history, like the history of other similarly organized systems, has demonstrated the inefficacy of "hyper-centralization, ignoring the laws of the market, and undervaluing incentives and efficiency." Monreal (2008) argued that "the economic system that exists in the country today cannot serve as the starting point" of a model, because it does not perform the most basic functions to foster economic development. Omar Everleny Pérez Villanueva (2008a, 2008b) added that the current system is "a dead-end street" and urgently requires deep and comprehensive economic reform: decentralization of decisionmaking and a larger role for the market; the possibility of investing remittances in small and medium-sized family enterprises; the creation of cooperatives in services industries and in activities that complement state industrial enterprises; and limitation of the role of the state to policy design and development of instruments to support the operation of nonstate actors. Moreover, Hernández stated: "there is consensus on the importance of transforming the Cuban model, the need for the socialist system to persist under a different model . . . that would have the capacity for self-correction"; the 1993–1996 reforms that were interrupted should be continued (interview by E. García, 2007b).

The Chinese and Vietnamese models should be appealing to the Cuban leadership, because they combine strong economic performance and improvement in the population's standard of living through one-party (communist) rule. Nevertheless, Fidel rejected the Chinese model several times, arguing that China had several characteristics not present in Cuba: large territory and economic importance, great physical distance from the United States, and a domestic market large enough to attract large amounts of foreign investment, including from the United States (this view was also shared by José Luis Rodríguez [2007a]). During a visit to Cuba in 2003, Xu Sicheng, member of the Chinese Academy of Social Sciences, stated that "Cuba needs to establish a socialist market economy and put an end to egalitarianism" (cited by Contreras, 2007). In a trip to China in 2005, Raúl said: "It is really heartening to see all that you have been able to accomplish. . . . [T]here are people who are concerned about China's evolution, but I am untroubled [by what I see]" (*Granma,* April 21, 2005).

Pedro Monreal opined: "The Chinese and Vietnamese experiences are very interesting; I do not think that they need to be copied, but one can learn from them because these are countries that had similar problems to those that Cuba faces today in agriculture, and they were able to overcome them quite successfully." According to Monreal, the Cuban economy needed comprehensive reforms, along the lines of what China and Vietnam had undergone, to promote decentralization and the existence of private markets, confront the lack of motivation, allow markets to determine prices, and provide incentives to enterprises and encourage them to take economic risks (interview by Davies, 2007; E. García, 2007a). According to Pérez Villanueva (2008a), "Vietnam has been able to introduce the market into its model and has become an economy with high rates of growth, improving the welfare of its citizens, and becoming a leader in world exports."

A comparison of reforms in the three countries is revealing (Perkins, 2004). At the very heart of China's and Vietnam's reforms was the breakup of state farms and the granting of property rights to peasants, which also gave them autonomy over use of the land and control over to whom they sold their output; Cuba's more modest steps converted a portion of state farms into basic units of cooperative production (UBPCs), which lacked decisionmaking autonomy and were dependent on the state. Similarly, at the outset of its reforms, China transferred the bulk of state industries to local village enterprises and subsequently to foreign-invested firms; the bulk of Vietnam's exports were generated by foreign-invested firms. Only 25 percent of industrial enterprises in China and Vietnam were owned by the state in 2004. In contrast, in Cuba the industrial sector is state-owned except for joint ventures, and the legalization of self-employment that has occurred to date is on an exceptional basis and a far cry from an endorsement of small private enterprises. Based on foreign-investment laws that provided a secure legal framework, Vietnam attracted US$2 billion in foreign direct investment (FDI) in 2007; in Cuba, FDI fell by 41 percent between 2002 and 2006 as a result of state restrictions on investors and cancellation of contracts, and in 2002 was equivalent to about 5 percent of Vietnam's FDI. Imports by the two Asian countries were financed by fast-growing hard-currency goods exports. China did away with state monopoly over foreign trade and devalued its currency to make exports more competitive, while Vietnam allowed its currency to float with the same objective. On the contrary, in 2003 Cuba reversed the modest decentralization of foreign trade that had occurred in the 1990s and concentrated foreign trade decisionmaking in the Ministry of Foreign Trade and the Central Bank of Cuba, while maintaining an unrealistic exchange rate.

Property

Researcher Luis Marcelo Yera argued that the state currently makes fundamental decisions affecting Cuban enterprises that should be transferred to workers and that state enterprises should compete with other property types (Orta et al., 2006). In a symposium on socialist transition published in the journal *Temas,* most of the participants rejected the proposition that socialist property is equivalent to state property. The problem with state property, according to jurist Narciso Cobo, "is that what belongs to everyone does not belong to anyone, and therefore no one is accountable for it." Philosopher Isabel Monal stated that "workers do not feel that they own the means of production, and instead they say that the state is the owner," while historian Jorge Luis Acanda posited that it is essential to look for ways in which enterprises "can become in reality the property of workers." Sociologist Aurelio Alonso argued that the state "should have regulatory functions, and retain ownership of natural resources and large public services, otherwise permitting the creation of a mixed economy that would support private productive and service activities where they are efficient, as well as cooperatives ("Sobre la transición," 2007). Monreal postulated that "a socialist state can accommodate a private property sector much larger than what is currently being contemplated. . . . There are certain areas in which large state enterprises should predominate, such as nickel, steel, electricity . . . but the state does not have necessarily to take responsibility for repairing automobiles or shoes, or producing food. . . . [A] very long list of activities is inefficiently carried out by state enterprises, where it has been proven that the private sector and cooperatives can do much better." Many of these activities are based on the skills and experience of individuals and do not require a great deal of capital investment; a special bank could be established to make loans that would help them (interview by E. García, 2007a). Hernández supported the creation of cooperatives beyond agriculture as well as the legalization of small private enterprises in many fields—not just small restaurants (*paladares*)—that are capable of hiring employees beyond the immediate family and selling their output to private markets (interview by Davies, 2007).[3]

Historian Pedro Campos submitted fifteen proposals to the PCC's Central Committee, and also made them available to the official news media (which did not publish them), in which he argued that the revolution had stagnated from the time that socialism was equated with state control due to excessive centralization in planning and decisionmaking, and a distribution of income that retards economic growth and improvement of living conditions. None of the proposals suggested "capitalist privatization of enterprises or the conveying of property to foreign capital," but rather "cooperatives and self-management," the distribution of land to farmers, and self-employment (interview by Ravsberg, 2007). Economist Camila Piñeiro Harnecker (2011) argued that state enterprises are ill-equipped to engage in mid- and small-size activities (including light industry) and that worker self-management is the optimal form of organization (see Chapter 6).

Agriculture

Armando Nova (2006, 2007) argued that the main challenge facing Cuba's agricultural sector is the concentration of land in the hands of the state. He recommended structural economic reforms to increase output and productivity, among them: turning ownership of land over to those who work it, granting autonomy in decisionmaking to UBPCs, promoting the participation of cooperatives in free agricultural markets, ending the *acopio* state monopoly over distribution and eliminating restrictions to expand competition, and permitting foreign investment in agriculture. He added that the state should establish a framework that allows demand and supply to operate freely, turn over a million hectares of idle lands to private farmers and their families, and facilitate sales to consumers by private farmers and cooperatives. Finally, he argued that it was essential to reactivate sugarcane production, key for feeding the population and livestock, generating electricity from bagasse, and building a biotechnology and ethanol industry.

For Monreal, the inability of the agricultural sector, as currently organized, to produce sufficient levels of foodstuffs to feed the population, is a function of an organizational structure and property relations that do not provide incentives for production even though labor and land resources are available. He made the case for transferring state lands to private farmers and their relatives, family enterprises, and cooperatives. He also called for measures to ease the constraints of lack of inputs and of credit faced by private farmers. It is essential for agricultural reforms to be bolder than they were in the 1990s, he argued, through dismantling the counterproductive *acopio* system and relegating the role of the state to that of regulator. Taxation of agricultural producers should not be so onerous that it would work against stimulating production and bringing prices down (interview by E. García, 2007a).

Oscar Espinosa Chepe (2008) suggested that land should be distributed to individuals and cooperatives through sale, usufruct, or lease with option to buy. Landowners should be able to purchase needed inputs and have the freedom to plant crops of their choice and sell them through whichever means they see fit, including intermediaries. The *acopio* system should be phased out, substituting it with free interactions between producers and consumers. These measures would modernize the sector and eliminate current subsidies to UBPCs, resources that could be better used to provide microcredits to individual farmers and cooperatives.

Monetary Duality

Since 2003 there has been a national debate in Cuba on the negative effects of monetary duality (the simultaneous circulation of the convertible peso [CUC] and the national peso [CUP]) and the desirability of unifying the two currencies. Jorge Máttar, of the Economic Commission for Latin America and the Caribbean (ECLAC), favored the elimination of duality, as it has caused fiscal and monetary policy distortions and prevented the establishment of a financial market (*Agence France-Press,* February 7, 2007). Hiram Marquetti (2006b) predicted that "monetary duality will continue to exist, at least in the short term," and contended that reaching monetary unification would require solid economic recovery, macroeconomic stability, balanced finances, an increase in monetary reserves, a reduction in the current account deficit, an improvement in the external financial balance, a rise in domestic capital formation, and achieving international recognition of the domestic currency. Most of these requirements have not been accomplished. Monreal pointed out that the productivity of the domestic economy—tied to the CUP—is low, and that unification in the absence of a substantial increase in production and productivity would put pressure on prices, salaries, and pensions, and therefore that structural reforms need to be carried out before tackling currency unification. He added that China unified its currency through increases in output and productivity, which allowed for revaluation of the domestic currency and eventually the adoption of a single currency that is traded in international markets (interview by E. García, 2007a). Pérez Villanueva (2008a) recommended the elimination of currency exchange controls affecting enterprises, while maintaining the status quo with respect to the monetary duality for the population. Pavel Vidal Alejandro (2008b, 2010c, 2011a) argued that the dual currency system is an impediment to improving the performance of the economy and recommended further devaluation of the CUC to promote import substitution and exports.

External Sector

Monreal (2007) deemed that the structural weaknesses of the Cuban export sector must be offset by import substitution policies that diversify the production base, including production of capital goods, and the replacement of raw materials exports by higher-value exports embodying technology and knowledge. Marquetti (2006a) endorsed export promotion policies to reduce the deficit in goods trade, accompanied by measures to promote international competitiveness such as reducing interest rates on export credits, creating incentives for new exports, and setting export quality standards and penalizing exporters that do not meet such standards (cited by Pérez Villanueva, 2006). There was strong consensus among experts about the desirability of increasing FDI. Pérez Villanueva (2006) reasoned that to attract significant FDI flows, it was necessary not only to have a healthy macroeconomic environment, but also to reform the financial sector; he further argued for opening to FDI sectors with export potential, such as sugar, transportation, and services.

Social Welfare

Viviana Togores and Anicia García (2006) claimed that "social policy decisions should be made . . . taking into consideration not only social outcomes . . . but also economic feasibility." Workers should also contribute to the cost of social security, and retirement ages should be raised. In order to finance social services and enhance their efficiency, Pedro Campos proposed administration at the local level and self-management of the social security budgets. He also recommended the elimination of the rationing system and its substitution by a system of subsidies targeted to low-income persons who need assistance, coupled with salaries adjusted by inflation (interview by Ravsberg, 2007). Alexis Codina suggested that price subsidies for rationed goods should remain only for the most vulnerable population, with all other consumers relying on markets—and market prices—for their needs ("Sobre la transición," 2007). Monreal pointed out that "it is not possible to live on the [goods available through the] rationing card, but a segment of the population cannot live without them either." The elimination of the rationing system is likely to take a long time and will depend on a substantial increase in food production and a reduction in prices (interview by E. García, 2007a).

Pérez Villanueva posited that it was essential to establish a direct link between wages and profits of state enterprises: "it is not credible that in exchange for a salary of 200 pesos, a worker would turn in a good work performance" (cited by Orta et al., 2006). The low unemployment rate was achieved through excessive employment in social services sectors rather than in productive sectors, and therefore it is necessary to reverse this trend (Pérez Villanueva, 2008b). Vidal Alejandro (2008b) called for decentralization of decisionmaking regarding salary levels, for workers to share to some extent in enterprise profits, and for the state to use the "growing revenues in hard currency being received from exports of professional services to meet the demand for CUC that would be generated by salary increases." To reduce poverty, Lía Añé (2007) called for eliminating the dual currency system, reducing market segmentation, increasing salaries of those at the low end of the salary scale, and consolidating and evaluating the effectiveness of new social programs. Mayra Espina (2008) proposed a new social policy to eliminate poverty and reduce inequality in a sustainable manner.

Juan Triana Cordoví (2007) recommended higher investments in technical education and in careers that contribute to knowledge, even if they are more costly than those in other disciplines such as the humanities, social sciences, and pedagogy. Hernández argued that since Cuban citizens own their homes, they should be free to buy or sell them, and the state should facilitate housing construction and repair by individuals (interview by E. García, 2007b). Espinosa Chepe (2007a) recommended allowing homeowners to use their properties as collateral to secure loans to improve them or to invest in small businesses. Espina (2008) proposed decentralizing housing construction, increasing production of construction materials, and supporting the population in building their own homes.

Citizen Participation and Role of Youth

José Luis Toledo, president of the Constitutional and Legal Affairs Commission of the ANPP, criticized the impunity with which Cuban public officials "transform into a caricature the essential aspirations of our society, and the spirit and letter of our Constitution"; he complained about the poor record of claims and complaints by citizens against the state's powers, and the many ways in which public officials obstruct the resolution of citizens' problems as well as the indifference and inefficiency of government officials and members of the ANPP. With respect to the latter, he expressed that "overwhelming unanimity reigns [within the ANPP] and there are few instances when views are actually debated and contested . . . particularly at a time when debate is indispensable in the process of taking decisions . . . given the very complex circumstances the country faces. . . . [Ignoring this reality] would be a regrettable demonstration of ignorance or half-heartedness." He said that ANPP delegates "should stop complaining and concentrate on exercising their power to remove managers and executives of enterprises who do not meet their obligations" (*Juventud Rebelde,* November 25, 2007). Randy Alonso Falcón meanwhile argued that citizen participation was unsatisfactory: "the process of oversight by the ANPP . . . does not permit real interaction. . . . [R]ather than promoting discussion of the problems facing communities, it promotes lack of communication" ("Sobre la transición," 2007). Journalist Soledad Cruz (2007) stated that "citizen participation is relegated to obeying, accepting directions from above, which eliminates a sense of being responsible. . . . [C]itizens need to feel that they actually participate in decision-making, . . . that they are listened to and that their views are taken into account." Hernández pined for a socialist society in which citizens contribute more effectively to decisions, where public opinion and participation go beyond mobilization and extend to decision-making and oversight of state policies, and where the Organs of People's Power, workers, and mass organizations truly have the capacity to decide how to resolve fundamental problems (interview by E. García, 2007b). The official media were also subject to criticism.[4]

In 2006, newspaper *Juventud Rebelde* published the results of a survey of 280 youth. Among the statements from interviewees was: "We continue to make many errors. . . . There are many things that ought to be straightened out . . . [and] for this reason we need efficient leaders. [We ought to promote criticism] because if we do not, things will not improve; although some say that criticism is practiced, in fact this is only demagoguery, as real criticism does not really happen. The double morality needs to disappear altogether; there are some leaders who call for honesty, savings and sacrifice, while they do not practice them." Survey respondents sought a nation in which salaries are sufficient to cover basic needs, with a single currency, better public transportation, paved streets and reliable water distribution, no electricity shortages, and no prostitution (cited by D. Pérez et al., 2006). In 2007, students asked Universidad de Oriente rector Zaida Valdés to address problems such as availability of food, public safety concerns, lack of potable water, and poor lighting; she refused to listen to their demands, and the protest extended to the Julio Antonio Mella Secondary Institute, where students used placards to ask for a more open dialogue at universities; faculty supported the students and refused to sign a letter backing the administration (Bravo, 2007). During a meeting with students of the University of Information Sciences in Havana, ANPP president Ricardo Alarcón was questioned by students about the insufficiency of salaries to support purchases at foreign-currency stores (TRDs), the ban on Cuban citizens patronizing tourism hotels and restaurants, the inability to travel abroad, and the lack of access to the Internet; the students demanded closer oversight of the work of ministries and the removal of officials who failed to meet performance targets (*BBC News,* February 6, 2008). Carlos Lage Cordoniú, president of the Federation of University Students, contended that "participation channels are not credible and students do not trust institutions or their leaders as a way to communicate with the Revolution. . . . Many persons have been excluded and accused of being counter-revolutionaries because they had points of view that differ from the norm. . . . Some sectors have recognized the imperative to integrate the youth, but others still resist" ("Sobre la transición," 2007). Singer Pablo Milanés (2008) put it as follows: "I do not trust any Cubans older than 75 years because they are all ready to be retired. . . . [Their] socialism stagnated . . . their revolutionary ideas of yore have turned into reactionary and . . . they do not allow the new generation to advance," forcing youth to emigrate; "we must undertake reforms in many different areas. . . . It is essential to pass [the torch] to new generations so that they can create another socialism."

Raúl's Reforms

The aforementioned debate was followed by a period of inactivity in the reform arena. At a time of damaging hurricanes and a global economic crisis, Raúl warned that it was necessary "to adjust all dreams to real possibilities." Thus, he had to give "secondary priority" to the reforms, but doing so "did not mean a change in economic strategy"; reform proposals would not be forgotten but would be implemented gradually "as circumstances allow, and we will advance slowly but steadily, without excessive idealism, as resources become available" (R. Castro Ruz, 2008b, 2008c). Pedro Campos (2007) complained about the delayed policy response to the debate: "The hopes of citizens that have been awakened by the debates cannot be underestimated. Very important ideas and suggestions have been presented. Not to act on them would be dangerous for the future of Cuba. . . . What would be the sense of holding national consultations . . . if their purpose is only to keep people busy and offer them an escape valve, as is argued by skeptics and enemies of the revolution?" An alternative to the official view that hurricanes and the global financial crisis required the slowdown of reforms is that those same external factors in fact made the need for reforms even more urgent, as happened in the 1990s after the collapse of the Soviet Union. The lack of progress of reforms, the alternative view posits, was attributable to resistance from the more conservative top and mid-level officials, who were concerned that changes would curb their economic power through the emergence of actors independent from the state that might compete with inefficient state enterprises.

The changes implemented by Raúl in 2007–2009 were of three types: administrative measures, nonstructural changes, and structural reforms. The administrative measures did not entail systemic changes and sought to improve efficiency and reduce costs, along the line of measures adopted before Raúl gained control. They included the merging of state agencies, implementation of the *perfeccionamiento empresarial* (enterprise improvement system) and start of decentralization, campaigns against corruption and labor indiscipline, and broader acceptance of criticism (the most innovative of the measures). Nonstructural changes involved bolder and more creative measures, but of secondary order, as they did not change the core of the system; they included allowing citizens access to hotels and restaurants formerly accessible only to foreign tourists, payment of arrears to farmers and members of cooperatives, increases in prices under the *acopio* procurement system, sale of certain goods (such as electric appliances) to the population, authorization for the operation of private taxis, raises in salaries, pension reform, and reduction in free goods and services (gratuities). These measures sought to reduce government expenditures and the amount of money in circulation, increase production and productivity, create incentives for workers and farmers, diminish costly food imports, and improve transportation. They favored the high- and middle-income population through access to the convertible peso, while ignoring the low-income population, who could not afford to buy the goods and services sold in convertible pesos. The majority of the administrative measures and nonstructural changes were fairly simple and could be implemented in a relatively short period of time. In contrast, structural reforms "are very complex transformations that modify the material and organizational bases of the economy and require relatively long periods of time to implement" (Monreal, 2008). The only structural reform implemented through 2010 was the distribution of idle state lands in usufruct, but others were subsequently introduced, principally during the Sixth Congress of the PCC and thereafter. The three types of changes are described below, listed roughly in order of importance and chronology. Other structural reforms are addressed in later in the chapter.

Administrative Reorganization

Raúl proclaimed the formation of a more compact government structure, with fewer state administrative entities, in order to reduce the enormous number of meetings, permits, regulations, and other bureaucracy, and to consolidate economic activities that were under different organizations. For example, the Ministry of Agriculture absorbed what was left of the Ministry of Sugar after the creation of the AZCUBA Sugar Group, the Ministry of Fisheries became part of the Ministry of Food Industry, and a new Ministry of Industries consolidated the activities of the former Ministries of Light Industry and of Steel Industry and Metalworking. The Ministry of Basic Industries was eliminated and its functions were transferred to the Ministry of Energy and of Mining; the Ministries of Foreign Trade and of Foreign Investment and International Cooperation were combined; the National Institute of Housing was integrated into the Ministry of Construction. The state postal service was transformed into a group of enterprises. A number of entities affiliated with the Council of State were transferred to the relevant ministries, whereas numerous enterprises within ministries and other state entities were eliminated (see list in Roque, 2010). Plans were announced to merge and rationalize enterprises that were physically spread out (e.g., foundries) and operated at low capacity, in order to reduce costs (*Granma Internacional,* December 23, 2010).

Perfeccionamiento Empresarial and the Start of Decentralization

Decree-Laws nos. 252 and 281, both approved in August 2007, directed all state enterprises to implement the *perfeccionamiento empresarial* system that Raúl had championed since 1987 in productive enterprises under the Ministry of the Revolutionary Armed Forces and that had been extended since 1998 to civilian state enterprises. This management improvement system provides more autonomy in decisionmaking to enterprises, imposes strict accounting standards and performance requirements, and offers material incentives to workers and managers. Implementation of this system was essentially stopped by Fidel in 2003 with his return to centralization, despite the fact that only 7 percent of enterprises that had adopted the improvement system suffered losses in 2006 (compared to a national average of 38 percent), and despite the fact that these enterprises made proportionally larger contributions to sales and had higher productivity than those outside the *perfeccionamiento empresarial* system (*El País,* February 11, 2007; *Granma,* December 25, 2007). Statistics on the number of firms that applied the system vary: 11 percent of all enterprises in 2002, fifteen years after *perfeccionamiento empresarial* was created; between 22 percent and 32 percent in 2006–2007; but only 40 enterprises (out of a total of 3,000) were considered to be in an "experimental process" prior to their approval by the government in 2008 (Espinosa Chepe, 2007c; Lee, 2007). Within agriculture, local organizations were created in all municipalities to "decentralize decisionmaking" in transportation and marketing of agricultural output (*Granma,* April 1, 2008; *Reuters,* September 20, 2010; Nova, 2012).

Campaigns Against Labor Indiscipline and Corruption

Fidel warned that the revolution could self-destruct because of corruption (F. Castro Ruz, 2005b; for background, see Díaz-Briquets and Pérez-López, 2006). In September 2006, during the Nineteenth Congress of the Workers' Central Union of Cuba (CTC), Raúl blamed labor indiscipline and corruption for the economic ills of the country, including inefficiency and scarcity of goods.[5] Inspections conducted by the National Inspectorate of Labor in May–June 2006 in 2,207 enterprises found that 55.4 percent had mediocre or poor compliance with labor standards (*Granma,* April 3, 2006; *Agence France-Press,* November 26, 2006). In October 2006, the press published a series of articles denouncing instances of theft, waste, and overall lack of administrative controls in state enterprises and informing about sentences of four to twenty years of imprisonment meted to public officials engaging in such crimes (*Juventud Rebelde,* October 1, 2006, October 15, 2006, October 22, 2006).

In August 2006, the Ministry of Labor and Social Security issued new regulations to tighten labor discipline, addressing the following problems: lack of punctuality; unauthorized absences from the workplace during the workday and meal breaks longer than authorized; failure to follow supervisor instructions and disrespectful behavior toward supervisors; negligence in the use of resources; unauthorized release of information about the workplace; introduction of unauthorized software programs or files into workplace computer systems; loss or theft of goods from the workplace, failure to report those observed engaging in theft, and failure to take preventive measures to avoid loss or theft; and hiring or promotion of friends or relatives and failure to verify previous labor history of new hires. Managers of workers found guilty of these misbehaviors could also be prosecuted if it could be shown that they were negligent in demanding appropriate behavior or, once informed, did not take action to remedy the misbehavior or bring it to the attention of superiors. Sanctions included reprimand and temporary or permanent removal from the workplace or from employment in the sector. Sanctions against disciplined workers could be appealed to the most immediate higher authority; if the appeal was denied, workers had the right to appeal to the highest-level organ within their enterprise, but not to the court system (Resoluciones nos. 187 and 188, 2006).

There are a number of obstacles to the implementation of these regulations: it is virtually impossible to arrive to work on-time because of the chronic failures by the public transportation system; retail stores and government offices are closed before and after the normal workday and during weekends, requiring workers to shop and conduct other business during work hours; the shortage of childcare facilities makes it difficult for mothers with young children to meet regular work schedules; low salaries create an incentive to steal from the workplace; workers have to dedicate a great deal of time and resources to meet their basic needs, which takes up much of the energy they could otherwise devote to work; excessive meetings and mobilization to other tasks reduce productive labor time (*Granma,* April 3, 2006; Pérez Villanueva, 2010c; Martín, 2010). These problems delayed implementation of the regulations, which were superseded by Decree-Law no. 251 of 2007. Instruction no. 188 of the Popular Tribunal, issued on September 22, 2008, stipulated that in cases of theft of state property and corruption, the penalty would be twice that prescribed in the penal code.

A survey conducted in 2008 by the Ministry of Labor and Social Security of 2,042 enterprises found 26,622 violations of labor regulations: 46 percent of workers arrived late to their jobs, 19 percent took lunch periods and breaks that exceeded legal limits, 10 percent left work before the scheduled quitting time, 5 percent carried out unauthorized tasks during the workday, and 4 percent left their workplace without proper authorization (*Granma,* February 11, 2009). In that same year, the Operational Group to Combat Crime was created, composed of inspectors, prosecutors, Ministry of Interior agents, and police officers supported by special courts that process anticorruption cases rapidly (*Agence France-Press,* July 9, 2008, October 6, 2008). Despite these efforts, in April–May 2011 the Sixth National Verification of Internal Controls audited 132 enterprises in Havana and found that 45 percent showed deficiencies such as accounting problems, superficial controls, violations of laws and regulations, and crime and corruption (*Cubanet,* July 8, 2011). Factors that contribute to corruption include centralization in decisionmaking and state control over resources that give unfettered power to government officials, lack of transparency and accountability by managers, social mores that discourage questioning of leaders' decisions, and government-controlled media that lack the initiative to denounce corrupt behavior (Ravsberg, 2011a).

In an essay circulated within the National Union of Writers and Artists of Cuba (UNEAC), Esteban Morales (2010), honorary director of the Center for the Study of the United States, candidly stated: "There are individuals in state and government positions who are setting themselves up financially for the time when the Revolution ends, and others that might have things almost ready to transfer state property to private hands, as happened in the former USSR. . . . Corruption is more dangerous than the so-called internal dissidence, [as it is] the true counterrevolution, one that can cause the most damage because it is within the state, which is truly the manager of the country's resources." He added that "nearly all" leaders participate in corrupt activities, including members of the armed forces and of the Ministry of Interior, and criticized the state import monopoly, the commissions received from foreign transactions, and accounts held in foreign banks. Morales was removed from the PCC as a result of his essay, but the criticism caused by that removal led to his reinstatement.

Subsequently, Raúl agreed with several of the key points made by Morales: "Corruption is one of the principal enemies of the Revolution today, more harmful than subversive and interventionist activities by the government of the United States. . . . Corruption today is tantamount to counterrevolution" (R. Castro Ruz, 2011c; *Granma,* December 23, 2011). In the First National Conference of the PCC, in 2012, Raúl deplored that, in the past, actions to fight corruption had been "ephemeral," and warned that PCC leaders involved in corruption would be expelled (a sanction heretofore reserved for acts of treason or of very serious nature). He called on the PCC to be a "battering ram" against corruption and predicted that the revolution "would cease to exist, without the enemy firing a single shot, if the direction of the country were to fall in the hands of corrupt leaders" (R. Castro Ruz, 2012a). This was followed by the screening to high-level PCC and government officials, as well as to enterprise managers, of a video in which a number of officials confessed to accepting bribes and participating in illegal business transactions. Another video, titled "Metastasis" because it "spread like a cancer" within the higher echelons of the government, showed the payment of bribes by Canadian company Tokmakjian Group, one of the largest foreign enterprises operating on the island, with an annual turnover of US$80 million (*Reuters,* February 21, 2012).

In mid-2009 the office of the comptroller general, reporting to the Council of State, was created to exercise financial oversight of state entities. The agency has broad authority to supervise all government institutions, including ministries. It is reported that more than 300 high-level officials and executives of joint ventures and of state enterprises—including important foreign officials—have been arrested or sentenced to jail terms.[6] An audit of 750 state enterprises conducted in 2011 by some 3,000 auditors from the comptroller general's office deemed that 63 percent had financial controls that were satisfactory or acceptable, with the rest having deficient or unacceptable controls, a small improvement over 2010 (*Reuters,* June 20, 2011). In order to detect financial mismanagement sooner, the Central Bank of Cuba began to require all state entities to supply it with quarterly reports of all financial transactions (Resolución no. 19, 2012).

Openness to Criticism Within Socialism and the PCC

Juan Triana Cordoví (2011) recalled that for several decades, the national political culture discouraged disagreement and dissent, limiting spaces for criticism of state policies and giving rise to the situation currently faced. Raúl affirmed that the PCC, "the supreme leading force of society and the state," should be "more democratic, so that every citizen has the right to express his or her views . . . without fear . . . provided they are within the law and socialism. . . . Leaders need to be able to listen and to create an environment within which all can express their views with complete freedom. . . . Criticism, when properly expressed, is essential to move forward. . . . The Party and the Government will determine collegially, and subject to available resources, the priorities and the pace of addressing the main problems that affect the nation, after consultation with the citizenry . . . when matters rise to that level. . . . All opinions shall be analyzed and when consensus cannot be reached, different views should be raised to higher authorities in order to make decisions." He added that it was "essential to dismantle the colossal psychological barrier" impeding open discussion and to promote "debate without dogmatic constraints or bound by unviable schemes." Finally, he promised "to eliminate the excessive degree of secrecy to which we have become accustomed in the last fifty years" and make economic information more readily available (R. Castro Ruz, 2007b, 2010c, 2011d).[7]

Access by Cuban Citizens to International Tourism Hotels

In 1993, Cuban citizens were banned access to hotels and restaurants that catered to foreign tourists, even when they were invited by family members visiting from abroad, a policy that was harshly criticized inside and outside the country. Raúl accepted the existence of "excessive restrictions and legal measures that create more harm than good" (R. Castro Ruz, 2007b). In April 2008 the restriction on access by Cuban citizens to hotels and restaurants was lifted (limitations on automobile rentals were similarly removed); as payment at such locales must be made in convertible pesos, the impact of these measures is limited: hotel rates range from US$45 to US$200 per day, and restaurant meals from US$15 to US$30, while the average monthly salary of a Cuban worker is about US$20. Moreover, Cuban citizens who patronize hotels have to pay full fare and are not able to take advantage of special rates for tourism packages. The lifting of the access restrictions, which eliminated a blatantly discriminatory policy, could have the effect of helping to generate customers to fill vacant hotel rooms, particularly during the summer season.

Payment of Arrears, Rise in Prices, and Increase in Sales to Farmers and to the Population

In 2006, Raúl blamed bureaucratic red tape and *acopio* payment delays to cooperatives and private farmers—who produced 65 percent of agricultural output—for the poor performance of the agricultural sector and the high need for food imports (*Granma,* December 24, 2006). In 2007 the government developed a system to streamline payments to farmers and cooperatives upon submission of proper documentation; in May the *acopio* agency increased procurement prices for milk and beef and in June arrears of 1.4 billion CUP were paid (*Granma,* March 26, 2007, May 25, 2007, April 28, 2007). Despite price increases, milk *acopio* prices were still 6 percent of the retail price whereas meat *acopio* prices were 1–4 percent of the retail price, depending on the cut of the meat (Espinosa Chepe, 2007b). A second increase (of 150 percent) in the *acopio* price for milk was implemented in 2008, and prices of root crops, vegetables, tobacco, coffee, and coconuts were similarly raised (Lugo, 2008).[8] The government also opened stores in the countryside where farmers could purchase, using CUP, inputs such as seeds, fertilizers, herbicides, tools, work clothes, and gloves (Reuters, August 16, 2010).

In May 2007, Cuba allowed the importation of electrical equipment, motors, and spare parts for vehicles, photographic and video equipment, and spare parts for bicycles. Beginning in March 2008, sale in CUC of computers, mobile telephones,[9] video and DVD equipment, microwave ovens, electric pressure cookers, wide-screen televisions, automobile alarms, and other products was allowed (*Reuters,* March 14, 2008, March 16, 2008, March 31, 2008, May 3, 2008).

Private Transportation Services

In 2008 the government approved the use of private transportation services, including taxis, which had been banned since 1999. The regulations issued by the Ministry of Transportation in January 2009 distinguish between transportation within cities, where private vehicles can operate only along routes not covered by public transportation, prices can be set based on demand and supply (with caps set by the state), and service providers must purchase fuel at the prevailing rate; and transportation in the interior of the island, where private providers can operate wherever they wish, rates are set by the state, and fuel can be purchased at subsidized prices; violations of regulations are punished by a fine of 1,000 CUP (US$42) for the first offense and seizure of the vehicle for the second offense (*Associated Press,* January 12, 2008). Private drivers pay the government a monthly fee of between 600–800 CUP (US$23–37) depending on the type of vehicle, and are responsible for maintaining and repairing their own vehicles. It has been reported that owners of automobiles illegally rent them to private drivers, receiving up to 1,000 CUP per day in rental fees, which make for a tidy profit for the vehicle owners (even after paying for gasoline and maintenance) and a good income for the drivers (I. García, 2012). In 2010, state enterprise Cubataxi began to rent taxis and small vans to individuals to provide transportation services rather than employing these individuals as drivers. By mid-2011, 47,652 licenses had been issued to self-employed passenger and freight transportation operators (*Reuters*, July 31, 2011).

Salary Increases and Meeting Basic Needs

Raúl acknowledged that salaries were insufficient to meet basic needs and announced measures to compensate for price increases. In 2007 the government permitted compensation in convertible pesos or in other convertible currencies to employees of foreign companies (legalizing a de facto practice), with an annual progressive tax of 10 percent charged on earnings of over 2,400 CUC and up to 50 percent on earnings beyond 60,000 CUC (Resolución no. 277, 2007). During a meeting with 1,200 employees of foreign companies to explain the new tax system, Vice Minister of Finance Nelly Cubillas faced hostility from the foreign businessmen and the meeting was cut short (*BBC News*, February 6, 2008). In 2008 the salary cap for production workers was eliminated as a way to encourage overtime and higher production; by 2011, though, few enterprises had implemented this cap, as salaries were still set through the mechanism of the central plan (Vidal Alejandro, 2011a). Since 2009, workers have been permitted to hold more than one job, and to earn more than one salary, provided the second job does not affect performance on the first (main) job. Excluded from this option are managers, medical personnel, teachers, and auditors; students can hold part-time jobs outside school hours (Decreto Ley no. 268, 2008). Also approved was pay based on performance, which connected salaries with individual effort and outcome rather than basing them on enterprise performance (Resolución no. 9, 2008). Salaries of employees of the judicial branch were increased as well (Vicent, 2008b).

Pay based on performance was supposed to be implemented nationally by August 31, 2008, but only "modest progress" was reported even in November. Implementation was postponed until January 2009, for several reasons: resistance from managers, workers, and unions because the new system is more demanding of workers and would result in lower salaries than previously earned; absence of reliable information, and deficient accounting practices in enterprises; lack of studies about how to link salaries to results, and lack of trained personnel to undertake the studies; delay in the publication of the methodology; lack or delay in the delivery of inputs, breakage of equipment, and interruption of electricity service, which hamper worker performance of stop work altogether; and the need to control quality in order to avoid production of defective or useless goods (*Granma*, October 28, 2008; *Trabajadores*, November 24, 2008, December 1, 2008, December 8, 2008; Calves, 2010). In April 2009 only 18 percent of the labor force was under the system of pay based on performance and in October

2009 only 13.8 percent of salaries were calculated on the basis of performance (*Bohemia,* April 29, 2009; *Granma,* October 2, 2009).

The construction sector illustrates the problems faced in the application of salary based on performance. In 2008 there was a national shortage of some 2,200 construction workers, particularly in Havana city and the provinces of Matanzas and Holguín. In 2007–2008 the Ministry of Construction lost 5,000 workers—equivalent to the construction labor force in Santiago de Cuba—who shifted to other occupations for several reasons: managers did not understand or did not apply salary based on performance and were unable to evaluate performance; the system was only applied where labor shortages were most severe; workers complained that it was more demanding to work in the upper floors of a building compared to the lower levels, as it was necessary to set up scaffolds, lift materials, and so on, which added two to three hours to the workday; and there were numerous delays, beyond workers' control (e.g., shortage of cement), which reduced the number of work hours and the salary paid. The vice minister of the Ministry of Construction, Resibel Rosquete, acknowledged that self-employed bricklayers had higher productivity and produced better-quality work compared to their state counterparts, because of higher earnings; and that the performance of state construction workers was of comparatively lower quality, and often it was necessary to undo work they had done because it was defective (*Granma,* August 20, 2008; *Bohemia,* October 4, 2008).

Reform of Social Security Pensions

Social security pensions in Cuba were increased in 2008 between 0.2 percent and 22 percent, depending on the amount of the pension,[10] with the top monthly pension set at 400 CUP (about US$17), although the increase still does not compensate for the 50 percent fall in the real value of pensions since 1989. The cost of this measure, which benefited 2 million persons, was 1 billion CUP (Vicent, 2008a, table 4.4). The 2008 pension reform, analyzed in Chapter 4, reduced somewhat the enormous deficit faced by the pension system, but did not bring long-term financial balance to the system. The reform's mandatory inclusion of the self-employed in the social security system makes Cuba one of only five countries in the region that does so; pensions for the self-employed are calculated on the basis of contributions that they make to the system (Decretos-Leyes nos. 278 and 284, 2011; Mesa-Lago, 2012).

Monetary Duality

Raúl proposed the "progressive, gradual and prudent revaluation of the peso [CUP]," noting that elimination of monetary duality was a complex problem that required "profound study" in order to avoid "traumatic impacts on the population": "it is necessary to eliminate the dual currencies," he stated, "but little by little, perhaps in 4 or 5 years" (*Granma,* September 18, 2008). Full convertibility will require a marked increase in production and productivity, combined with an overall price reform that is bound to adversely affect the Cuban population, requiring adjustment of retail prices, salaries, and so on. At the end of 2007, 10,800 individuals signed a petition submitted to the ANPP calling for unification of the currency. Believing that currency unification was imminent, in February 2008 Cubans exchanged massive quantities of convertible pesos (CUC) for national pesos (CUP), essentially clearing out stocks of CUP in exchange houses; subsequently, the rumor was quelled by the government, which clarified that unification would be achieved gradually (Terrero, 2008). If the decision were made to lower the exchange rate of the CUP for the CUC, it would have to be done slowly. For example, if the exchange rate were suddenly cut from 24 CUP for 1 CUC to 8 CUP for 1 CUC, without an increase in the supply of goods, consumers would see a two-thirds reduction in prices of goods at foreign-currency stores, resulting in a rush to buy those goods that would wipe out supplies and require new rounds of imports, which in turn would quickly disappear from the shelves as well.

Elimination of Gratuities, Rationing, and Subsidies

Raúl cautioned in 2008 that "no one, neither an individual nor a country, can consistently spend more than it receives," and therefore it is essential to "adjust our expenditures in convertible currency to our revenues." It is not possible to "increase non-productive [social] expenditures by contracting debts that our children and grandchildren will have to pay." To balance the country's finances, he announced the "elimination of improper gratuities and excessive subsidies" that are "irrational and unsustainable." Rationing is "an expression . . . of egalitarianism that benefits those who do not work . . . or work but do not need the benefits of the rationing system" (R. Castro Ruz, 2008a). Thus, high- and middle-income households, as well as those that receive remittances, benefit from rationed goods that are priced below the market and benefit from free social services that should properly be targeted to low-income households and others who need them (Soberón, 2005, 2006). But the 35 percent of households that do not receive remittances, or receive them in small amounts, and the households that do not receive payments in CUC or hard currencies, would not be able to survive without the roughly ten days of consumption of foodstuffs provided by rationing at subsidized prices; if the rationing system were eliminated, it would be necessary to grant social assistance to all destitute persons (Mesa-Lago, 2006). Mario González-Corzo (2009) argues that elimination of the rationing card would bring about a significant decline in the purchasing power of Afro-Cubans, pensioners, and residents of the eastern provinces. Arnaldo Ramos Lauzurique (2010) estimates that the elimination of the rationing system would result in a fivefold increase in the monthly food expenditures of the average consumer. Ernesto Hernández-Catá (2007) favors eliminating the rationing card at once, arguing that the effect of doing so would be positive, but under the assumption that structural reforms will create a full market economy.

At the end of 2009, 24,700 cafeterias at workplaces that served meals at subsidized prices to some 225,000 workers were closed; the cost of the meal service was estimated at US$170 million per annum. Quality of the meals was poor and food products were regularly stolen from the kitchens and sold on the black market. The government currently provides workers a stipend of 15 CUP (US$0.75) per day for them to buy their lunches, an amount deemed to be insufficient to buy a proper meal, particularly since there are few cafeterias near workplaces; workers who bring their meals from home do not have access to appliances to refrigerate and heat their food (*Bohemia*, June 29, 2010; *Granma*, June 11, 2010).

Distribution of Idle State Lands in Usufruct

Raúl stated in 2007 that "land and resources [should be] in the hands of those who can use them to produce efficiently . . . [who should receive] a just reward . . . [for] satisfying the needs of the population." He reported that Cuba imported 80 percent of the foodstuffs that the population consumed, at an annual cost of US$1.5 billion, and that nearly 30 percent of the 6.6 million hectares of land controlled by the state was idle (R. Castro Ruz, 2007b). Orlando Lugo (2008), then-president of the National Association of Small Private Farmers (ANAP), stated that 51 percent of the land in the state's hands was idle or being poorly used, and that a significant portion was infested with marabú (*Granma*, April 1, 2008).

Decree-Law no. 259, passed in 2008, stipulated the distribution of idle state lands in usufruct to individuals, cooperatives, and nonagricultural state entities. This was the most significant structural reform up until that time. The distribution of lands was subject to the following restrictions, requirements, and obstacles: (a) a maximum of 13.42 hectares per grantee, which is too small to allow crop rotation; (b) a ban on building a dwelling on the parcel (which may require the grantee to travel from a long distance away to cultivate the land), as well as on constructing a barn for seeds, tools, animals, and barnyard birds; (c) ownership of the land remains in state hands, with individuals having the nontransferable right of usufruct for only ten years (twenty for cooperatives and state entities), renewable for a second period of ten years if the grantee meets all obligations; (d) 50–60 percent of lands are infested with marabú and others are of low quality for cultivation and often lack water, which together with lack of resources for preparing the lands and digging wells makes it challenging to clear, cultivate, and irrigate lands in a "rational and sustainable manner," as required by the law; (e) grantees are obligated to sell to the state a portion (*acopio*) of production (up to 70 percent) at below-market prices; (f) the contract can be canceled if the grantee fails to meet legal obligations or infringes against environmental rules, or in the interest of the public need; (g) clarity is lacking on whether, should a contract be rescinded, the state is obligated to reimburse the grantee for improvements to the land; (h) 80 percent of grantees lack experience in land cultivation, although they must begin to sell produce to the state within two years and to pay taxes (land use, labor force, social security, and personal income) immediately; and (i) credit is lacking for grantees to acquire seeds, fertilizer, tools, and equipment (some of these restrictions and requirements were subsequently relaxed, as discussed later). Implementation of the law was delayed by three months; in June 2010, 73 percent of 100,000 land applications had been processed and distributed to 38 percent of applicants (*Reuters,* October 9, 2008, November 17, 2008; *BBC Mundo,* November 11, 2008; *Agence France-Press,* March 3, 2009; *Juventud Rebelde,* March 22, 2009; *Granma,* June 12, 2009). Raúl stated that the idea was not to "rush out to distribute land without any controls . . . it has to be done efficiently," but was critical of delays and of bureaucratic red tape, as only one-third of distributed land was being cultivated (R. Castro Ruz, 2009b).

Resistance and Criticism of Reforms

In some of his Reflections, Fidel criticized directly or indirectly the reforms that were being implemented: on April 16, 2008, he complained about "making shameful concessions to the ideology of the enemy"; on October 2, he said that some government leaders "dream of satisfying all the 'wish lists' of the people" and stated that the government "needs to apply rigorous discipline and an absolutely rational set of priorities," to align dreams and realities. On January 22, 2009, Fidel promised to scale back his Reflections in order "not to interfere or hinder the continuous flow of decisions that comrades in the Party and in the state need to be taking to address the global economic crisis" (F. Castro Ruz, 2008, 2009). Although Fidel did not stop the Reflections, henceforth they generally were not focused on internal matters.

Former minister of economy José Luis Rodríguez (2007a) stated that the transfer of power to Raúl had not generated significant changes, but rather continuity, albeit with some adjustments to make the socialist economic model more efficient. Rodríguez added that he did not conceive of other forms of property that would contribute to development to the same extent as state property, that collectivization would be maintained and strengthened, that self-employment would disappear gradually as state efficiency improved, and that small businesses would not be allowed, as they could not be the basis for economic development of the nation. Others defended the virtues of central planning: it establishes priorities and maintains close control over performance, prioritizes strategic investments and uses existing capital stock most efficiently, and permits prompt decisionmaking to confront crisis (Terrero, 2009; *Granma,* June 25, 2010).

Some of the opposition to reforms took the form of inertia and obstructionism. In the months leading to the Sixth Congress of the Cuban Communist Party, the official press published numerous news articles and opinion pieces regarding incompetence and bureaucratic resistance to change. On September 9, 2011, *Juventud Rebelde* called for the deepening of reforms, moving from words to deeds, and combating "plagues" such as excessive centralization, onerous regulations and prohibitions, lack of initiative by state enterprises and local institutions, and lack of participation of workers in decisionmaking.

Through one of his Reflections, Fidel engaged in a polemic with two leftist US social scientists who had written in mid-2007 about Cuba's accomplishments but also identified a number of critical problems facing the island's economy and society (Petras and Eastman-Abaya, 2007). Fidel derisively referred to them as self-described extreme-left "super-revolutionaries" who felt entitled to criticize the revolution and suggest neoliberal policies that were totally inappropriate for Cuba (F. Castro Ruz, 2007). In several Reflections in 2008, Fidel directly or indirectly criticized reform measures being implemented: on April 16 he "rejected" the idea of Cuba having to make "shameful concessions to the enemy's ideology," while on October 2 he stated that some comrades "dream of meeting all the 'unbounded' demands of our people. What we need in our state is a strict discipline and an absolutely rational order of priorities," focusing not on dreams but on what can be accomplished through intensive and quality work. In 2009, on January 22, Fidel promised to cut back on his Reflections in order "not to interfere or obstruct comrades in the government or the PCC who are continuously making decisions on how to address difficult problems arising from the global economic crisis" (F. Castro Ruz, 2008, 2009). Fidel continued to write his Reflections, but tended to focus them on foreign policy issues.

Agreements of the Sixth Party Congress: Limitations and Adjustments

Raúl announced that the Sixth Congress of the Cuban Communist Party would be held in the second half of 2009 (the Fifth Congress was in 1997, and party congresses should have been held at five-year intervals) to adopt guidelines for economic and social development for 2010–2014. By mid-2009, the official call for the Congress had not been issued, and it was postponed until 2011, due to alleged reasons such as the global economic crisis but with the implication that there were disagreements among the leadership with regard to potential reforms. The Sixth Congress, finally held in April 2011, ratified the reform measures proclaimed by Raúl and announced a number of additional ones.

In November 2010, a comprehensive set of economic and social policy guidelines ("Lineamientos") for public discussion was published and circulated widely; the guidelines were the subject of a national debate prior to being submitted to the Sixth Congress in April 2011. The Congress changed or added to 68 percent of the original 291 guidelines, increasing the total number to 313 agreements (92 percent dealing with economic matters and 8 percent with social matters).[11] Most of the changes were relatively minor language corrections and merging of guidelines. More radical proposals, for example those that would allow concentration of private property, were rejected because they ran counter to the essence of socialism (*Proyecto, 2010;* "Información," 2011; R. Castro Ruz, 2011a). The agreements from the Sixth Congress admitted that the "changes" that had been made earlier (the term "reform" does not appear in the document) were insufficient to address the country's problems, and additional policy actions (*actualización,* or updating of the model) were required. The reforms embodied in the Congress's agreements are positive, but plagued by obstacles and disincentives that would limit their effectiveness in addressing national problems (Espinosa Chepe, 2011a). This section describes the principal agreements, their limitations, and subsequent adjustments to mitigate some of the limitations (based in part on Mesa-Lago, 2011a, 2011c).

Updating of the Economic Model

In updating the economic model, Raúl called for avoiding "risks of improvisation and rush to take action"; although he was conscious of the expectations for "prompt and deep changes," it was essential to proceed at a firm and steady pace because "we do not have the right to make mistakes." He added that it was "more necessary now than ever to return to five-year plans," and that planning was "vital in order to avoid the risk of improvisation" (R. Castro Ruz, 2009d). Thus the agreements reached by the Congress do not substantially transform the current economic model, but rather propose updating it in a gradual and programmed way.

Central planning remains as the main economic management instrument in Cuba, although it would be modified to take into account the market and "nonstate" economic activity (the term "private" does not appear in the agreements of the Sixth Congress), the latter remaining under the plan and subject to strict state regulation and financial and administrative controls.

The relationships between the plan and the market as well as the participation level of each are not clearly defined, and there are contradictions among some agreements. For example, Pavel Vidal Alejandro (2011a) asks: "the plan is superior to the market, but up to what point?" Armando Nova (2011) states: "In economics, nothing is absolute, and the problem [rests] with the complementarity that should exist between both elements [plan and market] and it is critical to have a clear definition of which of the two is the determinant one." Armando Chaguaceda and Ramón Centeno (2011) note that the agreements are silent with respect to the relative shares of the economy subject to plan and market; the participation of producers and consumers in the planning and managerial process; and how reforms will be financed.[12]

The state enterprise continues to prevail, though the agreements ratified nonstate activities that existed prior to the Congress as well as those introduced by Raúl.[13] Management of state enterprises will become more decentralized,[14] based on self-financing and without fiscal subsidies; nonprofit enterprises or cooperatives will be shut down or transferred to the private sector. Using their profits, state enterprises may open investment funds and incentive plans for their workers. The agreements forbid "concentration of property," as well as the sale or lease of cooperative property to other cooperatives or to the private sector, or its use as collateral for investment. The Congress did not alter the previous policy on foreign investment, which remains "complementary" to domestic investment in "activities that are of interest to the nation," a policy that resulted in a fall in the number of joint ventures in the 2002–2009 period despite the dire need for investment and technology transfer in all economic sectors.

Price policy will be set "in accordance with the updating of the economic model," without explaining how. Centralized price-setting of goods and services will continue in the areas "the state has interest in regulating," and decentralized price-setting will continue "in the rest," though neither of these two areas are specified. The guidelines deferred greater price-setting "flexibility" by enterprises to a later date, to follow the issuance of regulations that "guarantee the interests of the nation," but this provision was omitted from the Congress's agreements. The latter call for "the integral revision of the price system," but do not provide guidance on how to accomplish this.

Nova (2011) deems the guidelines more advanced than the agreements on the degree of decentralization and autonomy granted to agricultural producers. The guidelines would permit cooperatives to make direct sales to the public and the nonstate sector, but the agreements added the caveats "after fulfillment of quotas to the state" and "without intermediaries." The agreements also eliminated two important proposed changes: "seeking management autonomy of different forms of cooperatives" and "price-setting for the majority of products [by usufructuaries] based on supply and demand."

The agreements call for the elimination of monetary duality but merely state that the complexity of the problem will demand careful preparatory work and implementation, without any elaboration regarding key elements of such action: time frame for unification of the two currencies, the role that the market might play in determining the equilibrium value of the currencies, how convertibility of the CUP would be achieved, and whether monetary unity will be achieved using the CUP or the CUC (Vidal Alejandro, 2012a).

There is a long list of objectives in the agreements concerning the external sector, with no guidance on how to reach them:[15] promote import substitution (which would require an increase in domestic production), "create an export vocation," promote export diversification and improve the quality of exports, diversify geographic markets (an indirect reference to Cuba's commercial dependence on Venezuela), protect international commodity prices, and strictly comply with all international commitments, including payment of the foreign debt. There is also a call for maintaining international solidarity—in the form of assistance to other countries—but now recognizing the need to take into consideration its costs and seeking compensation whenever possible (Pérez-López, 2011).

Prior to his visit in March 2012, Pope Benedict XVI stated that in Cuba "it is evident that Marxist ideology, as it was conceived, does not match today's reality. . . . [I]t is essential to seek new models, with patience and in a constructive manner"; the church wishes to cooperate "in a spirit of dialogue in order to avoid traumas and help in creating a just and fraternal society" (*Associated Press,* March 23, 2012). To which Vice President Marino Murillo responded: "the updating of the Cuban economic model seeks to find sustainable economic development and preserve the achievements of the Revolution and of socialism. . . . [W]e will address economic problems within a socialist framework." He added that Cuba has studied the economic experiences of other countries, such as China, Vietnam, and Russia, in order to "understand methodologically what these countries have done," but "this does not mean that we are planning to copy automatically what others have done. . . . [W]e are not making political reforms."[16] With respect to the pope's offer of cooperation, Murillo said: "anyone who offers . . . truly to help us in updating our model . . . not to impose their views on us, is very welcome; we are ready to analyze the cooperation" (*Granma,* March 29, 2012; *La Jornada,* March 28, 2012).

Expansion and Greater Flexibility of Usufruct

Distribution of idle state lands in usufruct began in September 2008. Statistics are few and not always consistent: 56,000 usufructuaries and 560,751 hectares distributed in March 2009; 111,715 and 1 million, respectively, in

June 2010; 146,000 and 1 million in May 2011; and 147,000 and 1.2 million in October 2011 (*Juventud Rebelde,* March 22, 2009, July 11, 2011; *Associated Press,* June 27, 2010; *Granma,* May 26, 2011; *Inter Press Service,* November 1, 2011). The share of the distributed land in usufruct that was being cultivated rose from 33 percent in 2009 to 46 percent in 2011, but the National Center of Land Control alleged that the share was 77 percent for 2011 (R. Castro Ruz, 2009b; ECLAC, 2011b; *EFE,* July 16, 2011).

The Sixth Congress agreed that the remainder of idle state lands (some 600,000 hectares) would be distributed in usufruct, but did not change significantly the legal limitations and disincentives. Still in place are the ban on sale and purchase of land and its lease to third parties, as well as the requirement that farmers sell a portion of their output through the state's *acopio* procurement system, although the expectation was that "more agile management mechanisms" would be developed to allow producers to go directly to the market without intermediaries. The guidelines proposed that *acopio* prices be set by supply and demand, but the agreements did not incorporate this suggestion and instead maintained that *acopio* prices be set administratively. In 2009, *acopio* functions were transferred from the Ministry of Agriculture to the Ministry of Domestic Trade (Nova, 2012) and a pilot project was launched in twenty-three state enterprises that contracted directly with agricultural producers, providing working capital, containers, and transportation services and receiving produce directly, without having to go through *acopio;* this system was expected to avoid loss of crops, as happened with tomatoes (*Juventud Rebelde,* June 12, 2009).

After the Sixth Congress, Orlando Lugo (2011)[17] raised concerns about regulations affecting land distributed in usufruct and made recommendations to create incentives for improving the land and making investments: eliminate the ten-year limit on usufruct and make it permanent; allow heirs of usufructuaries to inherit the land; permit producers to build a house in the parcel; make credit available to usufructuaries to purchase needed inputs; and abolish *acopio* and authorize producers to sell their output directly.

Due to poor results in agricultural production (see Chapter 6), some of the mentioned restrictions were eliminated or relaxed. Raúl promised that the state would compensate usufructuaries for investments and improvements made to the land (R. Castro Ruz, 2010c). The high prices of inputs sold to farmers and usufructuaries[18] were reduced by up to 60 percent (*Associated Press,* August 5, 2011; *BBC Mundo,* September 27, 2011). State banks were authorized to give small loans to private farmers, usufructuaries, and self-employed workers, as well as to allow them to open bank accounts (discussed later) (*Reuters,* December 2, 2011; *La Jornada,* December 19, 2011, March 28, 2012). In 2010, agricultural producers (private farmers, cooperatives, usufructuaries) were permitted to sell their output at roadside stands near their production sites, subject to a 5 percent sales tax, a 5 percent tax for the use of the stand, a 2 percent tax for use of the land on which the roadside stands are sited, plus the contribution to social security (Acuerdo no. 6853, 2010; Resolución no. 206, 2010). As of late 2011, usufructuaries, private farmers, and cooperatives can sell directly their unprocessed output (except for milk and dairy products, coffee, and meats) to hotels and tourism restaurants; the price is agreed in CUP between the parties; usufructuaries can also sell their output directly in markets (Resolución no. 122, 2011). In all of these instances, commitments to *acopio* need to be met first (*Granma,* November 21, 2011; *Bohemia,* November 24, 2011).

Decree-Law no. 300 of October 2012, which entered into force in December, regulated usufruct and introduced several important positive changes that had been recommended earlier: (a) allows the construction of one house on the land parcel for use by the usufruct grantee and construction of other dwellings for the grantee's family-member workers, as well as construction of stables for animals and storage; (b) those buildings, as well as woody trees, fruit trees, and other permanent plantings are considered to be the grantee's investment (*bienhechurías*); (c) the state may sell or rent existing facilities (based on their assessed value) to the grantee and the latter can build, expand, and improve them, in which case these too will be considered investments; (d) if the contract is rescinded, the state must assess the value of the grantee's investments and reimburse the grantee; (e) in case of the grantee's death, family-member workers may inherit the usufruct land and investment (employees may inherit the value of investment if there are no heirs); and (f) the grantee can hire nonfamily temporary workers, most of whom are self-employed (Decreto-Ley no. 300, 2012; *Juventud Rebelde,* November 10, 2012).

The law did not modify other key aspects of usufruct or changes tied to certain requirements. The parcel size for individual usufructuaries continues to be small (13.42 hectares), but it could be expanded to 67 hectares for usufruct granted to state entities and cooperatives; however, individuals could also obtain such an extension if they establish a link to a state farm or cooperative in order to receive supplies and market their produce. Contrary to several calls to expand the contract period, it remains at ten years for individuals but was increased from twenty years to twenty-five years for state entities and cooperatives. As before, production must be "rational" and "sustainable" and the grantee must fulfill their obligations with the state, including *acopio* obligations; otherwise the contract is rescinded (Decreto-Ley no. 300, 2012).

Despite the noted improvements, some key obstacles and disincentives remain: (a) the size of investments is limited to 1 percent of the parcel size and investments cannot be sold to third parties; (b) to expand the parcel size to 67 hectares, the individual grantee must be tied to a state farm or cooperative (in 2011 it was said that such expansion would be subordinated to an increase in production); (c) state credit cannot be used for eradicating marabú infestation from the parcel; (d) *acopio* remains and the price of produce is set by the state at below the market price; (e) in order to qualify to receive land in usufruct, the individual must have skills to till the land (the state may provide training); (f) new complex and detailed regulations require several documents and government resolutions for granting of usufruct land, signing and extension of contracts, and approval of investments and construction of houses; and (g) additional prohibitions can result in termination of the contract, such as hiring of nonauthorized employees, investment without previous state approval, and lack of ties to a state farm or cooperative (Decreto-Ley no. 300, 2012).

The tax reform of 2012 (discussed later) seeks to stimulate the private agricultural sector and agricultural production in four ways: (a) the income tax rate for agricultural production is lower than that for other economic activities; (b) usufructuaries are granted a two-year exemption from the payment of personal income tax, property tax on the value of the land, and the work force utilization tax from the time the land is granted; (c) such tax exemption may be extended for an additionaltwo years if the grantee has cleared the land of marabú and other invasive plants; and (d) in order to increase production, a tax is imposed on agricultural and forestry lands granted in usufruct that are kept idle (Ley no. 113, 2012).

Expansion of Private Employment and State Sector Dismissals

Raúl asserted that the growth of the nonstate sector of the Cuban economy did not mean privatization of social property, but rather was an enabling factor that would facilitate the construction of socialism by permitting the state to shed nonstrategic activities (R. Castro Ruz, 2011a). The Sixth Congress introduced some positive innovations: (a) approval of 178 categories for self-employment, 21 more than previously approved; (b) authorization to employ up to five nonfamily individuals in 50 percent of the 178 occupations;[19] (c) the possibility for self-employed workers to sell goods and services to state enterprises, and more flexibility in leasing space and equipment from the state or from individuals; (d) availability of small loans from the Central Bank of Cuba to self-employed workers for the purchase of goods, equipment, and inputs; (e) development of wholesale markets in which workers can sell inputs and rent equipment to the private sector; (f) mandatory enrollment in a special system of social security pensions; and (g) an increase in the number of chairs allowed in small restaurants (*paladares*) from twelve to twenty (Vidal Alejandro and Pérez Villanueva, 2010; *Granma*, March 30, 2011; *Agence France-Press*, April 5, 2011).

There is some uncertainty about the potential impact of these measures, given the fluctuations of self-employment during the revolution: banned initially, permitted at the start of the 1980s, subsequently shunned and

reduced, expanded during the crisis of the 1990s, and restrained during recovery from the crisis (Mesa-Lago, 2010b). The peak number of self-employed workers was reached in 2005 (see Table 5.1), twenty-five years after
self-employment was first authorized, when 169,400 such individuals were
recorded (3.6 percent of the labor force); by the end of 2010, their number
had fallen to 147,400 (2.9 percent of the labor force). Similarly, the number
of members of agricultural cooperatives fell steadily, from 323,400 in 2000
(7 percent of the labor force) to 217,000 in 2010 (4.2 percent), while the
number of other private workers (farmers and salaried employees) increased from 361,300 in 2000 (7.8 percent) to 500,900 in 2004 (10.6 percent), and subsequently fell to 442,000 in 2010 (8.6 percent). Total nonstate
employment grew from 18.1 percent of the labor force in 2000 to 20 percent in 2004, and slipped back to 15.7 percent in 2010.

Cuban and foreign economists had recommended that the state permit
self-employment throughout the economy except for selected strategic
areas, but instead the agreements took a different approach and authorized
self-employment in only 178 well-defined categories, as mentioned earlier.
Some of the occupations have certain economic significance (e.g., electri-
cian, producer and seller of certain products, operator of passenger and
freight vehicles, repairman, translator, interpreter), but most are of relatively low importance and low-skilled (e.g., water deliverer, shoe shiner,
clown, push cart operator, collector of empty cans, fruit peeler, bathroom
attendant). Advertising for these occupations is banned and university graduates are still not allowed to engage in self-employment in the professions
for which they are trained and may do so only in unskilled, authorized jobs.
They may be dismissed from state employment in their professions and are
permitted to work only in such unskilled jobs.

Another serious obstacle is the excessive level of taxation and other
costs, which act as disincentives for the creation of formal employment and
prolong informal employment: (a) high cost for a work license; (b) a progressive income tax (25 percent applied to earnings of 5,000–10,000 CUP,
equivalent to US$208–417, and rising to 50 percent for income exceeding
50,000 CUP, or US$2,080),[20] although deductions are allowed for some ex-
penses; (c) a 25 percent labor force utilization levy; (d) contribution of 25
percent to social security, a higher rate than is assessed on wage earners; and
(e) a 10 percent sales tax and an additional 10 percent levy for the use of
public services. Minister of Finance and Prices Lina Pedraza (2010) stated
that the average tax burden on self-employed workers in 2010 was between
30 and 35 percent of income, and that average profits were in the range of
20 to 25 percent of income. In contrast, Archibald Ritter (2011c) estimates
that the effective taxation rate of the self-employed can exceed 100 percent
of net income and is higher than the rate applied to joint ventures. Pedraza
(2010) further stated that the tax on labor force utilization rises with the

Table 5.1 Nonstate Employment, Including Self-Employment, Cooperatives, and Other Private Employment, 2000–2011

	Total Nonstate Employment[a]		Self-Employment		Cooperatives		Other Private Employment[b]	
	Thousands of People Employed	Percentage of Labor Force	Thousands of People Employed	Percentage of Labor Force	Thousands of People Employed	Percentage of Labor Force	Thousands of People Employed	Percentage of Labor Force
2000	838.0	18.1	153.3	3.3	323.4	7.0	361.3	7.8
2001	903.4	19.2	152.3	3.2	318.5	6.8	432.6	9.2
2002	910.7	19.3	152.9	3.2	316.9	6.7	440.9	9.4
2003	941.8	19.9	151.0	3.2	292.7	6.2	498.1	10.5
2004	947.7	20.4	166.7	3.6	280.1	6.0	500.9	10.8
2005	936.9	19.5	169.4	3.6	271.3	5.6	496.2	10.3
2006	866.0	17.9	152.6	3.2	257.0	5.3	456.4	9.4
2007	833.5	16.8	138.4	2.8	242.1	4.9	453.1	9.1
2008	835.9	16.6	141.6	2.8	233.8	4.6	460.5	9.2
2009	822.9	16.2-	143.8	2.8	231.6	4.6	447.5	8.8
2010	806.4	15.7	147.4	2.9	217.0	4.2	442.0	8.6
2011	1,137.2	22.7	391.5	7.8	652.1	13.0	93.6	1.9

Sources: Authors' estimates based on ONE, 2001b, 2002, 2005, 2006, 2007, 2008a, 2011a, 2012a.
Notes: a. Excludes workers in joint ventures.
b. Private farmers and private wage earners.

number of workers, as a way to discourage hiring of workers (only 33,000 were hired in 2011) and to prevent businesses from generating higher profits and accumulating wealth.[21] In 2009, taxes on self-employed generated revenues of 247 million CUP, and revenues were projected to rise fourfold in 2011, to 1.1 billion CUP (*Granma,* October 28, 2011; Pedraza, 2011).

The tax reform of 2012 seeks to simplify taxation of self-employed workers and provide incentives. Annually, the Ministry of Finance and Prices will issue a list of occupations of "low complexity" that would be eligible for treatment under a simplified taxation system and set minimum the tax rate applicable to occupations. Self-employed workers are exempt from taxes on sales, the special tax on products and services, and taxes on services, work force utilization, and personal income during their first three months of activity. Also exempted from the work force utilization tax are self-employed workers, agricultural workers, and other individuals who hire up to five workers. The law set the tax on sales and services by self-employed workers at 10 percent (Ley no. 113, 2012).

The bureaucracy hinders self-employment: it asks for documents not required by law; delays the issuance of health licenses mandated for food handling activities such as in *paladares,* cafeterias, and home delivery of meals (the license should be issued within seven working days, but it sometimes takes weeks), and delays the mental and physical health certificate required for childcare occupations; and establishes strict rules for food preparation, utensils used, general condition of kitchens; in addition, inspectors are quick to find faults and shut down businesses (*Granma,* December 28, 2010, February 8, 2011, May 17, 2011; *Juventud Rebelde,* March 19, 2011; *Bohemia,* September 21, 2011). Bureaucrats are motivated to use delay tactics because "it is not in their interest to change a system rife with red tape, impunity and delays," nor to eliminate the possibility of getting bribes; "they enjoy playing the role of the executioner . . . making it difficult for anyone who wishes to obtain a license to be on their own" (*Granma,* January 21, 2011, May 21, 2011). Raúl urged support for the self-employed, calling on the PCC and the government not to "demonize them" through for the creation of "stigmas or prejudices," but rather to change "the negative impression toward them" (R. Castro Ruz, 2010c). A spokesperson for the Catholic Church has stated that small businesses should not be rejected because of ideological reasons or envy, as punishing those who wish to succeed and prosper would only increase poverty (Márquez, 2011a).

In mid-2011, the Council of Ministers approved measures to address some of the aforementioned problems: it (a) froze state employment and extended the time frame for the dismissals without setting specific dates; (b) authorized the employment of nonfamily individuals in the 178 approved self-employment occupations, increased the number of seats in *paladares* from twenty to fifty, and announced that state restaurants with low sales volume would be leased to self-employed workers; (c) suspended the payroll tax in 2011 for businesses that employed five workers (but not for enterprises that employed more than five), reduced monthly fees and taxes levied on several categories of self-employment, and increased the deductible amount for the income tax; (d) eliminated the mandatory affiliation to social security for self-employed women sixty years or older and for men sixty-five years or older, and offered to return contributions to those self-employed who returned their licenses; (e) allocated US$120 million for the sale of goods to the self-employed through the industrial goods and services markets, facilitated imports and sales of inputs for the self-employed (stoves, fryers, ovens, air conditioners), and reduced the price of some inputs by 15 to 20 percent, but postponed the creation of a wholesale market to which self-employed workers could turn; (f) added three occupations (insurance agent, party organizer, wedding planner, for a total of 181 followed by six more in September 2012) to the list of authorized self-employment occupations; and (g) granted maternity benefits to dismissed workers who were pregnant and did not find another job (*Granma*, May 17, 2011, May 27, 2011; *Trabajadores*, July 18, 2011; Decretos-Leyes nos. 278, 284, and 285, 2011).

These measures seemed to be working, because in 2011 the number of self-employed grew to 391,500 (7.8 percent of the labor force), whereas the number of members of all types of cooperatives (including those in services) jumped to 652,100 (13 percent) and the number of nonstate employees rose to 1,137,200 (22.7 percent). Conversely, the number of other private workers dropped sharply, to 93,600 (only 1.9 percent) (see Table 5.1). The latter is difficult to explain, because the number of wage earners hired by the self-employed and cooperatives must have increased, unless those wage earners were reported as part of those who hired them.

Sergio Díaz-Briquets (2011) developed a typology for the 181 occupations authorized for self-employment at the time, based on forward and backward linkages, dependence on domestic and imported inputs, employment creation, and education level. He concluded that most of the occupations authorized for self-employment do not align well with the profile of well-educated workers; exclude individuals with the highest levels of human capital; are slanted toward low-productivity occupations; and will be more likely to attract informal workers than dismissed state workers. Exceptions are occupations in construction, some personal services, and small-scale manufacturing.[22]

Production and Services Cooperatives

The agreements of the Sixth Party Congress expanded the scope of cooperatives, previously limited to the agricultural sector, and created two "grades": production and services cooperatives; and value-added cooperatives, such as those in sales, procurement, or joint sales. Cooperatives of barbers, hair-dressers, and manicurists, which were first authorized in 2010, were reor-ganized in November 2011, subject to the following rules: the state leases the premises to cooperative members for ten years, which can be extended, for a customer seating allowance of up to three chairs, and initially sells certain products and inputs to the cooperative.[23] Cooperative members pay the monthly rent[24] plus electricity, gas, water, telephone, and advertising fees, and are assessed income taxes similar to those of self-employed work-ers (including social security payments). Cooperatives must buy needed in-puts, maintain the locale, and offer quality services. Prices of services are set by demand and supply and the members determine how to distribute income—according to former minister of economy Marino Murillo, profits are to be distributed based on individual work (Resoluciones no. 333 and 434, 2011; *Granma,* July 24, 2012). In December 2011, cooperative agree-ments were extended to another twenty-four production and services activ-ities, ranging from repair shops for electric appliances to shoe repairers (Resolución no. 516, 2011).[25] In July 2012, Murillo announced a program to create 222 cooperatives in sectors other than agriculture by the end of 2012, with the government setting aside US$100 million to provide fi-nancing to them. Subsequently, Internal Commerce Minister Ada Chávez Oviedo reported that a pilot project to lease state-owned restaurants to workers would start in December in the provinces of Artemisa, Villa Clara, and Ciego de Avila following terms similar to those applied to barbershops and beauty shops leased to workers (*Associated Press,* July 23, 2012, No-vember 9, 2012). Monthly fees paid by individuals who rent rooms in their houses to tourists were reduced from 200 to 150 CUP per room (*Associated Press,* November 2, 2011). Due to the opening of service cooperatives, the number of cooperative members jumped from 217,000 to 652,100 between 2010 and 2011, or from 4.2 percent to 13 percent of the labor force (see Table 5.1).

Turning government-owned shops into cooperatives results in benefits for all parties: the government saves money of the costs of salaries, mainte-nance, public utilities, and inputs that are frequently stolen (all of which are the responsibility of the cooperative), while receiving income from rent and income tax paid by cooperative members; the cooperatives are self-managed and their members, arguably led by the profit incentive, repair their shops, buy better products, and offer better services, hence improving their income; and consumers receive better personal attention and quality of services. But the barber and hairstylist cooperatives have already faced challenges: some have not been able to make enough money and have gone out of business; cooperative members complain about long work hours, the limit of only three chairs for customers, and high rent; and customers grumble about the high prices for haircuts and other services (a haircut that cost 3 CUP before the increase in 2010, when cooperatives were created, increased to 10 CUP or even 1 CUC), although competition should bring prices down (*Reuters,* October 3, 2010; Piñeiro Harnecker, 2012). Jorge Martín (2010) worries that "capitalist elements," such as cooperatives, will grow at the expense of the state sector, and that the "socialist elements" will retreat: "sooner or later, whichever sector is able to attract the largest amount of productive investment and increase productivity will prevail."

Microcredits and Private Bank Accounts

Through 2011 in Cuba, state credits were available primarily to state enterprises and cooperatives (especially UBPCs), with private farmers and usufructuaries receiving small shares; credits were also available to state employees and pensioners to purchase electric household appliances.[26] In March 2011 the Metropolitan Bank, whose branches operate in each of Havana's municipalities, and the Credit and Commerce Bank (BANDEC), whose branches operate in the rest of the country, were authorized to offer small credits to private farmers and usufructuaries, at interest rates of 3 percent and 5 percent respectively during the first two years of the loans; by June, some 13,000 credits had been issued to 9 percent of usufructuaries (*Juventud Rebelde,* July 10, 2011; *Reuters,* September 28, 2011).

　　Decree-Law no. 289 of 2011 increased the amounts that private farmers could borrow, expanded credits to self-employed workers, and offered loans to individuals to finance the purchase of construction materials to build and repair homes. The loan application process takes seven to twenty-one days, depending on the amount; borrowers must prove the economic feasibility of the business, income estimates, potential market for sales, and collateral guarantees (including mortgages), submitting also the activity license and the most recent tax payment receipt. Credits can be used to improve permanent crops or undertake activities that increase production, but not to eradicate marabú, build fences, or buy animals. The minimum credit amounts are 500 CUP (US$21) to private farmers, 1,000 CUP (US$42) to buy construction materials, and 3,000 CUP (US$125) to self-employed workers; there is no cap on the loan amount, with limits determined between the two parties based on capacity to repay. Loans are dispersed in tranches and the lender confirms at each step the proper use of the funds; payment arrears are subject to additional interest, and persistent failure to repay can result in legal action (*Reuters,* October 18, 2011; *Granma,* December 25, 2011).

　　At the close of 2011, the total amount of credits issued for the purchase of construction materials was small: US$150,000 loaned out to 516 borrowers, for an average loan size of US$290; 17 percent of those who applied were successful in obtaining loans (*Associated Press,* January 20, 2012). There is no information on other loans. Because of the limitations on domestic microcredits, donations from abroad for this purpose are important. The European Union (particularly Spain), Brazil, and the Cuban Study Group (a group of Cuban American businesspeople from Florida) have offered about US$20 million in financial assistance and business advice to the self-employed; these funds would be dispersed through BANDEC rather than going directly to nonstate actors (*El Financiero,* October 11, 2010). To date, the Cuban government has not stated publicly that it has accepted the offers.

Representatives of the Central Bank of Cuba informed the ANPP in July 2012 that in the previous six months, loans to individual Cuban citizens amounting to 250 million CUP had been approved, representing 80 percent of loan applications received. The objective of the credit policy is to promote self-employment and other nonstate activities, support the activities of small farmers, and finance the purchase of materials and labor for construction. The bulk of the loans were made by the Popular Savings Bank (BPA), and over 99 percent of the loans were destined for construction. Commenting on the report, a Cuban government analyst remarked about the low rate of participation of agricultural workers and self-employed workers in the loan program: as of July 2012, only 79 loans had been requested by individual agricultural producers to buy tools, materials, and inputs, out of a total of 7,162 loan applications for investments, while the number of applications from self-employed workers was described as "modest" (*discreto*), indicating that the banking system was reviewing the requirements and mechanisms associated with the loan program to determine the factors that might be responsible for such low participation (Alonso Falcón, 2012b).

In 2011, private farmers, self-employed workers, and other nonstate actors were permitted to open accounts in pesos as well as convertible pesos at three state banks; such accounts are mandatory for those with gross earnings above 50,000 CUP (US$208). These groups can use checks, credit cards, bank transfers, drafts, and promissory notes in their financial transactions, and can also pay taxes, utility bills, and social security contributions through banks, thus reducing transaction costs and risks; bank deposits may be given as collateral. Using the banking system would allow the state to increase tax control and reduce fiscal evasion. But bottlenecks may arise due to low bank capacity to provide the offered services, poor training of bank employees, and the overall lack of telebanking, magnetic cards, and automatic-teller equipment (Vidal Alejandro, 2012b).

Social Welfare

Cuba's rationing system received the greatest attention at the Sixth Congress, with opinions ranging from elimination of the system at once, to strong support for continuation in its current form or with changes that would prohibit those who do not work or have high incomes to continue to receive benefits. Raúl pledged that the social welfare system would not be abolished "without previously creating the conditions for its elimination. . . . Rather than subsidizing products . . . we will move progressively toward supporting persons [who lack] other means" (R. Castro Ruz, 2011a). The agreements of the Sixth Congress set forth that rationing should be eliminated in an "orderly and gradual manner" alongside a promise to guarantee social assistance "to those who need it." Several food items have been removed from the ration card, which now covers only about ten days of consumption, and the rest of the monthly food needs must be purchased at agricultural markets and the TRDs at increasingly high prices. It is reasonable to do away with subsidized prices for people with high income, but such subsidies are fundamental for the survival of the poor and for others in need who do not receive remittances, which would require a strengthening of social assistance prior to taking any action.

One of the agreements calls for a gradual increase in salaries, but in order to increase their real value (which fell 73 percent between 1989 and 2010; see Table 4.4), it would be essential to boost production and productivity, which in turn would require deeper reforms than those already approved. In April 2012, nearly four years after the announcement that salaries would be set based on performance, there were no data on implementation of this policy (the most recent data are for October 2009), nor was there information on multiple employment and elimination of wage caps.

The Congress confirmed that the high and rising cost of social services (53.1 percent of the state budget and 34 percent of GDP in 2010; see Table 4.7) was unsustainable and that the solution was to reduce social services and link their growth to increases in production and in available fiscal resources to pay for them. The agreements incorporate the sound principle that enrollment in university curricula should correspond with socioeconomic development needs. The export of physicians and other medical personnel, particularly to Venezuela, has generated substantial hard-currency revenue for Cuba, but has also given rise to a domestic deficit of these professionals, as a third of physicians are stationed abroad. One of the agreements promises to guarantee that the annual graduation of physicians will be sufficient to cover "the needs of the country as well as those generated by international commitments." Another agreement calls for a reduction of the fiscal subsidy to cover the deficit in the pension system, by expanding the affiliation of the self-employed and state sector contributors.

The agreements call for the elimination of "improper gratuities" and for social assistance to be targeted at "persons who really need it"; if the latter were done properly, current recipients who are not poor would be excluded and resources would be saved overall. The agreements also stipulate "the elimination of benefits that could be financed . . . by the relatives of the beneficiaries." These policy modifications have led to the aforementioned reduction in the number of beneficiaries and amount of social assistance benefits, an outcome inconsistent with the expansion of the vulnerable population resulting from the structural reforms. Samuel Farber (2011) argues that the cuts to the rationing system and to the social assistance budget, coupled with dismissals, will mean the end of the implicit social pact—already deteriorated since the 1990s—whereby the government guaranteed a low but stable standard of living to the population in exchange for support of the regime, which could generate discontent and threaten the status quo.

Sale and Purchase of Homes

Although not part of the economic and social policy guidelines, the Sixth Congress authorized citizens to buy and sell homes. As discussed, the ban on sales of homes had led to a system of swaps (*permutas*) laden with red tape and corruption, which was not eliminated by the agreements, although they legitimized private construction of homes and committed the state to meeting the population's need for construction materials to repair and maintain their houses.

About 87 percent of Cuban homes are private property (*Juventud Rebelde,* November 3, 2011). The housing reform law, which took effect in November 2011, allows citizens and permanent foreign residents to buy and sell homes at a price in CUP freely established by the buyer and the seller; own a second home for recreation or rest; donate homes and idle land; transfer property from those who permanently leave the country; and legally engage in property swaps and associated payments. Nonrelatives have the right to inherit a home and to continue living in a house after five years of residence. The law also addresses the issue of divorced couples who jointly own a home, allowing its sale by mutual agreement (Decreto-Ley no. 288, 2011).

The housing law imposed a 4 percent fee on the transfer of a dwelling based on its updated value or the sale price. The tax reform of 2012 assesses a levy on homes and vacant residential lots equivalent to 2 percent of their assessed value; the tax becomes effective at the time the owner is issued a property title by the authorities. Homes built by individuals through their own efforts are exempt from the property tax for five years; also exempted are homes deemed not fit for occupancy (Ley no. 113, 2012).

Benefits of the housing reform include elimination of the massive red tape associated with swaps and permission to transfer real estate with relatively few restrictions; authorization to legally sell the billions of dollars worth of housing that had been frozen for more than fifty years, whose sale can be used to generate the capital needed by the private sector to launch and expand small private businesses and repair deteriorated housing; permission to have bank accounts, which together with the allowed sale of real estate could contribute to an expansion of the banking sector; and authorization to own a second vacation home, which creates an incentive for Cubans living abroad to buy homes through relatives in Cuba, although this is illegal within Cuba itself and in the United States. But there are concerns about the reform: ownership of real property is limited to a main home and a vacation home; it is illegal to sell property to foreigners who are not permanent residents; only 6 percent of homes are duly registered in real estate property registries; and there is limited access to the Internet and it is difficult to advertise home sales through other means (*Juventud Rebelde,* November 4, 2011; *Reuters,* January 9, 2012). Mario Coyula, director of the journal *Urbanismo y Arquitectura* in the 1970s and 1980s, foresees inequalities regarding housing, as people who have greater assets will be able to purchase houses in the better neighborhoods while those with fewer assets will be condemned to remain in poor neighborhoods. Moreover, the owner of a home that has been rented can still sell the property, leaving the tenant without a place to live (Cave, 2011).

Sale and Purchase of Automobiles

Effective as of October 2011, Cuban citizens and permanent foreign residents are permitted to buy and sell automobiles from individuals and from car dealerships (Decreto-Ley no. 292, 2011). The first category of automobiles that may be bought and sold comprises the pre-1959 stock of US-made cars (so-called *almendrones*) as well as the Soviet Ladas and Moskvichs that were made available to key state officials prior to 1990; all of these are old and difficult to repair, mainly because of the lack of spare parts.[27] It is also possible to buy more recently manufactured secondhand cars brought into the country legally by artists, athletes, intellectuals, and professionals who worked abroad. Cuban citizens who emigrate permanently may transfer the ownership of a vehicle to immediate family members; the procedure calls for the state initially to take possession of the vehicle and then transfer it to the designated individual, unless there are compelling reasons of public utility or social interest not to do so. The buyer must declare that the money for the transaction comes from a legal source and also declare the number of vehicles that he or she has.

The second category comprises new automobiles. The regulation permits Cuban citizens and permanent residents to purchase, every five years, a new car paid in convertible pesos or foreign currency, through a car dealership or through direct importation. Foreigners who are temporary residents can own up to two automobiles during their stay on the island. The purchase of new automobiles is initiated through the regional government authorities, who in turn obtain permission from the Ministry of Transportation, a process that can take up to four months. The buyer must demonstrate that his or her funds in hard currency or CUC come from services to the state. Intellectuals or artists who have received international awards or royalties through official entities may also purchase new automobiles, as can fishers, merchant mariners, airline personnel, employees at the Guantánamo naval base, and workers in the tobacco industry. Not eligible for purchase of automobiles are citizens who have accumulated CUC or hard currencies through remittances, through self-employment, or through works as health professionals involved in international missions in Venezuela, Bolivia, Nicaragua, and Ecuador.

Migration Policy

A 1997 decree prohibited residents of provinces, particularly those in the eastern provinces, to settle in Havana without permission. Tens of thousands of these internal migrants (referred to as *palestinos*) were deported back to their place of origin in order to avoid massive internal migration to the capital city, although this did not stop them from migrating again because of the poor conditions in the areas from where they originated (Ravsberg, 2011c).

Another regulation, one that is highly disliked by the population, requires that Cuban citizens obtain permission from the government (a "white card") to travel out of the country for one month, after first having obtained permission from their workplace and a letter of invitation from relatives or friends abroad. Once these permits are obtained, those seeking to travel must pay US$150 for processing of the exit authorization, whereas those sending the letter of invitation must pay US$200 and a monthly fee of US$150 to extend the visit of the relative. Finally, travelers must return within eleven months or risk being deemed as permanently departed and having all their assets on the island confiscated by the government (Cruz, 2007). Minor children are not permitted to leave the island, nor are their parents. Revenues received by academic and technical professionals from work at foreign institutions are taxed at 50 percent. Cuban émigrés must request a visa to travel to the island to visit relatives or for tourism, at a cost of US$200–400 according to the date of their emigration; those émigrés who maintain Cuban passports must renew them periodically, at high cost. One of the "errors" committed by former vice president Carlos Lage and former foreign minister Felipe Pérez Roque was that, without informing Fidel and Raúl, they championed new Ministry of Foreign Affairs regulations that would permit Cubans living in Cuba and abroad to enter and exit the island without the need to negotiate permits, and they announced these changes abroad in a manner deemed as "collaborat[ing] with the enemies of the revolution" (PCC, 2009).

Prior to the Sixth Congress of the Cuban Communist Party, Raúl stated that the government was engaged in changing the migration policy and progress had been achieved in the development of regulations "to contribute to the deepening of linkages between the nation and its community of emigrants"; he added that the relaxation of migration policy would need to take into account the imperative to defend against US interference and to preserve human capital and protect the nation from brain drain (R. Castro Ruz, 2010b). During the discussion of the economic and social policy guidelines, proposals were tabled, among other things, to eliminate the "white card," the concept of permanent departure, and the associated confiscation of assets; to grant citizens a passport that would permit travel at the discretion of the individual; to permit professionals to emigrate once they had compensated the nation for the resources expended in their education; and to eliminate the 50 percent income tax on payments to academics and professionals (Ravsberg, 2011b; Triana, in Dossier, 2011). Jesús Arboleya maintained that the existing restrictions did not stop emigration (for example, by deserters and rafters) and called for "a totally open migration policy . . . that would allow a person who wishes to emigrate to do so, and he or she who wishes to return to do the same" (interview by Ramy, 2011). Armando Chaguaceda (2011) noted that the existing regulations were used to generate hard currency and to punish or reward nationals and émigrés rather than to protect against US interference.

Despite the expectations created, the Sixth Congress did not address migration policy. After the Congress, Raúl said: "many consider as an urgent matter the application of a new migration policy . . . forgetting the circumstances under which Cuba lives . . . under the [US] siege"; he added that all of the issues raised would eventually be addressed, carefully taking into account positive and negative aspects (R. Castro Ruz, 2011c). New expectations regarding migration policy were raised by the First National Conference of the PCC, in 2012, but that forum did not address migration policy either. At the start of 2012, the issue was back in play, with ANPP president Ricardo Alarcón saying that a "radical and profound reform of migration policy . . . was being considered, with some regulations modified and others eliminated altogether" (interview by Lamrani, 2012).

Finally, Decree-Law no. 302, on migration, was approved in November 2012 and entered in force in January 2013. The law has several positive aspects: (a) it terminates the "white card," the letter of invitation, and corresponding high fees and charges for Cubans to travel abroad, and henceforth Cuban citizens need only a passport to enter and leave the country; (b) the period that Cubans are allowed to stay abroad is extended to two years, renewable twice, for a maximum of six years; (c) the cost of the passport has been set at 100 CUC (the law is ambiguous on whether the fee is payable in CUP or CUP); (d) Cubans who leave with proper authorization can accumulate vacation payments, and pensioners who leave can collect their pensions; and (e) Cuban émigrés may stay up to three months in Cuba, and authorized residents up to six months.

The law has several negative provisions, however. A large number of Cuban citizens can neither leave the country nor obtain a personal passport for the following reasons: (a) national defense or internal security issues or protection of official information, as well as involvement in the penal system; (b) preservation of the skilled labor force, which applies to government high officials, managers in vital activities (economic, social, scientific), graduates of higher education in vital careers (specifically healthcare personnel), middle-level technicians in key occupations, and "high yield" athletes and trainers; and (c) other reasons of public interest as decided by the Cuban authorities. Cuban citizens who fall within any of the previous categories are subject to complex procedures in order to travel or leave the country: an official request to the manager of their workplace; a Ministry of Labor and Social Security database analysis from a work force perspective; and final approval by the Council of Ministers (to the best of our knowledge, the latter requisite is unique in the world). Cubans living permanently abroad still need an entry visa issued by the Cuban government, valid for only one visit and for a specific period of time; banned from returning are those whom the Cuban authorities judge as "hostile" to the state or as otherwise representing a threat to defense and security. The Ministry of Interior is in charge of passports, visas, and similar procedures (Decreto-Ley no. 302, 2012).

Tax Reform

Law no. 113, an overarching reform of Cuba's taxation system that came into effect at the start of 2013, partially repeals the previous tax code, passed in 1994—enacted in the midst of the economic crisis of the 1990s—and supplemented with a patchwork of decrees that had been enacted to address changes to the economic system. The preamble of Law no. 113 states that the new taxation system is intended to be "coherent with the new economic and social scenarios of the nation," and it is gradual, flexible, and effective application will support implementation of the development model currently being pursued (Ley no. 113, 2012). A Cuban government analyst stated that the new taxation system "provides the government with an important general economic policy tool intended not only to raise the levels of revenue required by the state, but also to stimulate those sectors and activities that contribute the most to the socio-economic development of the nation and de-stimulate those that do not" (Alonso Falcón, 2012a).

The new taxation system consists of nineteen taxes (including import duties), three contributions (two related to the social security system, the other a local development contribution), and three user fees (road tolls, airport use, and advertising in public spaces). The reform seeks to make the desirable change of shifting the burden of taxation from indirect taxes (sales taxes, turnover taxes) toward direct taxes on income, profits, and assets held. The taxes, contributions, and user fees set out in the law seek to increase government revenue. As already noted, private agriculture and self-employment in Cuba are subject to preferential tax treatment to stimulate their development.

Conclusion

The three types of reforms promoted by Raúl, together with those approved by the Sixth Congress and issued subsequently, are the broadest and deepest undertaken in Cuba during the revolution. But three important topics still have not been addressed: eradication of monetary duality, elimination of the rationing system, and increases in real salaries to satisfy basic needs. Raúl characterized these three areas of reforms as "complex . . . requiring deep study and to be implemented with aplomb"; they need to be preceded by an increase in production and productivity, basic for the advancement of structural reforms (R. Castro Ruz, 2007b). New laws on usufruct, migration, and tax reform enacted in 2012 are positive steps, though they still endure significant restrictions and disincentives. Several policy initiatives advanced by reformists have been implemented, but not others, among them: granting true autonomy to agricultural cooperatives, eliminating or substantially modifying the *acopio* procurement system, opening up the economy to foreign investment, and designing and implementing a development strategy that will improve the balance of payments.

Chapter 6 evaluates the effects of the principal reforms, examines the possible reasons for the slow pace of the reform process or for the failure to implement key reforms, and makes recommendations for the future.

Notes

1. According to a PCC report, Lage and Rodríguez allowed themselves "to be seduced by . . . the failed policies implemented in the former socialist camp." In the 1990s, Rodríguez proposed reforms that would permit small private enterprises, in opposition to true revolutionary thought. Raúl stopped him and gave him an opportunity to rectify, which he did not take. Both officials "dusted off proposals" predicated on "economic freedom" and "private enterprise" necessary to "save socialism," but socialism "is saved through rigor, more control, more revolutionary oversight, and more discipline." They also wanted to "allow farmers to sell their output at whatever price" and it was necessary to stop them from "turning over the country to capitalism" (PCC, 2009).

2. The armed forces have a significant representation in governance structures: they compose 53 percent of the Political Bureau membership, nearly 30 percent of the Central Committee membership, and one-third of joint posts in the Council of State and the Political Bureau (Mujal-León, 2011).

3. Hernández stated that the leaders "no longer have the same standing and leeway" as they had in the 1990s: "At that time, it was evident that 'the roof of the house was coming down' and the population understood that it was not the right time to remodel the building, but now there are 'no excuses to delay certain changes'" (interview by E. García, 2007b).

4. According to Hernández, Cuban media "suffers from the officialism syndrome": everything has to be approved or represent the point of view of official institutions (interview by E. García, 2007b). Soledad Cruz (2007) revealed that at the newspaper where she worked (*Juventud Rebelde*), she could not write the truth because "among the Stalinist defects that Cuban socialism has not been able to overcome is a form of journalism that is unrelated to the realities of life and conflicts."

5. In 2006, the Ministry of Domestic Trade lost 185 million CUP because of poor internal controls and lack of discipline. It conducted 33,483 inspections and found irregularities in 90 percent; it detected 125,000 deficiencies and imposed 5,742 sanctions (*Associated Press*, February 23, 2006).

6. Cuban citizens and foreigners involved in prominent corruption cases include the president of Canadian corporation Tri-Star Caribbean, a firm that did US$30 million in business annually with seventeen Cuban state enterprises and several ministries; the director of Spanish corporation Provimar S.A., which supplied duty-free shops; the director and executives of the corporation Tecnotex, which was managed by members of the armed forces and executives of British and Canadian corporations with which it did business; directors of Chilean corporations Río Zaza and Sol y Son; the director of the British investment fund Coral Capital; officers of ETECSA, which is responsible for the underwater communications cable between Cuba and Venezuela; the minister of food industry; the minister of tourism and the president of Cubanacán; the vice minister of Sugar; the president of the Cuban Institute of Civil Aeronautics and of Cubana de Aviación; two vice ministers, one of them vice director of external relations of the PCC; the vice president and ten executives of Habanos SA; eleven executives of CIMEX; and 47 percent of the leadership of the National Construction Union (*Bohemia*, November 8, 2006; *La Vanguardia*, May 24, 2010; *Juventud Rebelde*, September 23, 2011; *Reuters*, December 13, 2011; Farber, 2011; Pérez-López, 2011).

7. *Juventud Rebelde* published a report that showed a trend of increasing complaints submitted to and processed by state entities: 26 percent of complaints submitted were processed in 2003, increasing to 87.7 percent in 2007–2008, albeit followed by a decline to 73 percent in 2011; 48 percent of the complaints were solved after their publication, 39 percent were postponed, and 13 percent were not solved (J. A. Rodríguez, 2011).

8. An increase in the price of milk stimulated domestic production from 2006 to 2010, but output declined in 2011 (see Table 2.2).

9. Mobile telephones cost US$100 and each call costs US$0.40; the average monthly salary is equivalent to thirty-eight minutes of mobile use (Vicent, 2008b).

10. The minimum pension of 164 CUP (US$7) per month was increased by 22 percent; pensions between 200 and 360 CUP (US$8–$15) were increased by 11–20 percent; and those between 361 and 399 CUP (US$16–$17) were increased by 0.2–10 percent.

11. Part of the discussion of the economic and social policy guidelines by the Sixth Congress was published in *Granma Internacional*, December 23, 2011. For an interesting debate on the guidelines, see Dossier, 2011.

12. In a debate published in the journal *Temas* ("El Período Especial," 2011), the majority of participants supported decentralization, with the exception of former

minister of economy José Luis Rodríguez, who defended central planning and referred to market mechanisms as "concessions" that ultimately undo socialist systems. See the subsequent debate between Mesa-Lago (2011b) and Rodríguez (2011).

13. There are four key sectors: the state sector, anchored on the state budget and consisting of enterprises, companies, and entities; joint ventures and other enterprises with foreign capital; cooperatives, formerly only in the agricultural sector but now expanded to nonagricultural production and services; and the private sector, comprising private farms, self-employment, usufruct, and the like.

14. Raúl promised to promote decentralization, from the central government to local administrations, and from ministries to autonomous state enterprises (R. Castro Ruz, 2011a). ANPP president Ricardo Alarcón predicted that provinces and municipalities would be allowed to raise revenue to finance local production and social initiatives (interview by Ramy, 2011). In the new provinces of Artemisa and Mayabeque (formerly La Habana), a pilot experiment transferred state control over public enterprises to provincial and municipal governments (Guanche, 2012).

15. Jorge Sánchez-Egozcue (2011a) states that many of the agreements "express a political response" and that there is a long way to travel in order to achieve their real implementation.

16. Raúl said: "We are not contemplating copying again what anyone else has done; doing so brought us enough problems and moreover we copied badly; however, we do not ignore the experiences of others and learn from them" (R. Castro Ruz, 2010c).

17. Lugo, seventy-eight years old, who had been president of ANAP since 1987, was removed from that post on September 30, 2012, and replaced by his second in command, Félix González Viego, age fifty.

18. Examples of prices in 2012: water pump, 1,680 CUP; milk can (forty liters), 855 CUP; roll of barbed wire, 800 CUP; pick, 200 CUP; shovel, 175 CUP.

19. A Marxist view to the left of the government criticizes permanent employment of workers by private enterprises because that is a form of capitalism and proposes to set a maximum number of workers who can be employed, regulate such employment tightly, and impose taxes that increase with the number employed (Piñeiro Harnecker, 2011). The First National Conference of the PCC, in 2012, approved this form of employment.

20. In China, the progressive income tax assessed on annual earnings is 5 percent up to US$900, and 45 percent for income in excess of US$189,120.

21. For up to ten workers employed, the rate is 37.5 percent of the average monthly salary; from ten to fifteen workers it is 50 percent; and beyond fifteen workers it is 75 percent.

22. According to domestic and foreign surveys taken in Cuba in 2011, key characteristics of the self-employed were: 78 percent were men and 22 percent were women; 67 percent were white and 33 percent were Afro-Cubans; and only 29 percent had lost a state job prior to becoming self-employed (*Granma,* May 21, 2011, December 22, 2011; *Juventud Rebelde,* July 29, 2011; Orozco and Hansing, 2011; Moreno and Calingaert, 2011).

23. Prices of products in 2011 were quite low: 250 CUP (US$10) for a barber or hairdresser chair; 120 CUP for body cream; 40 CUP for hair-coloring products; 35 CUP for mascara; and 10 CUP for lipstick.

24. The amount of rent depends on the province where the shop is located and whether it is an urban or rural setting. Example monthly rents in 2012 were: hairdressing salon, 70–400 CUP; barbershop, 60–220 CUP; manicure salon, 40–220 CUP. Payment of rent can be waived for up to one year in lieu of repair of the premises.

25. Among them knife or scissors sharpener, woodcutter, carpenter, locksmith, electric-motor winder, photographer, tinsmith, clothing washer, upholsterer, machine-shop operator, and repairers of office equipment, electrical appliances, jewelry, watches, mattresses, bicycles, umbrellas, cigarette lighters, and shoes.

26. In 2007 the distribution of credits was as follows: state enterprises, 68.2 percent; UBPCs, 23.2 percent; CPAs, 4.7 percent; private farmers and CSSs, 1.6 percent; and for purchase of electric household appliances, 2.3 percent. More recent information is not available (Vidal Alejandro, 2012b).

27. The dire need for spare parts to repair Soviet-era cars still being used in Cuba has opened business opportunities for entrepreneurs in the United States. According to a report in the *Miami Herald,* an entrepreneur of Cuban Russian origin residing in Hialeah, a suburb of Miami with a large population of Cuban Americans, stocks spare parts for Ladas and Moskvitchs that he obtains from Russia in his auto parts store. His customers in Hialeah buy the parts and either carry them to Cuba in their luggage or send them to Cuba through shipping services (Chávez, 2012).

6

Assessing the Reforms: Impact and Challenges

This chapter evaluates the effects of the reforms in Cuba, with emphasis on structural reforms, and offers recommendations to enhance them. It is based on a thorough analysis of the views of economists and other social scientists in Cuba and abroad, combined with our own assessment of the available data.

The Effects of Reforms

In 2012, Raúl stated that the reforms were "progressing . . . [with] many difficulties," moving "without haste, in order to avoid new errors," and that they would be implemented, although their outcome would depend "on many factors." Prior to passing a new law or issuing a regulation, he added, "hundreds of hours of study are needed" (*Granma,* January 12, 2012). Before the First National Conference of the Cuban Communist Party (PCC), held in January 2012, Raúl warned that the citizenry should not expect that new reform measures would emerge from that meeting ("it is important not to create more illusions . . . or raise expectations"), as the conference would focus on internal issues of the party (*Granma,* January 12, 2012).[1] In his closing speech he stated: "let's not fall in the trap of thinking that the decisions reached by this Conference . . . and the agreements of the VI Congress are a magic solution to all of our problems" (R. Castro Ruz, 2012a).

Evaluation of the reforms is difficult, for several reasons. First, the reforms that have been implemented for the longest period of time, and therefore the ones that might have some measurable results, are administrative changes rather than structural ones. Several of the structural reforms—the updating of the economic model, the authorization to sell homes and automobiles, the initial creation of production and services cooperatives, the availability of microcredits, and the ability to open bank accounts—were enacted in September–November 2011, and therefore had only been in force for about a year when we completed this book. Furthermore, the laws on usufruct, migration, regulation of production and services cooperatives, and tax reform were enacted in July–November 2012 and did not take force until December 2012 and January 2013, hence their results cannot be assessed here. Second, some of the structural reforms that actually were implemented in earlier periods (e.g., distribution of idle land in usufruct in 2008, expansion of self-employment in 2010) were significantly modified by the Sixth Congress of the PCC or by subsequent actions or laws, and therefore their assessment becomes more complicated as the time frame for it becomes shorter. Third, there are few statistics to properly measure the effects of the reforms; for example, official data on agricultural production and yields do not disaggregate for the land given in usufruct, thereby making it impossible to measure the direct impact of that reform. Finally, there are no public opinion surveys conducted by the government or Cuban research institutions that gauge the public's reactions to the reforms and their effects.[2]

The reform is an ongoing dynamic process with many laws and regulations still to be issued, and undoubtedly this book will not capture all there is to say about it or fully evaluate its impact. Nevertheless, we believe that there are many reform measures already implemented and enough documentation to assess their effects at least in a preliminary fashion. Furthermore, the causes underlying the reform, as well as the process of discussion, approval, and implementation, are worthy of analysis. Finally, no one knows how long it will take to complete the reforms, or even whether they can be truly "completed." In our analysis here, of those reforms that can be evaluated at this time, we rely on data and information mainly from Cuba itself.

Table 6.1 summarizes nineteen reforms, grouped by type, including for each reform its date of application, specific measures undertaken, objectives, and results (where available).

Openness to Criticism and Pluralism

Raúl's public pronouncements and ensuing national debate on the grave problems facing the nation and the socialist system are unprecedented, although they remain within socialist parameters. Academics have advanced the debate with critical analysis of socioeconomic issues and forward-looking approaches. Journals such as *Temas, Espacio Laical,* and others have published symposiums, dossiers, articles, and editorials that address key economic, social, and political issues, discuss their weaknesses, and

Table 6.1 Raúl's Reforms: Measures, Objectives, and Results, 2006–2012

	Date	Measures	Objectives	Results
Administrative changes				
Reorganization of state entities	2007–	Merging and closure of state entities, such as ministries	Reduce fiscal expenditures, improve coordination	About ten mergers of entities
Perfeccionamiento empresarial	2006–2007	Decentralization, control, accounting standards, incentives	Higher efficiency, production and productivity	No information available
Campaigns against labor indiscipline and corruption	2006–	Regulations to strengthen labor discipline, impose sanctions, combat corruption	Reduce losses, improve productivity and profitability, set positive examples	About 300 leaders, government employees, and managers arrested and/or convicted
Openness to criticism	2007–	Allow the official press to criticize problems, debates in journals, advance in scholars' analysis	Identify and resolve problems within the parameters of socialism and the PCC	Some elements of glasnost, but increase in arrests of dissidents in 2012
Nonstructural reforms				
Access to hotels and restaurants	2008	Allow Cubans access to hotels and restaurants formerly only available to foreign tourists	End discrimination, offer incentives to higher-income groups, fill hotels in summer	Positive results for high-income and medium-high-income groups, not accessible for low- and medium-low-income groups
Payment of arrears, increase in *acopio* prices, sale of inputs	2007–	State compliance of payments and incentives to farmers, members of cooperatives, and usufructuary grantees	Increase agricultural production, reduce imports, bring down prices	Payment arrears again in 2009–2012; increases in prices in 2011
Private transportation	2008	Permit private taxis and other transportation providers	Improve public transport; increase fiscal revenue	2011: 47,652 licenses granted; high fees
Salary increases	2007–2009	Multiple jobs allowed; salary cap dropped; joint venture workers' wages partly paid in convertible pesos or hard currency; pay based on results	Increase workers' efforts and stimulate output; close gaps between salaries and prices	1989–2010: real salary declined by 73 percent; the effects of four salary measures cannot be evaluated
Pension reform	2008	Raise retirement age, years of service, pension amount if delayed retirement; workers must contribute	Reduce fiscal subsidies to cover pension deficit; increase government revenues	Deficit fell in 2010; long-term balance not reached; real pension declined 50 percent between 1989 and 2010

(continues)

Table 6.1 Cont.

	Date	Measures	Objectives	Results
Reduction of gratuities and cost of social services	2008–2011	Cuts in social expenditures, better resource allocation, elimination of state subsidies	Increase financial sustainability of social services; reduce fiscal expenditures	2010: social expenditures cut by 1 percentage point in terms of state budget and 2 points in terms of gross domestic product
Structural reforms				
Updating of economic model	2011–	Predominance of central plan and state ownership, but some role for market and private sector	Develop a model that can be more effective in confronting socioeconomic challenges	Insufficient time to assess; need to specify model, role of market and private sector, and private sector's relations with state
End of rationing system	Pending as of November 2012	Elimination of some items from rationing card; cut of quotas	Promote fiscal savings; focus subsidies on the poor instead of on goods	Cut in social assistance is an obstacle to end rationing
Elimination of monetary duality	Pending as of November 2012	Gradual closing of the gap between CUP and CUC	Eliminate segmented market and related distortions; increase purchasing power	2011: small CUC devaluation; CUC/CUP exchange rate unchanged
Usufruct	2008–2012	Distribution of idle state lands to individuals, cooperatives, and state entities through contracts	Increase agricultural production; reduce food imports	Distribution of 1.5 million hectares and 174,271 usufructuaries in 2012; decrease in agricultural output in 2010 but increase in 2011 mainly in nonstate sector
Dismissals of state workers and creation of private jobs	2010–2012	Dismiss 500,000 to 1.3 million redundant state workers; create self-employment jobs and production and services cooperatives	Cut fiscal expenses, increase production and labor productivity; increase fiscal revenue	2011: 140,000 dismissals (14 percent of target); 244,100 newly self-employed individuals (24 percent of target), but insufficient to employ workers to be dismissed
Sale of homes	2011	Authorize sale and purchase of homes, forbidden since 1960	Increase housing mobility; permit alternative to swaps; develop a real estate market; increase fiscal revenue	By March 2012: 2,930 homes sold and 11,380 donated; boom of home repair-construction in Havana
Sale of automobiles	2011	Authorize sale and purchase of automobiles	Improve transport services; increase fiscal revenue	By March 2012: 11,700 cars sold and 7,774 donated
Migration flexibility	2012	Eliminate restrictions preventing Cubans to travel abroad	Respond to popular demand for freedom to travel abroad	Law introduced several key improvements, but with many exceptions and restrictions
Tax reform	2012	Comprehensive tax reform: nineteen types of taxes, three types of worker contributions, three types of user fees	Generate sufficient revenue to support efficient operation of the economy consistent with the "updated" economic model	Will become effective in 2013; incentives to self-employed, agricultural sector, small businesses; uncertain how reform will be implemented

Source: Authors' compilation.

make recommendations from different viewpoints and with heavy participation from younger generations. Although access to the Internet by the Cuban population remains the lowest in the region, there has been a proliferation of digital media—bulletins, blogs, videos—that provide dynamic means of expression and have opened new communication spaces (González Mederos, 2011b; Mujal-León, 2011). Intellectuals and other groups promote the elimination of discrimination based on race, religion, gender, migrant status, and sexual orientation.

Although the Cuban press is tightly controlled by the government, it has increasingly published articles critical of state officials and their actions. Still, Alfredo Guevara, in an interview with university students, referred to the official press as "very poor," stating that the struggle to create a new form of journalism needs to continue, which will require "getting rid of the idiots, the imbeciles and the ignoramuses who hold jobs today." He called on youth to express their views, confront risks, and create discussion groups to change the direction of the country without abandoning socialism (interview by Ravsberg, 2010b).

In 2010, through the mediation of Cardinal Jaime Ortega, the Cuban government freed 130 political prisoners and authorized the Sunday march of the Damas de Blanco (Ladies in White, a group of mothers, wives, and daughters of political prisoners), two actions that would have been unthinkable seven years earlier. In 2012, however, actions against peaceful dissidents and arrests intensified, and so did harassment of the Damas de Blanco, particularly on the eve of the visit by Pope Benedict XVI. Trade unions continue to be "transmission belts"; the Sixth Congress of the PCC neither mentioned trade unions explicitly nor discussed the role of workers in the operation of enterprise management and of the economy, instead merely stating that workers would be informed and their opinions heard (Dilla, 2011; Hernández, in Dossier, 2011).

The First National Conference of the PCC, in 2012, encouraged "the broadest and most open exchange of opinions" within the party and about the party's relations with workers and the citizenry, so that "differences in views would be considered as normal occurrences . . . within a framework of respect," with prompt attention given to complaints from the population (PCC, 2012). Raúl said that the media "should act . . . with strict veracity . . . objectivity, and root out useless secrecy" (R. Castro Ruz, 2012a). The effectiveness of these promises is supported somewhat by the modest expansion of discussion spaces mentioned earlier, but is contradicted by the crackdown on dissidents. Raúl warned that contrary to the hopes of "our enemies and some friends" Cuba would start to "dismantle [its] political system" and would reinstate a multiparty system; "we confirm the PCC's place as the highest leading force of society and the state . . . which we shall never renounce" (R. Castro Ruz, 2012a).

The results of the First National Conference of the PCC were subject to criticism within Cuba. While it did approve some changes,[3] many felt that the conference did not go far enough in launching the necessary political reform process and revealed the lack of a political mechanism to build consensus among those with different views about the future of the country (J. Pérez et al., 2012). Raúl's challenge is to lead a "political updating" parallel to the "economic updating" that has been ongoing (Márquez, 2011b). The PCC continues to latch on to dogmatic positions and to schemes that have failed everywhere. In order for economic reform to proceed on the island, enabling political changes are necessary; the "historical generation" will have a final opportunity to make these changes (González Mederos, 2011a). The conference did not set out clearly where the nation is going or what political changes are necessary to get there; neither did it create spaces for dialogue with certain segments of the population, such as youths and the emerging nonstate sector; it also ignored the growing ideological plurality of the nation (López-Levy, 2012). The objective of strengthening national unity around the PCC runs counter to official criticism of "false unanimity" (Guanche, 2012; see also Dossier, 2012). Many social scientists support deeper and swifter political reforms.

Labor Indiscipline, Corruption, and Payment of Arrears to Farmers and Cooperatives

Controlling labor indiscipline in Cuba presents important challenges; for example, punctuality at work is impossible to enforce due to the inefficient public transportation system. The establishment of the office of comptroller general is an important step in combating corruption. More than 300 arrests of high-level Cuban officials and representatives of foreign enterprises operating on the island have been made on corruption charges. The two most recent large-scale audits of state enterprises, conducted in 2011, found violations of law and regulations as well as corruption among 45 percent of those enterprises in Havana, while at the national level, 37 percent of state enterprises were found to have deficient or bad management. The anticorruption campaign is hindered by certain systemic factors—state monopoly, concentration of decisionmaking power, lack of transparency—that will be difficult to change.

Delays in payments to agricultural producers continued in 2009, although this was one of the first issues tackled by Raúl and at the time it seemed that it had been overcome. Former minister of agriculture Rosales del Toro revealed cheating by local entities who hide payment arrears when reporting to national authorities; Orlando Lugo, former president of the National Association of Small Private Farmers (ANAP), stated that these entities resort to underhanded approaches to hide payment delays, such as claiming that some of them are being contested through the legal system (*Granma,* September 28, 2009; *Trabajadores,* September 28, 2009). Raúl lashed out against state enterprises that did not meet the terms of their contracts and failed to pay their debts and to deliver essential products: "How are we going to take the moral high ground and demand that the population meet their obligations if our own [state] organizations consistently violate norms and regulations? We should meet our obligations first so that we have the authority to demand compliance by others" (R. Castro Ruz, 2011f). Arrears to agricultural producers amounted to some 6 million CUP in October 2011 (Amor, 2011).[4]

Updating of the Economic Model

As discussed in Chapter 5, the current economic model in Cuba is not to be substantially transformed but rather "updated" in a gradual and programmed manner. In his main report to the Sixth Congress of the PCC in 2011, Raúl stated that such "updating" would require "at least five years" and warned: "the agreements we reach in this Congress cannot suffer the same fate of those reached at previous Congresses, nearly all of them forgotten" (R. Castro Ruz, 2011a). And yet the agreements of the Congress failed to define "updating," left many important issues unresolved, and contained significant contradictions. Twenty months after the Congress, many key issues remained to be discussed, much less clearly defined, among them the relationship between plan and market (though the latter is explicitly subordinated to the former); the degree of decentralization in decision-making; the role of state enterprises within a process of shifting employment from the state to the nonstate sector; the method to set prices and the areas in which central pricing will prevail; and the strategy to accomplish many key economic goals set by the Congress. At the National Assembly meetings in mid-2012, former minister of economy Marino Murillo vaguely said that one of the actions proposed was "to conceptualize the economic model, which demands the design of a long-term program . . . along the lines of five-year projections and annual plans" (*Granma,* July 24, 2012). Raúl has also asserted the need to return to five-year central plans and the imperative of planning to avoid improvisation and mistakes. Nevertheless, the record of more than half a century of central planning in Cuba is one of numerous errors and failures, and some of the mechanisms for "updating" and improving central planning that have been tried before on the island— for example, self-financing, enterprise investment funds, and worker incentive plans—have all resulted in failure.

Pavel Vidal Alejandro (2011a) cautions: "I do not see significant structural change. . . . [I]n planning, a larger role has to be given to the market . . . regulating it through indirect incentives and disincentives . . . rather [than updating] a centralized system that has proven to be inefficient a thousand times in Cuba and abroad."[5] Jorge Sánchez-Egozcue (2011a) points out "the great difficulty in changing the vertical administrative culture that has prevailed for decades and has amply shown its unviability" and calls for adopting decentralized management at the level of local government and incorporation of the private and cooperative sectors.

In view of all this, it is probable that the current "updating" of the model will not succeed and that the leadership will have to go back to the drawing board and design a more feasible economic model with greater participation of the market and the private sector. The Chinese and Vietnamese market-socialism models, which give crucial roles to the market and the private sector, have been successful for decades. Adoption by Cuba of one of these models, adapted to its needs, would have carried a higher probability of success than updating the obsolete central-planning model.

Usufruct

Over a three-year period (September 2008 to November 2011), 1.2 million hectares of land were distributed to 147,000 usufructuaries; in November 2012 those figures were reported to have risen to 1.5 million hectares and 174,271 usufructuaries respectively (*Juventud Rebelde,* November 10, 2012). According to two different sources, between 33 percent and 54 percent of the distributed land was not under production at the end of 2011. In mid-2010, Minister Murillo expressed disappointment over production results from land distributed in usufruct, while Pedro Olivera, director general of the National Center of Land Control of the Ministry of Agriculture, stated that it would take two years to be able to evaluate the impact of land distribution on production (*Associated Press,* June 27, 2010). Agricultural output fell by 5 percent in 2010; production of raw tobacco, rice, beans, citrus fruits, vegetables, and most fruits fell between 15 and 20 percent; number of cattle rose by 2 percent; and production of coffee, milk, and corn increased as well (ONE, 2011a).

According to preliminary statistics, in 2011 agricultural production rose by 8.7 percent, nonsugar agricultural production by 11.5 percent, and livestock by 6 percent (ONE, 2012f), a significant improvement over 2010 and earlier years, suggesting that the distribution of land was yielding positive results. While overall economic performance statistics for 2011 had not been released in Cuba's statistical yearbook, the *Anuario Estadístico,* at the time we completed writing this book, the physical agriculture production data that are available confirm positive developments, with a few exceptions. Table 6.2 compares output for twelve production lines in 2010 and 2011: in nine of them output rose (ranging from 1.3 percent for tubers and plantains to 66.2 percent for beans), whereas it decreased in only two (milk and citrus

Table 6.2 Agricultural Production and Nonstate Sector Share, 2010–2011

	Production (thousand tons)		Change Between 2010 and 2011	Nonstate Sector (percentage of total)	
	2010	2011	(%)	Planted	Production
Sugarcane	11,500	15,800	37.4	97.4	96.8
Tubers and plantains	2,250	2,280	1.3	90.9	90.4
Vegetables	2,141	2,200	2.8	88.9	84.6
Rice	454	566	24.7	78.5	86.4
Corn	324	354	9.2	95.2	96.4
Beans	80	133	66.2	94.3	96.6
Citrus fruits	345	264	–23.4	54.6	40.0
Other fruits	762	817	7.2	88.0	94.0
Milk (cow)	630	600	–4.7		88.8
Eggs	2,430	2,620	7.8		
Tobacco	20	20	0.0	96.3	98.9
Cattle (thousands)	3,992	4,059	1.7		85.5

Sources: Authors' estimates based on Tables 2.2 and 2.8 and ONE, 2012a.
Note: Empty cells indicate that data are not available.

fruits).[6] Cultivated land in major crops largely contracted in the state sector but mostly expanded in the nonstate sector (ONE, 2012a). Table 6.2 shows that the nonstate sector had the largest shares in both planted land (79 percent to 97 percent for most crops) and production (86 percent to 99 percent for most crops). In 2011, production in the nonstate sector rose in ten out of twelve crops. Finally, the nonstate sector had higher yields than the state sector in 60 percent of the crops in 2011 (ONE, 2012a).

As noted, Cuba's statistical yearbook does not disaggregate usufruct land within the nonstate sector, although all evidence indicates that usufruct land has expanded since 2008. Hence a tentative conclusion is that usufruct has been mainly responsible for increases in the agricultural production, as in 2011, despite the disincentives it faces. If this analysis proves to be correct, then the 2012 usufruct law, provided it is properly implemented, should also increase agricultural production, but specific data on usufruct are needed to confirm this effect.

Dismissals, Self-Employment, and Production and Services Cooperatives

In February 2011 it was officially announced that the first tranche of dismissals of state employees would not occur as scheduled; although a revised schedule for dismissals was not announced, a reference was made to meeting the retrenchment goals during the 2011–2014 period. In 2011 an estimated 140,000 workers were dismissed from the state sector, 14 percent of the 1 million workers slated for retrenchment (*EFE,* April 30, 2012). There is no concrete information on how the dismissal committees operate, and whether they actually do so in a nondiscriminatory manner. Self-employment expanded by 166 percent in 2011, and according to the announced goals it was supposed to increase by 78 percent in 2012 and by 159 percent from 2012 to 2015; as a share of the labor force, self-employment rose from 2.8 percent in 2009 to 7.8 percent in 2011, and if the announced goals were met it was to reach 36 percent in 2015 (see Table 6.3 and Figure 6.1). At the close of 2010, some 147,400 self-employed workers were registered, 3,600 higher than in 2009, indicating a reversal of the downward trend since 2003 but still a small number compared to the number of state workers slated for dismissal.

Some 221,800 self-employment licenses were issued between October 1, 2010, and April 30, 2011; during the same time period, either 27,000 or 42,000 licenses (estimates from two sources) were returned by license holders. Of the new self-employed workers, 68 percent had not previously held a state job and 16 percent were retirees or state workers, so that only 16 percent (35,500) of new self-employed workers came from the ranks of dismissed workers (*Granma,* May 21, 2011). At the end of 2011, 391,500 self-employed workers were registered, more than twice the number at the end of 2010; subtracting the 147,400 self-employed workers registered in 2010 means that the net addition was 244,100, nearly meeting the goal of creating 250,000 new self-employment jobs by March 2011, but meeting only one-fourth of the goal of 1 million jobs set for December 2011. The share of self-employed workers who had been dismissed from state jobs grew slightly, from 16 percent in April 2011 to 18 percent in December 2011, still a small share of the total (*Bohemia,* April 10, 2012). By mid-2012 the National

Table 6.3 Self-Employment, 2009–2015

	Number of Self-employed Registered (thousands)	Growth Rate Compared to Preceding Year (%)	Share of Labor Force (%)[a]
2009	143.8	1.6	2.8
2010	147.4	2.5	2.9
2011	391.5	165.6	7.8
2012 (goal)	695.3	77.6	13.9
2015 (goal)	1,800.0	158.9[b]	35.9

Sources: Authors' estimates based on ONE, 2011a, 2012a; goals for 2012 and 2015 from Pedraza, 2010, and *Gaceta Oficial,* January 13, 2012.

Notes: a. For 2009, 2010, and 2011, labor force share is based on size of the economically active population in those years; for 2012 and 2015, no growth is assumed.

b. Growth compared to 2012.

Figure 6.1 Self-Employment, 2009–2015

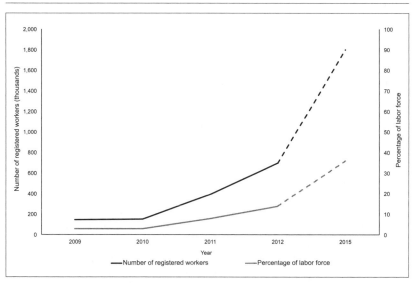

Sources: Authors' estimates based on ONE, 2011a, 2012a; goals for 2012 and 2015 from Pedraza, 2010, and *Gaceta Oficial,* January 13, 2012.

Assembly reported that 390,598 self-employed workers had been registered, lower than the number at the end of 2011 (395,300), and meeting 56 percent of the goal for the end of 2012 (695,300) (*Granma,* July 24, 2012).

Among the reasons given for the slowdown in dismissals and in the creation of private jobs is resistance from the bureaucracy and state managers. Raúl stated that "the largest obstacle we face in implementing the agreements of the VI Congress is the psychological barrier caused by inertia, immobility, double standards [*doble moral*], indifference, and lack of sensitivity. . . . I warn that all bureaucratic resistance [to changes] . . . will be useless" (R. Castro Ruz, 2011d).

The economic plan for 2012 projects the creation of 357,000 new self-employment jobs as well as 240,000 in cooperatives and in the nonstate sector, for a total of nearly 600,000 jobs, and a reduction of 170,000 state sector jobs (*Gaceta Oficial,* January 13, 2012). The minister of finance predicted that by 2015, 1.8 million additional workers would be employed by the nonstate sector (self-employed, private farmers, members of cooperatives), for a total of 2.6 million workers in the nonstate sector, roughly half of the labor force in 2010 (Pedraza, 2010; ONE, 2011a; A. García et al., 2011). The 166 percent rate of growth of self-employment in 2011 will be difficult to replicate in future years, and the 78 percent growth rate set for 2012 is questionable because the number of self-employed workers registered by mid-2012 was lower than at the end of 2011; therefore the target of 1.8 million for 2015 is unlikely to be met. It is expected that the growth of self-employment will decline as demand for certain occupations becomes saturated and competition grows, some businesses go bankrupt, and some workers decide to abandon self-employment.

Murillo has stated that the Permanent Commission, which reports to the president of the Council of State, is drafting a new law regarding non-agricultural cooperatives, and Raúl confirmed that such law would be brought before the ANPP for approval after an evaluation of the experiments in process (*La Jornada,* March 28, 2012; R. Castro Ruz, 2012b).[7] By mid-2011 there were reports that 1,500 cooperatives of barbers, hairdressers, and manicurists had been established (*Reuters,* July 30, 2011). At the National Assembly meeting in mid-2012, however, Murillo announced the approval of only about 200 production and services cooperatives; he added that some of them would start to operate by the end of 2012 and the rest gradually. He also stated that the drafting of regulations for cooperatives was in the final stage (*Granma,* July 24, 2012). In view of the modest approval number for new cooperatives, reported by Murillo, it is difficult to understand how the number of cooperative members, basically in services and nonagricultural production, jumped from 217,000 to 652,100 (from 4.2 percent to 13 percent of the labor force) between 2010 and 2011 (see Table 5.1). Because the number of "other" nonstate workers sharply declined at the same time, and it is possible that some of them were counted as cooperative members.

Social Welfare and Cuts in Social Services Expenditures

Income inequality in Cuba has increased as a result of the reforms. The recovery of real salaries accelerated after 2006, but in 2010 they were still 73 percent below their level in 1989 (see Table 4.4). There is no information on the implementation of salaries based on performance, multi-employment, or hard-currency payments to joint venture employees. Government revenue from direct taxes (profits, personal income) rose by 13 percentage points between 2006 and 2010, making the taxation system less regressive; nevertheless, more than half of government revenue is raised by indirect taxes, principally sales taxes (based on ONE, 2007, 2011a). The tax reform of 2012, which will shift taxation from indirect to direct taxes, should reduce the regressivity of the taxation system. The income gap between Afro-Cubans and whites will rise as state employment shrinks; Afro-Cubans are overrepresented in state employment compared to whites, and will be hit hard by the dismissals. In 2010, women continued to trail men on most labor force indicators, including participation in top leadership positions and in nonstate employment. Recently, Cuba finally recognized the existence of racial and gender discrimination, and the representation of Afro-Cubans and women in the PCC's Central Committee has risen.

After half a century of steady growth, social services expenditures were cut by 1 percentage point based on the budget and 2 percentage points based on gross domestic product between 2009 and 2010, mainly through cuts in public health and social assistance services. The health budget decreased by 18 percent between 2009 and 2011, driven by a reduction in the number of hospitals, family doctor offices, and Ministry of Public Health personnel, coupled with limits on the use of high-tech diagnostic tools and laboratory tests. Education expenditures have been flat as a result of the fall in enrollment at all education levels, the significant reduction in the number of municipal universities and secondary schools in the countryside, and the shutdown of schools for social workers. There was also a better allocation of resources devoted to education: enrollment in humanities and social sciences declined, while enrollment in natural sciences and mathematics rose; entrance exams were also made more rigorous. Medical school enrollment fell by 20 percent in the 2011–2012 school year compared to the previous school year, which is a concern for reaching the goal of graduating a sufficient number of physicians to cover the nation's needs as well as international commitments.

Housing construction fell 70 percent between 2006 and 2011, and from 9.9 to 2.8 units built per 1,000 inhabitants (see Table 4.15). Most of the dwellings destroyed or damaged by hurricanes since 2008 have not been rebuilt or repaired,[8] and the housing deficit has grown, probably exceeding 1 million units as of 2011. A positive measure is the unrestricted sale of construction materials to the population, though only 15 percent of the sales target was achieved in 2011 and prices were high.

The reform of the pension system cut the deficit financed by the state by nearly 2 percentage points in 2010; in the long term, the reform will not reduce the financial deficit significantly enough to reach actuarial equilibrium, which requires higher contributions by enterprises and workers. It has been officially reported that by 2021 there will be more pensioners than new workers entering the labor force (*Granma,* July 24, 2012). In 2011, 198,511 persons were enrolled in the social security (pension) system, mostly self-employed individuals who were already working in that capacity prior to the expansion of self-employment. Social assistance expenditures fell by 67 percent between 2008 and 2011 (a 78 percent decline of the state budget), whereas the overall numbers of beneficiaries, adults receiving assistance, and sick and elderly needing homecare shrank between 56 percent and 74 percent (see Table 4.13). These reductions in social assistance, the cutbacks in gratuities (e.g., lunches at the workplace) and in the scope of the rationing system, combined with new regulations that require families to support previous social assistance beneficiaries, affect vulnerable groups, who are expanding as a result of the reforms, and also weaken the social safety net that prevents citizens from falling into poverty.

Sale of Homes and Automobiles

From November 1, 2011 (October 1 for automobiles), through March 31, 2012, 2,930 homes were sold and 11,380 were donated; for automobiles, the respective figures are 11,700 and 7,774 (see Table 6.4). Between January and March 2012, the sale of homes accelerated compared to 2011, but the number of homes sold remained low compared with the number donated. The relatively low number of home sales may be a function of red tape in obtaining registry documentation and complexity of the transactions. Meanwhile, the high number of donations may reflect legalization of de facto arrangements that preceded the passage of the new regulations (*Granma,* April 26, 2012). A website listed the availability of the following properties in November 2011: a two-story home with five bedrooms in Havana's "Embassy Row" for US$200,000; a penthouse with swimming pool in Havana for US$280,000; and a five-bedroom home in Santiago de Cuba for US$200,000 (*Miami Herald,* November 20, 2011). In April 2012, another website listed a hundred homes and apartments for sale nationally at prices ranging between 16,000 and 75,000 CUC; among the properties offered was a penthouse in the Vedado neighborhood listed at 230,000 CUC (US$253,000) (Revolico.com). Small construction companies composed of an architect or engineer (working illegally) and a few workers have been organized; real estate agents, who formerly worked only in the arrangement of housing swaps, have reappeared as intermediaries in real estate transactions.[9]

Table 6.4　Sale and Donation of Homes and Vehicles, November 2011–March 2012

	November 1, 2011 to December 31, 2011[a]	January 1, 2012 to March 31, 2012	November 1, 2011 to March 31, 2012
Homes			
Sold	200	2,730	2,930
Donated	780	10,600	11,380
Total	980	13,330	14,310
Vehicles			
Sold	3,310	8,390	11,700
Donated	994	6,780	7,774
Total	4,304	15,170	19,474

Sources: Authors' estimates based on *Café Fuerte,* December 16, 2011; *Miami Herald,* January 1, 2012; *Granma,* April 26, 2012.

Note: a. Vehicles from October 1.

Implementation and Follow-Up

The Sixth Congress of the Cuban Communist Party did not provide a time-line to implement the reform agreements, nor did it set implementation priorities or a sequence of actions to be taken (Ritter, 2011b). As mentioned, the Permanent Commission, which reports to the president of the Council of State, was charged with overseeing, verifying, and coordinating implementation of the agreements. Marino Murillo, head of the commission and vice president of the Council of Ministers, reported that the commission has the authority to make changes to the agreements or propose new ones, as appropriate; he also stressed that the commission is developing a work plan through 2015 that "will be fulfilled to the letter" (*La Jornada*, March 28, 2012).

The First National Conference of the PCC, in 2012, set out that the party is responsible for fostering and overseeing compliance with the agreements of the Sixth Congress, particularly the updating of the economic model (PCC, 2012). Machado Ventura, second secretary of the PCC, opened the conference by stating that its principal objective was to ensure that the agreements did not become a "dead letter." Murillo stated that more changes were needed, but that there was a limit to changes, as "the socialist system is untouchable" (*Granma*, January 29, 2012). The Central Committee of the PCC is to meet twice annually to review progress and to prepare status reports on the implementation of the agreements. The leadership of the PCC and of the government will keep close oversight of the process and, when appropriate, make adjustments to correct negative trends. The press and other mass media have been asked to abandon their typical sycophantic pronouncements and play the role of critic, which will require enhancing the professionalism of journalists and providing them with reliable information regularly. The Cuban population will be informed about measures and adjustments adopted (R. Castro Ruz, 2011a, 2011b, 2012a). The creation of oversight entities to follow up on implementation of the agreements is an important step, but it is too early to assess whether these bodies will properly carry out their functions.

Recommendations to Enhance Reforms

Many of the recommendations offered here to enhance Cuba's reforms originate from economists and social scientists inside and outside the island, and we agree with the vast majority of them. In what follows, recommendations that are not attributed to specific individuals are ours, based on our previous research, which has been updated and considerably expanded (Mesa-Lago and Pérez-López, 2005; Mesa-Lago, 2008a, 2010a, 2010c, 2012).

Updating of the Model and Internal and External Economic Issues

Statistics and surveys. Evaluating the effects of Cuba's reforms will require a robust statistical base that is able to support economic analysis. It is likely that the Permanent Commission gathers such statistics, but so far they have not been publicly released, notwithstanding Raúl's call to do away with secrecy and to make more information available to the public. Concerning statistics published by the National Statistical Office (ONE), for example, to assess the impact of agricultural reforms it would be essential to disaggregate data on cultivated land, production, yields, sales, prices, and so on, distinguishing among types of producers: state farms, cooperatives of various types, private farms, and usufructuaries. Information should also be made public on credits given to farmers, their purpose, and repayment performance, and also on inputs sold to them. With regard to labor, salaries, and distribution, it is essential also that statistics be published on the impact of multi-employment, the elimination of salary caps, hard-currency payments to joint venture workers, and pay based on performance, as well as on indicators such as average salary by gender and race, incidence of poverty, and income distribution. Finally, the government should conduct and regularly publish public opinion surveys (or allow scholars to do this) in order to learn the population's views on the reforms and the desired changes.

Decentralization and regulation. The market and its system of economic signals should play a larger role in Cuba's economic development model, subject to some government regulation. Ricardo Torres Pérez (2011) recommends setting clear rules of universal application, backed up with legal instruments that would permit sanctioning of violations, even if committed by the state. A law is needed to guarantee private property rights, including for private enterprises, all types of cooperatives, and trade societies (de Miranda Parrondo and Pérez Villanueva, 2012). To enable enterprises to make the bulk of their decisions would require the decentralization of resource allocation and the progressive use of indirect regulation (see also Guanche, 2012). Jurist Ramón de la Cruz recommends that municipalities be assigned a budget for them to manage on their own, and be granted the ability to raise revenue and design and implement local development initiatives ("Sobre la transición," 2007). Yenisel Rodríguez (Dossier, 2011) calls for wide use of public referenda in important decisions made by communities, including budgets. G. H. Hagelberg (2011) does not believe that delegation of decisionmaking to provinces and municipalities would reduce bureaucratic meddling, and therefore calls for full deregulation, an action not contemplated in Cuba's reform agreements. With respect to the administrative structure, the Ministry of Economy and the Ministry of Finance and Prices could be merged, and their coordination with the Central Bank of Cuba enhanced; it would also be appropriate to merge the Ministry of Education and the Ministry of Higher Education in view of the reduction in university enrollment associated with population aging and budgetary pressures.

Self-management. As an alternative to the current central-planning model and to a potential market economy model, a group of Cuban Marxist social scientists have proposed a mixed economy model based on worker self-management. In this model, workers would play a leading role in the administration of enterprises, interacting with markets and with indicative (rather than central) planning mechanisms to promote autonomy, decentralization, and democratization. Three levels of worker participation in management are contemplated: full, shared with state or private sector managers, and indirect through consultation and veto power (Chaguaceda and Centeno, 2011). A Cuban economist has rejected the criticism that the worker self-management model is "utopian" and argued for fostering self-managed enterprises that respond to social interests and giving them preferential treatment over enterprises organized according to lesser forms of socialism (Piñeiro Harnecker, 2011). A broader conception of self-management, combined with cooperativism (participative socialism), would expand the model to society as a whole: workers would democratically manage all entities (even the PCC and labor unions), elect their leaders, and decide the distribution of earnings and profits. There would be a gradual shift in control over the means of production from the bureaucracy to workers and from state ownership to collective and individual ownership. The role of the state would shift from administrator and decisionmaker to facilitator of the model and to provider of such goods and services that cannot be accomplished by self-management (Campos et al., 2008).

Prices. An integral reform is fundamental in order for prices in Cuba to reflect supply and demand and play a key role in the allocation of scarce resources. This measure would eliminate the numerous distortions that are present throughout the economy. In the short term, price liberalization would bring about certain economic shocks, from which the most vulnerable population should be protected; in the middle to long term, it would have positive effects: efficient resource allocation, reduction in expenditures associated with subsidies, more competitive exports, and a basis for evaluating economic feasibility of import substitution. As part of a comprehensive price reform, the extremely high charges at foreign-currency stores (TRDs) should be reduced, ensuring that prices reflect import price plus a reasonable return, making such goods more accessible to middle- and low-income households, and positively affecting work incentives and income distribution (Betancourt, 2011; Triana, in Dossier, 2011; Vidal Alejandro,

2012a). The loss in state revenue from this source could be compensated by a progressive income tax with higher tax rates for the wealthiest and taxes on enterprise profits.

Monetary policy, monetary duality, and exchange rate. Pavel Vidal Alejandro (2010a, 2010c, 2011a, 2012a) points out that there is no generally accepted monetary policy to guide socialist economies that are seeking to incorporate market elements, and suggests that for Cuba, the Central Bank should develop such a policy. The "big bang" approach followed by Vietnam to reach monetary unification, despite its radical elements, still took several years to reach its objective. In Cuba, the huge gap between the value of the national peso (CUP) and the value of the convertible peso (CUC)—on the order of 2,300 percent—rules out a sudden devaluation and calls for a more gradual approach; it is important to start the process soon, however, to avoid prolonging it unnecessarily. Specific policy suggestions include: (a) gradually devaluate the overvalued CUC, unify its exchange rate with that in the hard-currency exchange houses (CADECAs), and make the CUP convertible with respect to the business sector, which would allow enterprises to buy hard currencies using CUP; (b) establish a more realistic exchange rate for the CUC so that it can be used in international markets, in a manner similar to that of the Chinese and Vietnamese currencies; and (c) adopt the CUP as the nation's only currency, based on the fact that the bulk of the economy operates with this currency (salaries, most savings, national accounts, the national budget, and key sectors such as agriculture).

Banking and insurance. Vidal Alejandro (2011a, 2012b) recommends comprehensive reform of the Cuban banking system: establish joint banks with participation from Latin American banks in order to meet the imperative for external capital and skirt the restrictions that the US embargo places on international banks; develop a domestic financial market and allow interest rates to be set by market forces; issue low-risk financial instruments that could be transacted through the domestic financial market; and, following the example of Vietnam, take the necessary steps to seek membership in the international financial institutions. Arturo López-Levy (2011) has also proposed the development of a competitive insurance market and of mortgages (on the latter, see also de Miranda Parrondo and Pérez Villanueva, 2012).

Taxation system. Cuba's comprehensive tax reform of 2012 seeks the desirable change of shifting the burden of taxation from indirect taxes toward direct taxes on income, profits, and assets held; hence, if properly applied, it should make the tax system less regressive. It also sets taxes, contributions, and user fees to increase government revenue needed for the reforms and provides incentives for the agricultural sector, self-employment, and small businesses. Since the law was not in force at the time we completed writing this book, we cannot assess whether the tax reform goals will be met. The possibility of a grace period or moratorium on taxing the emerging private sector until it has consolidated has already been partially incorporated into the new system, but could be further developed. It remains to be seen to what extent the new system is implemented; creating a culture of compliance requires not only convincing citizens to meet their obligations but also transparency on the part of tax authorities and accountability of the government vis-à-vis the citizenry (Betancourt, 2011).

Export and import strategy. Jorge Sánchez-Egozcue (2011a) argues that a successful foreign trade strategy "is not necessarily a function of structural policy changes, but rather of changes in rules affecting production of tradables." Among these changes as applied to Cuba would be: (a) a radical overhaul of enterprise management (independence in decisionmaking, elimination of unnecessary regulation, availability of financing, liberalization of prices, creation of incentives) to support increased productivity and achieve export potential; (b) relaxation of regulations that prohibit state enterprises from engaging directly in international trade, and eventual authorization for the private sector to do the same; and (c) identification of new export lines, in view of the stagnation of sugar and nickel exports, emphasis on high-value-added exports. Rafael Hernández (Dossier, 2011) focuses on the need to diversify foreign trade to reduce dependence on Venezuela. Juan Triana (Dossier, 2011) recommends shifting tourism from enclaves to the territory at large, in order to enhance both state and nonstate linkages with domestic production.

Foreign direct investment. Cuba is in dire need of foreign direct investment (FDI) in virtually all areas of the economy, and a new foreign investment law is essential (de Miranda Parrondo and Pérez Villanueva, 2012). Triana (Dossier, 2011) recommends reviewing rules on FDI to eliminate bottlenecks and involving provincial and local governments in decisionmaking regarding FDI; at the same time, he observes that, in some instances, foreign investors enjoy more privileges compared to domestic entities, and even enjoy monopolies in certain areas (e.g., cell telephony, with Cuba having among the highest charges for such service in the world); hence he advocates a law that is equal for all and open competition to other forms of ownership. Vidal Alejandro (2010a, 2011a) identifies areas of the economy where foreign investment is needed: the port of Mariel, the petrochemical complex in Cienfuegos, the oil refineries in Matanzas and Santiago de Cuba, projects to rebuild the manufacturing sector and the sugar industry in particular, the transportation sector, the cement industry, tourism, modernization of basic infrastructure, and export-oriented industries. Foreign investment is also needed in the agricultural sector, where the degree of de-capitalization has been high; there is a positive example in this sector, which is citrus production. Orlando Márquez (2011a) argues that Cubans should have the freedom to invest in their own country and that the stigma attached to accumulation of wealth should be overcome. A document issued by the Cuban Research Institute at Florida International University sets out several ways in which the Cuban American community could assist Cuba in developing its economic, human, and social capital (CRI, 2011).

Agriculture

The key to Cuban structural reforms is agriculture, as was the case in China and Vietnam; should changes in agriculture fail, the overall reform process would be severely jeopardized. A successful reform of agriculture would result in increased production, elimination of black markets for food, phasing-out of the rationing system, and reduction and eventual elimination of costly food imports. The lack of clear, significant positive results in agriculture as of 2011, three years after passage of the 2008 usufruct law, suggests that the policy changes to date have not been sufficient to generate a positive trend (Vidal Alejandro, 2011a).

Role of the state, cooperatives, acopio, and intermediaries. Centralized decisionmaking is counterproductive in Cuba's agricultural sector; the role of the state should shift from producer, overseer, and price-setter to regulator (with respect to the environment, food security, market failure) and promoter of economic growth (such as by investing in infrastructure, facilitating financing, promoting research and innovation, protecting against risks from natural disasters, and providing timely and reliable economic information) (Hagelberg, 2011). Agricultural cooperatives, whether basics unit of cooperative production (UBPCs), agricultural production cooperatives (CPAs), or credit and services cooperatives (CCSs), should have decisionmaking autonomy from the state, and their members should have the freedom to choose what crops to plant, to whom to sell their output, and at what price; enjoying these rights would make cooperative members feel like owners of their enterprises, encourage new members to join, increase production, and eliminate the need for government subsidies to cooperatives to cover their losses (Nova, 2011).[10] The *acopio* procurement system imposed on agricultural cooperatives, private farmers, and usufructuaries should be eliminated. According to Vidal Alejandro (2011a) *acopio* is "a bottleneck that must be dismantled"; believing that *acopio* could be fine-tuned to make it work more efficiently through increased controls and discipline, better forecasting, or enhanced contractual arrangements is a mirage that "drains the energy out of the reform process . . . and [out] of the imperative to effect structural changes." Producers should be able to sell their output to whomever they wish; should the state want to purchase part of the output, it could do so at prevailing market prices (or at least at prices substantially higher than it currently pays)[11] and without undue delays. Municipal *acopio* enterprises, which are notoriously inefficient and extract high profit margins, would be eliminated. Intermediaries, who play a useful and necessary role in the operation of markets, should be authorized to operate, subject to payment of taxes on their income (Nova, 2010a, 2011).

Expansion of property rights and elimination of restrictions on usufructuaries. The distribution of state lands in usufruct to private farmers has been a positive development in Cuba. Agricultural production fell in 2009 and 2010 because of existing restrictions; after some flexible norms were introduced in 2011, agricultural output rose in the nonstate sector. Disaggregated data on usufructuaries' cultivated land and output are not available and should be published so that their performance can be evaluated. Remaining obstacles and disincentives in the 2012 usufruct law should be removed. Evidence suggests that distribution of land in usufruct is not sufficient by itself to create a virtuous cycle of production and productivity growth, and must be accompanied by clarity with regard to property and economic rights and freedom on the part of usufruct grantees to make decisions (Nova, 2010a). Measures are needed to extend the term of usufruct contracts for individuals, further expand the amount of land distributed to farmers without forcing them to be tied to state farms and cooperatives in order to be able to obtain additional land, increase the share of usufruct parcels that can legally be devoted to investments and improvements, guarantee adequate state compensation to usufruct grantees for such investments and improvements, and allow usufructuaries to sell their output at a price set by supply and demand. Rather than distributing land for a fixed period of time, Cuba would be better off following the Chinese and Vietnamese example of granting the right to use land for an indefinite period, or selling state land to successful farmers under a time payment system, allowing mortgaging of land to raise capital, and making more explicit the transfer of land and improvements to heirs and family workers upon the death of the usufruct grantee (Espinosa Chepe, 2008).[12] Most usufruct grantees lack experience in agriculture and therefore it is essential that they receive training (as stipulated in the 2012 law) and improve their farming techniques through acquisition of the seeds, tools, fertilizers, herbicides, and other agricultural implements they need through the use of credit facilities. To eradicate marabú—which infests half of Cuba's idle lands—and to increase production, state credit should be made available for clearing land of marabú, and farmers should be encouraged to organize themselves into truly free cooperatives to buy or lease bulldozers and harvesting machinery. Nonstate agricultural producers should be allowed to freely contract any workers they might need, in accord with labor, taxation, and social security laws. These measures would increase production and eventually bring down retail prices of agricultural products (Nova, 2011).

Dismissals, Self-Employment, SMEs and Cooperatives, and Microcredits

Dismissals. The process to select workers to be dismissed should be transparent and based on objective factors. Raúl has called for avoiding favoritism and discrimination in dismissals, a tall order, as the decisions to retrench will be made by a committee composed of managers and members of the Workers' Central Union of Cuba (CTC) and of the PCC, and therefore will be state-controlled. A process for appealing or challenging dismissal decisions should be created. The compensation for dismissed workers is meager and paid for too short a period, and hence the compensation system should be improved. An alternative option could be to establish a temporary public assistance program for retrenched workers who might fall into poverty, possibly linked to retraining for occupations with high demand and acceptance of a suitable job offer. In the longer term, the possibility of an unemployment insurance scheme should be considered (Triana, in Dossier, 2011). Current options to absorb dismissed workers—self-employment, cooperatives, usufruct—are not capable of handling the magnitude of the dismissals; a larger and more vibrant private sector, spurred by foreign investment beyond joint ventures, is essential (Vidal Alejandro, 2012a).

Self-employment. Frequent policy changes on self-employment and small businesses have created confusion and distrust. Private activity carries with it a certain amount of risk that needs to be compensated by an adequate gain; regulation through stable and transparent rules that are not subject to arbitrary change is essential to a private sector that can grow, create jobs, and provide an environment for legalizing informal work (L. Pérez, 2010). It is essential to issue regulations that clearly spell out the rights and obligations of the self-employed, prevent excessive government control, and allow them to organize in unions (Hernández, in Dossier, 2011).

Rather than specifying occupations authorized for self-employment, it would be preferable to allow self-employment in broad categories that would infuse the flexibility needed to adapt to changes in demand, or to issue a list of occupations where self-employment would not be permitted (Vidal Alejandro and Pérez Villanueva, 2010; Espinosa Chepe, 2011a; Torres Pérez, 2011). Occupations currently authorized for self-employment have low knowledge requirements and do not match well the profile of workers to be dismissed, who are likely to be university graduates; to date, the only professionals authorized to engage in self-employment are information scientists, economists, and tutors (but only if they are retired teachers). As Triana (Dossier, 2011) has observed: "to limit the growth of the non-state sector to low-value-added services jobs or occupations would be wasting . . . investments made . . . in human development over the last 50 years." The labor force, if highly skilled, could support the creation and development of small- and medium-sized enterprises (SMEs), providing high-value-added technological services that would complement the activity of the state sector (Vidal Alejandro, 2010a). Therefore, it would make sense to authorize professionals to practice as architects, engineers, agronomists, accountants, and managers, in order to generate more employment, enhance productivity, and increase output of goods and services.

Issuance of self-employment licenses should be streamlined to avoid excessive paperwork and emphasize promptness. In order to take advantage of economies of scale, there should be no limits on the number of workers that a small business can hire, or on the number of customers it can serve, or on the volume of business it can generate (L. Pérez, 2010). Competition from SMEs would spur state enterprises to become more efficient. Self-employed workers should also have the freedom to set the price for the goods and services they provide and to decide where and how to invest their profits.

Critical to the success of the self-employed, SMEs, and cooperatives is the creation of a wholesale market that would be able to supply their needs. The availability of such a market would also ease the existing practice of stealing inputs from the state. Marino Murillo has predicted that in due course there will exist wholesale markets whose prices are below those of retail markets, but these will likely take some time to materialize.

SMEs and cooperatives. Expansion of SMEs could bring significant benefits to Cuba: lower investment per job created compared to large enterprises, relative ease in adapting to changes in inputs and demand, and positive effects at the local level on employment, consumption, and tax revenue. To stimulate SMEs and cooperatives, the following actions have been suggested: create a state entity to promote and facilitate the registration of SMEs and cooperatives; develop a legal regulatory framework for SMEs and cooperatives, include them within labor and social security laws, and permit them to have commercial relations with state enterprises; offer management training courses to SMEs at the secondary and vocational education levels; and set taxes at reasonable rates that would not provide incentives for managers to underreport the number of workers and level of salaries (A. García et al., 2011). Rafael Betancourt (2011) recommends that cooperatives be permitted to import inputs, export their output, and associate with foreign entities. Camila Piñeiro Harnecker (2012) identifies several areas of the economy for potential establishment of cooperatives: transportation, light industry, bakeries, savings and loans, street and building cleaning, trash removal, and collective housing. Triana (Dossier, 2011) has proposed the establishment of retail trade cooperatives with the capacity to import directly that could eventually replace the state retail network.

Microcredit. Self-employed workers, SMEs, usufructuaries, and other private sector actors have extremely limited credit options. Vidal Alejandro (2012b) recommends creating special institutions, in collaboration with banks from Latin American countries, to provide credit. López-Levy (2011) argues that microcredit agencies should be established at the municipal level to capitalize on their knowledge of local conditions. Both the Cuban government and the US government should allow and encourage remittances to be invested in small businesses.[13] The Cuba Study Group, headquartered in Miami, has proposed the creation of a US$10 million international fund to make small loans at low interest to SMEs on the island (Brazil and the European Union have offered monetary contributions to the fund and also technical assistance). The Cuban government is suspicious about such an initiative on the grounds that it would mean the intervention of Cuban American capital on the island, but this concern does not square with the opening to foreign investment in key sectors of the economy such as oil, nickel, and tourism.

Inequality, Social Services, and Social Welfare

Income inequality. The expanding income distribution gap in Cuba is connected to the lack of individual incentives resulting from egalitarian policies. To reverse the trend it would be necessary to find a balance between incentives and reasonable taxation policies—embodied to some extent in the new tax law—that would improve income distribution and generate fiscal resources to finance social assistance programs.

Regional development differences. The lack of recent statistical information on Human Development Index scores across Cuba's provinces does not permit an evaluation of whether there has been a reduction in the regional development differences that existed on the island in 2003; the scarce data available for 2006–2010 are contradictory. This information is essential for guiding policy on how to close the development gap between the eastern and western provinces (Íñiguez and Montes, 2010). The persistent lag in health indicators in the less developed provinces (Las Tunas, Granma, and Guantánamo) could be addressed by prioritizing assignment of resources to these provinces, particularly in the areas of health prevention and medical attention.

Race. Cutbacks in the rationing system and in the budget allocated to social services, dismissals from state employment, and reductions in social assistance affect Afro-Cubans to a larger extent than whites. Alejandro de la Fuente (2011) deems as important the increase in participation of Afro-Cubans in the ANPP and the Central Committee of the PCC, although he notes that this does not necessarily guarantee adequate representation within the top echelons of decisionmaking or increased access to better jobs or housing. He recommends an open debate about racial discrimination and measures for its eradication—in schools, workplaces, and through mass communication channels—accompanied by a set of actions including: (a) directing state prosecutors to implement effectively Article 259 of the penal code, which defines racial discrimination as a criminal act; (b) establishing an office to provide oversight regarding the racial impact of reforms; (c) designing affirmative action policies, particularly with respect to employment in the private sector, foreign enterprises, and the tourism sector; (d) putting in place a system to guarantee parity of access to higher education (where Afro-Cubans are affected by quotas, more strict entrance examinations, and the lack of assistance from "home tutors," whom only higher-income students can afford); (e) training police not to use racial profiling and stereotypes in their work; and (f) increasing the participation of Afro-Cubans in mass media, particularly in positive roles. It would also be important to legalize the formation of organizations of Afro-Cubans to protect their rights and promote their advancement, as has been done in South Africa and other nations.

Gender. A proactive policy to eliminate gender discrimination in the Cuban labor force should be implemented, focused on the emerging nonstate sector, to promote participation by females in the work force, prevent gender discrimination in state-sector dismissals, increase the share of women compared to men in managerial positions, expand childcare opportunities, strengthen the campaign against *machismo,* and publicize efforts to combat gender discrimination and their effects.

Salaries. The lack of recent data on multi-employment, pay based on performance, elimination of salary caps, and partial payment in convertible pesos or hard currency to joint venture employees makes it impossible to assess progress on salaries in Cuba. Vidal Alejandro (2011a) has argued that these measures would not succeed as long as the wage bill remains part of the central plan; he has called for enterprise autonomy, with a percentage of profits earmarked to finance the four incentive schemes, including rewarding managers and administrators. Foreign enterprises and joint ventures should be allowed to hire, promote, and pay their workers directly. Labor unions consider the government (the owner of enterprises) and workers as having common interests, an illusion that renders collective bargaining ineffective. Unions should be independent from the government and their leadership should be democratically elected so that they can perform their duty of defending workers' rights (Chaguaceda and Centeno, 2011; Dossier, 2011; González Mederos, 2011b; J. A. Rodríguez, 2011).

Education. The public education system should be maintained, although modified to make it financially feasible and more efficient, provide higher-quality services, and allow nonstate activities to coexist with state activities. Education is free for all Cuban citizens irrespective of family income, which increases costs, lowers quality, and makes the system financially unfeasible.[14] To confront these problems, the following are recommended: (a) focus education resources on the populations in greatest need, on the poorest provinces, and on areas with the largest demand for workers; (b) reduce resources devoted to primary and secondary education to reflect demographic trends and the smaller size of the student cohort at these levels; (c) reallocate resources to reflect domestic demand for trained workers and to allow competition in international markets, specifically by reducing enrollment in physical education and humanities and increasing enrollment in technical-vocational careers associated with economic development (science, technology, business administration, banking); (d) allow enterprises to finance higher education to their employees, which would increase labor productivity (Triana, in Dossier, 2011); (e) charge tuition for higher education to those who can pay it; (f) pay adequate salaries to teachers (despite recent salary increases, teachers continue to leave their profession for better-paying occupations); (g) reduce the school dropout rate, particularly in secondary education, and evaluate educational achievement using more rigorous standards; (h) permit teachers and professors to work as self-employed or in cooperatives; (i) authorize nonstate educational institutions (for example, religious schools) to operate under general standards and under supervision by the state; and (j) grant financial autonomy to research institutions so that they can receive resources through international cooperation (Y. Rodríguez, in Dossier, 2011).

Public health. Cuba's national health system should be preserved, although modified along the lines of the suggested modifications for education. Actions to reduce costs would include the following: (a) prioritize prevention over curative treatment, through more extensive vaccination against high-morbidity illnesses and improvements in potable water and sewage infrastructure; (b) convert underutilized hospitals (e.g., those specializing in gynecology and pediatrics) into geriatric hospitals and facilities for senior citizens needing special services; (c) reallocate resources aimed at reducing the already low infant mortality rate toward basic public health infrastructure and importation of medicines; (d) suspend the expensive free scholarship program to train foreign medical students on the island, and do the same with free medical assistance to foreign countries; and (e) consolidate within the national health system the costly programs that benefit members of the armed forces, internal security personnel, and top leaders. Measures to capture revenues to support the national health system would include the following: (a) implement a system of partial payment for services rendered in hospitals and laboratories based on patients' ability to pay, excluding prevention, primary health services, and treatment provided to low-income groups; (b) charge for the use of private rooms or special services in hospitals based on ability to pay; and (c) maintain and extend contracts of public service personnel working abroad (assessing taxes on their earnings) provided that this does not affect domestic medical needs. Pedro Campos (2012) has proposed imposing higher taxes on consumption of tobacco, alcoholic beverages, and luxury goods, with the proceeds used to improve salaries for medical personnel and therefore reduce their emigration and shift to other occupations. Authorizing health professionals to provide services privately would create competition with the state, permit high-income groups to receive personalized attention, and allow the national health system to focus on middle- and low-income groups and improve access and quality of services. This would require authorizing physicians, dentists, and other public health professionals to operate as self-employed workers or as members of cooperatives. Other potential actions include allowing religious institutions to provide primary healthcare services and requiring large enterprises to offer primary healthcare to their employees (while allowing enterprises to deduct such expenses as the cost of doing business).

Social security pensions. Measures taken to date have reduced somewhat the immediate deficit in the pension system financed by the state, but they have not balanced the system actuarially in the longer term. To address such imbalance and account for the aging of the population, Cuba's social security system requires additional actions: (a) request the International Labour Organization to conduct an actuarial study to determine the level of contributions that are necessary for the system to be solvent and also to evaluate the cost of expanding coverage to the self-employed and members of cooperatives; (b) raise contributions by employers and expand the number of workers that contribute; (c) gradually adjust the retirement age to take into account the rising life expectancy; (d) provide workers who are close to retirement age an option to take retirement early but with a reduced pension; (e) merge the expensive retirement schemes for the armed forces and internal security personnel with those of the general program; and (f) gradually increase the low value of pensions, with the funding for this increase coming from the savings realized from these recommended changes. Another potential action would be to shut down the current pension system, have the government take responsibility for the outstanding obligations, and create a new and mandatory public pension system for all new state employees funded from contributions by workers and employers plus the proceeds from an investment fund.

Housing. Recently enacted laws and regulations permit Cuban citizens to build homes and to purchase construction materials legally; they also provide credits to support home construction and repair by low-income groups. The housing deficit is so imposing, however, that additional measures are required: (a) budgetary allocations for housing should be significantly increased, and should target special forms of housing and groups; (b) the sale of construction materials should be regulated to prevent hoarding and resale at prohibitive prices; (c) credits for the repair of homes should be targeted to the needy, Afro-Cubans, single-mother heads of households, and residents of the least-developed provinces; (d) funds from abroad should be allowed to be used for the repair, construction, and sale of homes; and (e) a housing bank should be established to provide financing for real estate transactions, including management of fiscal subsidies. To create a domestic real estate market, it would be necessary to modernize the real estate property registries and upgrade the training of their staff, allow advertising of properties for sale, and foster the use of mortgages.

Social assistance. At least in the short term, structural reforms in Cuba will bring dismissals and increases in the prices of goods, public utilities, and housing, which will expand poverty. Given the drastic reduction in social assistance, it is critical to create a basic safety net to catch the vulnerable population and to train personnel on its application. An adequate safety net can facilitate other reforms by alleviating their potential adverse effects. Vidal Alejandro (2011a) recommends that social assistance be increased rapidly to avoid "very high social and political costs." The recent decision to purge from the social assistance rolls persons whose families are able to help them should be reconsidered, as providing such help is taxing for most families, who are already heavily burdened. Savings generated by the aforementioned changes in education, public health, and pensions should be allocated to fund social assistance for the poor. Shifting from general subsidies to assistance targeted to those who need help would ease inequality and help correct price distortions. A well-structured safety net could provide sufficient temporary supplementary income to needy households to guarantee that minimum needs are met; these transfers could be supplemented by improved public health and education services, as well as subsidies to repair homes.

Foreign Economic and Technical Assistance

Most of the suggested reforms will require the kind of economic and technical assistance that is generally offered by international organizations. Cuba is a member of the United Nations, but not of a member of the so-called international financial institutions (IFIs), such as the International Monetary Fund (IMF), the World Bank, and the Inter-American Development Bank (IADB). Therefore, Vidal Alejandro (2011a) argues, the island lacks an international lender of last resort to support it in times of economic and financial crisis, resulting in prolonged and deepened downturns and more extreme adjustment measures. He adds that current reforms, in contrast with those in the 1990s, are less open to influence from abroad, and that, moreover, the Cuban government has called for radical changes in the global financial architecture and for the elimination of the IFIs. Meanwhile, China and Vietnam are members of the IMF and the World Bank and participate actively in those organizations, drawing benefits without jeopardizing their national sovereignty on economic policy or altering their views on reform of the international financial system.

The possibility in the short term of Cuba becoming a member of the IMF, the World Bank, and the IADB is remote, given the prominent role that the United States plays in those organizations and the US economic embargo on the island.[15] In the middle to long term, there may be the possibility of Cuba's membership in the IFIs. Participation in the IFIs would allow Cuba to access financial and technical support from these institutions and also to participate in concessional programs, such as the World Bank's International Development Association and the IMF and World Bank's Heavily Indebted Poor Countries Initiative. Cuba may also be able to obtain access to economic and technical assistance from the European Union under the Cotonou Agreement, but such assistance is predicated on respect for human rights. Deepening of reforms, and improvements of political freedom and human rights, would facilitate Cuba's admission to several of these organizations, opening the door to grants and soft loans to finance reforms as well as a social safety net during a transition.

Democracy, Dialogue, and the Political Future

Democratic changes. To overcome the weaknesses of Cuba's political system, Carlos Alzugaray (2009a) proposes a "deliberative democracy" within which leaders would be forced to discuss their actions publicly and citizens would have the ability to participate in decisionmaking in an informed manner. Roberto Veiga and Lenier González, coeditors of the journal *Espacio Laical,* recommend broad political reforms that would guarantee the free expression of views held by all, within and outside the island, irrespective of ideologies, but joined in the common purpose of seeking consensus and dialogue; as organized in political parties, citizens would pursue a new social pact and establish decisionmaking based on majority rule, with rights for minorities. The PCC and the state must engage in a dialogue with society and become more democratic and participative. It is crucial that upon his exit from the scene, Raúl leave Cubans with a country that is institutionalized and as pluralistic as possible (Veiga, 2012; Veiga and González, 2012). Other recommendations include: separating the functions of the Council of State and the Council of Ministers; making the ANPP more active and independent from the executive; connecting the provincial and municipal assemblies more closely to the issues affecting their regions; fostering pluralism and competition within the PCC, with the requirement that at least two candidates compete for each position; introducing term limits and other measures for all public officials in order to promote rotation; and increasing transparency and accountability among public officials and establishing legal procedures to hold them accountable for poor management or for rights violations (Guanche, 2012; López-Levy, 2012).

An important issue, based on other socialist experiences, is whether economic reforms eventually result in political changes that are consistent with democracy and respect for human rights. Analyzing China's experience, Roger Betancourt (2007) posits that an expansion in economic and social options could be accompanied by an increase in civil liberties and first-generation human rights, but not necessarily of political rights. Based on Vietnam's experience, Kanako Yamaoka (2009) argues that as the government transfers economic functions to the nonstate sector, it loses some control over the citizenry. As the private sector generates income independently of the state, it grows less fearful of government actions. The growth of FDI and membership in the IFIs more fully exposes the country to outside influences. In Vietnam, the Communist Party has been pressured to evolve toward a multiparty system; civil liberties have improved in Vietnam, such as access to the Internet, ability to criticize the government through letters to the editor of official newspapers, and permission for private publications to operate. Freedom is more restricted in Cuba than in China or Vietnam because Cuba's reforms lag behind those of the latter. Cuban self-employed workers, for example, do not rely directly on the Cuban state for their income, but they are restricted to certain occupations, their employees have to follow state rules, they are heavily taxed, and the state limits the amount of resources they can accumulate. Land distributed to the private sector in Cuba is subject to more restrictions than in China and Vietnam, where contracts are granted for an indefinite time period. FDI in Cuba is small in comparison with such investment in China and Vietnam and, moreover, Cuba is not a member of the IFIs. Cuba needs to show more openness in the form of allowing the publication of critical views in official newspapers and allowing the circulation of independent journals. It remains to be seen whether the deepening of Cuba's reforms would have effects similar to those in China and Vietnam.

Expansion and strengthening of dialogue. Broadening and deepening of dialogue is essential to advance and strengthen reforms; dialogue can act as a mechanism to identify problems, develop alternatives, seek consensus, and legitimize changes. The Catholic Church plays an important role in this regard in Cuba: it supports dialogue on the country's problems, publishes journals with articles and debates that express different viewpoints, and promotes pluralism through a gradual approach (López-Levy and González Mederos, 2012). In 2008 the Cuban bishops called for "a dialogue among all Cubans, . . . frank, friendly, free, . . . not with the objective of silencing adversaries . . . but rather to allow questioning by each other. . . . In Cuba there is only one party, one press, one television. The dialogue we propose should take into account diversity regarding means of communications and individuals" (*Encuentro en la red,* November 15, 2008). The director of the journal *Palabra Nueva,* Orlando Márquez, called for more individual freedoms (November 8, 2002). Meanwhile, the editors of *Espacio Laical* noted that although dialogue does occur in Cuba in discrete public spaces and among an elite of thinkers and intellectuals, it has yet to become institutionalized in all strata of society and lacks the access to the mass media that is needed to affect the nation's decisionmaking (Veiga and González, 2012; Veiga, 2012). Dagoberto Valdés (2011), editor of the journal *Convivencia* (Coexistence), called for "ending the demonization of disagreement, eliminating the practice of condemning, disqualifying or labeling as a mercenary anyone who thinks differently, stopping the repudiation of one citizen by another following orders from above or because he or she has different views, [and] preventing anyone from being excluded from the negotiating table, which should be large, pluralistic and inviting." A significant gap is that peaceful political dissidents are excluded from discussions, as are their writings from most journals.

During Pope Benedict XVI's visit to Cuba in March 2012, the archbishop of Santiago de Cuba, Dionisio García, called for "a dialogue of mutual respect and reconciliation" to build "a prosperous republic, inclusive and participatory . . . an open and renewed society . . . with new criteria with respect to a way forward toward a better future." He further called for the elimination of intolerance, exclusion, and "violence among Cubans that brings suffering to all of us" (*La Jornada,* March 27, 2012). Though the pope deemed Cuba's reforms as positive, he noted that "still there are many aspects on which progress should be made" that will require "patience as well as resolve." He exhorted Cubans to unite "in a patient and sincere dialogue," respectful and free, in order to "solve differences" and overcome "rancor and enmity," and condemned "immobile positions and unilateral viewpoints that make understanding more difficult and collaboration efforts less efficient." He asked for respect for human rights and acknowledged the just aspirations, concerns, and sufferings of all Cubans, "wherever they are," particularly of youth, the elderly, workers, the poor, Afro-Cubans, and those serving prison sentences. The pope also indirectly criticized the US economic embargo (*El Mundo*, March 26, 2012; *La Jornada*, March 20, 2012, March 27, 2012, March 29, 2012; *El País*, March 28, 2012; González Mederos, 2012). Raúl stated that the pope's visit took place in an environment of "mutual understanding" with "many and profound points of agreement. While . . . we do not think alike on all issues . . . we agree that . . . dialogue and cooperation will allow us . . . to reach solutions to our gravest challenges" (*Juventud Rebelde*, March 28, 2012).

The political future. Raúl has been successful in consolidating his transition to power from Fidel, but what will happen when he and his brother disappear from the scene, having been the dominant figures for over five decades without challengers or successors? The Chinese and Vietnamese elites managed to survive beyond their founding leaders; Eusebio Mujal-León (2011) has analyzed whether the same might happen in Cuba, with the key being whether the coalition of the PCC, military leaders, and the emerging technocracy will persist. Cuba's armed forces are stronger than ever, but their multiple and heterogeneous functions may be their Achilles' heel as tensions rise with the PCC, whose role and importance will decline with the gradual phase-down of the state sector and its functions. In order to maintain stability and continuity, the coalition must succeed on its economic reforms; a failure would breed instability. Another unknown is who will succeed Raúl: he is promoting a younger generation that includes Miguel Díaz-Canel, Marino Murillo, and Adel Yzquierdo Rodríguez, but it is unpredictable whether any of them would be able to keep the coalition together and therefore maintain the stability of the regime (see also Farber, 2011).

Conclusion

Cuba's administrative and nonstructural reforms, which are less complex and significant than its structural reform, have had mostly positive effects: the merger of several ministries and state entities; some progress in combating corruption, with hundreds of public officials having been arrested and imprisoned; increased openness to criticism, within socialist parameters, and to some elements of glasnost; access of upper-income Cuban citizens to tourism hotels and restaurants; payment of arrears to private farmers caused by the *acopio* system (although arrears have begun to build up again); expansion in the number of private transportation providers; short-term reduction of the pension deficit financed by the state (although the long-term imbalance has not been addressed); and cuts in social expenditures. Because of lack of information, it is not possible to assess the results of the struggle against labor indiscipline or of the measures to increase salaries.

Structural reforms, however, have so far not shown clear positive results, because of their constraints and disincentives and insufficient depth. The success of updating the current economic model, based on central planning and state enterprises, is questionable in the light of five decades of numerous failed attempts to improve it. Meaningful changes to the model are expected to take at least five years. Despite the distribution of land in usufruct and other agrarian reforms, agricultural production fell in 2010; although it grew in 2011 in the nonstate sector, it is not possible to determine whether such recovery was attributable to usufruct, due to lack of disaggregated data. The targets for dismissals of redundant state workers were not met in 2011, while growth in self-employment and employment in cooperatives grew notably but not sufficiently to provide jobs for those projected to be dismissed. Measures allowing the sale of homes and of automobiles, as well as more flexible migration regulations, are significant but too recent for their effects to be assessed. Dismissals, elimination of gratuities, the gradual contraction of rationing, and cuts in social expenditures have proceeded in tandem with reductions in social assistance. Still to be addressed are two of the most difficult issues: elimination of monetary duality and elimination of the rationing system.

Why were design flaws in the reforms not detected and corrected during the long and massively attended discussions that occurred prior to the Sixth Congress of the Cuban Communist Party? That is, by the nearly 9 million citizens who debated the economic and social policy guidelines in over 163,000 meetings, in which 3 million interventions were made, during the Congress itself by the thousand delegates in attendance. Nor were flaws corrected during meetings of the Assembly of People's Power, the PCC's Central Committee and Political Bureau, the Workers' Central Union of Cuba, and other mass organizations. After the Sixth Congress, in light of the disappointing results of the structural reforms, the Council of Ministers made some adjustments on the distribution of land in usufruct and self-employment and passed legislation creating production and services cooperatives and allowing sale of homes and automobiles, but other fundamental problems remain. The First National Conference of the PCC, in 2012, did not delve into the structural reforms. Neither it nor the Congress addressed the issue of migration, which was finally passed at the end of 2012.

Why are Cuba's structural reforms not moving at a faster pace? In 2010, Raúl asked for patience: "Some comrades despair at times, wishing immediate changes" but fail to take into account the magnitude and complexity of the tasks; "we must avoid acting precipitously and in an ad hoc manner trying to solve a problem lest we might cause an even larger one." And he added in 2011: "It doesn't matter if we get criticized because we are moving too slowly; we are not going to act precipitously" (R. Castro Ruz, 2010c, 2011e). Armando Chaguaceda (2011) has observed that the state has granted itself the right to determine the depth and pace of the reforms, "with citizens . . . devoid of power to control the process or validate their results."

These questions might have different explanations: a split in the top decisionmaking echelon, contradictions among objectives, obstructions by the bureaucracy, lack of resources, damaging external events, fear of weakening the regime, lack of technical knowledge about the reforms, a desire to gain time in order to prolong the existence of the regime until oil in commercial quantities is discovered, or a combination of all of the above.

Raúl asserted that "the Cuban leadership is united [although this does not] exclude honest disagreements . . . and debates of different ideas, but with the same objectives." He criticized "false unanimity based on simulation and opportunism"; differences are not necessarily irreconcilable and it is important "to learn how to bring together divergent views" (R. Castro Ruz, 2010b, 2010c). However, this book suggests that there is dissent among the top leadership and at intermediate levels, in the form of contradictory objectives that obstruct the efficacy of reforms. Thus, on the one hand, principal objectives are to increase output, reduce imports, expand exports, and eliminate redundant state employment; and the key role of the market and the private sector in reaching these objectives is recognized. On the other hand, emphasis is also placed on the central plan, government controls, the need to fine-tune state enterprises to make them more productive, and heavy taxation levied on the private sector. It appears that some leaders support structural reforms as the way to improve economic and social development and preserve the revolution, while others resist them out of fear that they would unleash forces that would topple the regime or create competition from the private sector that would threaten their position and privileges. The result is a compromise that in practice breeds inefficiency and is unsustainable.

As currently designed and with some additions and corrections, the current reforms could yield modest successes. But until the internal dissent among the leadership that prevents the expansion and deepening of the reforms is resolved, and bureaucratic obstructions are removed, it will not be possible for these policies to achieve significant economic and social progress. Several alternative scenarios may be looming on the horizon: for example, a battle within the top leadership between reform and status quo proponents, with the prospect of a stalemate that would create economic and social deterioration with unpredictable outcomes; or the passing from the scene of the old guard and its gradual replacement by a young generation of technocrats who could facilitate unity and spur reforms. Significant oil discoveries would provide space for maneuvering, but given the lack of success of the first three attempts in deepwater offshore drilling, actual development of any oil field would take a considerable length of time, which is at a premium for the leadership. The death of Hugo Chávez and the negative economic impact this could have on Cuba have been recognized by Fidel, who has denied that a power struggle would occur in Venezuela in that case (F. Castro Ruz, 2012).

It is essential for Cuba to move firmly, swiftly, and with greater depth to implement the key structural reforms needed to increase production of goods and services, expand exports and import substitution, and achieve the kind of sustained economic growth that will improve the economic and social well-being of its people.

Notes

1. The background paper for the conference, published in 2011, was not as broadly discussed as were the guidelines for the Sixth Congress, since the conference's debate was limited to party militants; nevertheless, it was reported that 65,000 meetings were held, 1 million opinions were expressed, and 78 percent of the original proposals were modified (*Granma,* December 23, 2011; R. Castro Ruz, 2012a).

2. A survey conducted surreptitiously in Cuba in June 2011 by US-based human rights organization Freedom House found that 79 percent of respondents perceived the realization of changes in the previous six months (e.g., more self-employed workers), 63 percent had a favorable opinion about the reforms, and 41 percent felt that the country was advancing, compared to 15 percent in December 2010, when the previous survey was conducted (Moreno and Calingaert, 2011).

3. The conference set a maximum of two consecutive periods of five years each for major political and state positions, and separated the functions of the PCC from those of the government. In February 2013, Raúl Castro declared that maximum terms of office should be incorporated into the constitution and that he will retire after his second mandate ends in 2018 (*Granma,* February 25, 2013).

4. The Cuban press reported that in April 2012, a basic unit of cooperative production (UBPC) located in Artemisa was owed 1 million CUP by the state citrus enterprise, which in turn was owed 3 million CUP by other enterprises, indicating "chains of lack of payments . . . that constitute a generalized problem." Using the court system to collect overdue accounts is cumbersome, time-consuming, and expensive, and moreover, few entities have access to legal counsel; the most common solution is a contract to pay the arrears over a certain time period (*Granma,* April 10, 2012).

5. A US journalist asked Fidel whether the Cuban economic model was worth exporting, to which Fidel responded: "The Cuban model does not work even for us anymore" (interview by Goldberg, 2010). Fidel subsequently backtracked and attempted to reinterpret what he meant by this comment.

6. One statistical contradiction is in livestock, whose aggregate output reportedly increased 6 percent but only increased 1.7 percent in number of cattle.

7. After we completed writing this book, Decree-Laws nos. 305 and 306, on nonagricultural cooperatives, were published in the *Gaceta Oficial* on December 11, 2012.

8. Hurricane Sandy hit Santiago de Cuba and Holguín in October 2012, damaging 130,000 dwellings, 52,000 of which were totally or partially destroyed.

9. Mesa-Lago's conversation with Eugenio Balari, former director of Cuba's National Institute of Domestic Demand, about the housing boom, April 19, 2012.

10. In September 2012 the Executive Committee of the Council of Ministers approved seventeen measures to restructure the UBPCs (15 percent of which had deficits financed by the state) and grant them more autonomy (*Juventud Rebelde*, September 14, 2012).

11. An increase in the state *acopio* price would not bring about an instantaneous increase in output, because of the decades-long neglect by and distrust in the state; for instance, it would take at least five years for coffee production to recover to the levels reached in the 1970s (Hagelberg, 2011).

12. Antonio Rodiles (2011) has suggested the auctioning of all idle lands and has drawn up a detailed plan to carry this out.

13. According to Manuel Orozco, an expert on Latin American remittances, between 75,000 and 100,000 remittance-recipients in Cuba would like to invest in SMEs (*Reuters,* September 23, 2010).

14. To avoid the lack of integration of future generations, Roberto Veiga (2011) recommends that free compulsory education be extended through the ninth grade, with a more pluralistic curriculum and greater academic freedom.

15. For views and opinions regarding US-Cuba relations, see Alzugaray, 2009b; Brookings Project, 2009; Pérez-Stable, 2010; Domínguez, Hernández, and Barberia, 2011; Farber, 2011; and Feinberg, 2011.

Acronyms

ANAP	Asociación Nacional de Agricultures Pequeños (National Association of Small Private Farmers)
ANEC	Asociación Nacional de Economistas y Contadores de Cuba (National Association of Cuban Economists and Accountants)
ANPP	Asamblea Nacional del Poder Popular (National Assembly of People's Power)
ASCE	Association for the Study of the Cuban Economy
BANDEC	Banco de Crédito y Comercio (Credit and Commerce Bank)
BANDES	Banco de Desarrollo Económico y Social (Economic and Social Development Bank of Venezuela)
BCC	Banco Central de Cuba (Central Bank of Cuba)
BPA	Banco Popular de Ahorro (Popular Savings Bank)
CADECA	*casa de cambio* (hard-currency exchange agency)
CCS	*cooperativa de crédito y servicios* (credit and services cooperative)
CEEC	Centro de Estudios de la Economía Cubana (Center for the Study of the Cuban Economy)
CIMEQ	Centro de Investigaciones Médico-Quirúrgicas (Center for Medical-Surgical Research)
CIREN	Centro Internacional de Restauración Neurológica (International Center for Neurological Rehabilitation)
CMEA	Council for Mutual Economic Assistance
CPA	*cooperativa de producción agropecuaria* (agricultural production cooperative)
CPI	consumer price index

CTC	Central de Trabajadores de Cuba (Workers' Central Union of Cuba)
CUC	*peso cubano convertible* (convertible Cuban peso)
CUP	*peso cubano nacional* (Cuban national peso)
ECLAC	Economic Commission for Latin America and the Caribbean
EIU	Economist Intelligence Unit
FACI	Fondo Autónomo de Cooperación Internacional (Autonomous International Cooperation Fund) (Venezuela)
FDI	foreign direct investment
GDP	gross domestic product
HDI	Human Development Index (UNDP)
IADB	Inter-American Development Bank
ICAIC	Instituto Cubano del Arte y la Industria Cinematográficos Cuban Institute of Cinematographic Art and Industry
IFI	international financial institution
ILO	International Labour Organization
IMF	International Monetary Fund
INV	Instituto Nacional de la Vivienda (National Housing Institute)
OAS	Organization of American States
ONE	Oficina Nacional de Estadísticas (National Statistical Office)
OPEC	Organization of Petroleum Exporting Countries
PCC	Partido Comunista de Cuba (Cuban Communist Party)
SMEs	small- and medium-sized enterprises
TRD	*tienda de recuperación de divisas* (foreign-currency store)
UBPC	*unidad básica de producción cooperativa* (basic unit of cooperative production)
UNDP	United Nations Development Programme
UNEAC	Unión Nacional de Escritores y Artistas de Cuba (National Union of Writers and Artists of Cuba)

References

Acuerdo no. 15. 2005. Banco Central de Cuba, Comité de Política Monetaria. Havana, March 24.

———— no. 6853. 2010. Consejo de Ministros. Havana, June 24.

Alonso Falcón, Randy. 2012a. "Aprobada nueva Ley Tributaria por el Parlamento Cubano." *Cubadebate,* July 23. http://cubadebate.cu/noticias/2012/07/23/aprobada-nueva-ley-tributaria-por-el-parlamento-cubano.

————. 2012b. "Entrega la banca cubana más de 250 millones de pesos en créditos." *Cubadebate,* July 19. http://cubadebate.cu/noticias/2012/07/19/entrega-la-banca-cubana-mas-de-250-millones-de-pesos-en-creditos.

Alzugaray, Carlos. 2009a. "Cuba 50 años después: continuidad y cambio político." *Temas* 60, 37–47.

————. 2009b. "Diálogos para un nuevo tiempo." Inverview by Lenier González. *Espacio Laical* 55:1, 31–49.

Amor, Elías. 2011. "El sector cooperativo ante los incumplimientos e impagos." *Cubaeconomía,* December 13.

Añé, Lía. 2007. "Contribución a los estudios de pobreza en Cuba . . ." Paper presented at the twenty-eighth annual LASA Congress, Montreal, September 6–8.

Arias, Lianet, and Lourdes Pérez. 2010. "Con el agua al cuello." *Granma,* January 9.

Arreola, Gerardo. 2009. "Cuba reparte a ministerios el gasto en divisas para aligerar la centralización." *La Jornada* (Mexico), June 22.

————. 2012. "Venezuela, socio principal y pieza sensible de la economía cubana." *La Jornada,* January 16.

Bachelet, Pablo, et al. 2008. "La burbuja petrolera venezolana. . . ." *The Miami Herald,* January 27.

Barreiro, Georgina. 2007. "Presentación a la Asamblea Nacional del proyecto de presupuesto del estado para 2008." *Granma,* December 28.

————. 2008. "Presentación a la Asamblea Nacional del proyecto de presupuesto del estado para 2009." *Granma,* December 28.

Bayo, Francesc. 2010. "Las relaciones económicas entre España y Cuba: antecedentes y perspectives." *Boletín Económico del ICE* no. 2995, August.

BCV (Banco Central de Venezuela). 2012. "Información estadística." www.bcv.org.ve/c2/indicadores.asp.

Betancourt, Rafael. 2011. "Observaciones en torno al proyecto de lineamientos." *Temas*, February 3.

Betancourt, Roger. 2007. "Human Rights and Economic Growth: Why the Real China Model May Be Desirable in a Post-Fidel Transition." In *Cuba in Transition*, vol. 17. Washington, D.C.: Association for the Study of the Cuban Economy, 305–314.

BNC (Banco Nacional de Cuba). 1995. *Economic Report 1994*. Havana.

Borrego, Juan. 2006. "Pago luego exijo." *Granma*, February 22.

Bravo, Lisette. 2007. "Protestas en la Universidad de Oriente." *Cubanet*, September 28.

Brookings Project on US Policy Toward Cuba in Transition. 2009. *Cuba: A New Policy of Critical and Constructive Engagement*. Washington, D.C.

Brundenius, Claes. 2009. "Revolutionary Cuba at 50: Growth with Equity Revisited." *Latin American Perspectives*, March.

Burnett, Victoria. 2011. "Rusty Road to Riches in Cuba." *International Herald Tribune*, July 11.

Calves, Silvio. 2010. "¿Pago por resultados? ¿De quién son los resultados?" *Revista Bimestre Cubana* 6:3, 25–29.

Campos, Pedro. 2007. "Entrevista con motivo del discurso de Ramiro Valdés." *Kaos en la Red*, October.

———. 2012. "Socializar la medicina, actualmente estatizada." *SPD* no. 92, April 6.

Campos, Pedro, et al. 2008. "Cuba necesita un socialismo participativo y democrático: propuestas programáticas." *Kaos en la Red*, August.

Cancio, Wilfredo. 2008. "Disminuyen las firmas extranjeras en Cuba." *El Nuevo Herald*, March 19.

———. 2009a. "Crisis amenaza proyectos de refinerías en la isla." *El Nuevo Herald*, June 7.

———. 2009b. "Cuba refuerza control de su sistema bancario." *El Nuevo Herald*, April 21.

Carrobello, Caridad, and Vladia Rubio. 2011. "¿Motear con gato?" *Bohemia*, January 18.

Carrobello, Caridad, and Ariel Terrero. 2008. "Ganadería vacuna." *Bohemia*, January 28.

Castañeda, Rolando. 2010. "El insostenible apoyo económico de Venezuela a Cuba y sus implicaciones." In *Cuba in Transition*, vol. 20. Washington, D.C.: Association for the Study of the Cuban Economy, 127–142.

———. 2012. "Venezuela: el próximo ajuste económico fundamental—compleja situación en 20120 y perspectivas inmediatas." In *Cuba in Transition*, vol. 22. Washington, D.C.: Association for the Study of the Cuban Economy, 349–357.

Castro Ruz, Fidel. 2005a. "Discurso citado en Clarin.com." March 19.

———. 2005b. "Discurso en la Universidad de la Habana." November 17.

———. 2006a. "Discurso en acto de entrega de las primeras doce locomotoras chinas." *Granma*, January 15.

———. 2006b. "Discurso en el 47 aniversario de su entrada en Pinar del Río . . ." *Granma*, January 21.

———. 2007. "Reflexiones de Fidel: Los superrevolucionarios." *Granma*, September 3.

———. 2008, 2009, 2012. "Reflexiones de Fidel." *Granma*, February 18 and 22, April 16, May 25, October 2 and 11, November 3 and 14, and December 5, 2008; January 22, 23, and 30, February 5 and 6, March 8, April 4, 6, 8, 14, 15, 21, and 22, and May 22, 2009; and May 3, 2012.

Castro Ruz, Raúl. 2007a. "Discurso en el acto central con motivo del aniversario 54 del asalto al Cuartel Moncada . . ." *Granma*, July 27.
———. 2007b. "Intervención ante la Asamblea del Poder Popular . . ." *Granma*, December 29.
———. 2008a. "Discurso en las conclusiones de la sesión constitutiva de la VII legislatura de la Asamblea Nacional . . ." *Granma*, February 24.
———. 2008b. "Discurso en la Asamblea Nacional." *Granma*, July 11.
———. 2008c. "Discurso de clausura de la Asamblea." *Granma Internacional*, December 29.
———. 2009a. "Discurso en el 50 aniversario del triunfo de la revolución." *Granma*, January 2.
———. 2009b. "Discurso en conmemoración del asalto al Cuartel Moncada." *Granma*, July 27.
———. 2009c. "Discurso en la primera sesión del parlamento." *Granma*, August 1.
———. 2009d. "Discurso en la clausura de la Asamblea Nacional." *Granma*, December 22.
———. 2010a. "Discurso en la clausura del XI Congreso de la UJC." *Granma*, April 4.
———. 2010b. "Discurso en la clausura de la Asamblea Nacional." *Granma*, August 1.
———. 2010c. "Discurso en la clausura de la Asamblea Nacional." *Granma*, December 18.
———. 2011a. "Informe central al VI Congreso del PCC." April 16.
———. 2011b. "Discurso de clausura del VI Congreso del PCC." April 19.
———. 2011c. "Reunión ampliada del Consejo de Ministros." *Granma*, July 29.
———. 2011d. "Discurso ante la Asamblea Nacional." *Granma*, August 2.
———. 2011e. "Consejo de Ministros 25 Septiembre." *Granma*, September 29.
———. 2011f. "Reunión ampliada del Consejo de Ministros." *Bohemia*, November 4.
———. 2011g. "Discurso en el período ordinario de sesiones de la Asamblea Nacional." *Bohemia*, December 25.
———. 2012a. "Discurso en la clausura de la Primera Conferencia Nacional del Partido." *Granma*, January 30.
———. 2012b. "Discurso en la clausura de la Asamblea Nacional del Poder Popular." *Granma*, July 24.
Cave, Damien. 2011. "Cubans Set for Big Change: Right to Buy Homes" and "Cuba to Allow Buying and Selling of Property, with Few Restrictions." *New York Times*, November 4.
CEE (Comité Estatal de Estadísticas). 1991. *Anuario estadístico de Cuba 1989*. Havana.
Chaguaceda, Armando. 2011. "El VI Congreso: una evaluación preliminar." *Espacio Laical* no. 3, 23–26.
Chaguaceda, Armando, and Ramón Centeno. 2011. "El socialismo democrático ante las actuales reformas." *Viento Sur* no. 115 (March), 13–24.
Chávez, Juan Carlos. 2012. "Hialeah Business Supplies Spare Parts for Cuban Autos." *Miami Herald*, October 3.
CIA (Central Intelligence Agency). 2011. *The World Factbook 2011*. Washington, D.C.
CIECA (Centro de Investigaciones Económicas). 2009. *Gasto público anunciado por el gobierno de Venezuela*. Caracas, October 6.
Cojímar, Julia. 2008. "Cuba: que faire de la revolution?" *Cuestiones del Tiempo Presente*, April 25.

Contreras, Joseph. 2007. "Cuba's New Guiding Star: Beijing." *Newsweek International*, February 12.

"Controversia." 2010. "Cultura agraria, política y sociedad." *Temas* 61, 80–95.

Correa, Yania. 2011. "Economic Efficiency Also Applies to Education." *Granma International*, November 17.

CRI (Cuban Research Institute). 2011. *La diáspora cubana en el siglo XXI*. Miami: Eriginal.

Cruz, Soledad. 2007. "El revolucionario riesgo de la verdad . . ." *Kaos en la Red*, August.

Davies, Bob. 2007. "Cuban Economists Envision Role for Markets in Post-Castro Era." *Wall Street Journal*, January 10.

de la Fuente, Alejandro. 2001. *A Nation for All: Race, Inequality, and Politics in Twentieth-Century Cuba*. Chapel Hill: University of North Carolina Press.

———. 2011. "Race and Income Inequality in Contemporary Cuba." *NACLA Report on the Americas* (July–August), 30–43.

———. 2012. Correspondence with Carmelo Mesa-Lago, March 17.

de la Osa, José. 2010. "Hacia la racionalidad en la provincia de la Habana." *Granma*, October 15.

de Miranda Parrondo, Mauricio, and Omar Everleny Pérez Villanueva. 2012. "Los problemas actuales de la economía cubana y las reformas necesarias." In *Cuba: hacia una estrategia de desarrollo para los inicios del siglo XXI*. Cali: Pontificia Universidad Javeriana and SSRC, 190–224.

Decreto-Ley no. 251. 2007. Changes to disciplinary work rules. August 22.

——— nos. 252 and 281. 2007. Enterprise management (perfeccionamiento empresarial). August 6–7.

——— no. 259. 2008. Usufruct. July 10.

——— no. 268. 2008. Changes to multi-employment work practices. July 10.

——— nos. 278, 284, and 285. 2011. Work safety and social protection for self-employed workers. September 6.

——— nos. 287 and 294. 2011. Abolition of Ministry of Sugar and establishment of AZCUBA Sugar Group. November 10.

——— no. 288. 2011. General housing. November 2.

——— no. 289. 2011. Credit and bank accounts for the nonstate sector. November 21.

——— no. 292. 2011. Sale of automobiles. September 27.

——— no. 293. 2011. Internal migration. November 22.

——— nos. 300 and 304. 2012. Usufruct. October 22.

——— nos. 302 and 306. 2012. Migration. October 16.

del Valle, Amaury. 2008. "Sanciones ejemplarizantes . . ." *Juventud Rebelde*, January 23.

Díaz-Briquets, Sergio. 2009. "The Enduring Cuban Housing Crisis: The Impact of Hurricanes." In *Cuba in Transition*, vol. 19. Washington, D.C.: Association for the Study of the Cuban Economy, 429–441.

———. 2011. "Minimalism, Obsolescence, and Transferability: The Labor Market Impact of the New Self-Employment Regulations." In *Cuba in Transition*, vol. 21. Washington, D.C.: Association for the Study of the Cuban Economy, 463–474.

Díaz-Briquets, Sergio, and Jorge Pérez-López. 2006. *Corruption in Cuba: Castro and Beyond*. Austin: University of Texas Press.

Díaz Vázquez, Julio. 2008. "China-Cuba: Relaciones económicas." *Encuentro* no. 49, 87–93.

Dilla, Haroldo. 2011. "VI Congreso del PCC: ¿Qué pasó con la participación de los trabajadores." Santo Domingo, May 17.

Doimeadios, Yaima. 2007. "Un modelo de crecimiento económico para Cuba: análisis de productividad de factores." Havana: Universidad de la Habana, Facultad de Economía.

Domínguez, Jorge, Rafael Hernández, and Lorena Barberia. 2011. *Debating U.S.-Cuban Relations: Shall We Play Ball?* New York: Routledge.

Domínguez, Jorge, et al. 2012. *Cuban Economic and Social Development: Policy Reforms and Challenges in the 21st Century.* Cambridge. Harvard University Press.

Dorschner, John. 2007. "Cuban vs. U.S. Healthcare." *Miami Herald,* January 28.

Dossier. 2009. "¿Existe una problemática racial en Cuba?" [Víctor Fowler Calzada, Jesús Guanche, Rodrigo Espina Prieto, Alejandro de la Fuente, Tomás Fernández Robaina] *Espacio Laical* 2, 1–25.

———. 2011. "¿Hacia dónde va el modelo cubano?" [Rafael Hernández, Guillermo Rodríguez, Yenisel Rodríguez, Juan Triana]. *Espacio Laical,* February 10.

———. 2012. "Análisis a la Primera Conferencia Nacional del PCC" [Ovidio d'Angelo, Ariel Decal, Víctor Fowler, Lenier González, Orlando Márquez, Alexis Pestano]. *Espacio Laical,* April.

ECB (European Central Bank). 2012. "Reference Exchange Rate, US Dollar/Euro, Annual Averages, 2001–2011." http://sdw.ecb.europa.eu.

ECLAC (Economic Commission for Latin America and the Caribbean). 2000. *La economía cubana: reformas estructurales y desempeño en los noventa.* Mexico City.

———. 2007, 2008a, 2009a, 2010a, 2011a. *Preliminary Overview of the Economies of Latin America and the Caribbean 2007, 2008, 2009, 2010, 2011.* Santiago de Chile.

———. 2008b, 2009b, 2010b. *Cuba: evolución económica durante 2007, 2008, 2009.* Mexico City.

———. 2011b. *Cuba: evolución económica durante 2010 y perspectivas para 2011.* Mexico City.

———. 2010c, 2011c. *Social Panorama of Latin America 2010, 2011.* Santiago de Chile.

———. 2010d, 2011d. *Statistical Yearbook for Latin America Latina and the Caribbean 2010, 2011.* Santiago de Chile.

EIU (Economist Intelligence Unit). 2008. *Country Profile: Cuba.* London.

———. 2011. *Country Report: Cuba.* London.

"El Período Especial veinte años después." 2011. [Debate between Mayra Espina, José Luis Rodríguez, and Juan Triana, moderated by Rafael Hernández.] *Temas* 65, 59–75.

Espina, Mayra. 2008. *Políticas de atención a la pobreza y la desigualdad: examinando el rol del estado en la experiencia cubana.* Buenos Aires: CLACSO.

———. 2010. *Desarrollo, desigualdad y políticas sociales.* Havana: Acuario.

Espina, Mayra, and Viviana Togores. 2012. "Structural Change and Routes of Social Mobility in Today's Cuba: Patterns, Profiles, and Subjectivities." In Jorge Domínguez et al., *Cuban Economic and Social Development: Policy Reforms and Challenges in the 21st Century.* Cambridge. Harvard University Press, 261–289.

Espina Prieto, Rodrigo, and Pablo Rodríguez. 2006. "Raza y desigualdad en la Cuba actual." *Temas* 45, 44–54.

Espino, María Dolores. 2011a. "The Cuban Tourist Industry in the 21st Century: Current Problems and Future Challenges." Paper presented at the International Symposium on Cuba, City University of New York, March 31–April 2.

————. 2011b. "I'll See You in Cuba: Opportunities and Challenges of an Opening of the U.S. Market." Paper presented at the thirtieth annual conference of the International Society of Travel and Tourism Educators, Miami, October 20–22.

————. 2012. Correspondence with Mesa-Lago, February 1.

Espinosa Chepe, Oscar. 2007a. "Cuba: opciones para un futuro digno." In *Cuba in Transition*, vol. 17. Washington, D.C.: Association for the Study of the Cuban Economy, 21–27.

————. 2007b. *Cuba: revolución o involución*. Valencia: Aduana Vieja Editorial.

————. 2007c. "¿Regresa el perfeccionamiento empresarial?" *Cubanet*, February 7.

————. 2007d. "Salarios, pensiones y precios en la Cuba actual." *Cubanet*, November 7.

————. 2008. "Cuba: ¿Hacia una reestructuración agraria?" *Cubanet*, April 27.

————. 2010a. "Crecen las vicisitudes en el transporte cubano." *Reconciliación Cubana*, October 21. http://reconciliacioncubana.wordpress.com/2010/.../crecen-las-vicistudes-en-el-transporte-cubano.

————. 2010b. "Fuerte caída en la producción eléctrica de los grupos electrógenos." *Cubaencuentro*, September 2.

————. 2011a. "Cambios en Cuba: pocos, limitados y tardíos." http://reconciliacion cubana.files.wordpress.com/2011/03/cambios-en-cuba.pdf.

————. 2011b. "Comportamiento de la economía cubana en 2011." *Cubaencuentro*, December 29.

————. 2011c. "Lagunas educacionales al descubierto." *Cubaencuentro*, August 3.

Faguaga, María. 2008. "Afrocubanos en cambio de época." Havana, September 2. E-mail correspondence.

FAO (Food and Agriculture Organization). 2011. "Sugarcane Yields, 2000–2010." http://faostat.fao.org/?lang=en.

————. 2012. "Food Price Index." www.fao.org/worldfoodsituation/wfs-home/food pricesindex/en.

Farber, Samuel. 2011. *Cuba Since the Revolution of 1959*. Chicago: Haymarket.

Feinberg, Richard. 2011. *Cuba's New Economy and the International Response*. Washington, D.C.: Brookings Institution.

Ferrer, Darsi, and Carlos Ríos. 2007. "Autoridades sanitarias y la conspiración del silencio." Havana: Centro de Salud y Derechos Humanos, July 26.

Ferriol, Ángela. 2003. "Acercamiento al estudio de la pobreza en Cuba." Unpublished paper presented to the twenty-fourth annual LASA Congress, Dallas, March.

————. 2004. "Política social y desarrollo: una aproximación global." In E. Álvarez and J. Máttar, eds., *Política social y reformas estructurales: Cuba a principios del siglo XXI*. Mexico City: ECLAC/INIE, 57–90.

Fornés, Federico. 2007. "La luna de miel entre Pekín y La Habana . . ." *Encuentro en la Red*, December 27.

Frank, Marc. 2007. "Shroud of Secrecy Falls Over Cuba's Nickel Industry." *Reuters*, January 10.

————. 2008a. "Cuban Sugar Harvest Moves Into High Gear." *Reuters*, January 21.

————. 2008b. "Global Crisis, Storms Hit Cuban Finances." *Reuters*, December 17.

————. 2009. "Cuba Admits Nickel Prices Barely Cover Costs." *Reuters*, April 9.

————. 2010a. "Cuban Payment Crisis Goes On, Business In Limbo." *Reuters*, June 23.

————. 2010b. "Cuba Prepares for Another Bitter Sugar Harvest." *Reuters*, October 18.

————. 2010c. "Cuba Bows to Pressure to Reform Its Economy." *Reuters*, December 13.

————. 2011a. "Cuban Cellphones Hit 1 Million." *Reuters,* July 7.

————. 2011b. "Cuban Nickel Plant Offline After Breakdown" and "Cuba Says Nickel Venture to Top 37,700 Tons." *Reuters,* July 15 and December 21.

————. 2012a. "Cuba Drags Feet on Foreign Investment." *Reuters,* May 15.

————. 2012b. "Cuba Struggles with Foreign Investment Growth." *Reuters,* September 7.

Free Society Project. 2010. "Cuba's International Medical Missions." Summit fact sheet. New Jersey, April 19.

Gálvez, Karina. 2012. "Más que subsidios queremos ganar dinero con nuestro trabajo." *Convivencia* 5:25 (January–February).

García, Anicia. 2012. "Cuba's Agricultural Sector and Its External Links." In Jorge Domínguez et al., *Cuban Economic and Social Development: Policy Reforms and Challenges in the 21st Century.* Cambridge. Harvard University Press, 137–191.

García, Anicia, Betsy Amaya, and Camila Piñeiro. 2010. "El sector agropecuario, el desarrollo económico y su vínculo con el sector externo: el caso cubano." Havana, November.

García, Anicia, et al. 2011. "Reestructuración del empleo en Cuba." Paper presented at the CEEC seminar "Sobre economía cubana y gerencia empresarial," Havana, June 21–24.

García, Edmundo. 2007a. "Entrevista a Pedro Monreal." *La Noche se Mueve* (Montreal), September.

————. 2007b. "Entrevista a Rafael Hernández, director de la revista *Temas." La Noche se Mueve* (Montreal), September.

García, Fernando. 2007. "La Habana combate a duras penas el grave problema del transporte." *La Vanguardia,* September 17.

————. 2008. "La Cuba que teme a Obama." *La Vanguardia,* November 2.

García, Iván. 2012. "Cuba: taxis particulares, un buen negocio." *Martinoticias,* March 6.

García Méndez, Luis M. 2011. "Entrevista a Maida Donate: el suicidio entre los cubanos." *Cubaencuentro,* June 15, 2011.

Garrett, Laurie. 2010. "Castrocare in Crisis . . ." *Foreign Affairs,* July–August.

Goldberg, Jeffrey. 2010. "Fidel: Cuban Model Doesn't Even Work for Us Anymore." *The Atlantic,* September 8.

Gómez, Javier. 2008. "Sin techo pero con amo." *Encuentro en la Red,* January 28.

González, Ortelio. 2006. "Los golpes de la comercialización." *Granma,* February 21.

González-Corzo, Mario. 2009. "The End of Rationing in Cuba: Motivations and Socioeconomic Impact." *Focus on Cuba* no. 116. Miami: Institute of Cuban and Cuban-American Studies, November 9.

————. 2010. "The Reduction of State Sector Workers in Cuba." *Focus on Cuba* no. 133. Miami: Institute of Cuban and Cuban-American Studies, October 12.

González-Corzo, Mario, and Susel Pérez. 2009. *Analisis comparativo del poder adquisitivo en Cuba.* Prepared by the Institute for Cuban and Cuban-American Studies, University of Miami, for the Cuban Study Group and Fundación de Derechos Humanos.

González Mederos, Lenier. 2011a. "Rectificar el rumbo." *Espacio Laical* no. 4, December 5.

————. 2011b. "The Road to Patience." In *Desde la Isla* [From the Island]. Miami: Cuba Study Group, December 15.

————. 2012. *Iglesia católica y nacionalismo: los retos tras la visita del Papa Benedicto XVI.* Miami: Cuba Study Group.

Guanche, Julio César. 2012. "Esto no es una utopía: lo nuevo, lo viejo y el futuro de Cuba." *Temas,* Catalejo, February 20.

Guevara, Alfredo. 2011. "Dialogar, dialogar." Interview. *Espacio Laical* 152 (November), 11–12.

Hagelberg, G. H. 2011. "Agriculture: Policy and Performance." In *Cuba in Transition,* vol. 21. Washington, D.C.: Association for the Study of the Cuban Economy, 110–122.

Hernández, Rafael. 2009. "¿Debate o catarsis? El pensamiento crítico en la actual esfera pública cubana." Presentation at Florida International University, Miami, November 22.

Hernández-Catá, Ernesto. 2007. "Price Liberalization and the End of the Rationing System in Cuba: All We Have to Fear Is Fear Itself." In *Cuba in Transition,* vol. 17. Washington, D.C.: Association for the Study of the Cuban Economy, 43–49.

Hirschfeld, Katherine. 2007. "Re-examining the Cuban Health Care System: Towards a Qualitative Critique." *Cuban Affairs* 2:3 (July), 1–27.

Hoffman, Andy. 2010. "A Break-Through in China, Another Blow for Sudbury." *Toronto Globe and Mail,* June 11.

ICCAS (Institute of Cuban and Cuban-American Studies). 2008. *Islamic Investment in Cuba. Focus on Cuba* no. 99. Miami, August 11.

———. 2011. *Cuba's Debt Crisis: Foreign Debt, Unemployment, and Migration. Focus on Cuba* no. 147. Miami, August 9.

IMF (International Monetary Fund). 2011. *Primary Commodity Database.* www.imf .org/external/np/res/commod/index.aspx.

"Información sobre el resultado del debate de los lineamientos de la política económica y social del partido y la revolución." 2011. Havana: Sixth Congress of the Cuban Communist Party, May 1.

Íñiguez Rojas, Luisa. 2006. "Espacio, territorio y desigualdades sociales en Cuba." In Omar Everleny Pérez Villanueva, ed., *Reflexiones sobre economía cubana.* Havana: Editorial Ciencias Sociales, 420–470.

Íñiguez Rojas, Luisa, and Norma Montes. 2010. "Espacio y poblamiento." In Omar Everleny Pérez Villanueva, ed., *Cincuenta años de la economía cubana.* Havana: Editorial Ciencias Sociales, 363–405.

Isbell, Paul. 2007. *Hugo Chávez y el futuro del petróleo venezolano.* Madrid: Real Instituto Elcano, Documento de Trabajo.

ITU (International Telecommunication Union). 2010. *Yearbook of Statistics: Chronological Time Series, 2000–2010.* Geneva.

James, Harold. 2009. "The Making of a Mess." *Foreign Affairs,* January–February.

Kisting, Denver. 2012. "Namibia: Cuban Doctors Become Costly." *The Namibian,* September 22.

Krauss, Clifford, and Damien Cave. 2012. "Cuba's Prospects for an Oil-Fueled Economic Jolt Falter with Departure of Rig." *New York Times,* November 9.

Lacey, Marc. 2008. "Cuba's Housing Booms." *New York Times,* January 28.

Lamrani, Salim. 2012. "Entrevista a Ricardo Alarcón." *Huffington Post,* January 4.

Lee, Susana. 2007. "Perfeccionamiento empresarial: no es perfecto . . . pero ha demostrado su eficiencia." *Granma,* January 23.

Leiva, Miriam. 2008a. "Conclusiones de la Unión Europea hacia el gobierno de Cuba." *Convivencia,* Havana, July 15.

———. 2008b. "Reanudan cooperación la Unión Europea y Cuba." Havana, *Desde Cuba,* October 27. http://www.desdecuba.com.

———. 2009. "¿La Posición Común se irá con Luis Michel?" and "Conclusiones de la Unión Europea respecto a Cuba." Havana, May 13 and June 17.

Ley no. 113. 2012. Tax reform. *Gaceta Oficial,* November 21.

Leyva Martínez, Ivette. 2012. "Cuba cerrará la fábrica de níquel de Nicaro." *Café Fuerte,* September 13. www.cafefuerte.com.

López-Levy, Arturo. 2011. *Change in Post-Fidel Cuba: Political Liberalization, Economic Reform, and Lessons for U.S. Policy.* Washington, D.C.: New America Foundation.

———. 2012. "La Conferencia del PCC: ¿herramienta de cambio u obstáculo a las reformas?" *Infolatam* 26 (January). www.infolatam.com.

López-Levy, Arturo, and Lenier González Mederos. 2012. "Cuba espera a Benedicto XVI: el papel de la iglesia en el proceso de apertura de la isla." *Foreign Policy en Español,* March 21.

Lugo, Orlando. 2008. "Comparecencia en TV." Havana, April 1. Cited in "Cuban Government Looks to Restructure Food Marketing, Official Says," EFE News, World Service, April 15.

———. 2011. Interview. *Juventud Rebelde,* May 14.

Luis, Luis. 2012. "How Is Cuba Funding Its Rising International Bank Assets?" *ASCE Newsletter,* Winter.

Machado Ventura, José. 2010. "Discurso en conmemoración del asalto al Cuartel Moncada." *Granma,* July 27.

Marquetti, Hiram. 2006a. "El proceso de des-dolarización de la economía: impacto y perspectivas." Havana: Universidad de la Habana, CEEC.

———. 2006b. "Cuba: importancia actual del incremento de las exportaciones." In Omar Everleny Pérez Villanueva, ed., *Reflexiones sobre economía cubana.* Havana: Editorial Ciencias Sociales, 142–194.

Márquez, Orlando. 2011a. "Sin miedo a la riqueza." *Palabra Nueva,* January 31.

———. 2011b. "Un momento decisivo." *Palabra Nueva,* December 5.

Martín, Jorge, 2010. "¿Hacia dónde va Cuba, hacia el capitalimo o el socialismo?" *Kaos en la Red,* October.

Martín, Lucy, and Lilia Núñez. 2012. "Geography and Habitat: Dimensions of Equity and Social Mobility in Cuba." In Jorge Domínguez et al., *Cuban Economic and Social Development: Policy Reforms and Challenges in the 21st Century.* Cambridge. Harvard University Press, 291–320.

Martín, Marianela, and Dora Pérez. 2007. "Agricultura cubana: devolver el aliento a la producción agropecuaria." *Juventud Rebelde,* December 16.

———. 2008. "Viaje al centro de la tierra: por un cambio en la comercialización agropecuaria." *Juventud Rebelde,* January 27.

Martínez, Osvaldo. 2007. "Intervención sobre los temas del plan y presupuesto de la economía nacional." *Granma,* December 28.

———. 2008. "Intervención en la Asamblea Nacional del Poder Popular." *Granma,* December 29.

———. 2011a. "Dictamen de la comisión de asuntos económicos sobre el plan de la economía nacional y el presupuesto del estado." *Bohemia,* December 25.

———. 2011b. "Dictamen sobre la liquidación del presupuesto del estado de 2010." *Granma,* August 2.

———. 2012. "Dictamen soble el plan de la economía nacional y el presupuesto del estado para 2013." *Granma,* December 14.

Mayoral, María Julia. 2007. "Avances en las redes y mucho por hacer." *Granma,* August 18.

Méndez, Elier, et al. 2007. "Análisis territorial del desarrollo humano en Cuba, 1985–2004." *Comercio Exterior* 57:8, 643–656.

Mesa-Lago, Carmelo. 1994. *Breve historia económica de la Cuba socialista: políticas, resultados y perspectivas.* Madrid: Alianza Editorial.

————. 2000. *Market, Socialist, and Mixed Economies: Comparative Policies and Performance—Chile, Cuba, and Costa Rica*. Baltimore: Johns Hopkins University Press.

————. 2003. *Economía y bienestar social en Cuba a comienzos del siglo XXI*. Madrid: Editorial Colibrí.

————. 2005a. "The Cuban Economy in 2004–2005." In *Cuba in Transition*, vol. 15. Washington, D.C.: Association for the Study of the Cuban Economy, 1–18.

————. 2005b. "Social and Economic Problems in Cuba During the Crisis and Subsequent Recovery." *CEPAL Review* no. 86, 177–199.

————. 2006. "The End of Half a Century of Rationing in Cuba?" *Hemisphere*, Fall.

————. 2007. "The Cuban Economy in 2006–2007." In *Cuba in Transition*, vol. 17. Washington, D.C.: Association for the Study of the Cuban Economy, 1–25.

————. 2008a. "La economía cubana en la encrucijada: el legado de Fidel, el debate sobre el cambio y las opciones de Raúl." In *Cuba: presente y futuro*. Madrid: Real Instituto Elcano, 45–74.

————. 2008b. "Ventajas y desventajas de un posible restablecimiento de relaciones económicas de Cuba con los Estados Unidos." *Espacio Laical* 4:2, 36–38.

————. 2009a. "Economic and Social Balance of 50 Years of Cuban Revolution." In *Cuba in Transition*, vol. 19. Washington, D.C.: Association for the Study of the Cuban Economy, 368–386.

————. 2009b. "Historia y evaluación de medio siglo de políticas económico-sociales en Cuba socialista, 1959–2008." In Consuelo Naranjo Orovio, comp., *Historia de Cuba*. Madrid: Consejo Superior de Investigaciones Científicas, Ediciones Doce Calles, 507–537.

————. 2009c. "La economía de Cuba hoy: retos internos y externos." *Desarrollo Económico*, 49:195, 421–450.

————. 2009d. "La veleta económica cubana: huracanes internos, crisis mundial y perspectivas con Obama." *Encuentro* no. 51, 35–47.

————. 2010a. "Cincuenta años de servicios sociales en Cuba." *Temas* no. 64, 45–56.

————. 2010b. "El desempleo en Cuba: de oculto a visible." *Espacio Laical* 6:4, 59–66.

————. 2010c. "Estructura demográfica y envejecimiento poblacional: implicaciones sociales y económicas para el sistema de seguridad social en Cuba." *Espacio Laical* 6:3, 87–92.

————. 2011a. "Las reformas de Raúl Castro y el Congreso del Partido Comunista de Cuba: avances, obstáculos y resultados." Documento no. 35. Barcelona: CIDOB.

————. 2011b. "Sobre la 'inviabilidad del socialismo,' pero ¿qué tipo de socialismo?" *Temas*, September 19.

————. 2011c. "Will the Communist Party Congress Solve Cuba's Economic and Social Problems?" In *Cuba in Transition*, vol. 21. Washington, D.C.: Association for the Study of the Cuban Economy, 292–301.

————. 2012. *Reassembling Social Security: A Survey of Pension and Health Care Reforms in Latin America*. 2nd ed. Oxford: Oxford University Press.

Mesa-Lago, Carmelo, and Jorge F. Pérez-López. 2005. *Cuba's Aborted Reform: Socioeconomic Effects, International Comparisons, and Transition Policies*. Gainesville: University of Florida Press.

Mesa-Lago, Carmelo, and Pavel Vidal Alejandro. 2010. "The Impact of the Global Crisis on Cuba's Economy and Social Welfare." *Journal of Latin American Studies* 42:4, 689–717.

Messina, William, et al. 2008. "Cuban Agriculture and the Impacts of Tropical Storm Fay and Hurricanes Gustav and Ike." Gainesville: University of Florida, IFAS Extension.

"Miembros del Buró Político, el Secretariado y el Comité Central del Partido Comunista de Cuba." 2011. http://siemprecuba.wordpress.com.

Milanés, Pablo. 2008. "El socialismo cubano se ha estancado." Interview by Carlos Fuentes. *Público* (Madrid), December 29.

Ministerio de Finanzas y Precios. 2008. "Información a la población." Havana, September 8.

MINSAP (Ministerio de Salud Pública). 2010. Internet report. Havana, December 3.

————. 2011. *Anuario de estadísticas de salud 2010*. Havana, April.

"Modificaciones a la Ley de Seguridad Social." 2008. Havana: Ministerio de Trabajo y Seguridad Social, May 13.

Molina, Hilda. 2005. "Algunas consideraciones sobre el sistema de salud en Cuba." *Documentos del Centro para la Apertura y el Desarrollo de América Latina* 3:46, December 20.

Monreal, Pedro. 2006. "La globalización y los dilemas de las trayectorias económicas de Cuba." In Omar Everleny Pérez Villanueva, ed., *Reflexiones sobre economía cubana*. Havana: Editorial Ciencias Sociales, 447–473.

————. 2007. "Industrial Policy and Clusters in Cuba." Paper presented at the International Policy Forum, "The Cuban Economy: Challenges and Options," Carleton University, Ottawa, September 9–12.

————. 2008. "El problema económico de Cuba." *Espacio Laical* no. 2, 33–35.

————. 2009. "Comentarios en la Conferencia Internacional sobre Cuba." Comments at the conference "Cuba Today and the Road Ahead, sponsored by Tulane University and Centro de Investigación y Adiestramiento Político Administrativo," San José, Costa Rica, February 3–4.

Moody's Investors Service. 2011. "Moody's Disclosures on Credit Ratings of Cuba." Global Credit Research, December 23.

Morales, Emilio, and Joseph Scarpaci. 2011. "Washington, Havana Line Their Nests with Remittances." *Cuba News,* February.

————. 2012. "Opening on Both Shorelines Helps Increase Remittances to Cuba in 2011 by About 20%." Havana Consulting Group, March 12. www.thehavana consultinggroup.com.

Morales, Esteban. 2007. *Desafíos de la problemática racial en Cuba*. Havana: Fundación Fernando Ortiz.

————. 2010. "Cuba corrupción: ¿la verdadera contrarrevolución?" Havana: UNEAC, June 28. www.kaosenlared.net/noticia-cuba-corrupcion-verdadera-contrarrevolucion.

Moreno, Alejandro, and Daniel Calingaert. 2011. *Change Comes to Cuba: Citizens' Views on Reforms*. Washington, D.C.: Freedom House.

MPPS (Ministerio del Poder Popular para la Salud). 2011. "Proyectos de salud Cuba-Venezuela, Caracas." www.app.mpps.gob.ve/ADM/documentos/convenios%20 cuba-venezuela.pdf.

Mujal-León, Eusebio. 2011. "Survival, Adaptation, and Uncertainty: The Case of Cuba." *Journal of International Affairs* 65:1, 149–168.

Murillo, Marino A. 2009a. "Comparecencia en la TV." *Granma International,* May 23.

————. 2009b. "Resultados económicos del año 2009 y el plan de la economía para 2010." *Granma,* December 20.

————. 2010. "Resultados económicos del año 2010 y el plan de la economía para 2011." *Granma International,* December 23.

Nova, Armando. 2006. *La agricultura en Cuba: evolución y trayectoria (1959–2005)*. Havana: Editorial de Ciencias Sociales.

———. 2007. "La agricultura en Cuba, 2000–2006." Paper presented at the International Policy Forum, "The Cuban Economy: Challenges and Options," Carleton University, Ottawa, September 9–12.

———. 2010a. "El papel estratégico de la agricultura: problemas y medidas." *Temas*, April 9.

———. 2010b. "La agricultura en los últimos 50 años." In Omar Everleny Pérez Villanueva, ed., *Cincuenta años de la economía cubana*. Havana: Editorial Ciencias Sociales, 176–273.

———. 2011. "Valoración del impacto de las mediadas más recientes en los resultados de la economía cubana: el sector agropecuario y los lineamientos de la política económica y social." Paper presented at the CEEC seminar "Sobre economía cubana y gerencia empresarial," Havana, June 21–24.

———. 2012. "Cuban Agricultural Reforms After 2007." In Jorge Domínguez et al., *Cuban Economic and Social Development: Policy Reforms and Challenges in the 21st Century*. Cambridge. Harvard University Press, 75–105.

Núñez, Niurka, et al., eds. 2011. *Las relaciones raciales en Cuba: estudios contemporáneos*. Havana: La Fuente Viva.

ONE (Oficina Nacional de Estadísticas). 2001a. *Encuesta sobre la situación económica de los hogares*. Havana.

———. 2001b, 2002, 2005, 2006, 2007, 2008a, 2009, 2010a, 2011a, 2012a. *Anuario estadístico de Cuba 2000, 2001, 2004, 2005, 2006, 2007, 2008, 2009, 2010, 2011*. Havana.

———. 2008b. *El estado actual y perspectivo de la población cubana*. Havana.

———. 2008c. *Encuesta nacional de ocupación*. Havana.

———. 2008d. *Serie de cuentas nacionales de Cuba, años 1996–2007*. Havana.

———. 2008e. *Sondeo de precios en el mercado informal, febrero 2008*. Havana.

———. 2008f. *Uso y tenencia de la tierra en Cuba*. Havana.

———. 2010b. *Encuesta nacional de fecundidad*. Havana: CEP.

———. 2011b. *El envejecimiento de la población de Cuba y sus territories 2010*. Havana.

———. 2011c, 2012b. *Panorama económico y social de Cuba 2010, 2011*. Havana.

———. 2011d. *Reporte anual sobre empleo y salarios 2010*. Havana.

———. 2011e. *Turismo internacional: indicadores seleccionados, enero–septiembre 2011*. Havana.

———. 2012c. *Construcción de viviendas*. Havana.

———. 2012d. *Educación: resumen del curso escolar 2010–2011 e inicio del curso escolar 2011–2012*. Havana.

———. 2012e. *Sector agropecuario: indicadores, enero–marzo 2012*. Havana.

———. 2012f. *Sector agropecuario: indicadores seleccionados, enero–diciembre 2011*. Havana.

———. 2012g. *Turismo, llegada de visitantes internacionales, enero–diciembre 2011*. Havana.

———. 2012h. *Turismo internacional: indicadores seleccionados, enero–septiembre 2012*. Havana.

———. 2012i. *Ventas al mercado agropecuario: indicadores seleccionados, enero–diciembre de 2011*. Havana.

OPS (Organización Panamericana de la Salud). 2010. *Proyecto de información y análisis de salud. Iniciativa regional de datos básicos de salud*. Washington, D.C.

Orozco, Manuel, and Katrin Hansing. 2011. "Remittances Recipients and the Present and Future of Microenterpreneurship Activities in Cuba." In *Cuba in Transition,* vol. 21. Washington, D.C.: Association for the Study of the Cuban Economy, 302–308.

Orta, Yailin, Jorge Martínez Romero, and Roberto Suárez. 2006. "Iniciarán proyecto investigativo sobre propiedad en Cuba." *Juventud Rebelde,* October 22.

Ortiz, Gusel, Julieta García Ríos, Osviel Castro Medel, and Lisván Lescalle Durand. 2007. "Empleo juvenil en Cuba." *Juventud Rebelde,* November 27.

Pagés, Raisa, and René Castaño. 2006. "Orden para la comercialización." *Granma,* February 14.

PAHO (Panamerican Health Organization). 2010. *Proyecto de información y análisis de salud: iniciativa regional de datos básicos de salud.* Washington, D.C.

PCC (Partido Comunista de Cuba). 2009. Document circulated among the members of the PCC to explain the dismissals of Carlos Lage and Felipe Pérez Roque. Havana. Untitled document.

———. 2012. *Objetivos de trabajo del Partido Comunista de Cuba aprobados por la Primera Conferencia Nacional.* Havana, January 29.

Pedraza, Lina. 2010. "Intervención acerca de las propuestas para el perfeccionamiento y actualización del sistema tributario." *Granma,* December 16.

———. 2011. "Presentación de la Ley de Presupuesto del Estado para 2012." *Bohemia,* December 25.

———. 2012. "Informe del Proyecto de Ley de Presupuesto del Estado para 2013." *Granma,* December 14.

Peláez, Orfilio. 2011. "Raising Retirement Age Is Not Incompatible with Downsizing Staff." *Granma International,* May 5.

Pérez, Alfredo. 2006. "Reconocen crisis de cooperativas agrícolas." Las Tunas: Tuna Press, May 31.

Pérez, Dora, et al. 2006. "Dibujo de la Cuba futura." *Juventud Rebelde,* December 31.

Pérez, J. Ramón, Roberto Veiga, Lenier González, and Alexis Pestano. 2012. "Vírgen mambisa: ¡que seamos hermanos!" *Espacio Laical* no. 1 (March).

Pérez, Lorenzo. 2008. "Relaciones económicas internacionales de Cuba." Paper presented at the Fourth Congress on Creation and Exile. Valencia, November 17–21.

———. 2010. "Liberación del empleo en Cuba." *Palabra Nueva,* no. 201, November.

———. 2011. "Cuba: Banking Reforms, the Monetary Guidelines of the VI Party Congress, and What Needs to Be Done." In *Cuba in Transition,* vol. 21. Washington, D.C.: Association for the Study of the Cuban Economy, 37–47.

Pérez-López, Jorge. 2008. "The Rise and Fall of Private Foreign Investment in Cuba." *Cuban Affairs* 3:1, 1–30.

———. 2009. "Cuba's Wondrous Balance of Payments Turnaround." Working Document on the Cuban Economy, Tulane University. http://cipr.tulane.edu/articles/detail/812/Working-Documents-on-the-Cuban-Economy.

———. 2011. "Cuba's External Sector and the VI Party Congress." In *Cuba in Transition,* vol. 21. Washington, D.C.: Association for the Study of the Cuban Economy, 437–450.

———. 2012. "The Cuban Labor Market: Availability and Interpretation of Statistics." In *Cuba in Transition,* vol. 22. Washington, D.C.: Association for the Study of the Cuban Economy, 397–412.

Pérez-López, Jorge, and José Álvarez, eds. 2005. *Reinventing the Cuban Sugar Agroindustry.* Lanham: Lexington Books.

Pérez-López, Jorge, and Sergio Díaz-Briquets. 2005. "Remittances to Cuba: A Survey of Methods and Estimates." In *Cuba in Transition*, vol. 15. Washington, D.C.: Association for the Study of the Cuban Economy, 369–409.

———. 2011. "The Diaspora and Cuba's Tourism Sector." In *Cuba in Transition*, vol. 21. Washington, D.C.: Association for the Study of the Cuban Economy, 314–425.

Pérez-López, Jorge, and Carmelo Mesa-Lago. 2009. "Cuban GDP Statistics Under the Special Period: Discontinuities, Obfuscation and Puzzles." In *Cuba in Transition*, vol. 19. Washington, D.C.: Association for the Study of the Cuban Economy, 153–167.

Pérez-Stable, Marifeli. 2010. *The United States and Cuba: Intimate Enemies*. New York: Routledge.

Pérez Villanueva, Omar Everleny, ed. 2006. *Reflexiones sobre economía cubana*. Havana: Editorial Ciencias Sociales.

———. 2007. "La inversión extranjera directa en Cuba: ¿en qué momento se encuentra?" Paper presented at the International Policy Forum, "The Cuban Economy: Challenges and Options," Carleton University, Ottawa, September 9–12.

———. 2008a. "Entrevista a Omar Everleny." *La Jornada,* March 15.

———. 2008b. "La economía cubana: balanza actual y propuestas necesarias." *Boletín Cuatrimestral CEEC,* August.

———. 2008c. "La economía en Cuba: un balance actual y propuestas necesarias." Havana, CEEC.

———, ed. 2010a. *Cincuenta años de la economía cubana*. Havana: Editorial Ciencias Sociales.

———. 2010b. "Estrategia económica: medio siglo de socialismo." In Omar Everleny Pérez Villanueva, ed., *Cincuenta años de la economía cubana*. Havana: Editorial Ciencias Sociales, 1–24.

———. 2010c. "Notas recientes sobre la economía de Cuba." *Espacio Laical* 6:3, 75–81.

———. 2012. "Foreign Direct Investment in China, Vietnam, and Cuba: Pertinent Experiences for Cuba." In Jorge Domínguez et al., *Cuban Economic and Social Development: Policy Reforms and Challenges in the 21st Century*. Cambridge. Harvard University Press, 193–225.

Perkins, Dwight H. 2004. "Economic Reforms in China and Vietnam: Are There Lessons for Cuba?" In Jorge Domínguez, Omar E. Pérez Villanueva, and Lorena Barberia, eds., *The Cuban Economy at the Start of the Twenty-First Century*. Cambridge: Harvard University, Center for Latin American Studies, 199–206.

Petras, James, and Robin Eastman-Abaya. 2007. "Cuba: revolución permanente y contradicciones contemporáneas." *Rebelión*, August 24.

Piñeiro Harnecker, Camila. 2011. "Empresas no estatales en la economía cubana: ¿construyendo el socialismo?" *Temas* 67 (July–September).

———. 2012. "Ahora si van las cooperativas." *Temas,* February 20.

Piñón, Jorge. 2008. Presentation at the Brookings Institution conference "Cuba 2008: Opportunities and Challenges," Washington, D.C., February 6.

———. 2011. "Piñón on Energy: Analyzing Sherritt." CubaStandard.com, February 23. www.cubastandard.com/2011/02/23/pinon-on-energy-analyzing-sherritt.

———. 2012. Correspondence with Mesa-Lago, January, February, and March.

Pollitt, Brian. 2010. "From Sugar to Services: An Overview of the Cuban Economy." *Monthly Review,* June 10.

"Proceso de reducción de plantillas." 2010. E-mail correspondence, August 24.

"Proyecto de lineamientos de la política económica y social." 2010. Havana: Sixth Congress of the Cuban Communist Party, November 9.

Pujol, Joaquín. 2011. "Main Problems Faced by the Cuban Economy and What the Government Is Doing to Try to Solve Them." In *Cuba in Transition,* vol. 21. Washington, D.C.: Association for the Study of the Cuban Economy, 1–17.

Ramos Lauzurique, Arnaldo. 2010. "El dilema de la libreta de racionamiento." Sancti Spíritus, Misceláneas de Cuba, May 31. www.miscelaneasdecuba.net.

Ramos Lauzurique, Arnaldo, and Marta Beatriz Roque. 2011. "Situación de la familia en Cuba." Havana: Instituto Cubano de Economistas Independientes, December 20.

Ramy, Manuel A. 2011. "Entrevista a Ricardo Alarcón." *Espacio Laical* no. 3, 37–39.

———. 2012. "Entrevista a Jesús Arboleya." *Espacio Laical* no. 1, 85.

Ravsberg, Fernando. 2007. "La revolución sufre un estancamiento." Interview of Pedro Campos. *BBC Mundo,* September 25.

———. 2010a. "Con veintiocho centavos." *BBC Mundo,* November 18.

———. 2010b. "Cuba's Battle of Ideas." Meeting between Alfredo Guevara and journalism students. *BBC Mundo,* July 1.

———. 2011a. "Los cinco elementos." *BBC Mundo,* August 12.

———. 2011b. "Los escurridizos materiales." *BBC Mundo,* November 3.

———. 2011c. "Migraciones internas y externas." *BBC Mundo,* December 1.

Remón, José. 2012. "En funcionamiento cable submarino que conecta a Cuba y Venezuela." *Café Fuerte,* November 25. www.cafefuerte.com.

Research and Markets. 2011. "Cuba Oil Markets." June. www.researchandmarkets .com/research/b79a21/cuba_oil_markets.

Resolución no. 9. 2008. Salaries. Ministerio de Trabajo y Seguridad Social. Havana, February 2.

——— no. 19. 2012. Financial reporting. Banco Central de Cuba. *Gaceta Oficial,* March 20.

——— no. 32. 2007. Public transportation fares. Ministerio de Finanzas y Precios. January 31.

——— no. 122. 2011. Sale of agricultural products.*Gaceta Oficial,* November 15.

——— nos. 187 and 188. 2006. Labor discipline. Reglamentos disciplinarios laborales, Ministerio del Trabajo y Seguridad Social. Havana, August 21.

——— no. 206. 2010. Sale of agricultural products.Ministerio de Finanzas, July 23.

——— no. 263. 2009. Private taxis. Ministerio de Transporte. *Gaceta Oficial,* January 12.

——— no. 277. 2007. Payments in convertible currency. Ministerio de Finanzas y Precios. Havana, December 13.

——— no. 321. 2011. Payments to professionals working abroad.Ministerio de Salud Pública, October 30.

——— nos. 333 and 434. 2011. Services cooperatives (barbers, hairdressers, manicurists). *Gaceta Oficial,* November 11.

——— no. 516. 2011. Services cooperatives (extension to twenty-four production and services activities). *Gaceta Oficial,* December 23.

Ritter, Archibald. 2010. "Has Cuba's Catastrophic Decline in Real Wage Levels Been Reversed?" *The Cuban Economy,* June 22. www.thecubaneconomy.com.

———. 2011a. "Can Cuba recover from its de-industrialization?" *The Cuban Economy,* September 27. www.thecubaneconomy.com.

———. 2011b. "El VI Congreso del Partido y los lineamientos: ¿un punto de viraje para Cuba?" *Espacio Laical* no. 3, 18–22.

————. 2011c. "Microenterprise tax reform, 2010." *The Cuban Economy*, January 11. www.thecubaneconomy.com.

————. 2011d. "Up-date on Canadian-Cuban economic relations." *The Cuban Economy*, May 27. www.thecubaneconomy.com.

Robles, Frances. 2008. "Cubans Can Stay at Hotels, but Rates Will Deter Most." *Miami Herald*, April 1.

Robles, Frances, and Wilfredo Cancio. 2009. "La economía detrás de las destituciones en Cuba." *El Nuevo Herald*, March 8.

Rodiles, Antonio. 2011. "Liberalización de las tierras ociosas y propiedades ruinosas." November 30. http://periodistas.impela.net/2011/11/liberalización-de-las-tierras-ociosas-I.

Rodríguez, José Alejandro. 2011. "Menos respuestas cuando más se necesitan." *Juventud Rebelde*, July 6.

Rodríguez, José Luis. 2007a. Cited in "Ministro de Economía niega modelo chino." EFE, April 30.

————. 2007b. "Presentación a la Asamblea Nacional del informe sobre los resultados económicos del año 2007 y los lineamientos del plan económico y social para el 2008." *Granma*, December 28.

————. 2008. "Presentación a la Asamblea Nacional del informe sobre los resultados económicos del año 2008 y los lineamientos del plan económico y social para 2009." Havana, December 27. http://www.cubagob.cu.

————. 2011. "A propósito del socialismo, ¿de que inviabilidad se habla?" *Temas*, September 19.

Rojas, Luis F. 2007. "La odisea de viajar entre provincias." Havana, August 16. Cubaencuentro.

Romero, Carlos. 2011. "La política, el comercio y la economía entre Cuba y Venezuela." In *Cuba in Transition*, vol. 21. Washington, D.C.: Association for the Study of the Cuban Economy, 423–434.

————. 2012. Correspondence with Mesa-Lago, February 8.

Roque, Marta Beatriz. 2010. "La ley y el orden." Havana, September 20. www.marthabeatrizbloginfo.blospot.com

Roy, Joaquín. 2012. "La EU y Cuba: ¿fin de la posición común?" *El País*, November 20.

Sánchez, Fabiola. 2006. "Objetan la inversión de PDVSA en Cuba." *Associated Press*, April 18.

Sánchez, Maritza. 2012. "Resumen sobre la labor de Cáritas en Cuba." Havana, June 7. E-mail correspondence.

Sánchez, Víctor. 2007. "Encuesta sobre pobreza rural." Santiago de Cuba, September 19. www.cubanet.org.

Sánchez-Egozcue, Jorge M. 2007. "Economic Relations—Cuba-US: Bilateralism or Geopolitics?" Paper presented at the twenty-eighth annual LASA Congress, Montreal, September 6–8.

————. 2011a. "Cuba: el camino interno y la política norteamericana en busca de la racionalidad perdida." In Luis Fernando Ayerbe, ed., *Cuba, Estados Unidos y América Latina frente a los desafíos hemisféricos*. Barcelona: Icaria, 11–46.

————. 2011b. "La relación crecimiento económico y sector externo." Paper presented at the CEEC seminar "Sobre economía cubana y gerencia empresarial," Havana, June 21–24.

Sánchez-Egozcue, Jorge M., and Juan Triana. 2010. "Panorama actual de la economía, transformaciones en curso y retos perspectivos." In Omar Everleny Pérez Villanueva, ed., *Cincuenta años de la economía cubana*. Havana: Editorial Ciencias Sociales, 83–192.

Santamaría, Antonio. 2011. "Dos siglos de especialización y dos décadas de incertidumbre: la historia económica de Cuba, 1800–2010." In Luis Bertula and Pablo Gerchunoff, eds., *Institucionalidad y desarrollo económico en América Latina*. Santiago de Chile: CEPAL-AECID, 135–184.

"Sitio del gobierno de la República de Cuba." 2012. List of members of the government. www.cubagob.cu.

Soberón, Francisco. 2005. "Intervención en el Congreso de la Asociación Nacional de Economistas de Cuba." *Granma*, November 27.

———. 2006. "Que los sistemas de distribución vinculen el estándar de vida con el esfuerzo de cada cual." *El Economista de Cuba*, February 6–10.

"Sobre la transición socialista en Cuba: un simposio." 2007. *Temas* nos. 51–52, 126–162.

Spadoni, Paolo. 2009. "U.S. Financial Flows in the Cuban Economy." Working Document on the Cuban Economy, Tulane University. http://cipr.tulane.edu/articles/detail/812/Working-Documents-on-the-Cuban-Economy.

Tamayo, Juan. 2012a. "As Misery Grows, Church Steps In to Help." *Miami Herald*, March 16.

———. 2012b. "Cuba Sentences 12 Public Officials in Corruption Scandal." *Miami Herald*, August 21.

Terrero, Ariel. 2007. "El huevo, la gallina y el ómnibus." *Bohemia*, November 10.

———. 2008. "Comparecencia en TV Buenos Días." Channel 10 news program, February 27.

———. 2009. "Paradigmas." *Bohemia*, June 1.

———. 2010. "Cuentas claras: ante el dilema de las plantillas infladas" and "Vieja deuda." *Bohemia*, June 15 and September 20.

Theis, Reyes. 2010. "Venezuela: gasto anunciado para Cuba ascendió a $34 mil millones de dólares." *El Universal*, November 13.

Togores, Viviana. 1999. "Cuba: efectos sociales de la crisis y el ajuste económico de los 90s." In *Balance de la economía cubana a finales de los 90s*. Havana: Universidad de la Habana, CEEC.

Togores, Viviana, and Anicia García. 2006. "Algunas consideraciones acerca del acceso al consumo en los 90." In Omar Everleny Pérez Villanueva, ed., *Reflexiones sobre economía cubana*. Havana: Editorial Ciencias Sociales, 281–282.

Torres Pérez, Ricardo. 2011. "La actualización del modelo económico cubano: continuidad y ruptura." *Temas*, June 8.

Triana Cordoví, Juan. 2007. "Crecimiento económico, conocimiento y cambio estructural." Paper presented at the twenty-eighth annual LASA Congress, Montreal, September 6–8.

———. 2011. "Cuba 2010–2012: del crecimiento posible al desarrollo necesario." Paper presented at the CEEC seminar "Sobre economía cubana y gerencia empresarial," Havana, June 21–24.

UNDESA (United Nations Department of Economic and Social Affairs). 2011. *World Economic and Social Survey 2011: The Great Green Technological Transformation*. New York. www.un.org/en/development/desa/policy/wess/index.shtml.

UNDP (United Nations Development Programme). 2005, 2007, 2010a, 2011. *Human Development Report 2005, 2007/2008, 2010, 2011*. New York: Palgrave Macmillan.

———. 2010b. "Cuba: Explaining HDI Value and Rank Changes in the *Human Development Report 2010*." New York.

UNESCO (United Nations Educational, Scientific, and Cultural Organization). 2011. Montreal: Institute for Statistics Data Center.

UNSD (United Nations Statistics Department). 2011. *National Accounts Main Aggregates Database*. New York. www.unstats.un.org/unsd/snaama.asp.

UNWTO (United Nations World Tourism Organization). 2012. *UNWTO Tourism Highlights*. New York.

USGS (US Geological Survey). 2005. "Assessment of Undiscovered Oil and Gas Resources of the North Cuba Basin, Cuba 2004." Fact Sheet no. 2005-3009. Washington, D.C., February.

US Trade and Economic Council. 2012. "2011–2001 U.S. Export Statistics for Cuba." Washington, D.C., February 22.

Valdés, Dagoberto. 2011. "¿Actualizar el modelo cubano?" *Convivencia* 19 (January–February), www.convivenciacuba.es.

Veiga, Roberto. 2011. "Cuba: urgencias del presente, imperativos del futuro." *Espacio Laical* 130 (April).

———. 2012. "Palabras en el panel sobre la esfera pública en Cuba." *Espacio Laical* 172 (April).

Veiga, Roberto, and Lenier González. 2012. "La relación iglesia-estado en Cuba ha dado un salto cualitativo." *Espacio Laical* 171 (March).

Vicent, Mauricio. 2008a. "El gobierno de Cuba sube un 20% las jubilaciones." *El País*, April 28.

———. 2008b. "La fiebre de la telefonía móvil hace estragos en Cuba." *El País*, April 15.

Vidal Alejandro, Pavel. 2007. "La inflación y el salario real." *Economic Press Service* 20:5, 18–20.

———. 2008a. "La disyuntiva actual de la política económica cubana." *Economic Press Service*, September 30.

———. 2008b. "Los salarios, los precios y la dualidad monetaria." *Espacio Laical* 4:2, 22–26.

———. 2009. "La macroeconomía cubana en 2008: datos de cierre del año." *Economic Press Service*, January 15.

———. 2010a. "Cuban Economic Policy Under the Raúl Castro Government." Tokyo: Institute of Developing Economies.

———. 2010b. "La crisis bancaria cubana actual." *Espacio Laical* (X Semana Social Católica) no. 3.

———. 2010c. "Política monetaria, 1989–2009." In Omar Everleny Pérez Villanueva, ed., *Cincuenta años de la economía cubana*. Havana: Editorial Ciencias Sociales, 153–175.

———. 2011a. "Desarticular el monopolio de la centralización estatal." Interview by Lenier González. *Espacio Laical* 7:2, 46–52.

———. 2011b. "La inflación, CADECA y la crisis global." *Economic Press Service*, August 15.

———. 2012a. *Monetary and Exchange Rate Reform in Cuba: Lessons from Vietnam*. VRS Series no. 473. Tokyo: Institute of Developing Economies and Japan External Trade Organization.

———. 2012b. "Pasos hacia la bancarización del sector no estatal cubano." In *Desde la Isla* [From the Island]. Cuba Study Group, Havana, February 1.

Vidal Alejandro, Pavel, and Annia Fundora. 2008. "La relación comercio-crecimiento en Cuba." *Revista de la CEPAL* 94 (April), 101–120.

Vidal Alejandro, Pavel, and Omar Everleny Pérez Villanueva. 2010. "Se extiende el cuentapropismo en Cuba." *Espacio Laical* 6:3, 53–58.

Whitefield, Mimi. 2012. "Is Oil Drilling in Cuban Waters Safe?" *Miami Herald*, January 26.

World Bank. 2011. *World Development Indicators and Global Development Finance Database.* Washington, D.C. www.data.worldbank.org/data-catalog/world-development-indicators.

Yamaoka, Kanako. 2009. "The Feasibility of a Cuban Market Economy: A Comparison with Vietnam." Tokyo: Institute of Developing Economies.

Yzquierdo Rodríguez, Adel. 2011. "Informe sobre los resultados económicos del 2011 y el plan económico y social para 2012." *Bohemia,* December 25.

Index

Abortion, 146, 164
Acanda, Jorge Luis, 175
Acopio procurement system, 251,
254(n11); agricultural decline, 66–
67; agricultural machinery debt, 68;
defense of, 74(n33); nonstructural
changes, 182; reform implementation
and evaluation, 238–239; reforming,
188; Sixth Congress expansion of
usufruct, 198; socialism debate,
176–177; usufruct requirements, 193
Acupuncture, 152–153
Acute diarrhea, 149, 150(table)
Acute respiratory diseases, 149,
150(table)
Administrative measures, 182–186,
221–222(table), 250–251
Afro-Cubans, 127, 135–138, 156–157,
163–164, 192, 230–231, 243, 246, 250
Aging population, 153–154, 153(table),
164
Agricultural diversification, 6
Agricultural markets, 15, 23–24
Agricultural production cooperatives
(CPAs), 59, 60(table), 238–239
Agricultural reforms, 234, 238–240
Agricultural sector: agricultural
production and nonstate sector share,
2010–2011, 227(table); cooperatives
and privates farmers, 187–188;
deterioration of, 66–71, 73(n18);

distribution of agricultural land by
state and nonstate sectors, 60(table);
distribution of harvested land and
agricultural production, 62(table);
foreign investment, 238; GDP
composition, 31–33; higher
education graduates, 143–144;
hurricane damage, 48–49(box);
land tenure and production, 59–61;
microcredit loans, 207; nonsugar
agriculture, livestock, and fishing,
58–59, 61–64; performance of
nonsugar production, 44–46;
physical production in mining,
manufacturing, and agriculture, 1989
and 2005–2011, 35(table); private
property rights and usufructuaries,
239–240; real and hidden
unemployment, 122; socialism
debate, 176–177; structural reform
in China and Vietnam, 175. *See also*
Cooperatives; Sugar production;
Usufruct
Aircraft imports, 56–57
Alarcón, Ricardo, 181, 215(n14)
Alcoholic beverages, 81
Almeida, Juan, 169–170
Almendrones (old automobiles), 210
Alonso, Aurelio, 175–176
Angola: Cuban intervention in, 9; oil
leases, 72(n11)

286 *Index*

Migration policy, 211–213
Milanés, Pablo, 181
Milk production, 65, 67, 130(table),
215(n8), 227(table)
Mining, 23; economic performance,
37, 69; foreign investment, 89;
GDP composition, 31; labor force
differentials, by gender, 138(table);
physical production in mining,
manufacturing, and agriculture, 1989
and 2005–2011, 35(table); salaries,
134, 137. *See also* Nickel; Oil and
natural gas
Ministry of Agriculture, 67, 183, 198,
226
Ministry of Labor and Social Security,
122, 127, 165(n2), 184–185, 213
Ministry of Sugar, 47, 73(n18), 183
Ministry of the Revolutionary Armed
Forces, 183
Monal, Isabel, 175
Monetary duality, 90–91; negative
economic effects, 114; proposed
reforms, 190–191; Raúl's reform
measures, 222(table); reform
implementation and evaluation,
236; Sixth Congress agreements,
197
Monetary liquidity, 16, 22–23;
Canadian-Cuban economic relations,
106; domestic macroeconomic
indicators, 1989 and 2005–2011,
30(table); economic crisis, 29;
economic policy areas, 3; events
creating, 114; foreign debt, 87;
idealist and pragmatist cycles, 10–11,
14; price stability, 34; unemployment
figures, 121
Monetary policy, 236
Moore, Michael, 145
Morales, Esteban, 185–186
Moratinos, Miguel, 106
Morbidity, 149–151, 150(table)
Mortality rates, 135, 145–146,
147(table), 151, 164, 167(n18)
Mulas (professional travelers), 96
Multi-employment, 129, 243–244
Murillo, Marino: capital formation, 33;
Chinese trade, 104–105; Cuba's
political future, 250; dismissal plan,
123; electricity production and

consumption, 53; housing shortage,
162; medicine production, 115(n6);
nonagricultural cooperatives, 230;
production and services cooperatives,
205; reform implementation, 233;
self-employment expansion, 241;
succession of power, 171–172;
updating the economic model, 197,
225; usufruct, 226

National accounts methodology, 30–31
National Assembly of People's Power
(ANPP), 4, 10, 19, 88, 169–170, 180
National Statistical Office (ONE), 27,
29, 34, 56–57, 75, 134, 234
National Union of Writers and Artists
of Cuba (UNEAC), 185
Nationalization policies, 9–10
Natural medicine, 152–153
Netherlands: distribution of Cuban
foreign trade, 97(table)
"New man," 8–10
Nickel pig iron, 41
Nickel production, 40–41; Brazilian
investment, 110; Canada trade,
105–106; China trade, 103; foreign
investment, 89–90; goods terms of
trade, 80–81; hurricane damage,
48–49(box); idealist and pragmatist
cycles, 10, 13; increasing value,
115(n5); physical production in
mining, manufacturing, and
agriculture, 1989 and 2005–2011,
35(table); physical production of
selected products, 1989 and 2005–
2006 to 2010–2011, 36(fig.); Russian
investment, 112
Nixon, Richard, 5
Nonstructural changes: changes for
cooperatives and private farmers,
187–188; citizens' access to tourism
hotels, 187; distributing idle state
lands in usufruct, 192–193;
gratuities, rationing, and subsidies,
191–192; labor indiscipline and
corruption, 184–186; monetary
duality, 190–191; openness to
criticism, 186–187; private
transportation services, 188–189;
Raúl's changes, 182; salary increases
for meeting basic needs, 189–190;

About the Book

What led to the dramatic social and economic reforms introduced by Cuba's president Raúl Castro? How effective have those reforms been? And what obstacles does Raúl Castro face in overcoming the country's chronic socioeconomic woes? *Cuba Under Raúl Castro* addresses these questions, offering a comprehensive analysis of the president's efforts during his first six years in office.

Carmelo Mesa-Lago is Distinguished Service Professor Emeritus of economics and Latin American studies at the University of Pittsburgh. He is the author of numerous books on Cuba, most recently *Cuba's Aborted Reform: Socioeconomic Effects, International Comparisons, and Transition Policies* (with Jorge Pérez-López). **Jorge Pérez-López** is executive director of the Fair Labor Association in Washington, D.C. His recent publications include *Corruption in Cuba: Castro and Beyond.*